A.D.

NEW ORLEANS

AFTER THE DELUGE

A.D.

NEW ORLEANS
AFTER THE DELUGE

JOSH NEUFELD

PANTHEON BOOKS
NEW YORK

Although based on real people and events, some names and details have been changed for dramatic purposes or to protect the privacy of individuals.

 Published in the United States by Pantheon Books, a division of Random House, Inc., New York, and in Canada by Random House of Canada Limited, Toronto.

Pantheon Books and colophon are registered trademarks of Random House, Inc.

Originally published in hardcover in the United States by Pantheon Books, a division of Random House, Inc., New York, in 2009.

Portions of this work originally appeared, in different form, in SMITH Magazine (www.smithmag.net).

Publication design by Josh Neufeld and Charlie Orr

Library of Congress Cataloging-in-Publication Data

Neufeld, Josh.
A.D.: New Orleans after the deluge / Josh Neufeld.
p. cm.
ISBN 978-0-375-71488-7
1. New Orleans (La.) -- Biography -- Comic books, strips, etc.
2. Disaster victims -- Louisiana -- New Orleans -- Biography -- Comic books, strips, etc.
3. Hurricane Katrina, 2005 -- Comic books, strips, etc.
4. Hurricane Katrina, 2005 -- Social aspects -- Louisiana -- New Orleans -- Comic books, strips, etc.
5. New Orleans (La.) -- Social conditions -- 21st century -- Comic books, strips, etc.
6. New Orleans (La.) -- History -- 21st century -- Comic books, strips, etc.
7. Graphic novels. I. Title.
F379.N553A26 2009 976.3'350640922--dc22 [B] 2008055687

www.JoshComix.com
www.PantheonBooks.com

Printed in China

First Paperback Edition

1 3 5 7 9 8 6 4 2

To Denise, Leo, Michelle, Brobson, Abbas, Darnell, and Kwame --
the beating hearts and souls of "A.D."

HURRICANE KATRINA

 HURRICANE KATRINA struck Louisiana on August 29, 2005, bringing winds of 140 miles per hour. The worst hurricane in a generation, it caused tremendous devastation in Louisiana and Mississippi, as well as in parts of Florida and Alabama.

Even though the hurricane struck east of New Orleans, the powerful storm surge breached the city's levee systems. By August 30, eighty percent of the city was flooded with water from Lake Pontchartrain, with some areas as much as 15 feet underwater. The storm surge devastated the Lower Ninth Ward and other low-lying areas of the city, with whole blocks of buildings swept away. Days later, dead bodies lay in city streets and floated in still-flooded sections. The floodwaters lingered for weeks.

Although ninety percent of New Orleans' residents had evacuated before the storm, many -- mainly the elderly and poor -- remained behind. Scores of people who tried to stay in their homes were forced to swim for their lives, or wade through deep water. Others were trapped in their attics or on their rooftops. Thousands who sought shelter at the Ernest N. Morial Convention Center and the Louisiana Superdome were abandoned to their fate.

In the end, more than 700 New Orleanians died as a direct result of the hurricane and the flooding. And tens of thousands who evacuated or lost their homes are still unable to return.

WHO'S WHO

 DENISE is a sixth-generation New Orleanian with a master's degree in guidance and counseling. When Katrina strikes, she is living with her mother, Louise (a surgical tech at Memorial Baptist Hospital), her niece Cydney, and Cydney's daughter, R'nae, in an apartment above a boxing club in Mid-City.

 LEO and MICHELLE are twenty-somethings who grew up in New Orleans. Leo is the publisher of "AntiGravity," a local music zine; he also works with mentally challenged youth. He is a huge comic book fan, with a collection of more than 15,000 comics. Michelle is a waitress and gymnastics instructor.

 ABBAS is an Iranian-born longtime New Orleanian, the father of two, and the owner of a family-run convenience store in Uptown. Along with his fishing buddy DARNELL, Abbas decides to weather the storm in his store.

 KWAME, the son of a pastor from New Orleans East, is just entering his senior year of high school when Katrina strikes. He flees to his older brother's Tallahassee college dorm with his family the day before the storm.

 THE DOCTOR (Brobson) is a medical man-about-town often found at the legendary restaurant Galatoire's. Secure in the knowledge that his French Quarter home has withstood many previous storms, the Doctor refuses to evacuate. In fact, he hosts a hurricane party.

THE STORM

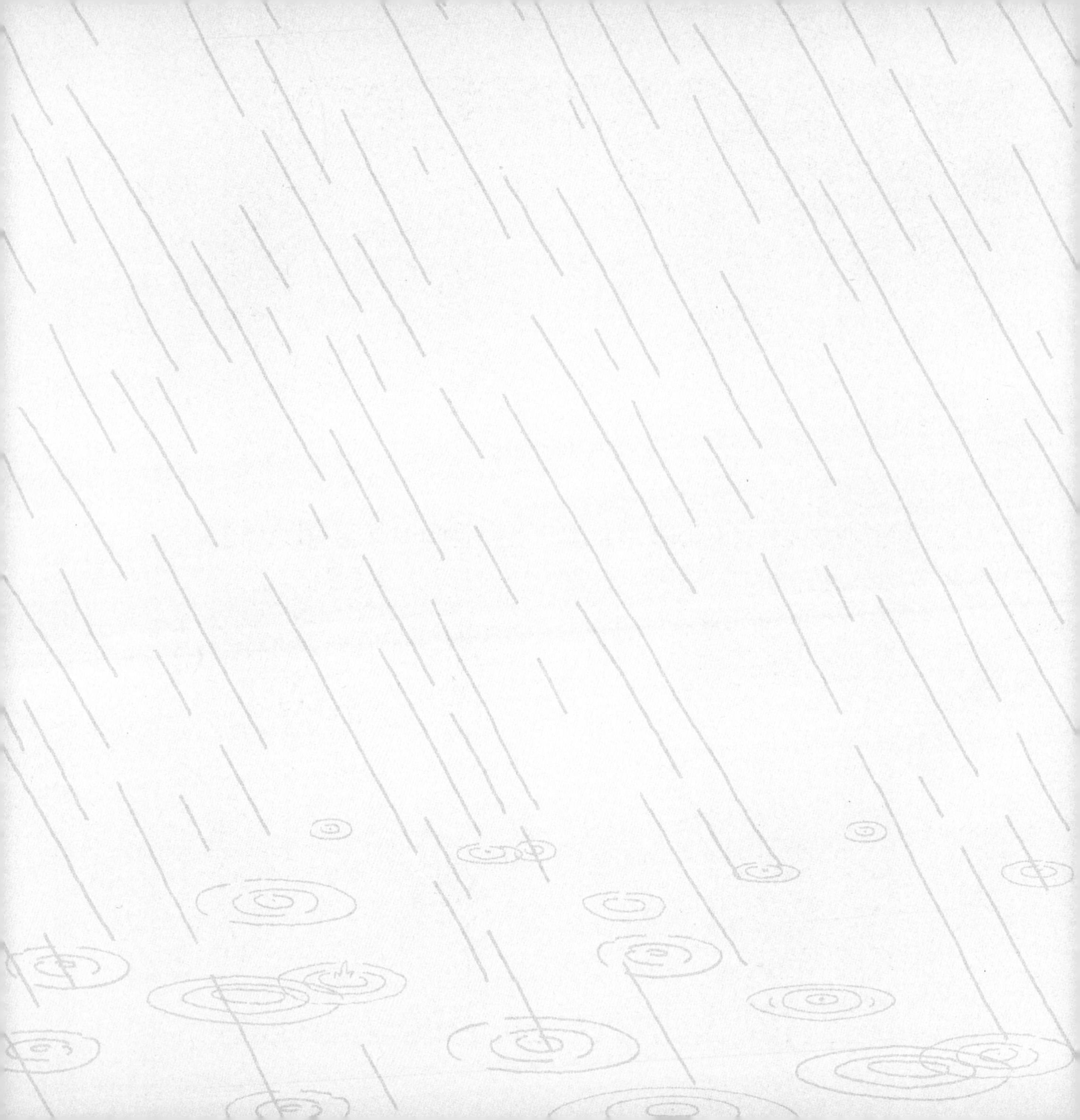

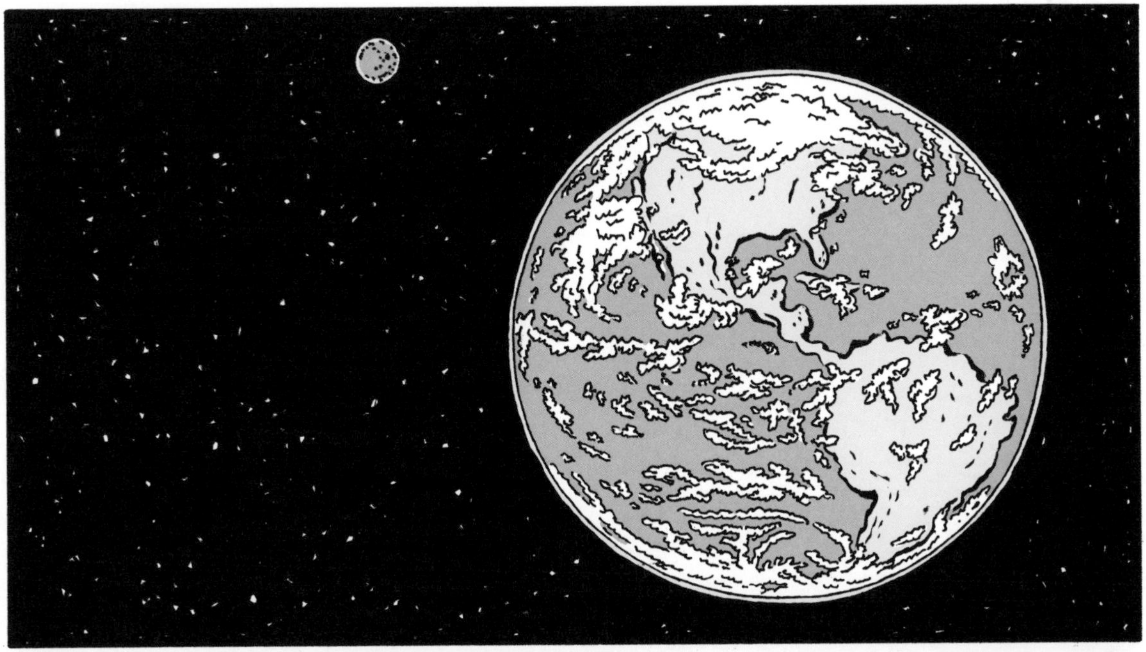

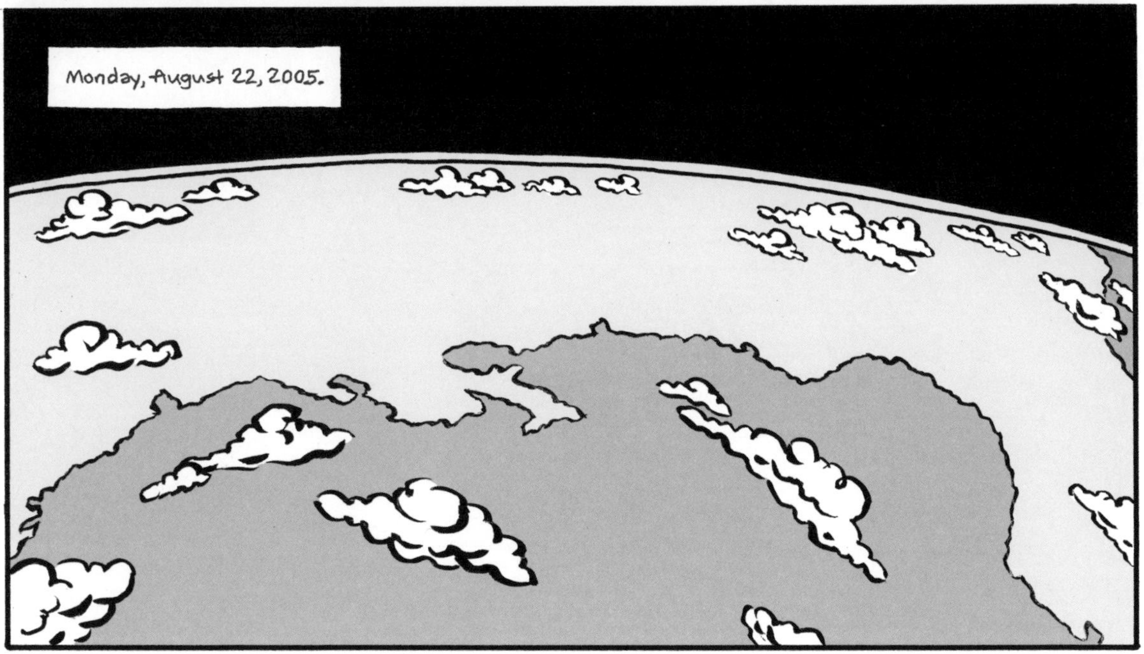
Monday, August 22, 2005.

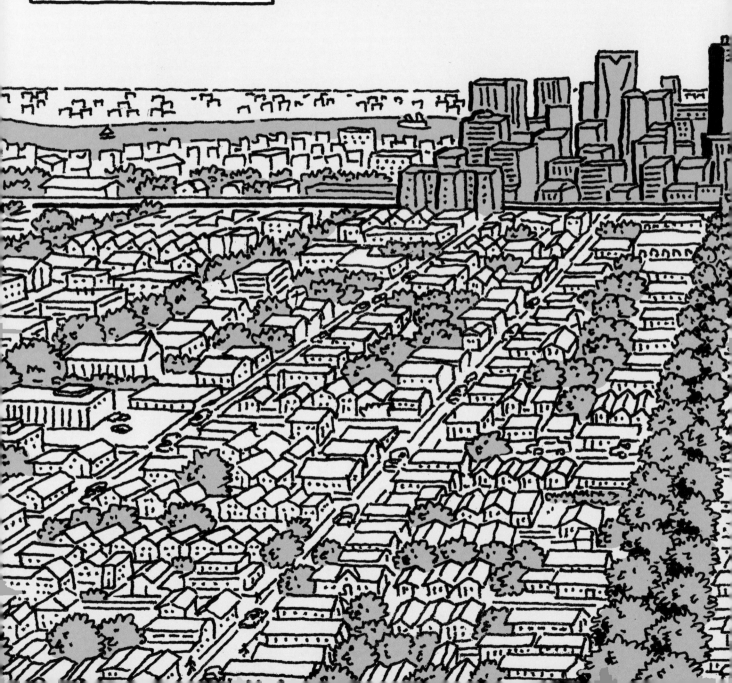
New Orleans, Louisiana.

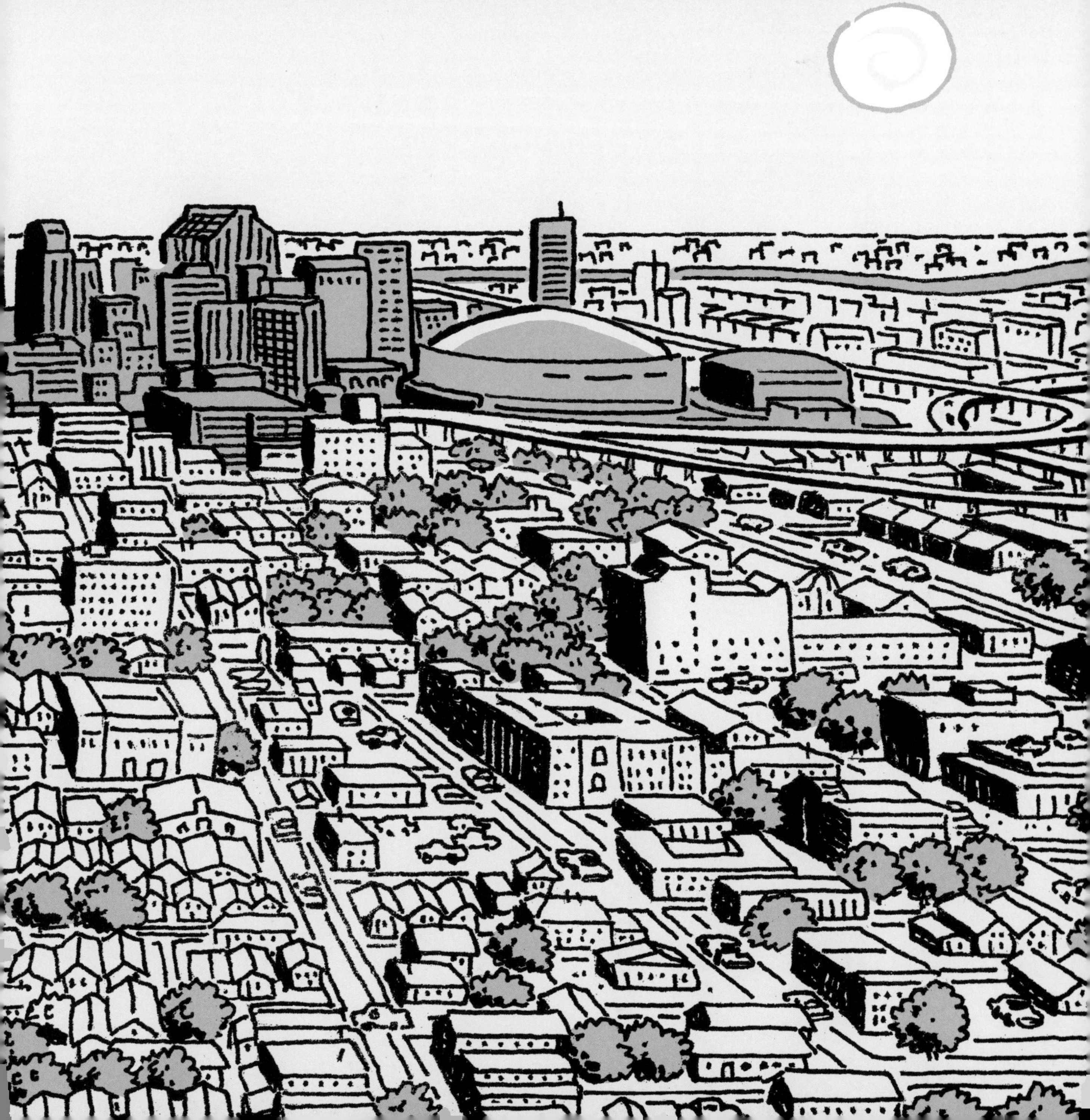

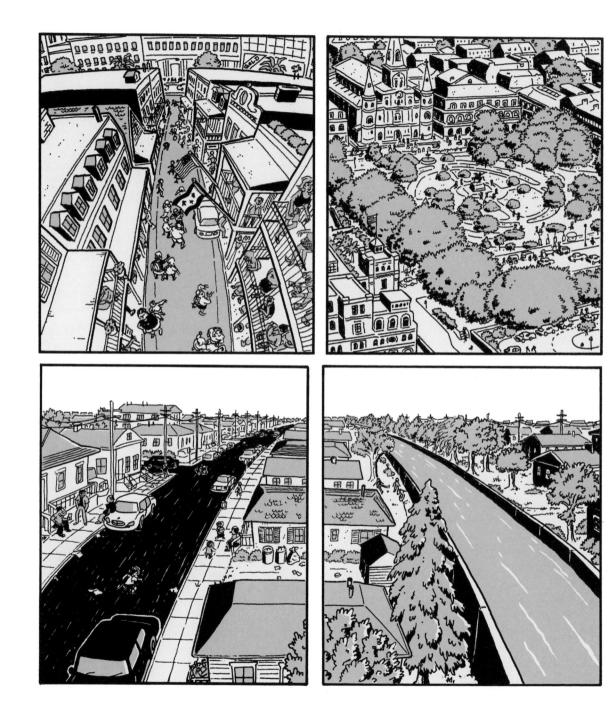

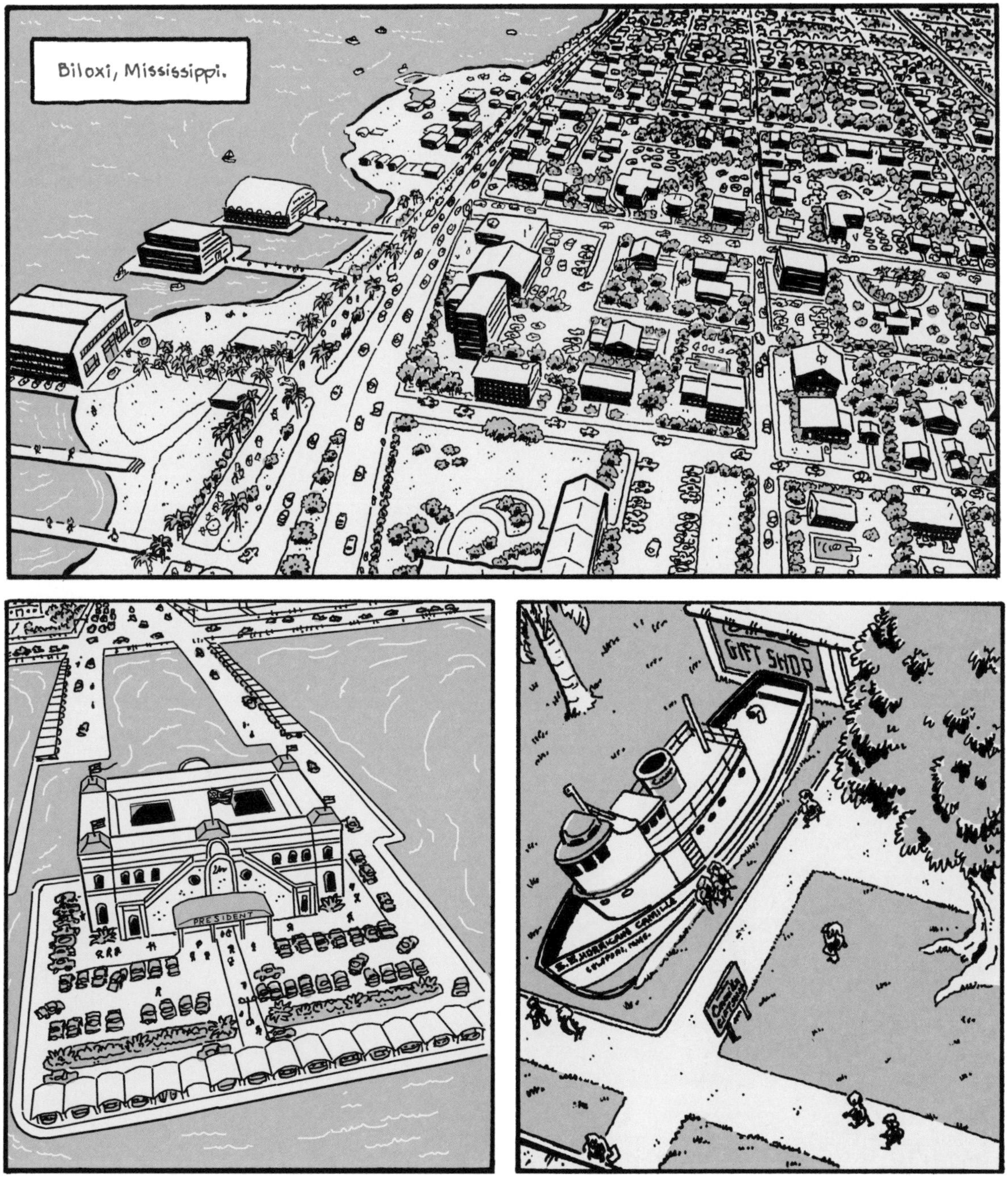
Biloxi, Mississippi.
PRESIDENT
GIFT SHOP
HURRICANE CAMILLE

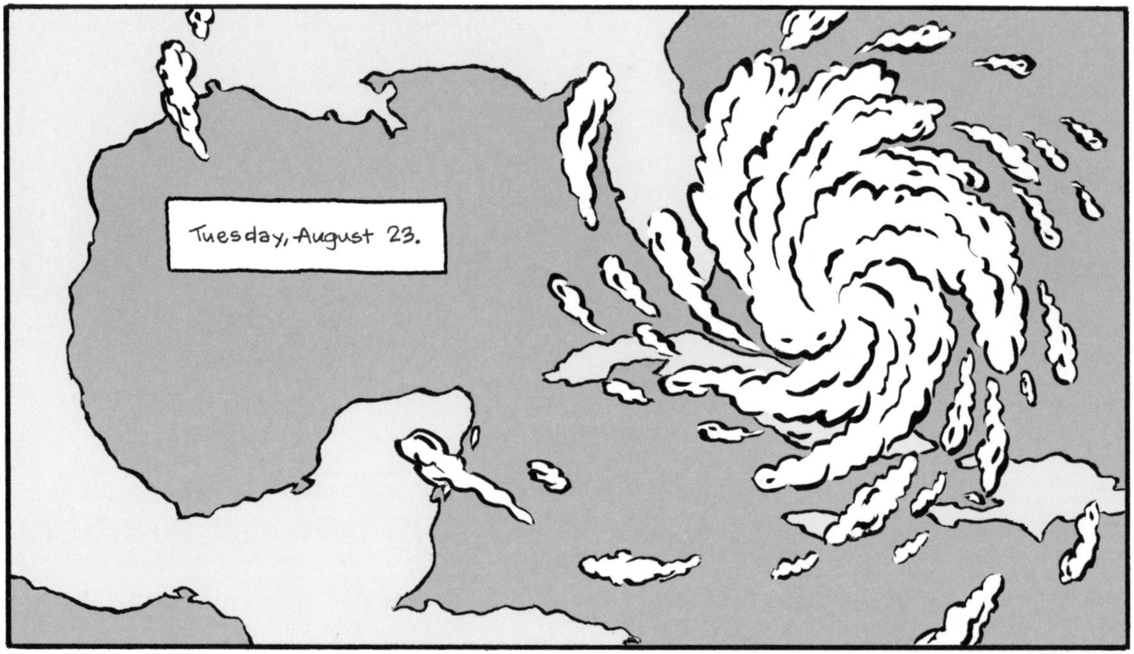
Tuesday, August 23.

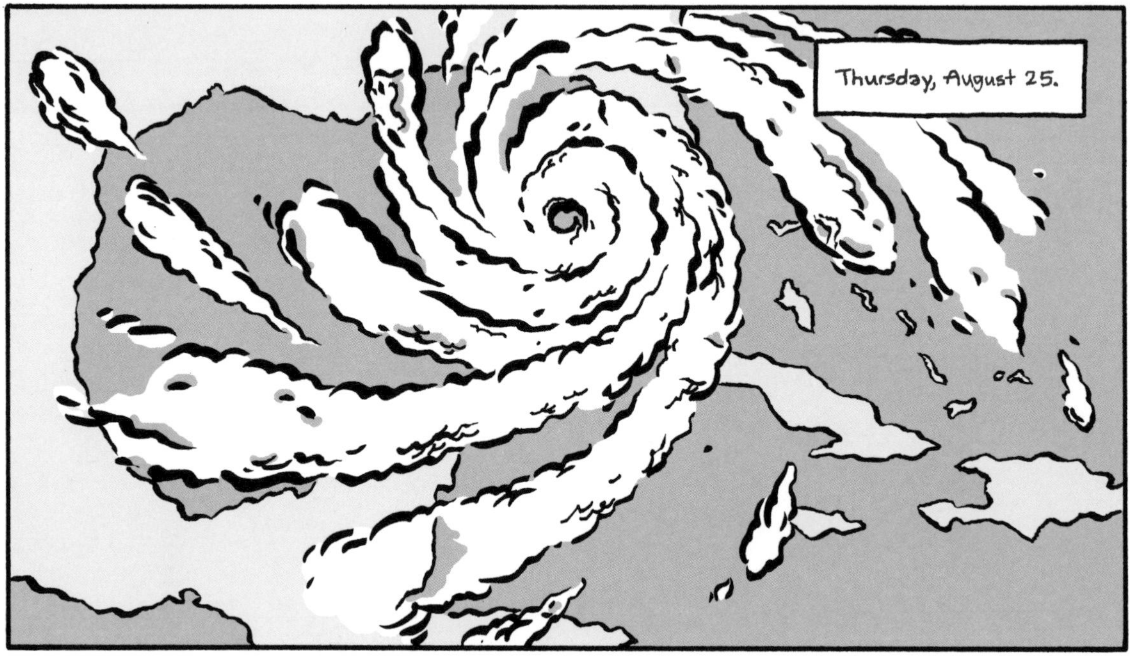
Thursday, August 25.

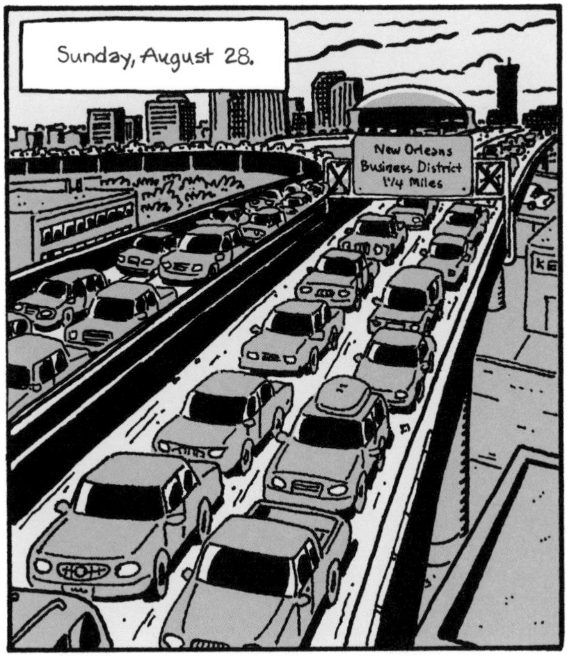
Sunday, August 28.
New Orleans
Business District
1 1/4 Miles

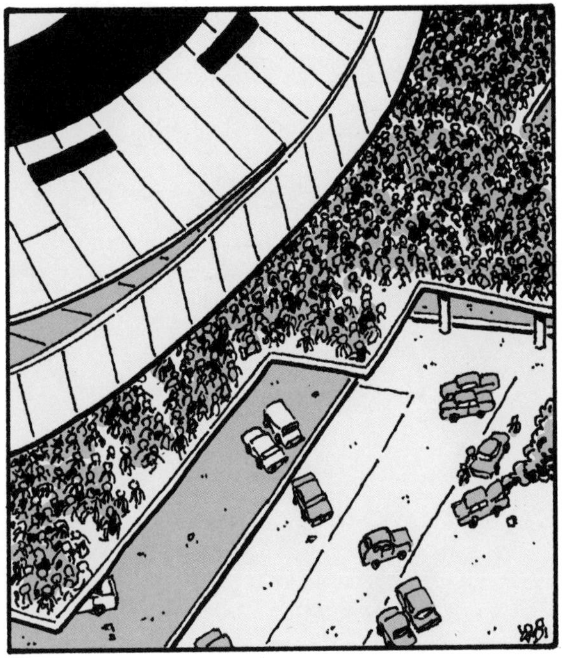

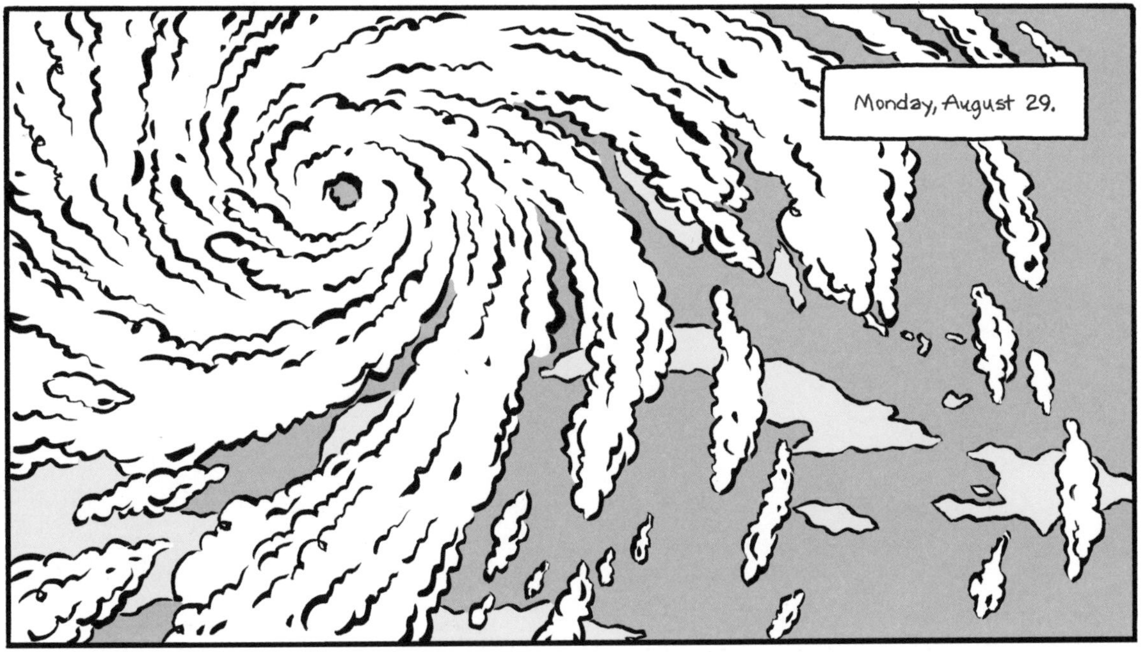
Monday, August 29.

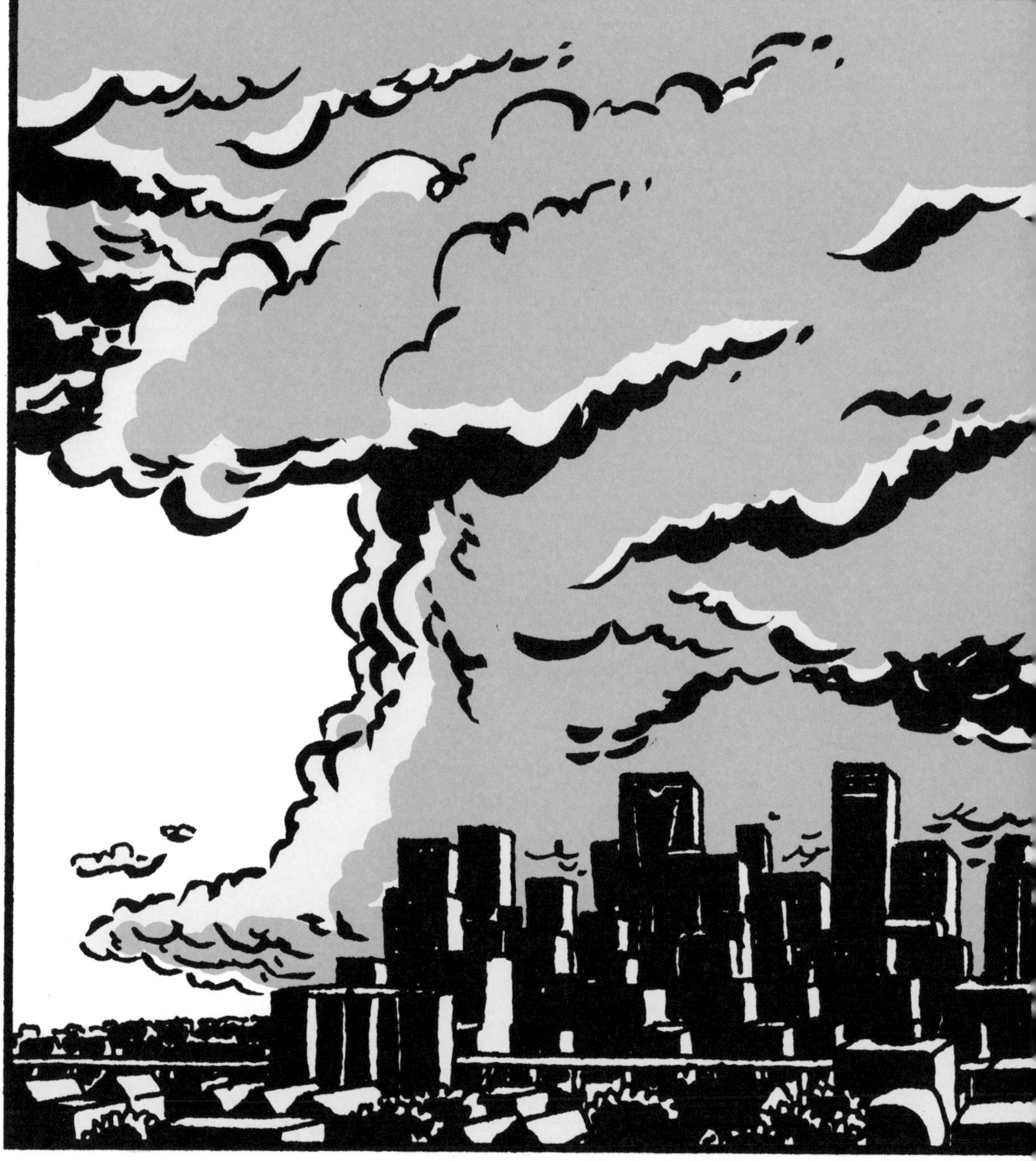

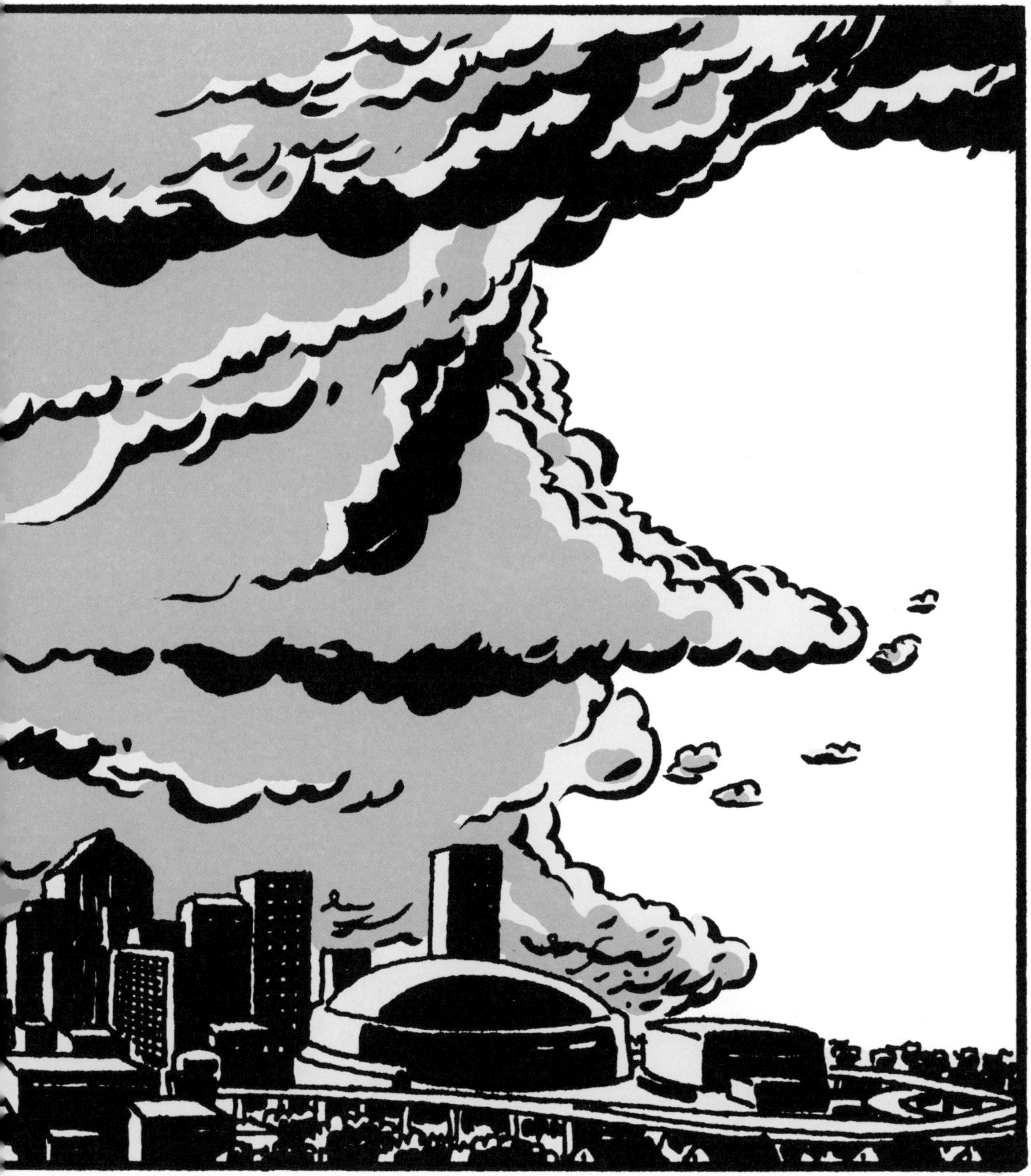

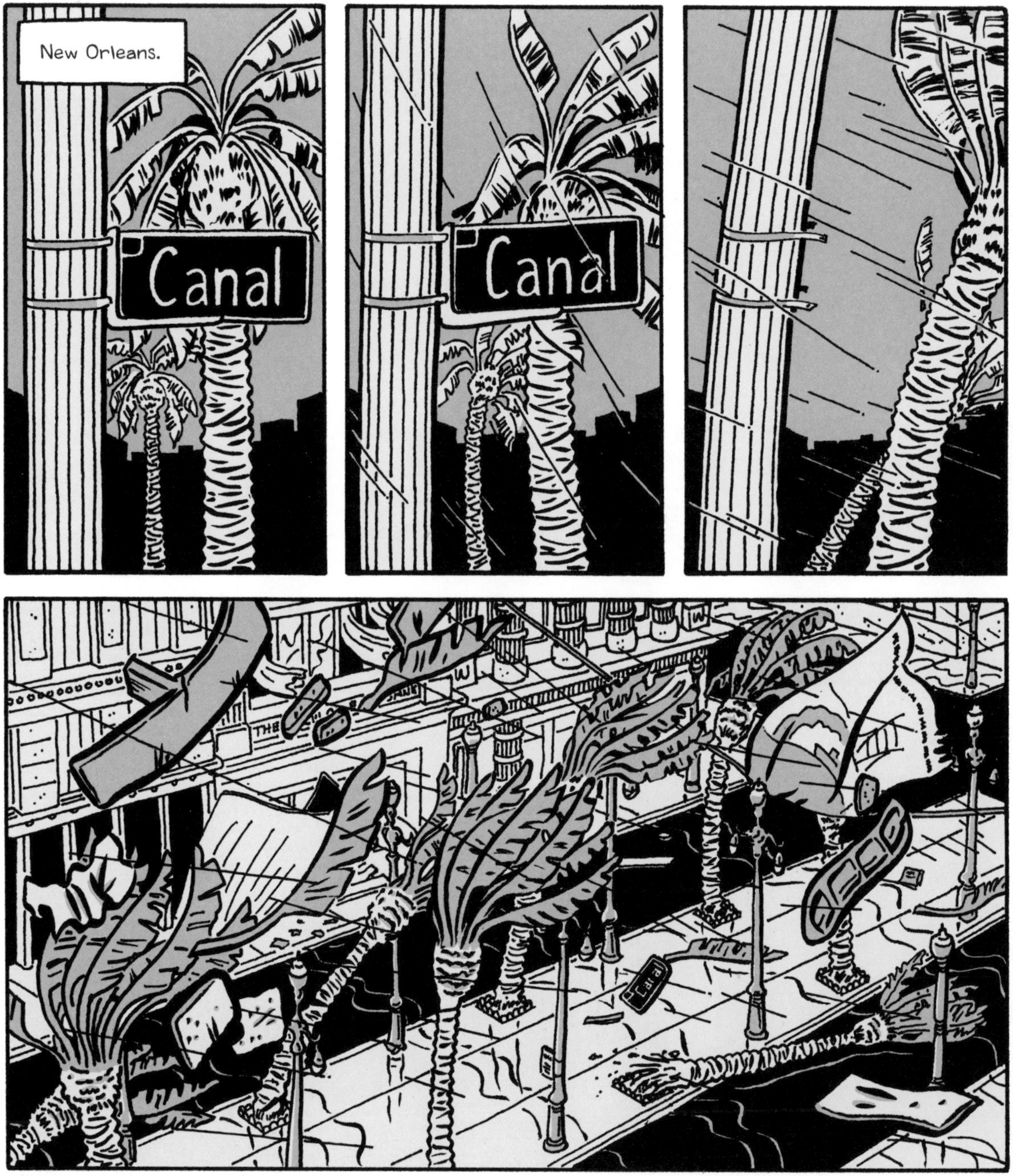
New Orleans.
Canal
Canal

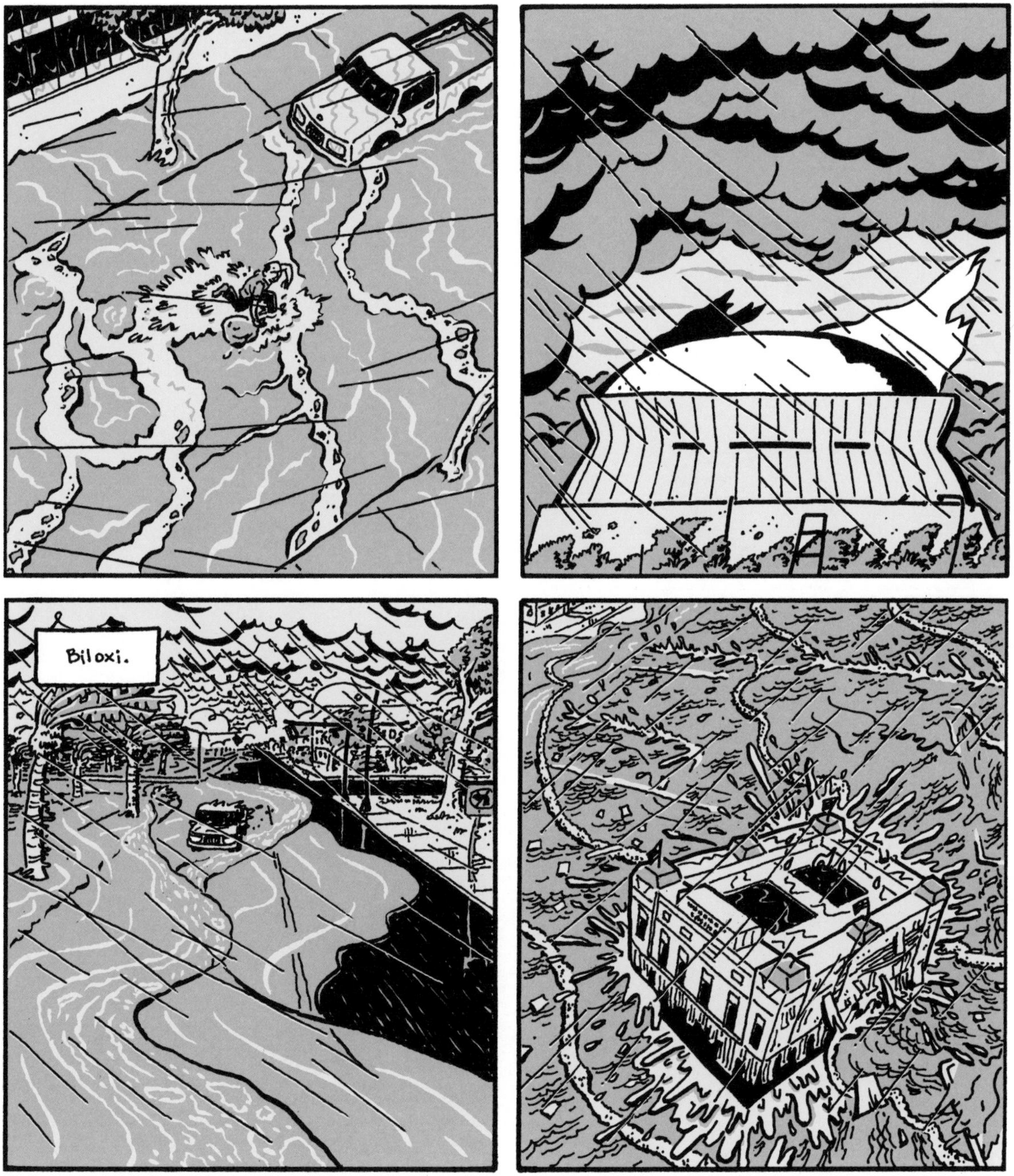
Biloxi.

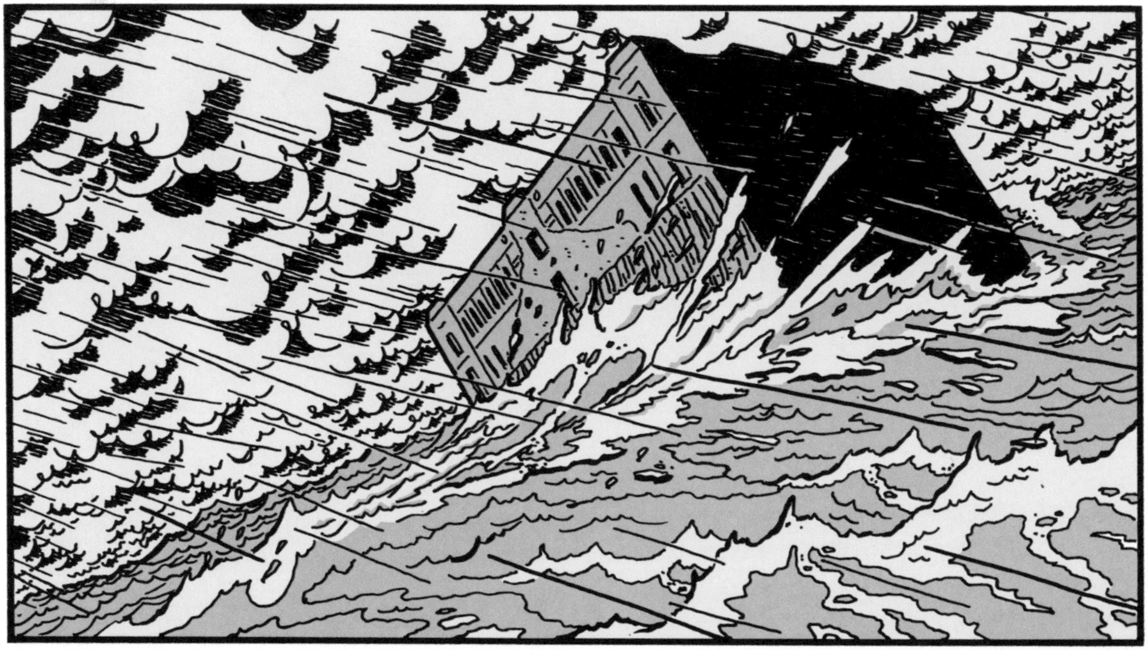

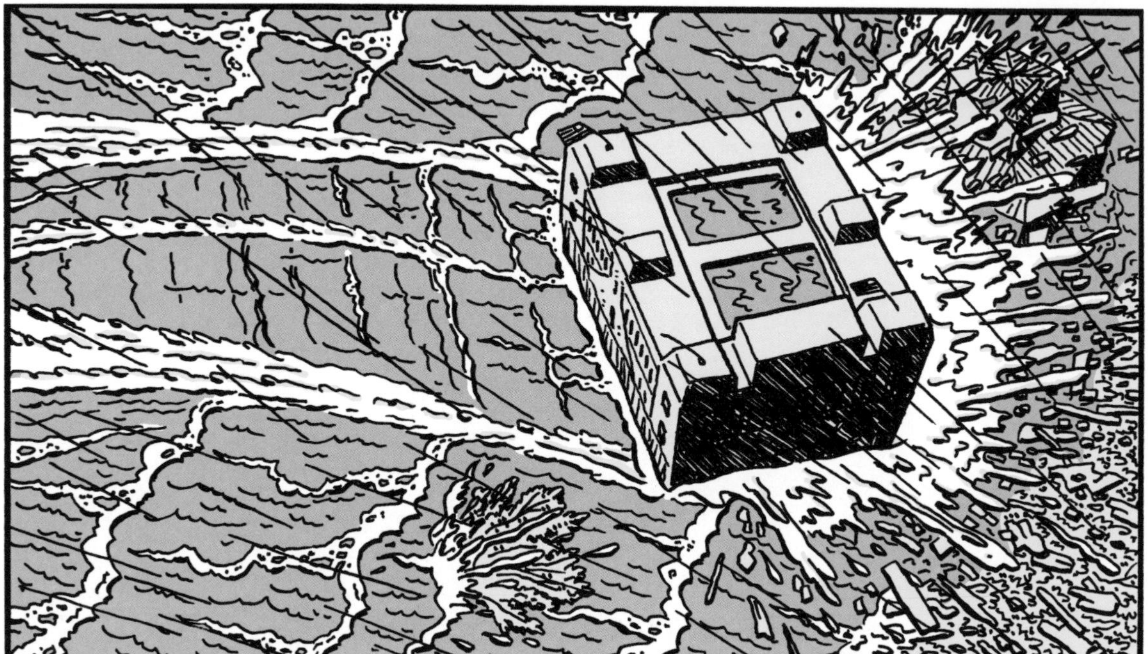

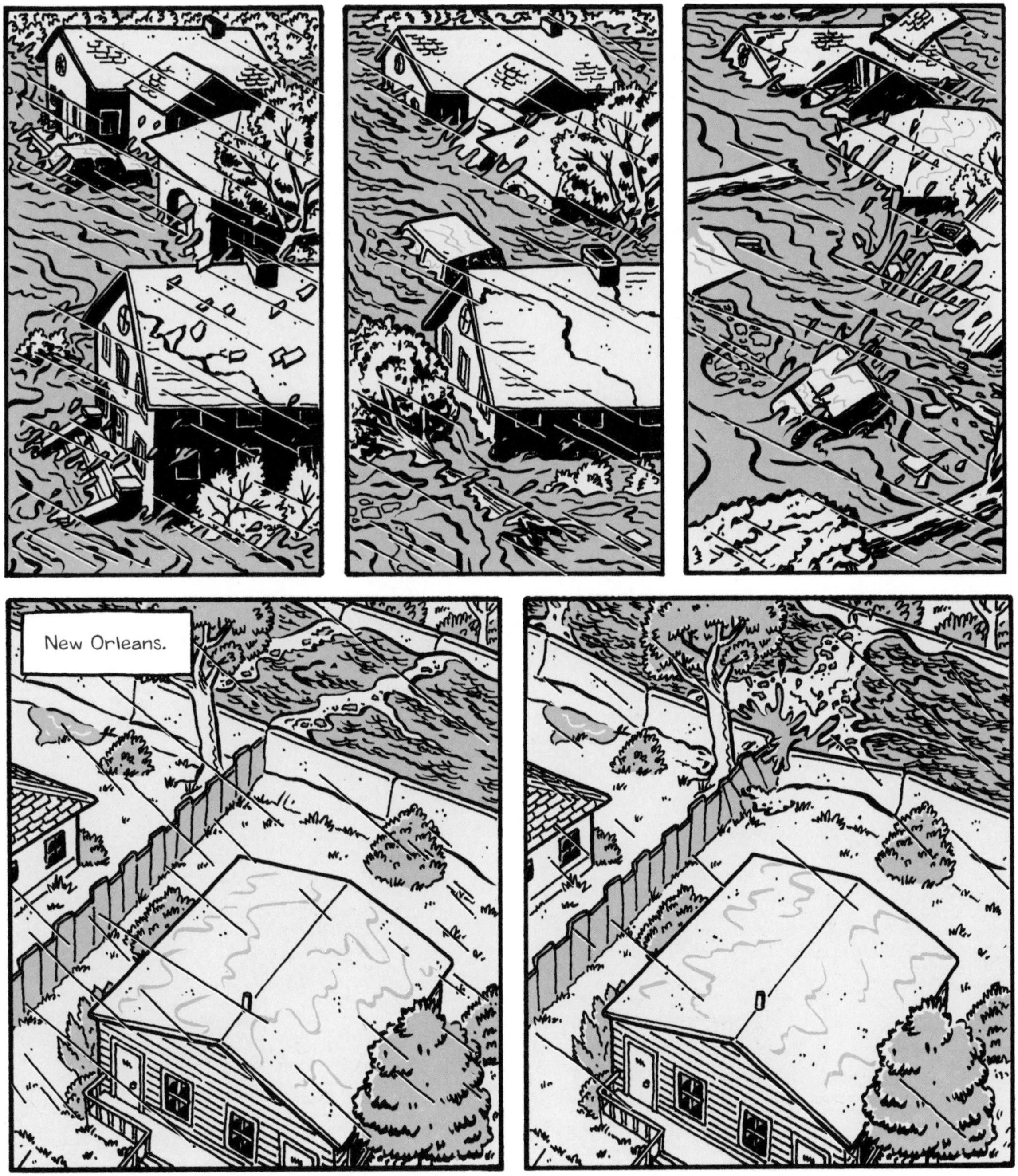
New Orleans.

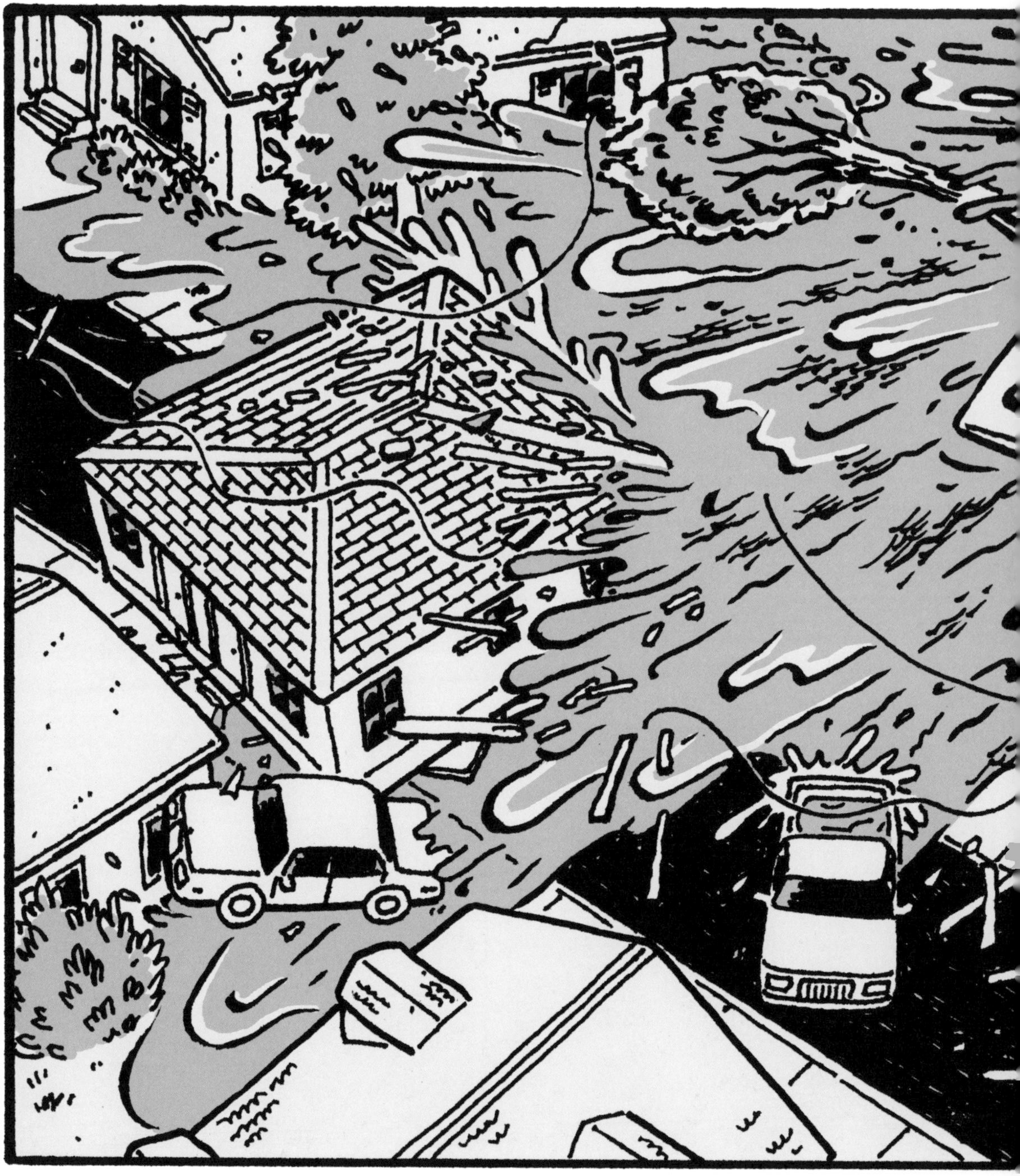

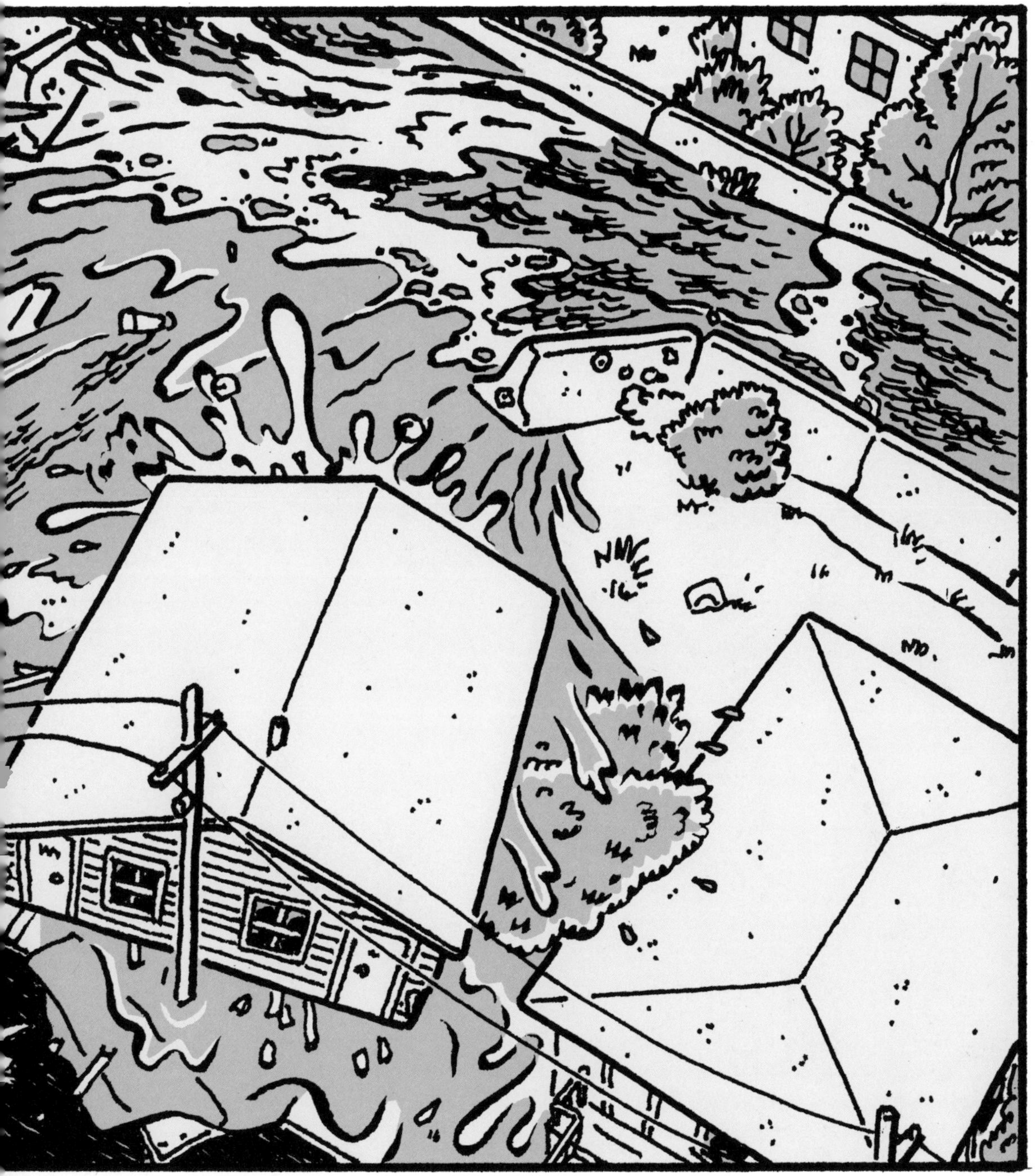

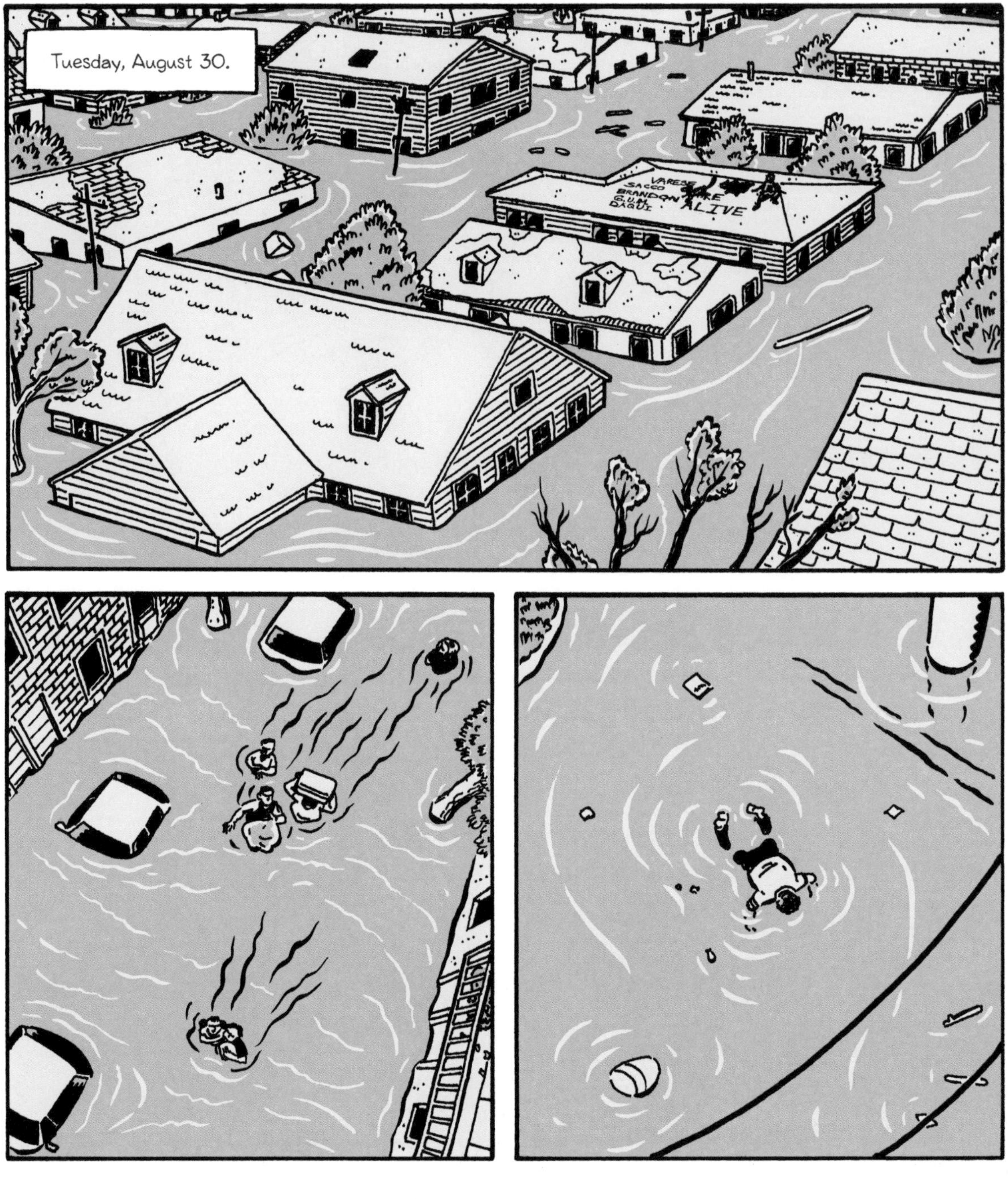
Tuesday, August 30.
VARESE
SACCO
BRANDON
G.U.M.
DAQUI
ALIVE

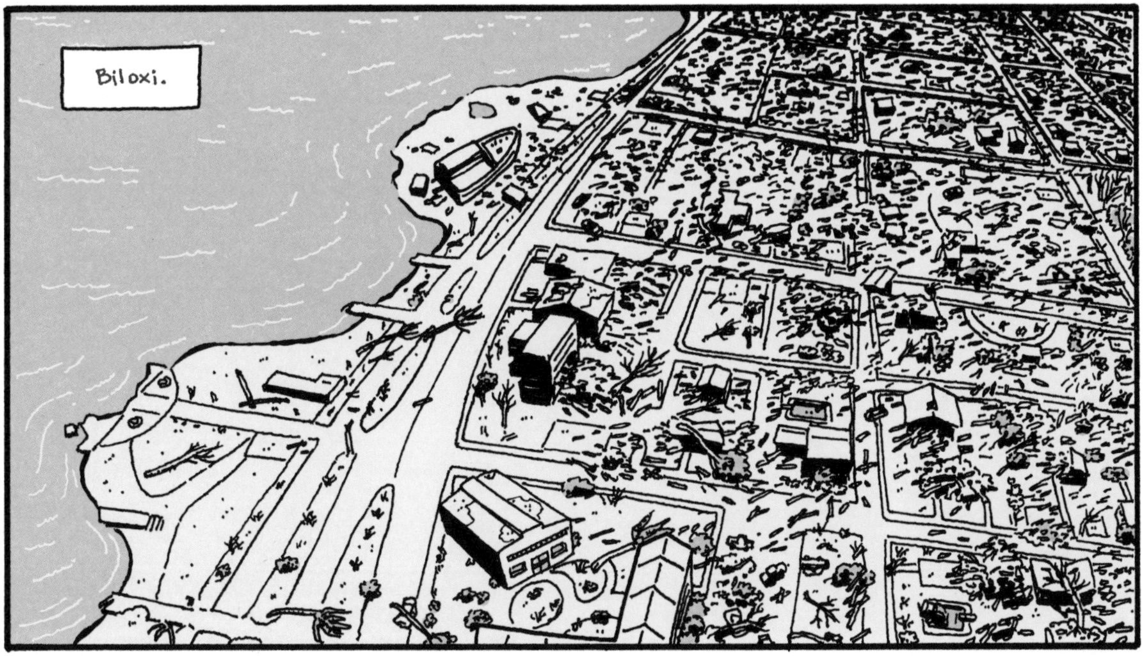
Biloxi.

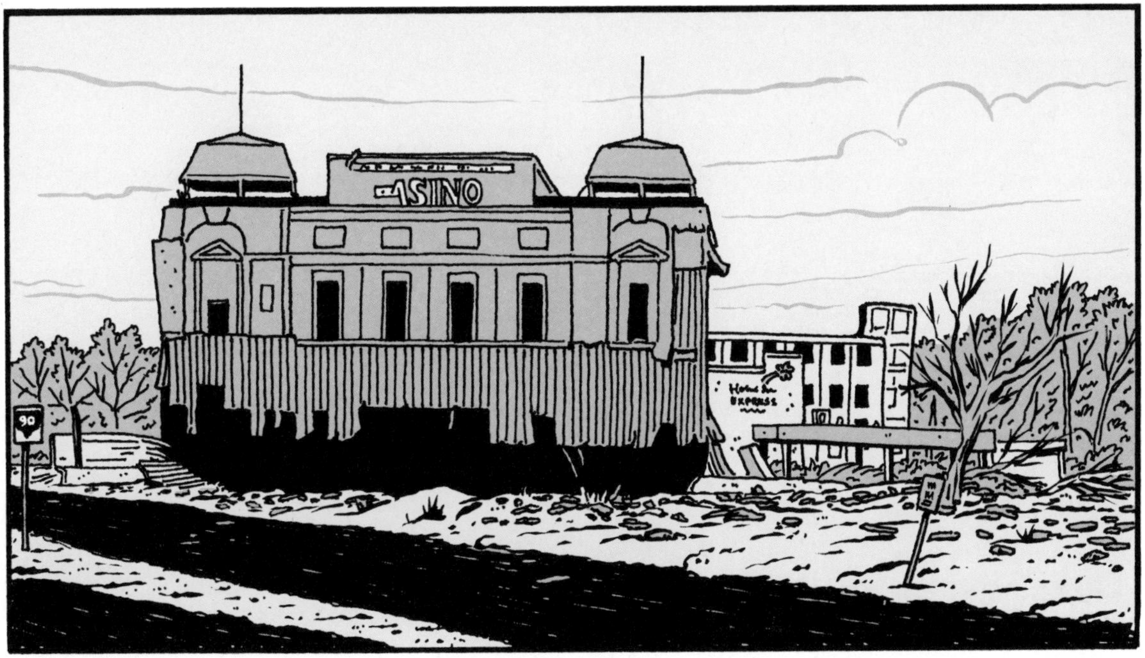
ASINO
90

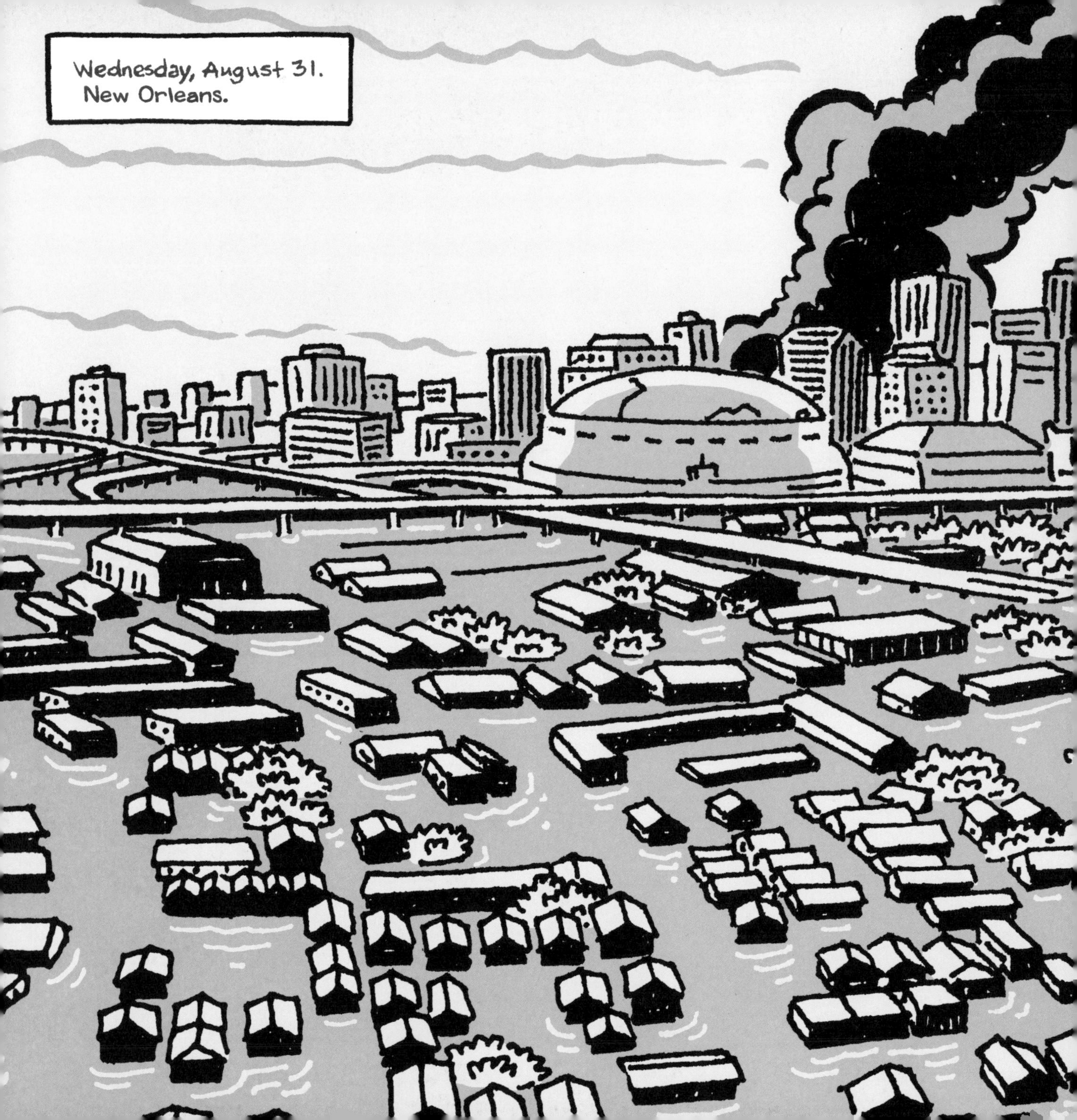
Wednesday, August 31.
New Orleans.

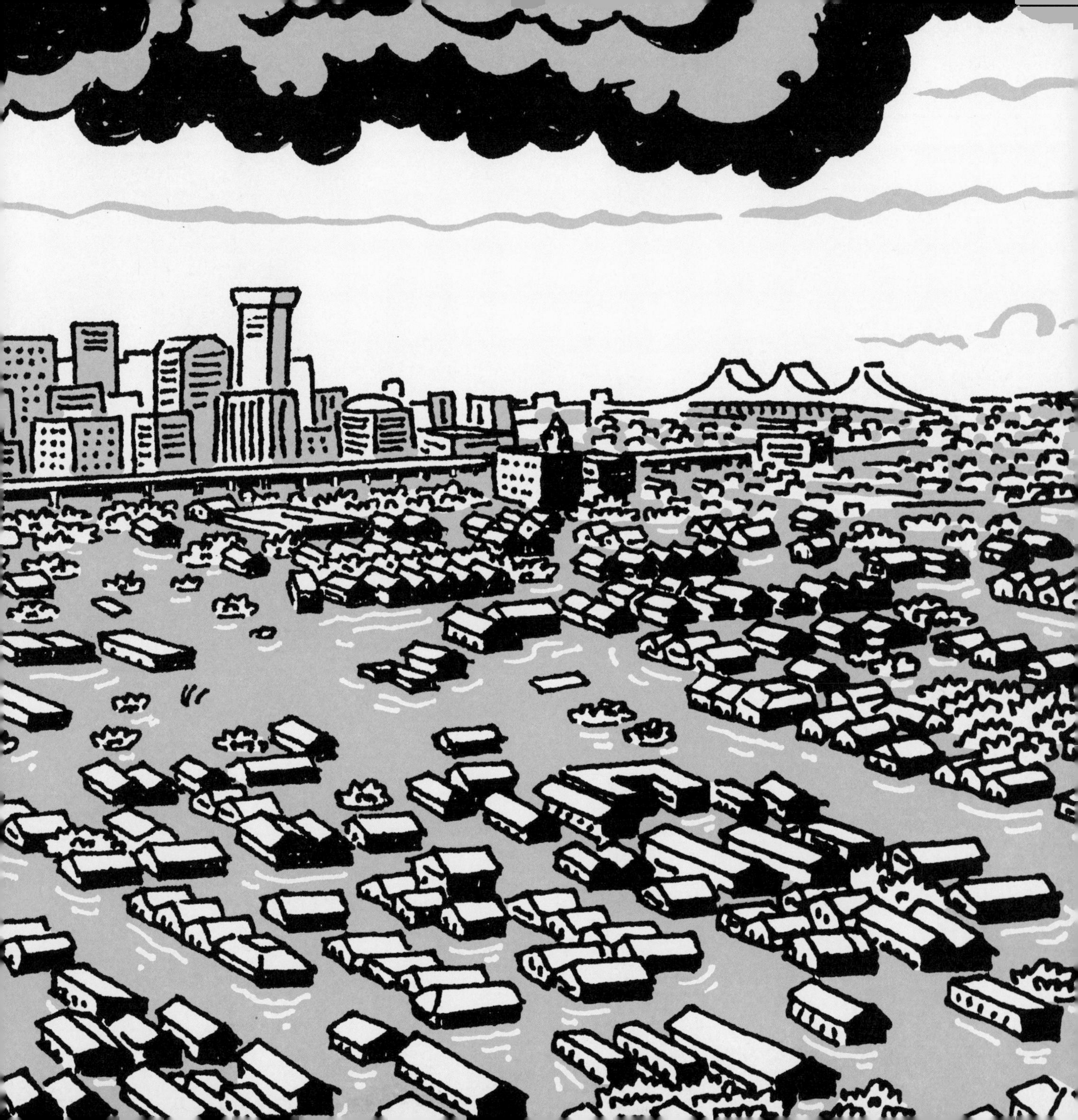

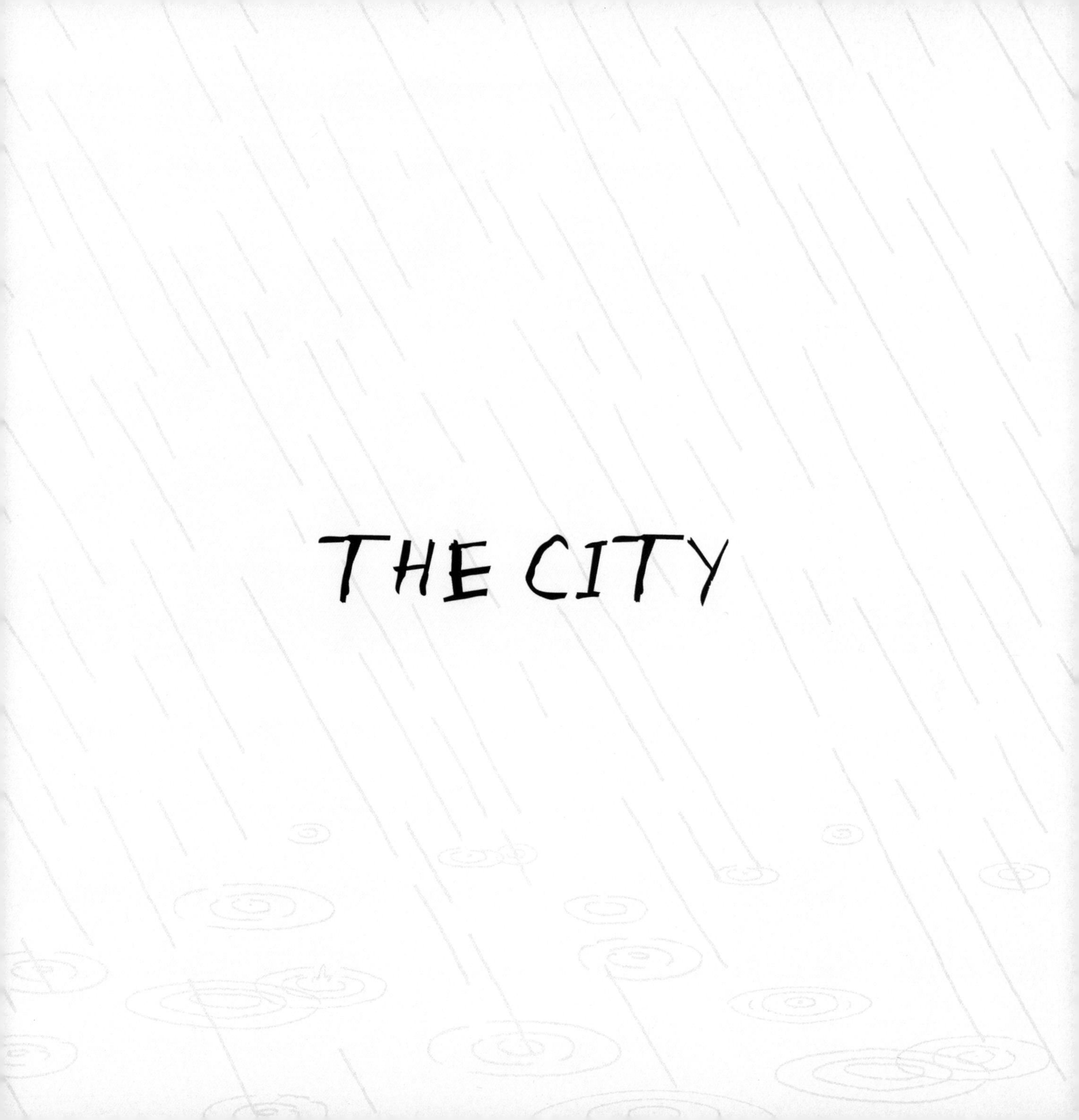
THE CITY

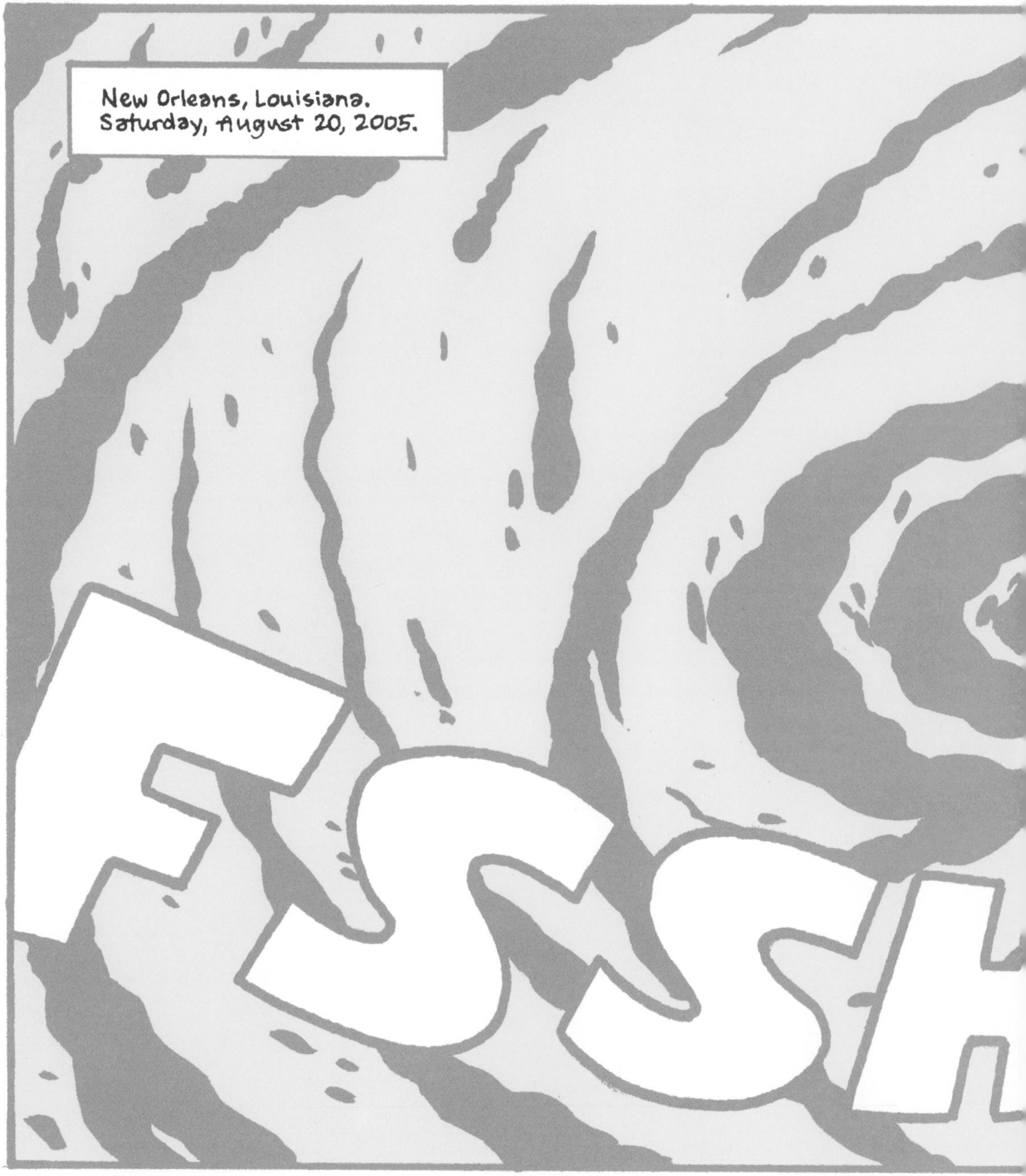
New Orleans, Louisiana.
Saturday, August 20, 2005.
FSSH

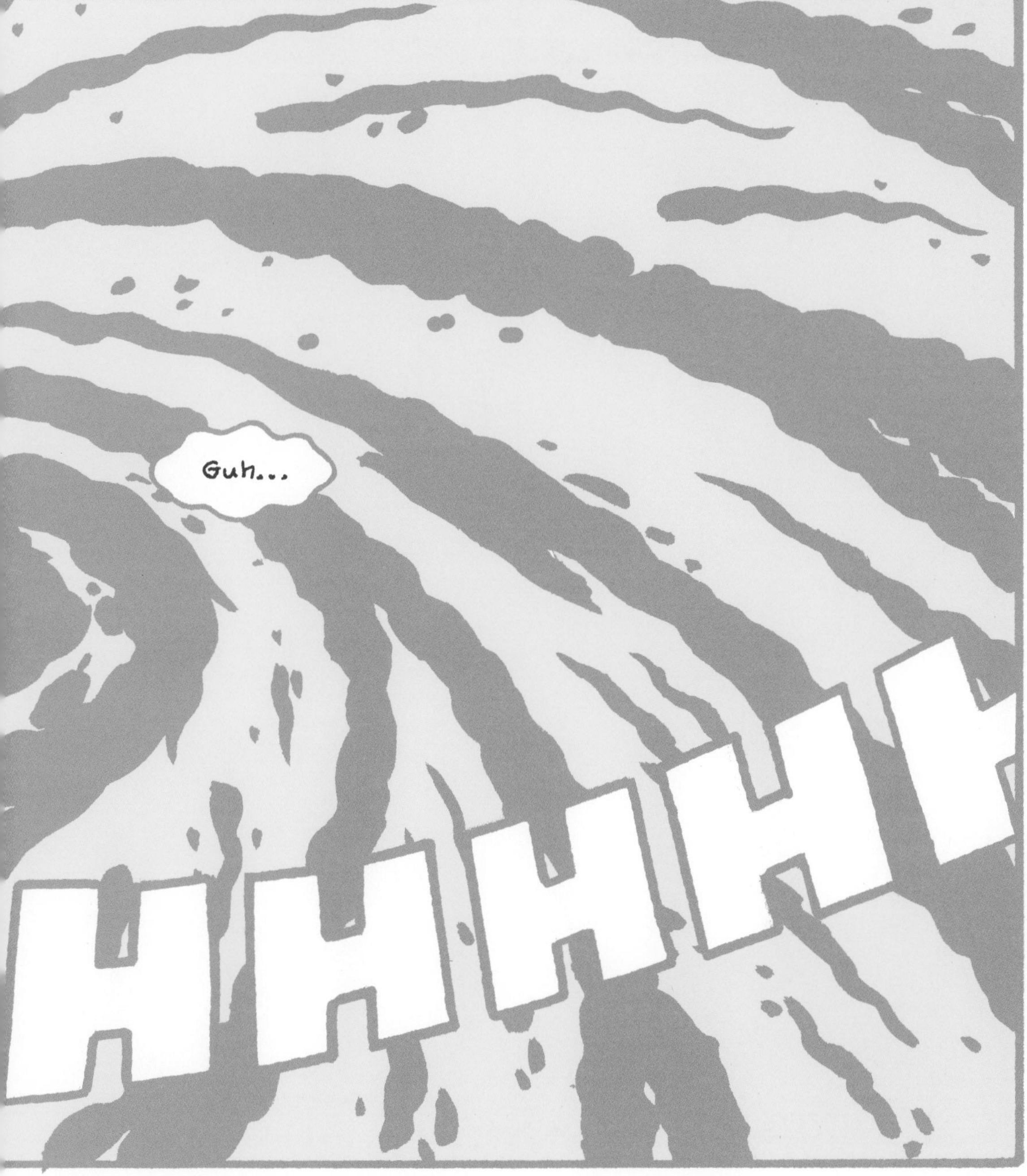
Guh...
HHHHHH

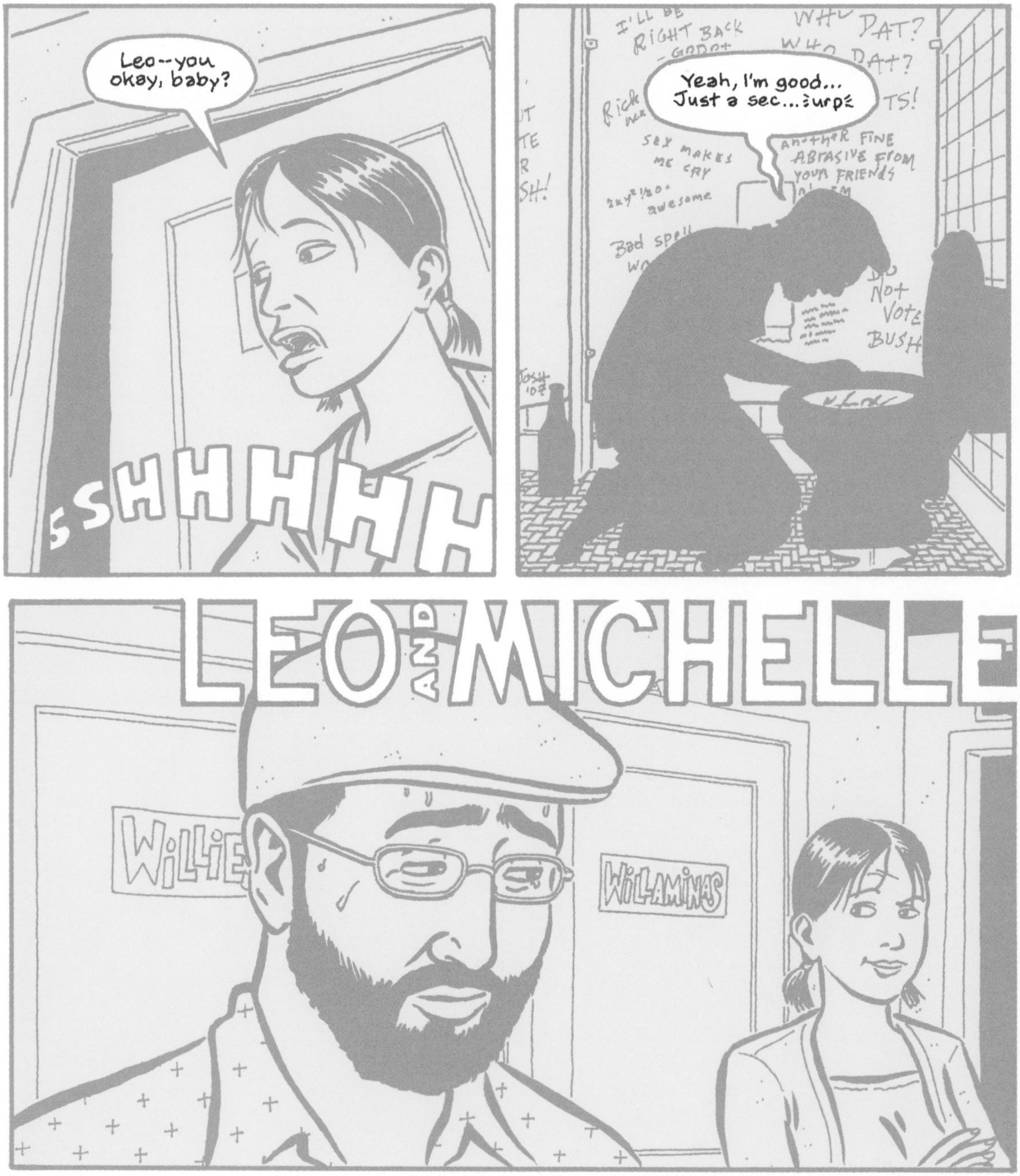
Leo--you okay, baby?
SSHHHHHH
Yeah, I'm good... Just a sec...urp
I'LL BE RIGHT BACK
WHO DAT? WHO DAT?
SEX MAKES ME CRY
awesome
ANOTHER FINE ABRASIVE FROM YOUR FRIENDS
NOT VOTE BUSH
LEO AND MICHELLE
Willies
Willaminas

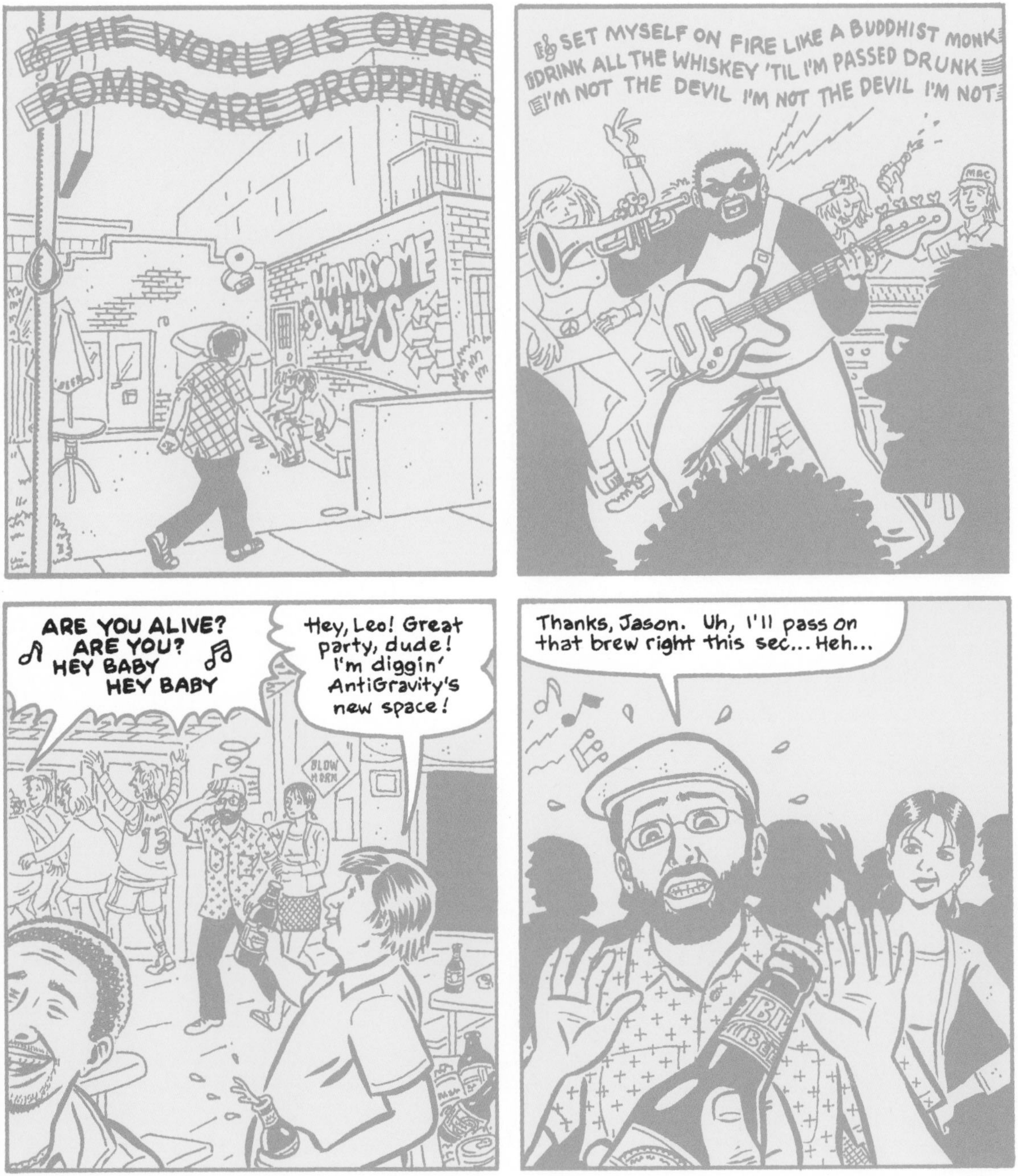
THE WORLD IS OVER
BOMBS ARE DROPPING
HANDSOME WILYS
SET MYSELF ON FIRE LIKE A BUDDHIST MONK
DRINK ALL THE WHISKEY 'TIL I'M PASSED DRUNK
I'M NOT THE DEVIL I'M NOT THE DEVIL I'M NOT
ARE YOU ALIVE? ARE YOU? HEY BABY HEY BABY
Hey, Leo! Great party, dude! I'm diggin' AntiGravity's new space!
BLOW HORN
Thanks, Jason. Uh, I'll pass on that brew right this sec... Heh...

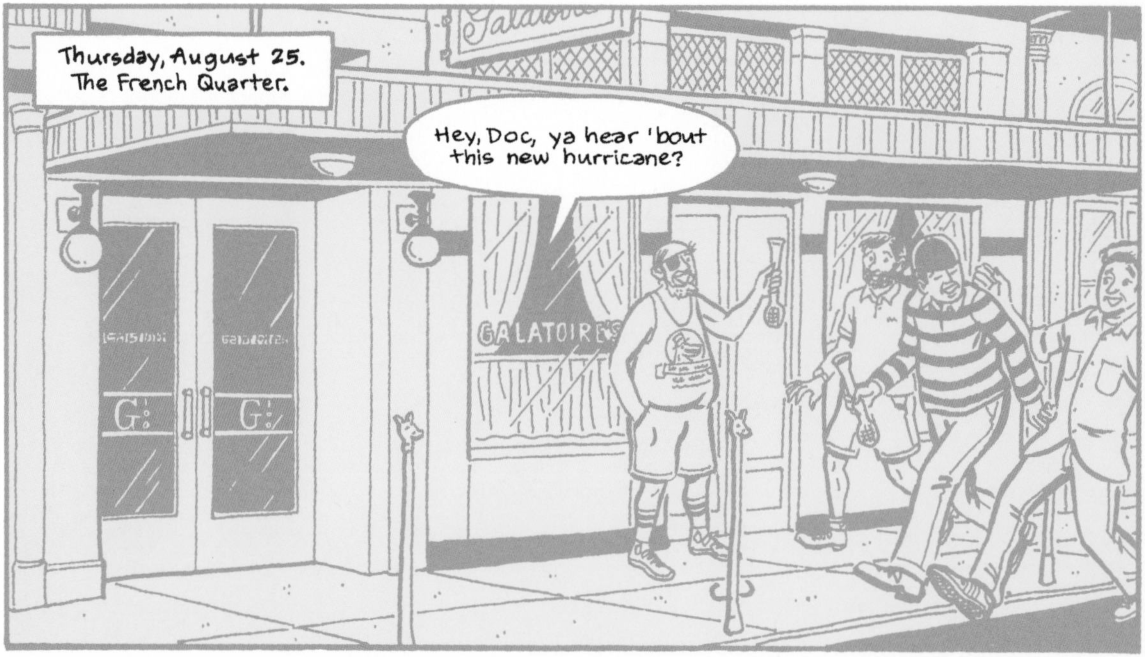
Thursday, August 25.
The French Quarter.
Hey, Doc, ya hear 'bout this new hurricane?
GALATOIRE'S

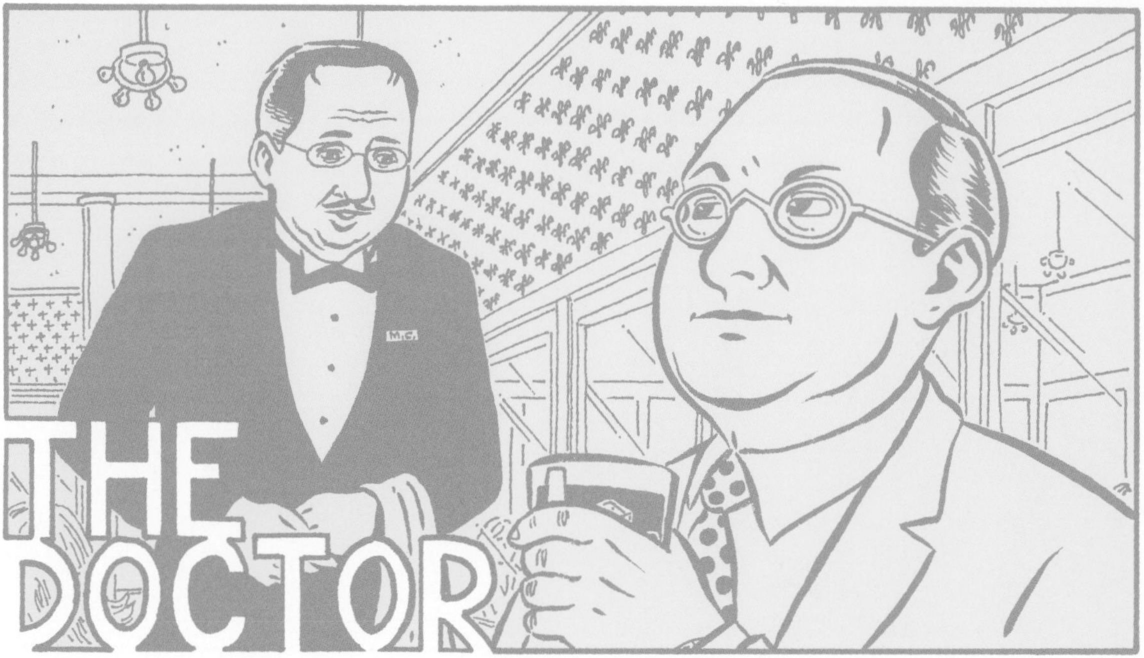
THE DOCTOR

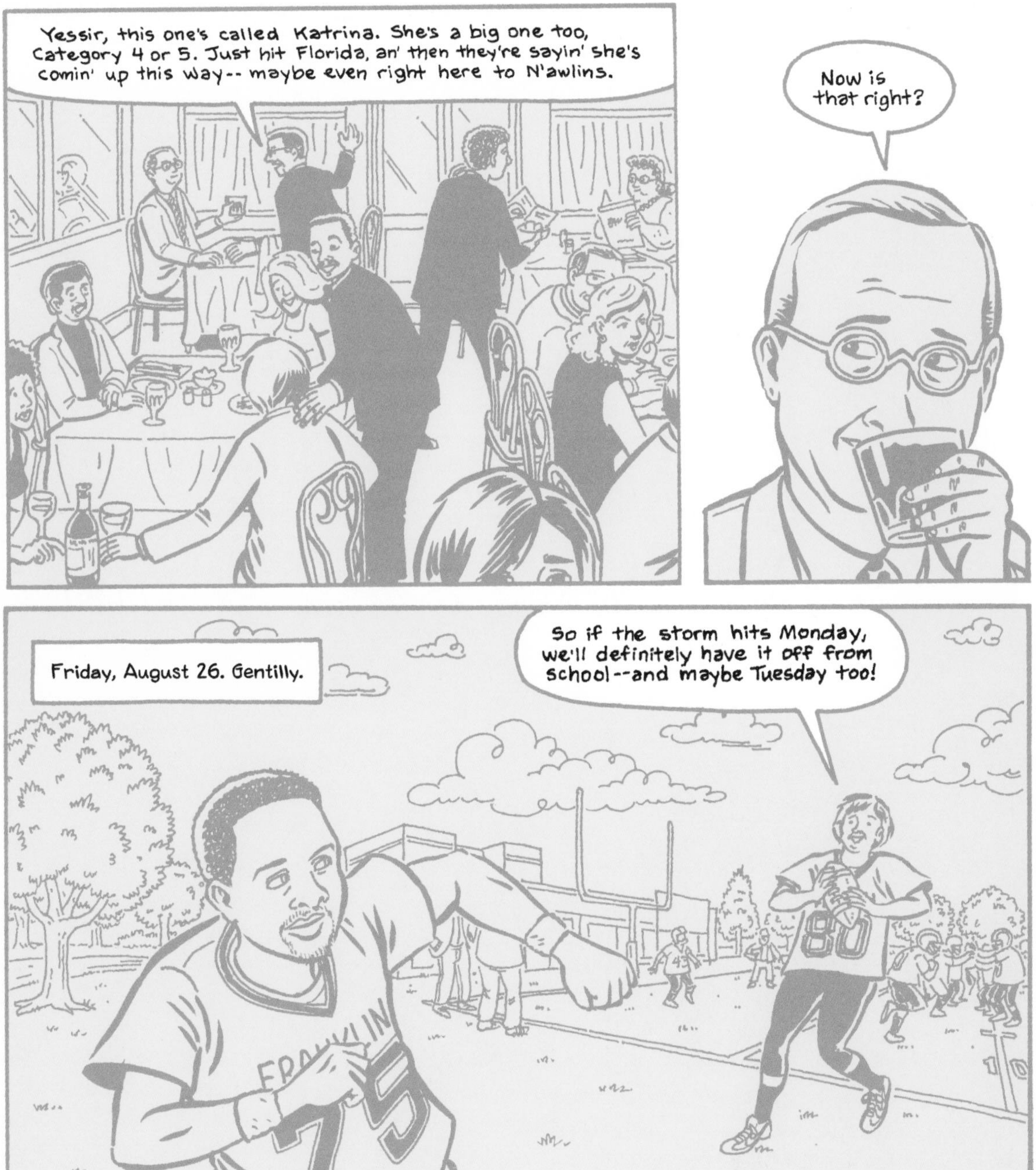
Yessir, this one's called Katrina. She's a big one too, Category 4 or 5. Just hit Florida, an' then they're sayin' she's comin' up this way-- maybe even right here to N'awlins.
Now is that right?
Friday, August 26. Gentilly.
So if the storm hits Monday, we'll definitely have it off from school--and maybe Tuesday too!
FRANKLIN
75
80

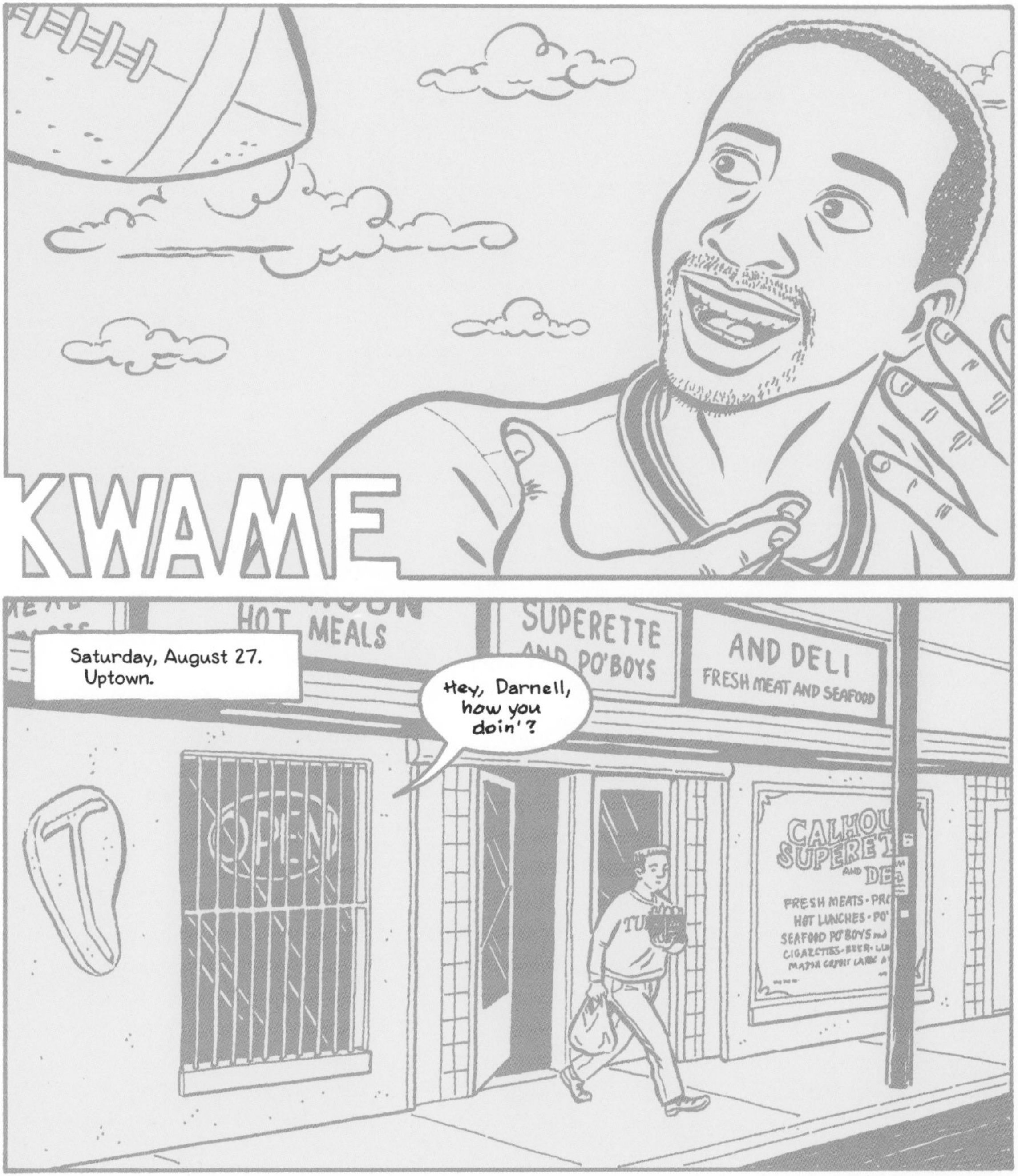
KWAME
HOT MEALS
SUPERETTE
PO'BOYS
AND DELI
FRESH MEAT AND SEAFOOD
Saturday, August 27.
Uptown.
Hey, Darnell, how you doin'?
OPEN
HOT LUNCHES

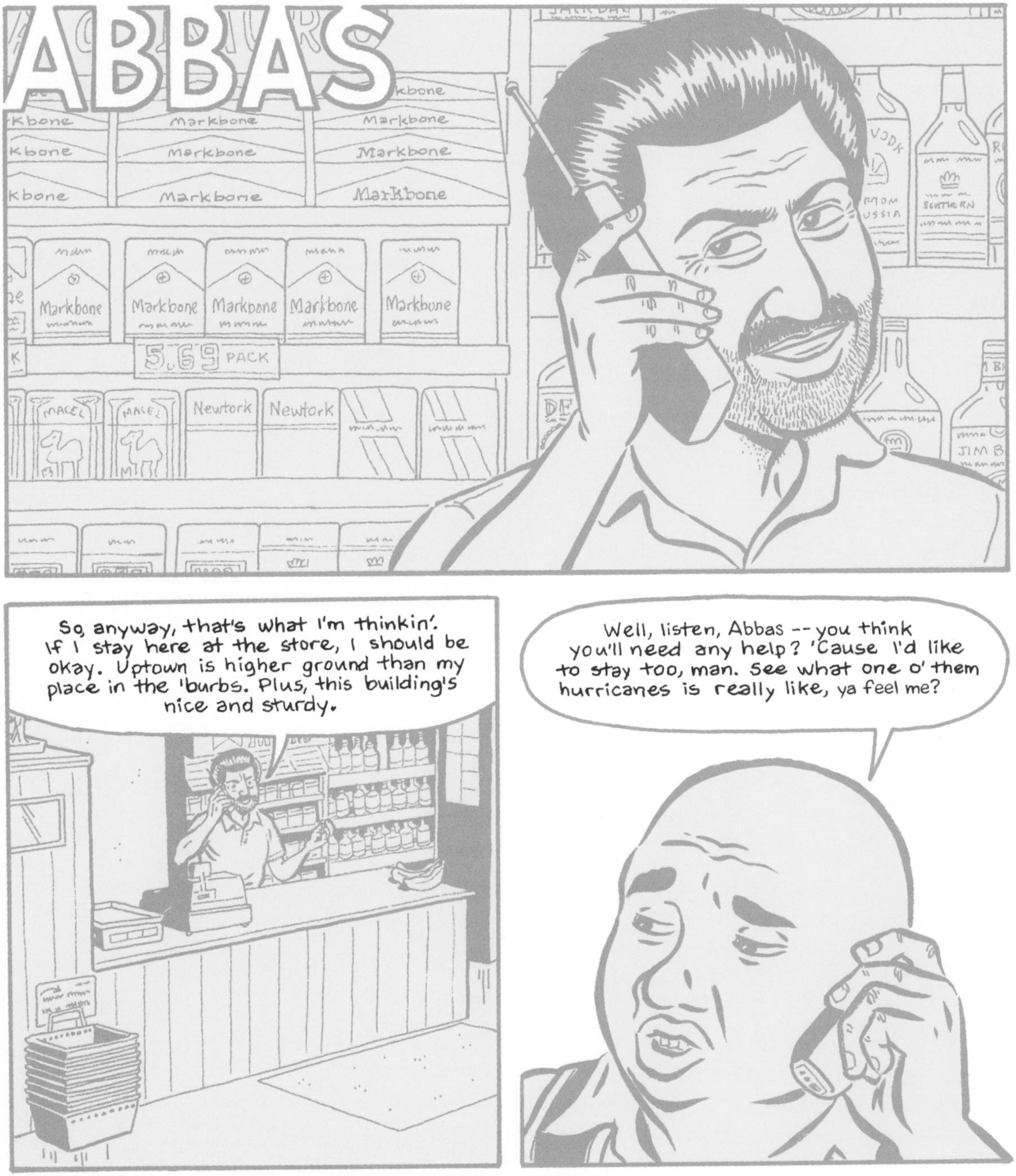
ABBAS
So, anyway, that's what I'm thinkin'. If I stay here at the store, I should be okay. Uptown is higher ground than my place in the 'burbs. Plus, this building's nice and sturdy.
Well, listen, Abbas -- you think you'll need any help? 'Cause I'd like to stay too, man. See what one o' them hurricanes is really like, ya feel me?

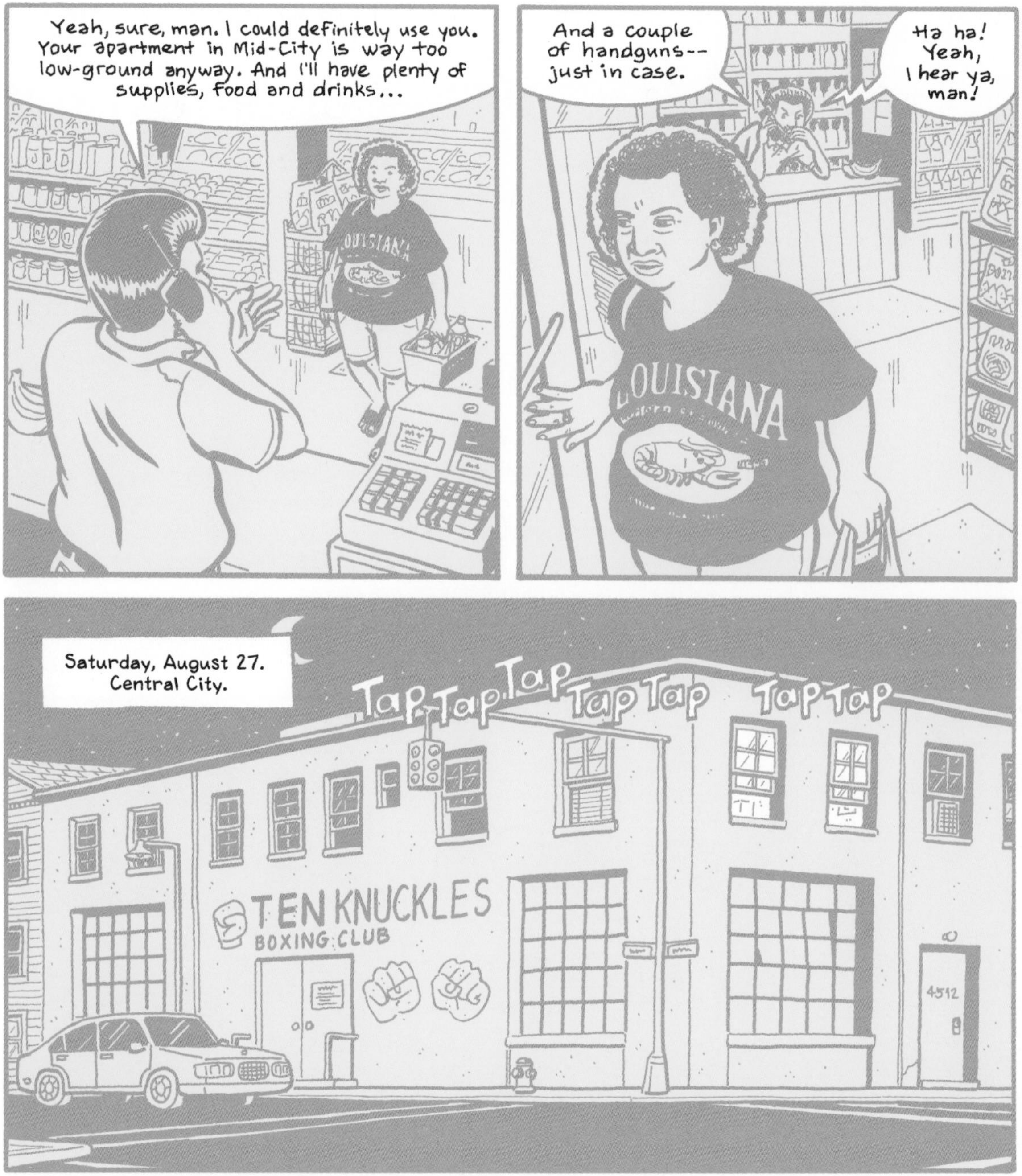
Yeah, sure, man. I could definitely use you. Your apartment in Mid-City is way too low-ground anyway. And I'll have plenty of supplies, food and drinks...
LOUISIANA
And a couple of handguns-- just in case.
Ha ha! Yeah, I hear ya, man!
LOUISIANA
Saturday, August 27. Central City.
Tap Tap Tap Tap Tap Tap Tap
TEN KNUCKLES
BOXING CLUB
4512

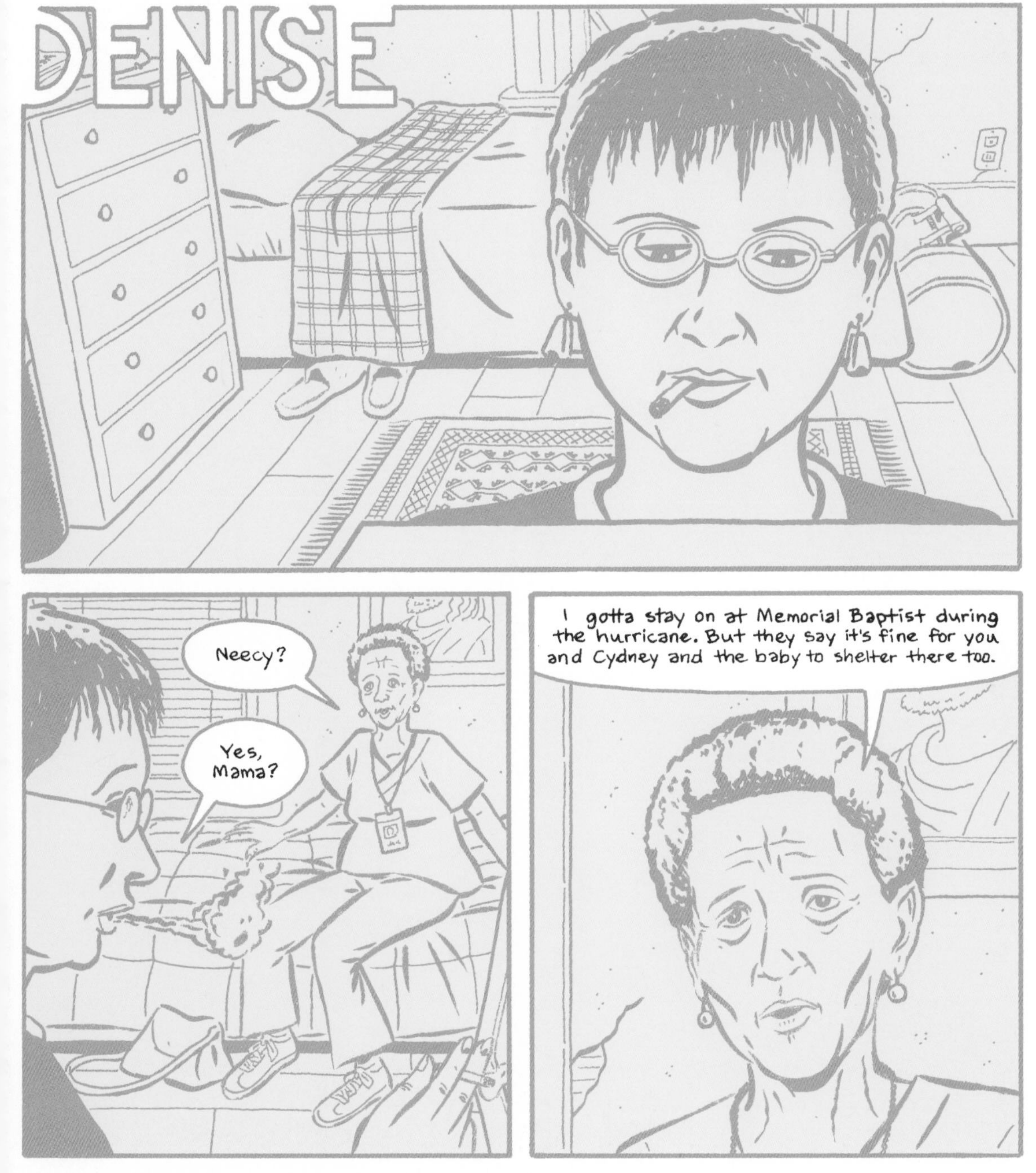
DENISE
Neecy?
Yes, Mama?
I gotta stay on at Memorial Baptist during the hurricane. But they say it's fine for you and Cydney and the baby to shelter there too.

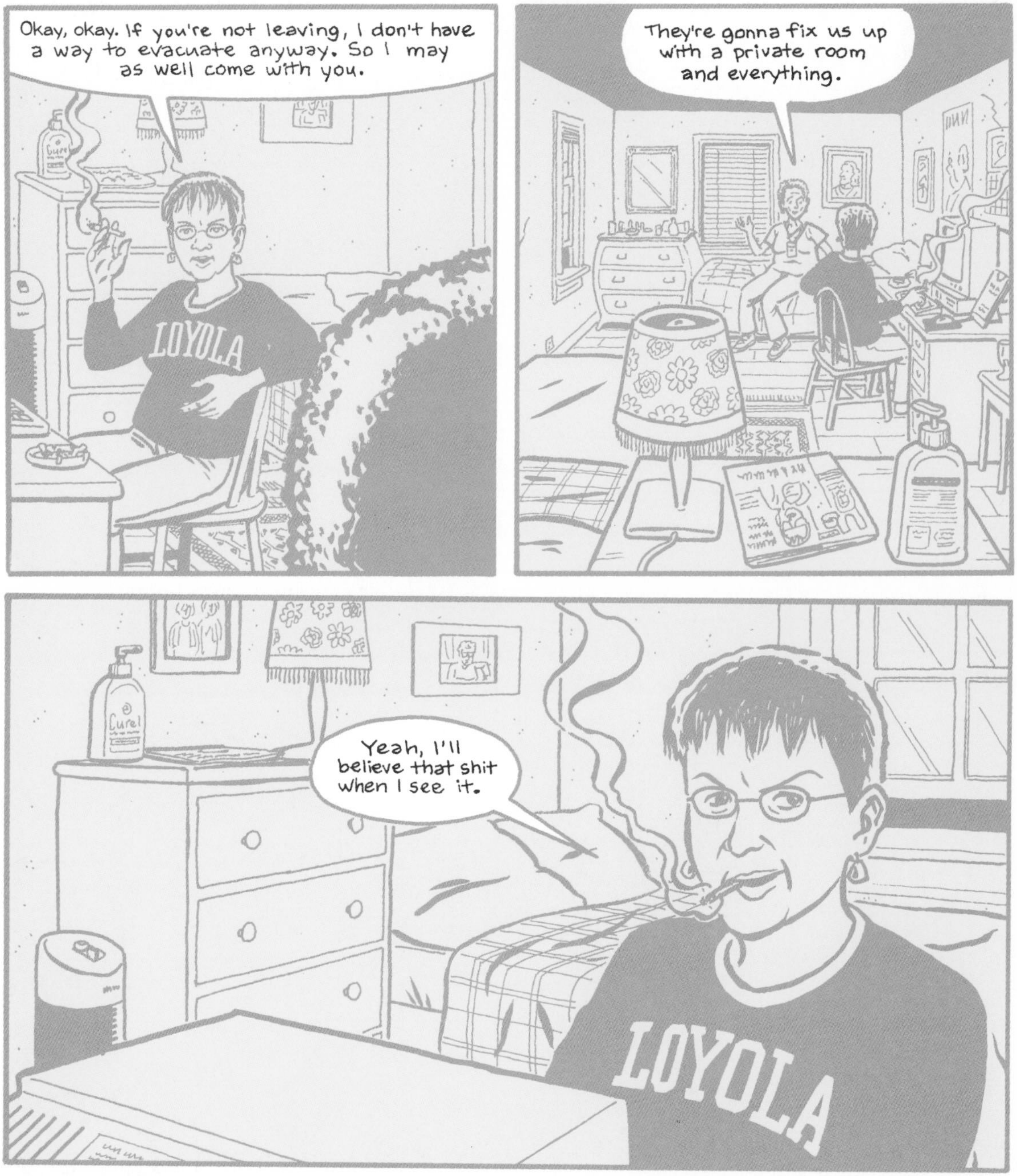
Okay, okay. If you're not leaving, I don't have a way to evacuate anyway. So I may as well come with you.
LOYOLA
They're gonna fix us up with a private room and everything.
Yeah, I'll believe that shit when I see it.
LOYOLA

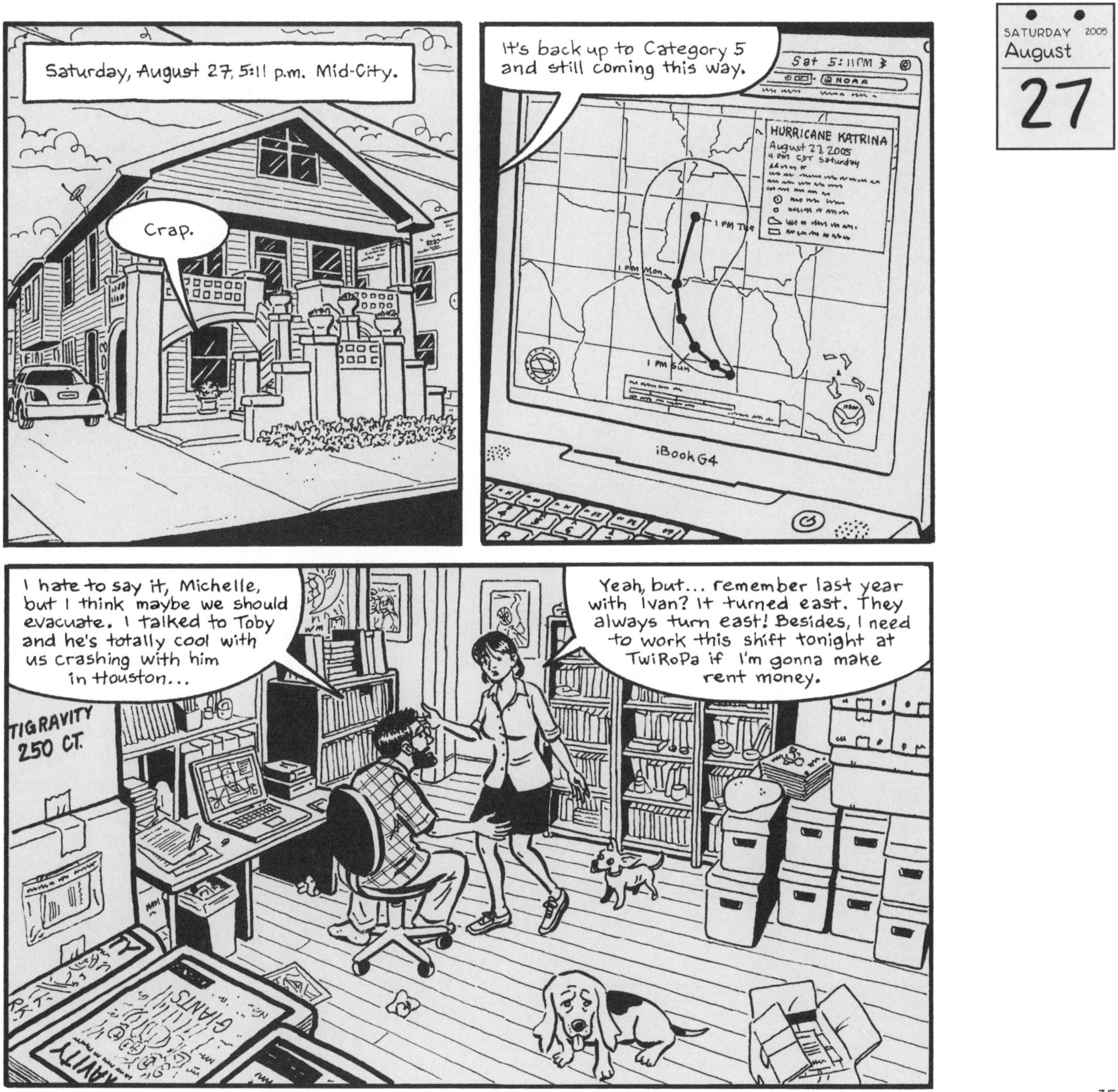
SATURDAY 2005
August
27
Saturday, August 27, 5:11 p.m. Mid-City.
Crap.
It's back up to Category 5 and still coming this way.
Sat 5:11PM
HURRICANE KATRINA
August 27, 2005
4 PM CDT Saturday
1 PM Tue
1 PM Mon
1 PM Sun
iBook G4
I hate to say it, Michelle, but I think maybe we should evacuate. I talked to Toby and he's totally cool with us crashing with him in Houston...
Yeah, but... remember last year with Ivan? It turned east. They always turn east! Besides, I need to work this shift tonight at TwiRoPa if I'm gonna make rent money.
TIGRAVITY 250 CT.

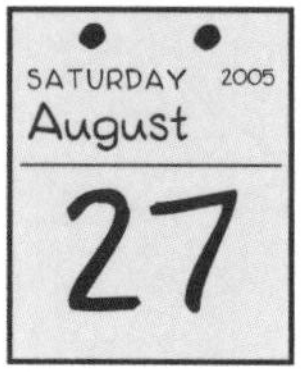
SATURDAY 2005
August
27

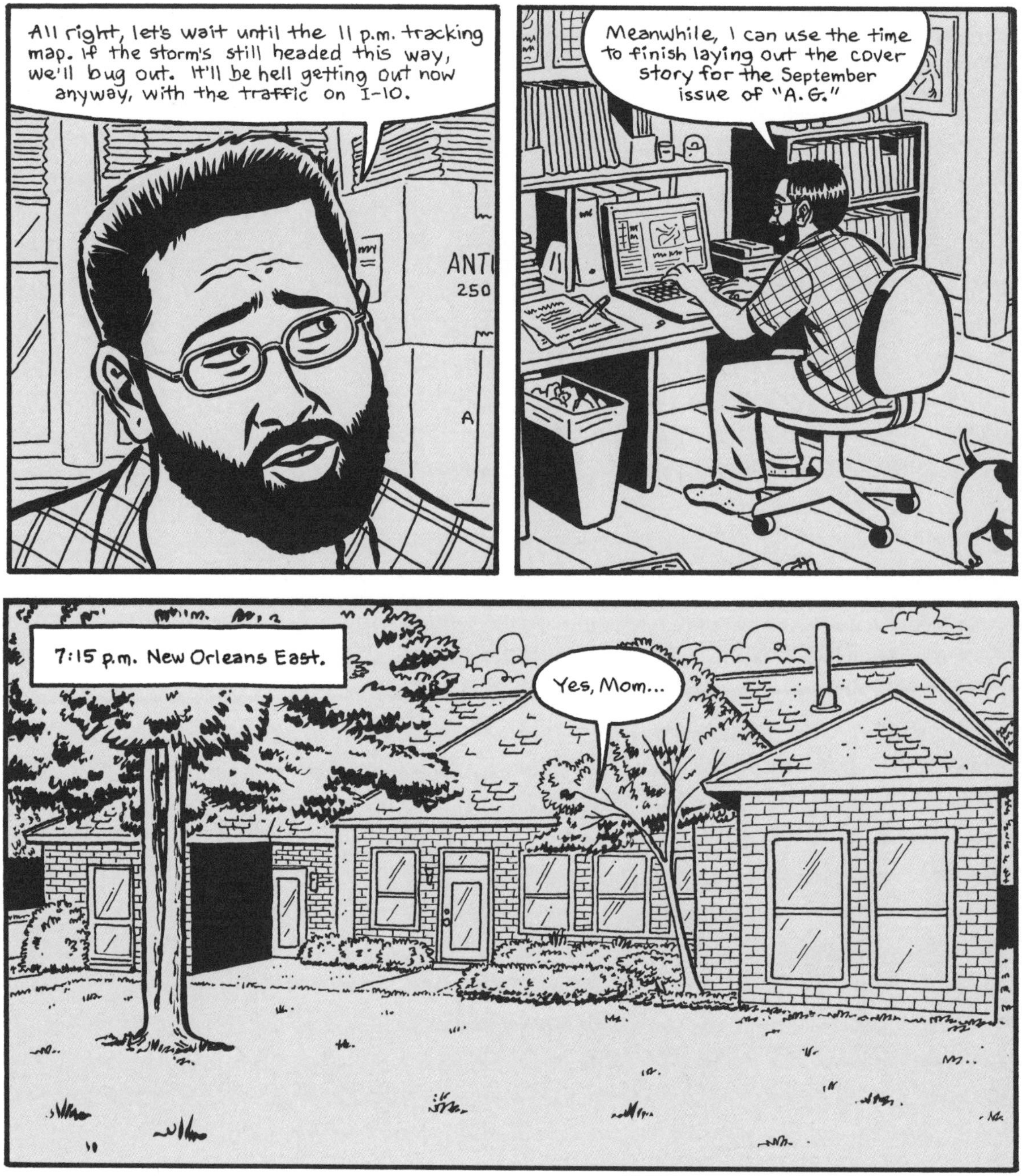
All right, let's wait until the 11 p.m. tracking map. If the storm's still headed this way, we'll bug out. It'll be hell getting out now anyway, with the traffic on I-10.
Meanwhile, I can use the time to finish laying out the cover story for the September issue of "A.G."
7:15 p.m. New Orleans East.
Yes, Mom...

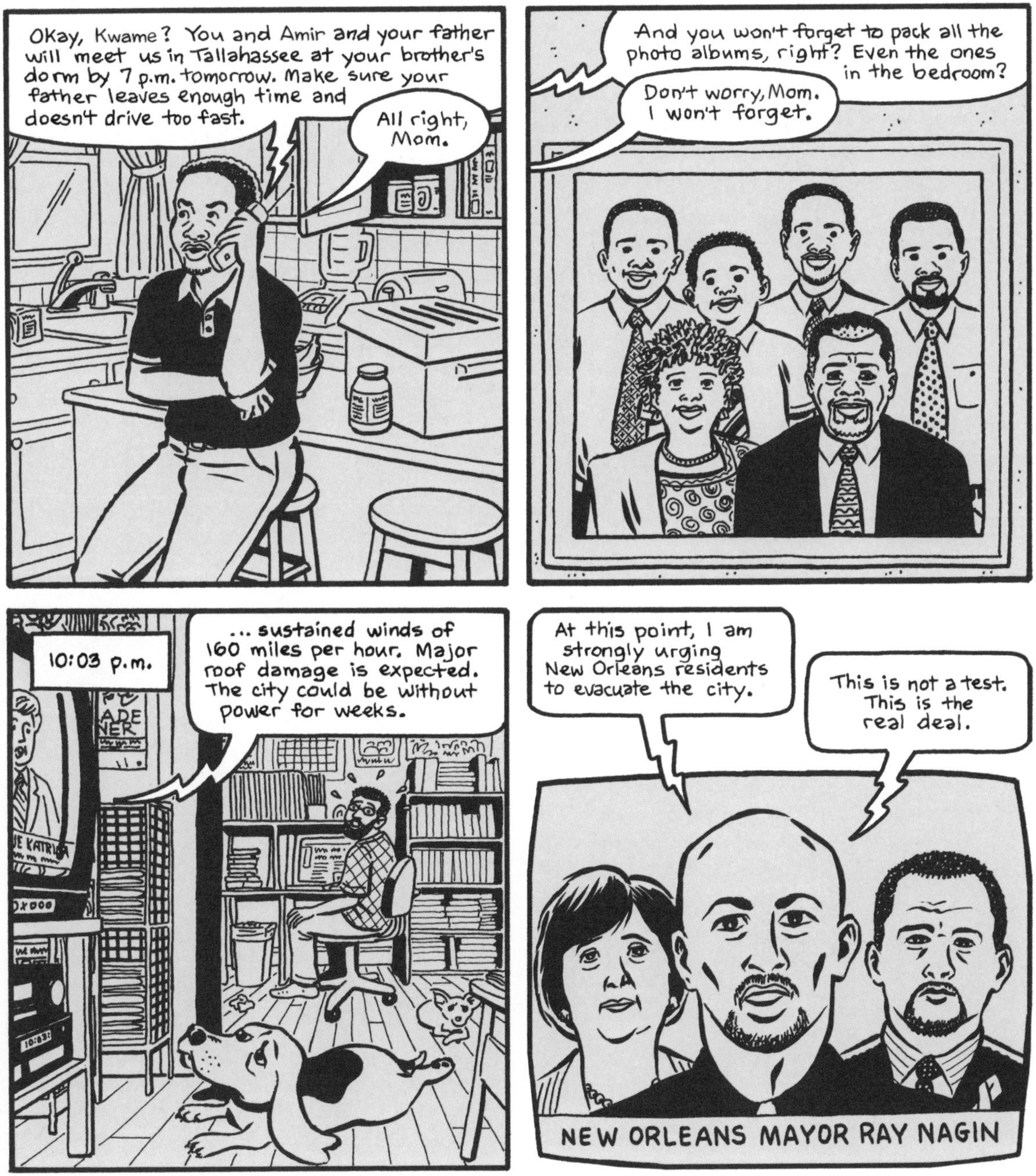
Okay, Kwame? You and Amir and your father will meet us in Tallahassee at your brother's dorm by 7 p.m. tomorrow. Make sure your father leaves enough time and doesn't drive too fast.
All right, Mom.
And you won't forget to pack all the photo albums, right? Even the ones in the bedroom?
Don't worry, Mom. I won't forget.
10:03 p.m.
... sustained winds of 160 miles per hour. Major roof damage is expected. The city could be without power for weeks.
At this point, I am strongly urging New Orleans residents to evacuate the city.
This is not a test. This is the real deal.
NEW ORLEANS MAYOR RAY NAGIN

SATURDAY 2005
August
27

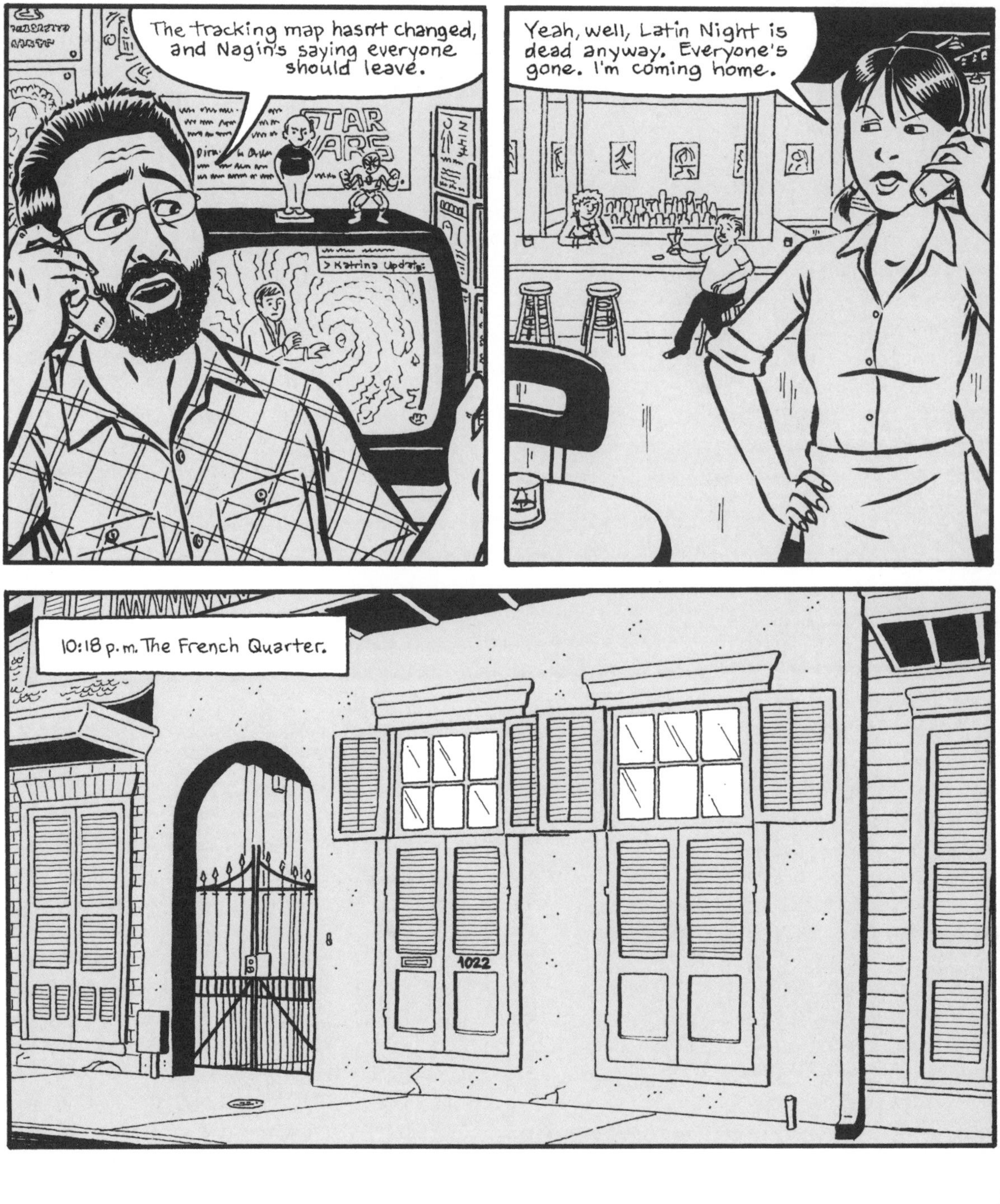
The tracking map hasn't changed, and Nagin's saying everyone should leave.
STAR WARS
Katrina Update:
Yeah, well, Latin Night is dead anyway. Everyone's gone. I'm coming home.
10:18 p.m. The French Quarter.
1022

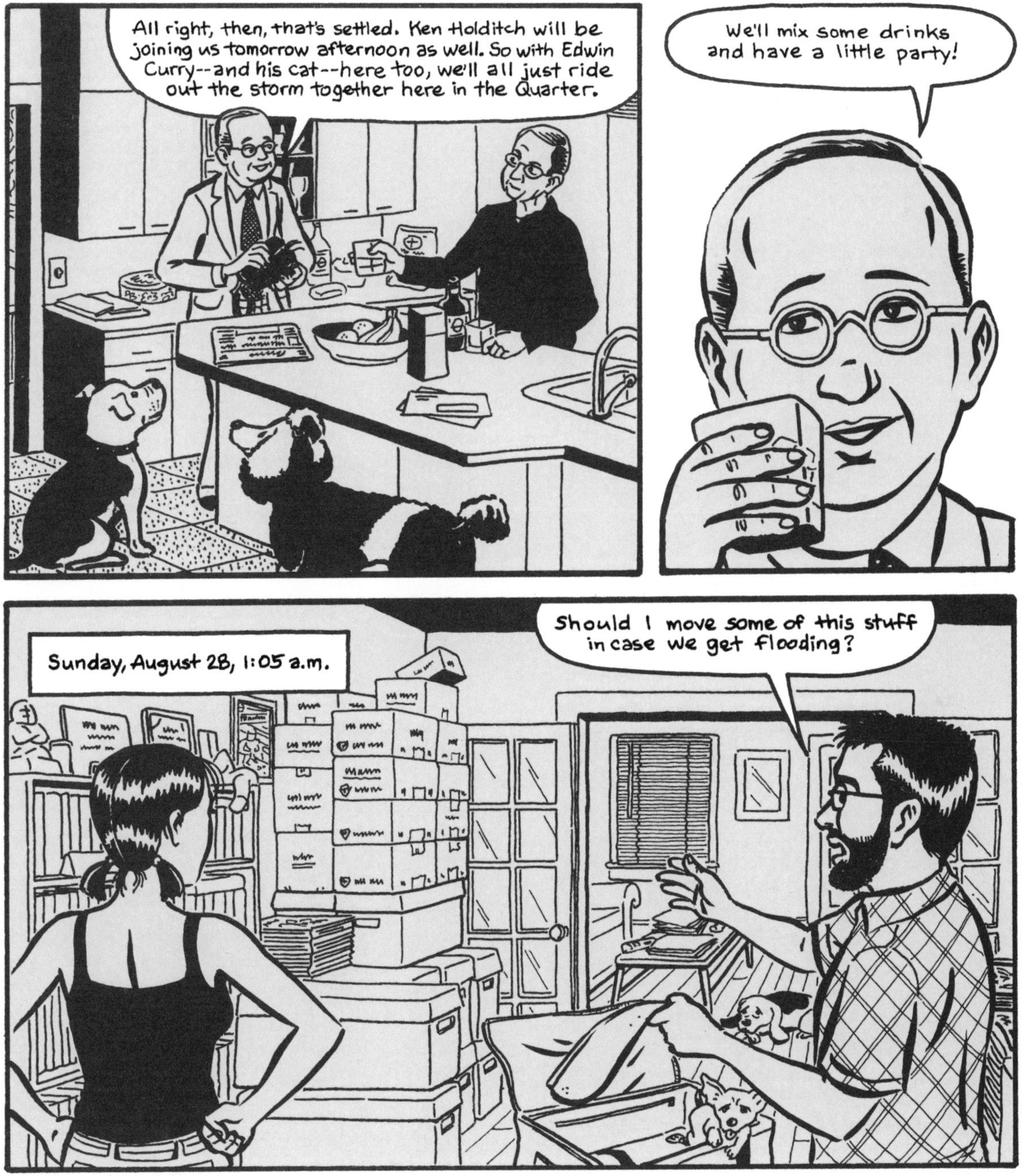
All right, then, that's settled. Ken Holditch will be joining us tomorrow afternoon as well. So with Edwin Curry--and his cat--here too, we'll all just ride out the storm together here in the Quarter.
We'll mix some drinks and have a little party!
Sunday, August 28, 1:05 a.m.
Should I move some of this stuff in case we get flooding?

SUNDAY 2005
August
28

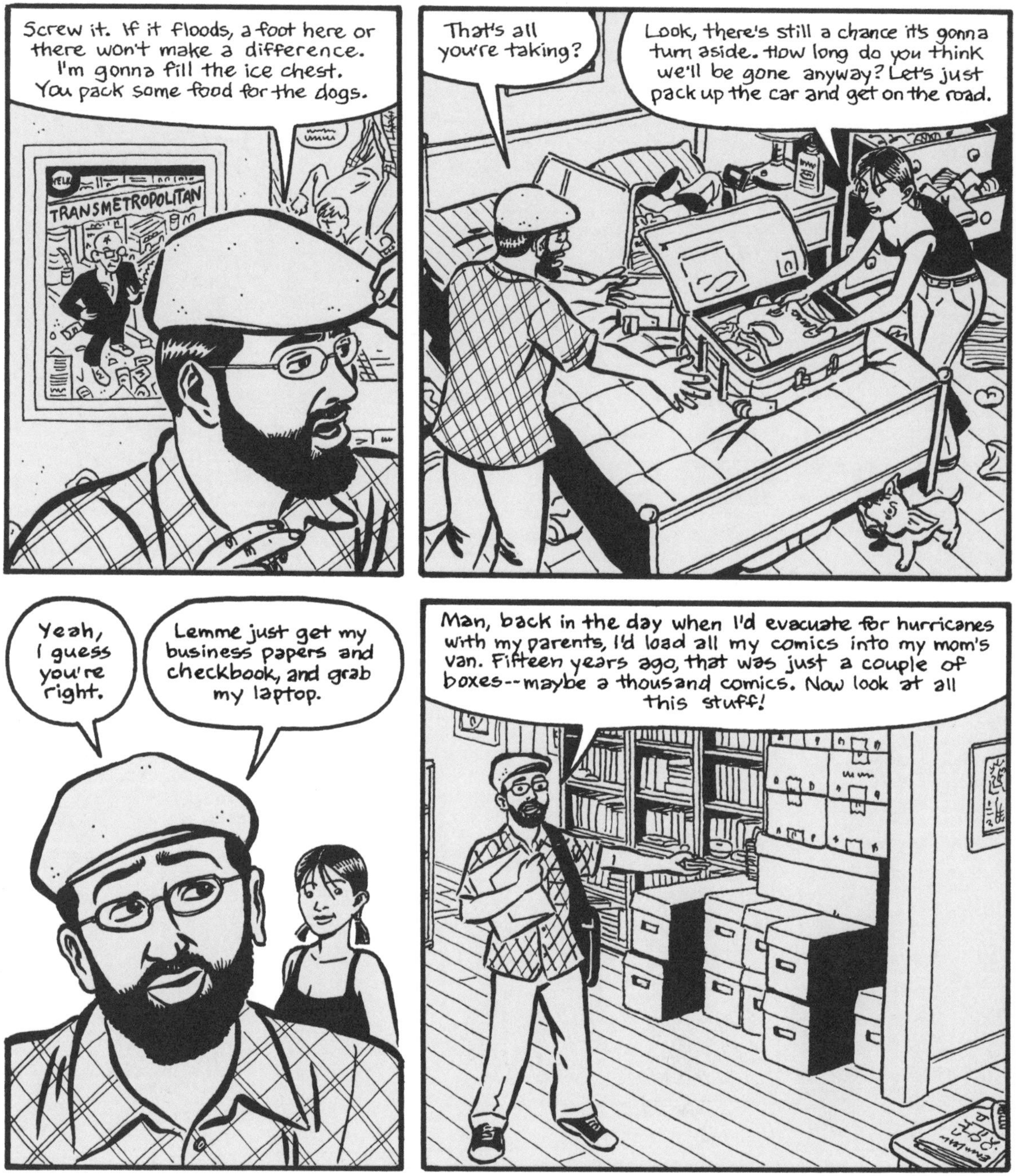

Screw it. If it floods, a foot here or there won't make a difference. I'm gonna fill the ice chest. You pack some food for the dogs.
TRANSMETROPOLITAN
That's all you're taking?
Look, there's still a chance it's gonna turn aside. How long do you think we'll be gone anyway? Let's just pack up the car and get on the road.
Yeah, I guess you're right.
Lemme just get my business papers and checkbook, and grab my laptop.
Man, back in the day when I'd evacuate for hurricanes with my parents, I'd load all my comics into my mom's van. Fifteen years ago, that was just a couple of boxes--maybe a thousand comics. Now look at all this stuff!

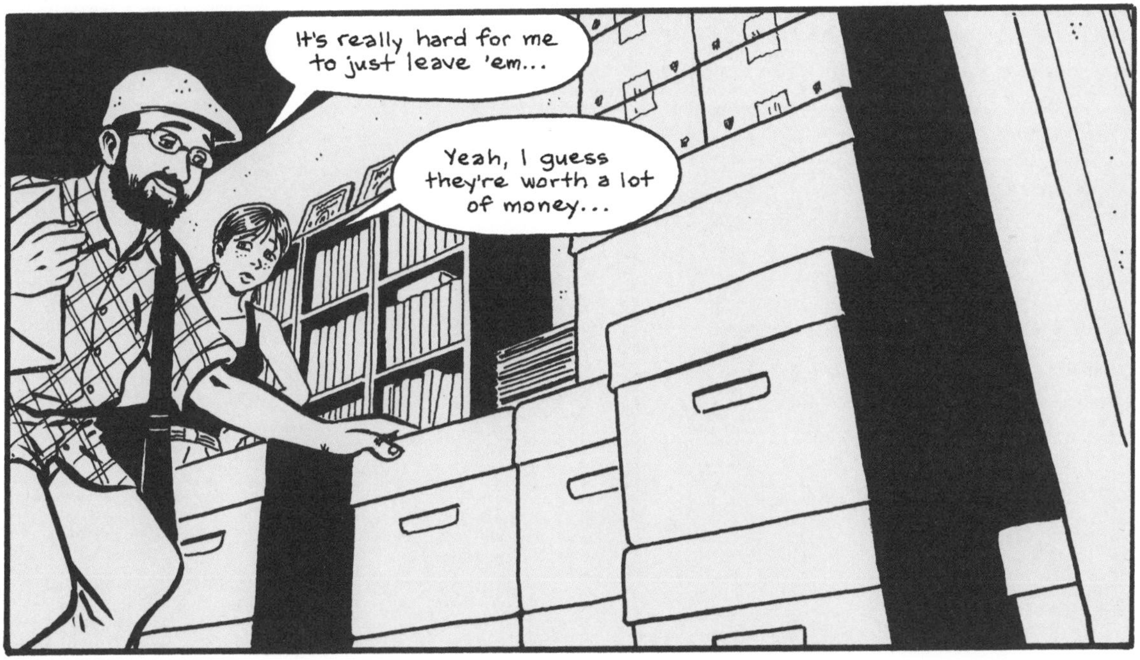
It's really hard for me to just leave 'em...
Yeah, I guess they're worth a lot of money...

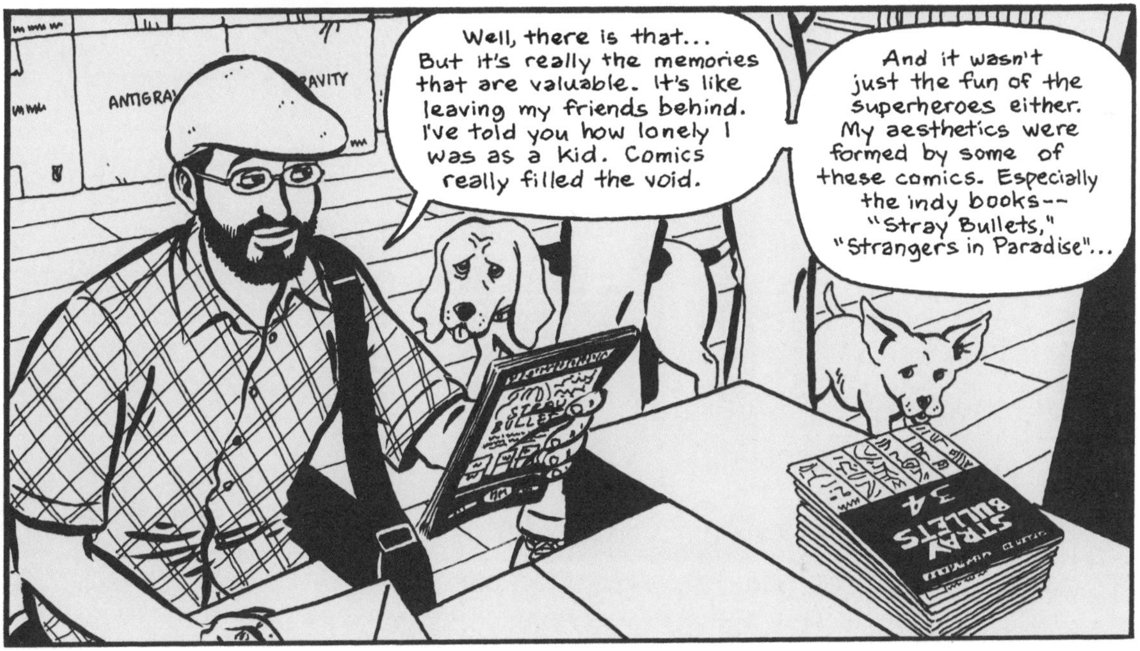
Well, there is that... But it's really the memories that are valuable. It's like leaving my friends behind. I've told you how lonely I was as a kid. Comics really filled the void.
And it wasn't just the fun of the superheroes either. My aesthetics were formed by some of these comics. Especially the indy books-- "Stray Bullets," "Strangers in Paradise"...
STRAY BULLETS
34

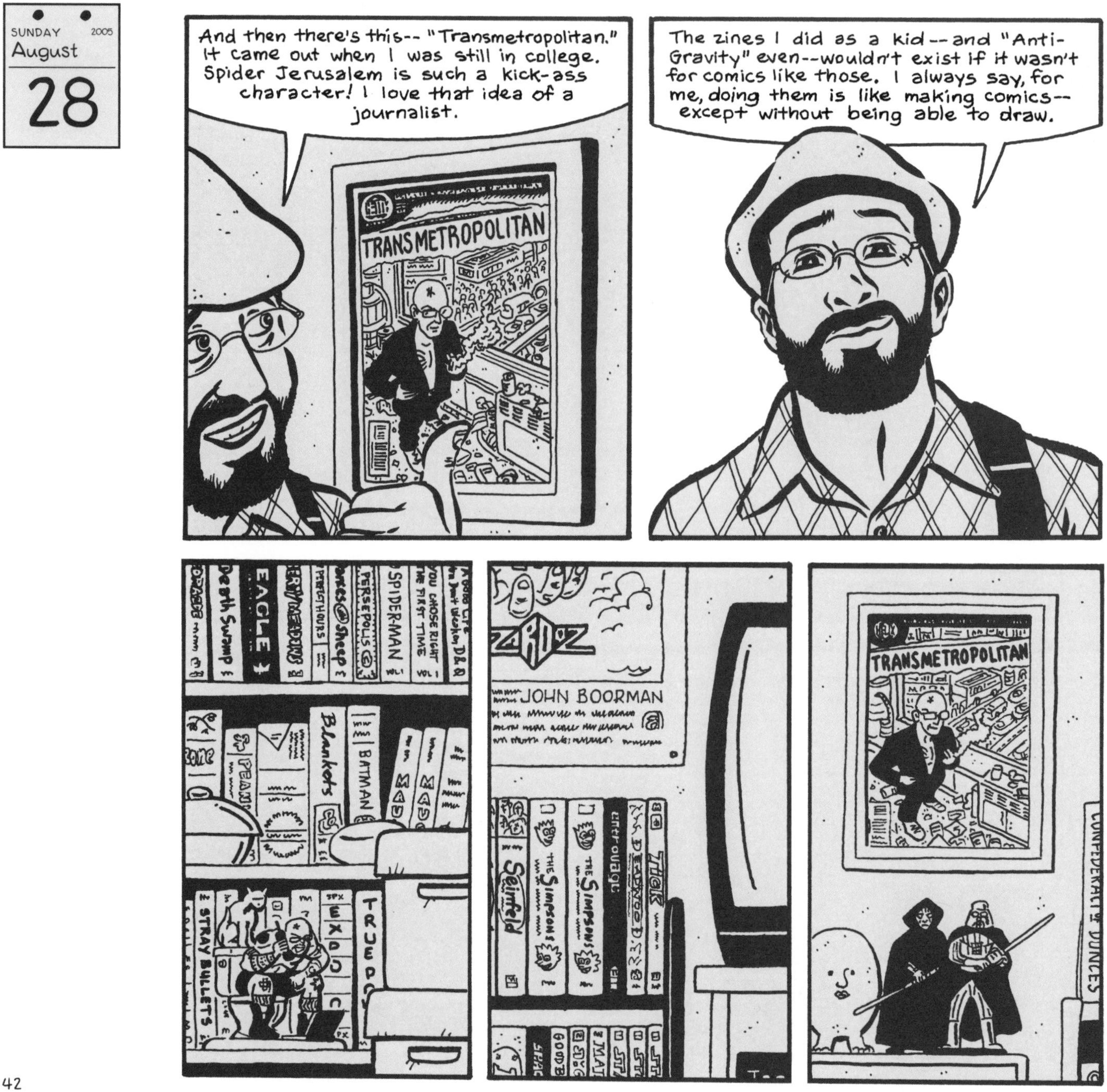
SUNDAY 2005
August
28
And then there's this-- "Transmetropolitan." It came out when I was still in college. Spider Jerusalem is such a kick-ass character! I love that idea of a journalist.
TRANSMETROPOLITAN
The zines I did as a kid--and "Anti-Gravity" even--wouldn't exist if it wasn't for comics like those. I always say, for me, doing them is like making comics--except without being able to draw.
Death Swamp
EAGLE
PERSEPOLIS
SPIDER-MAN
Blankets
BATMAN
STRAY BULLETS
JOHN BOORMAN
Seinfeld
THE SIMPSONS
THE SIMPSONS
TRANSMETROPOLITAN
CONFEDERACY OF DUNCES

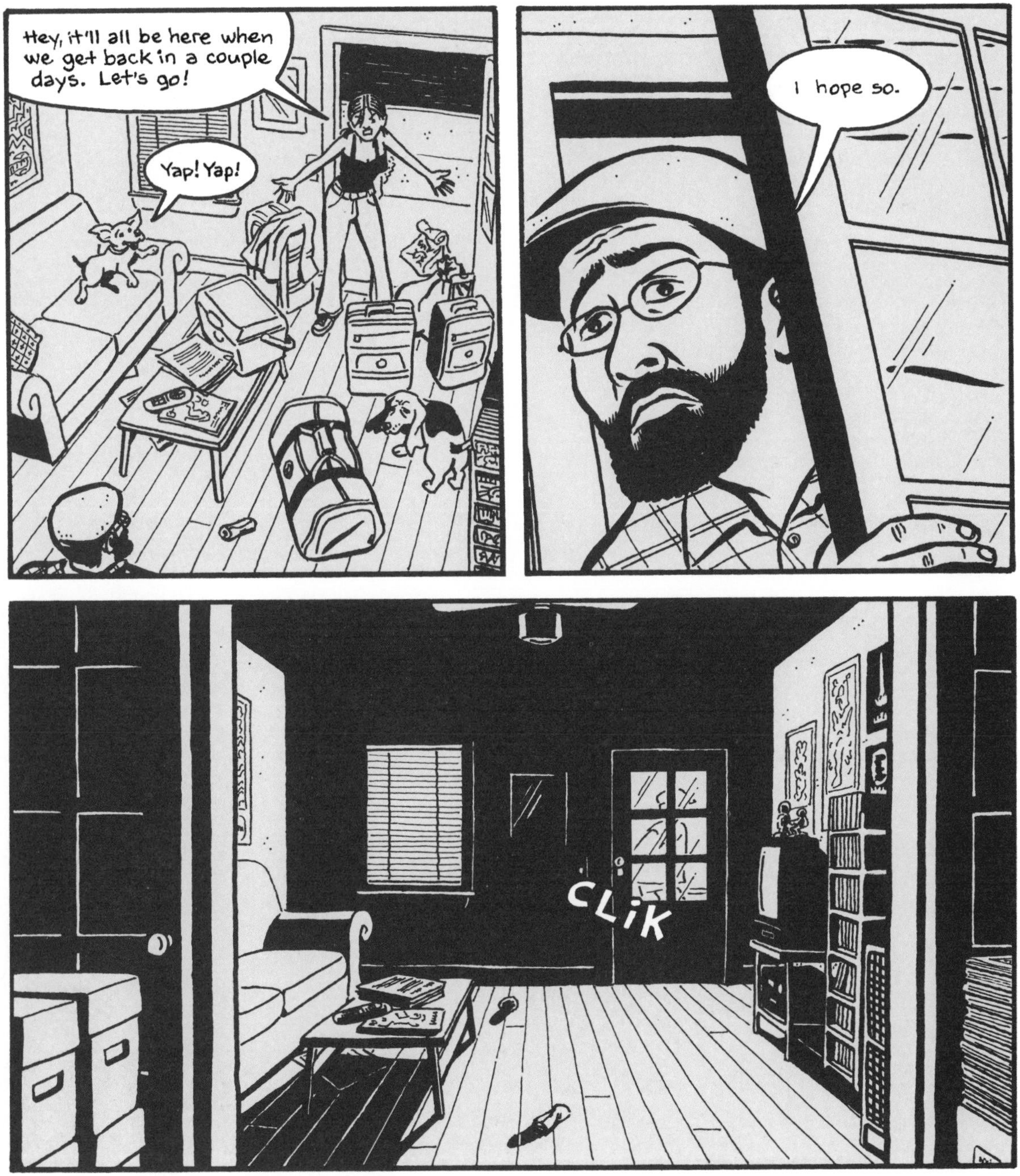
Hey, it'll all be here when we get back in a couple days. Let's go!
Yap! Yap!
I hope so.
CLiK

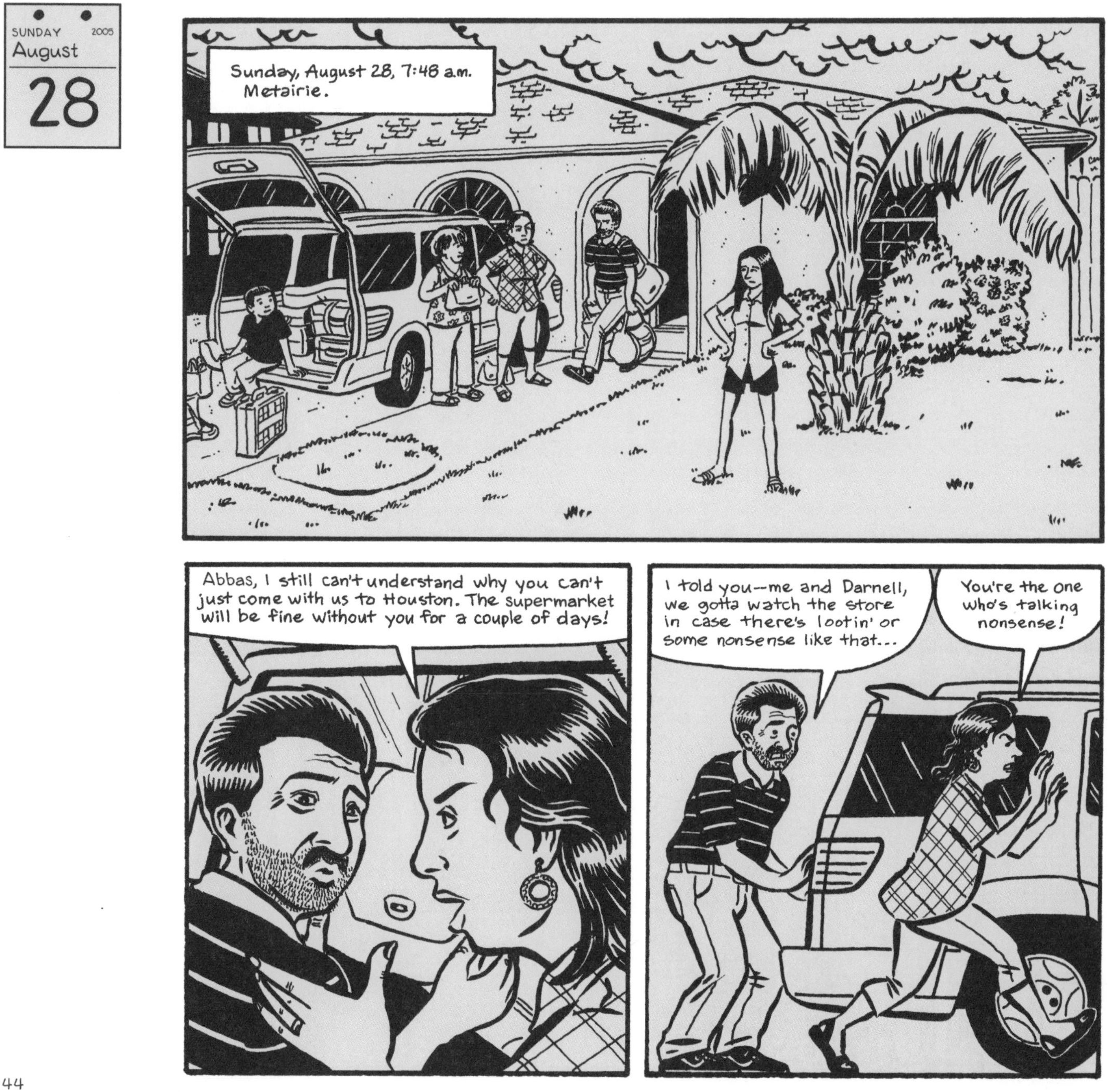
SUNDAY 2005
August
28
Sunday, August 28, 7:48 a.m.
Metairie.
Abbas, I still can't understand why you can't just come with us to Houston. The supermarket will be fine without you for a couple of days!
I told you--me and Darnell, we gotta watch the store in case there's lootin' or some nonsense like that...
You're the one who's talking nonsense!

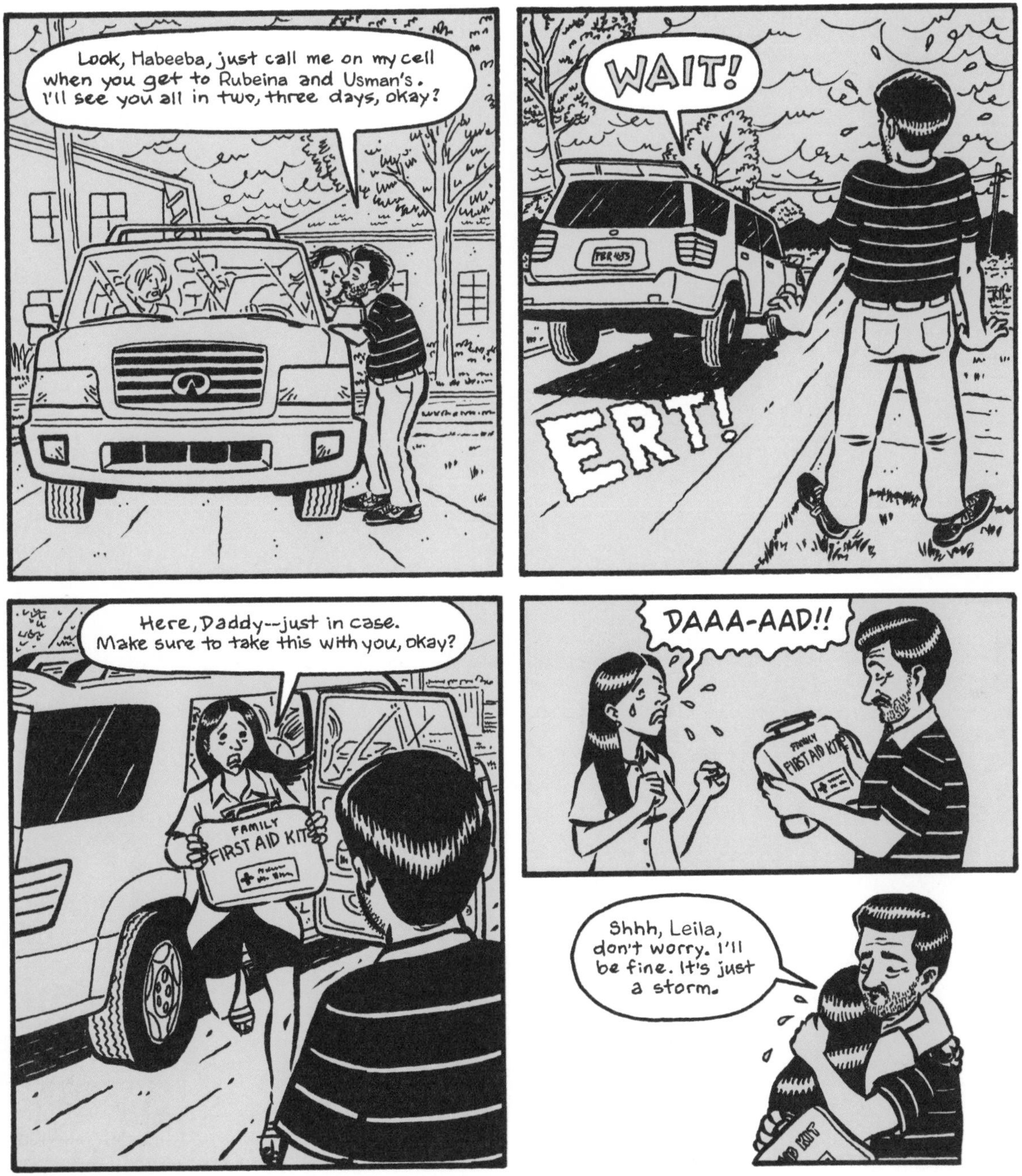
Look, Habeeba, just call me on my cell when you get to Rubeina and Usman's. I'll see you all in two, three days, okay?
WAIT!
ERT!
Here, Daddy--just in case. Make sure to take this with you, okay?
FAMILY FIRST AID KIT
DAAA-AAD!!
FAMILY FIRST AID KIT
Shhh, Leila, don't worry. I'll be fine. It's just a storm.

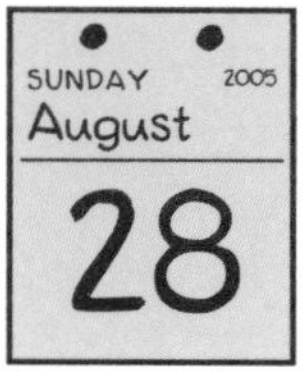
SUNDAY
2005
August
28

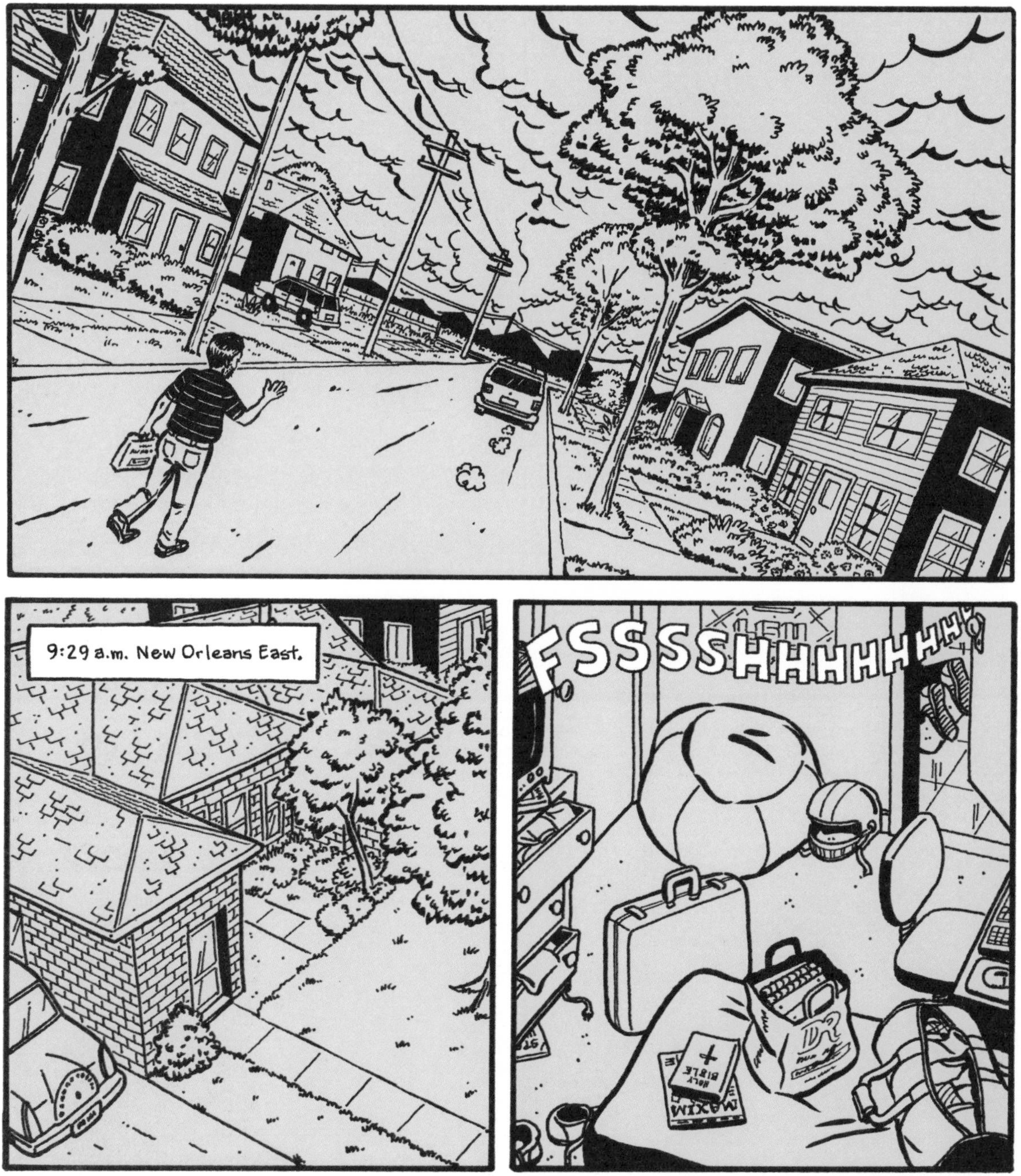
9:29 a.m. New Orleans East.
FSSSSHHHHHHHH

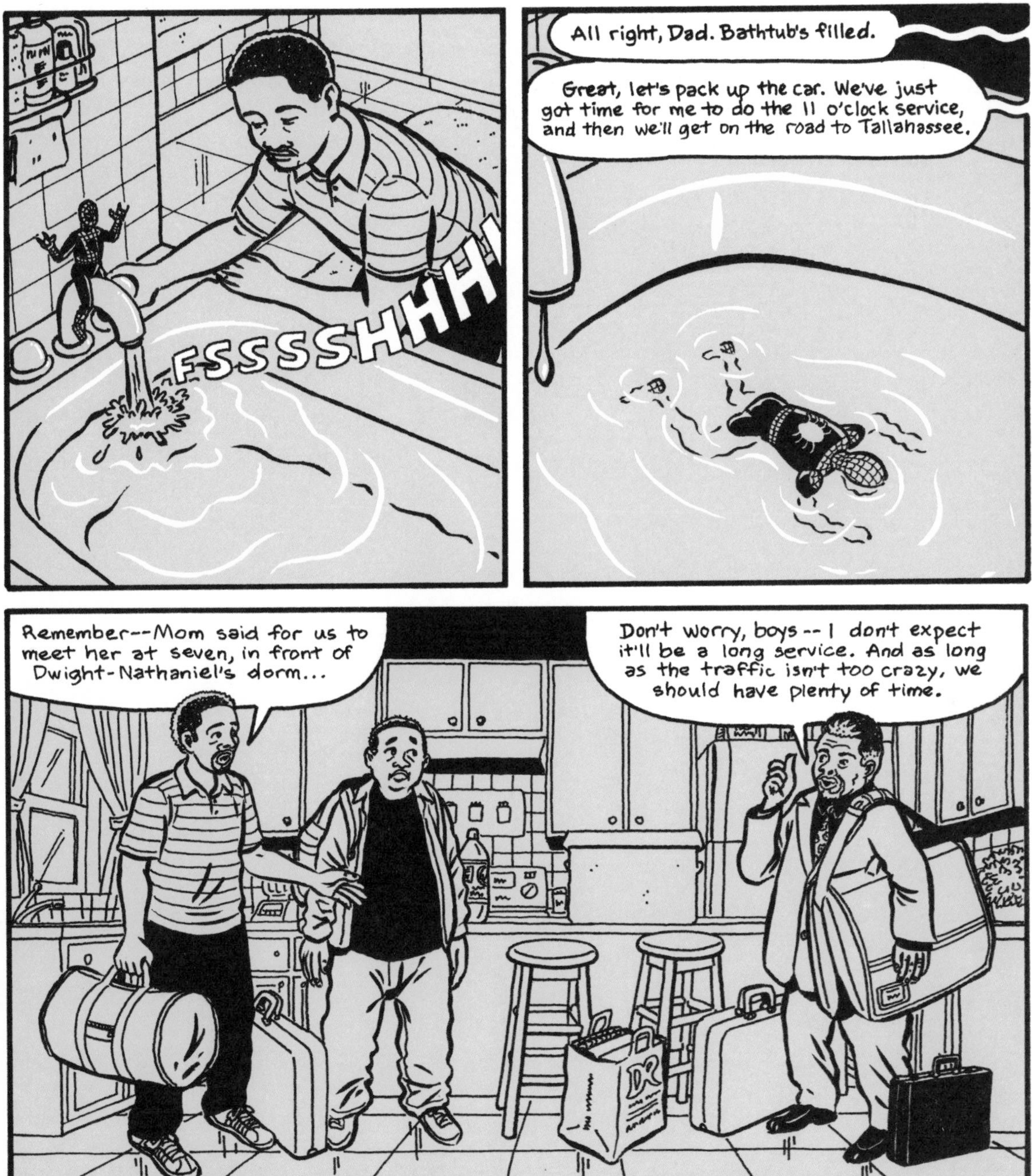
FSSSSHHHH
All right, Dad. Bathtub's filled.
Great, let's pack up the car. We've just got time for me to do the 11 o'clock service, and then we'll get on the road to Tallahassee.
Remember--Mom said for us to meet her at seven, in front of Dwight-Nathaniel's dorm...
Don't worry, boys -- I don't expect it'll be a long service. And as long as the traffic isn't too crazy, we should have plenty of time.

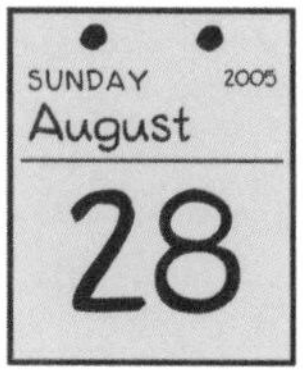
SUNDAY
2005
August
28

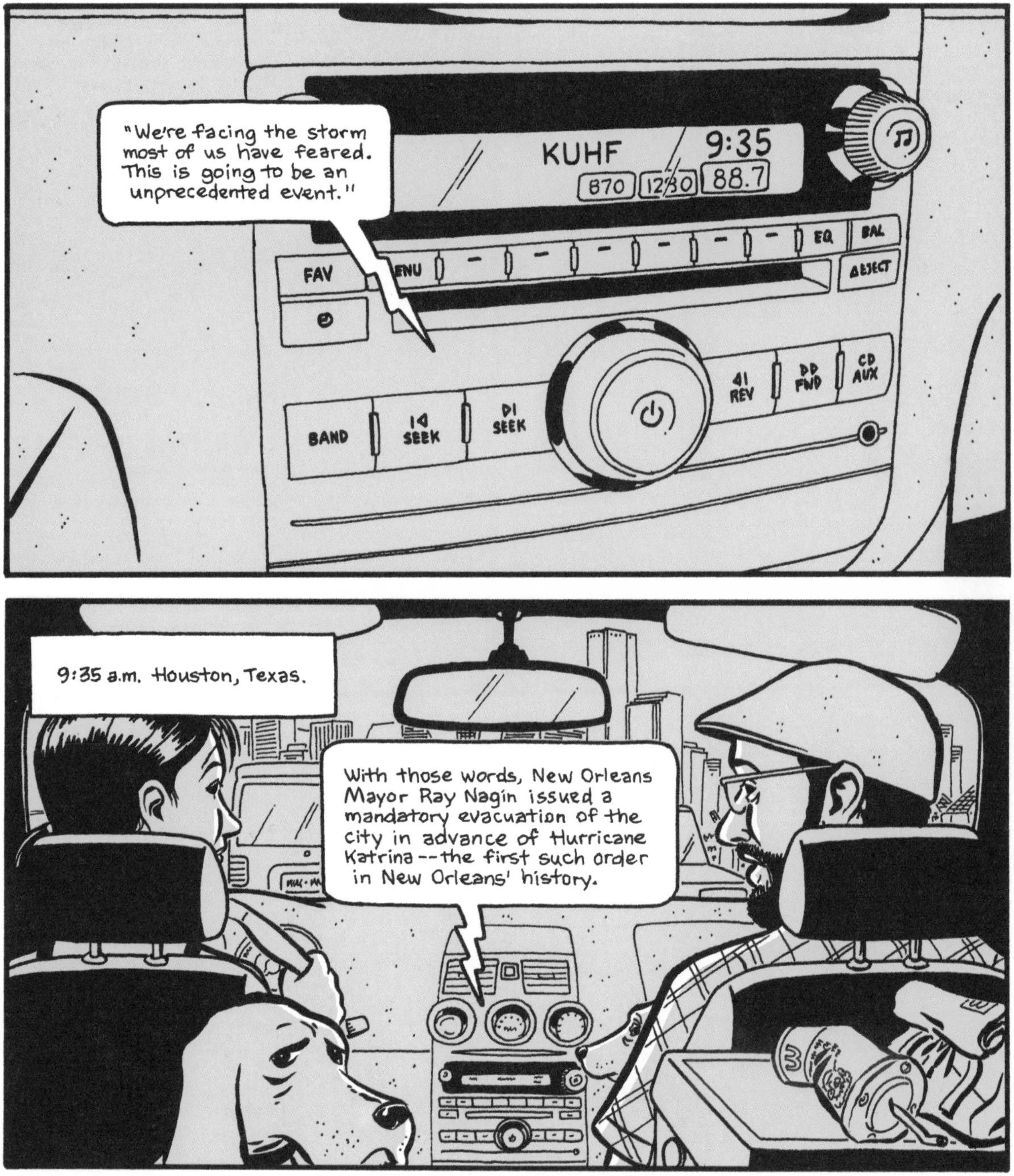
"We're facing the storm most of us have feared. This is going to be an unprecedented event."
KUHF
9:35
870
1230
88.7
9:35 a.m. Houston, Texas.
With those words, New Orleans Mayor Ray Nagin issued a mandatory evacuation of the city in advance of Hurricane Katrina--the first such order in New Orleans' history.

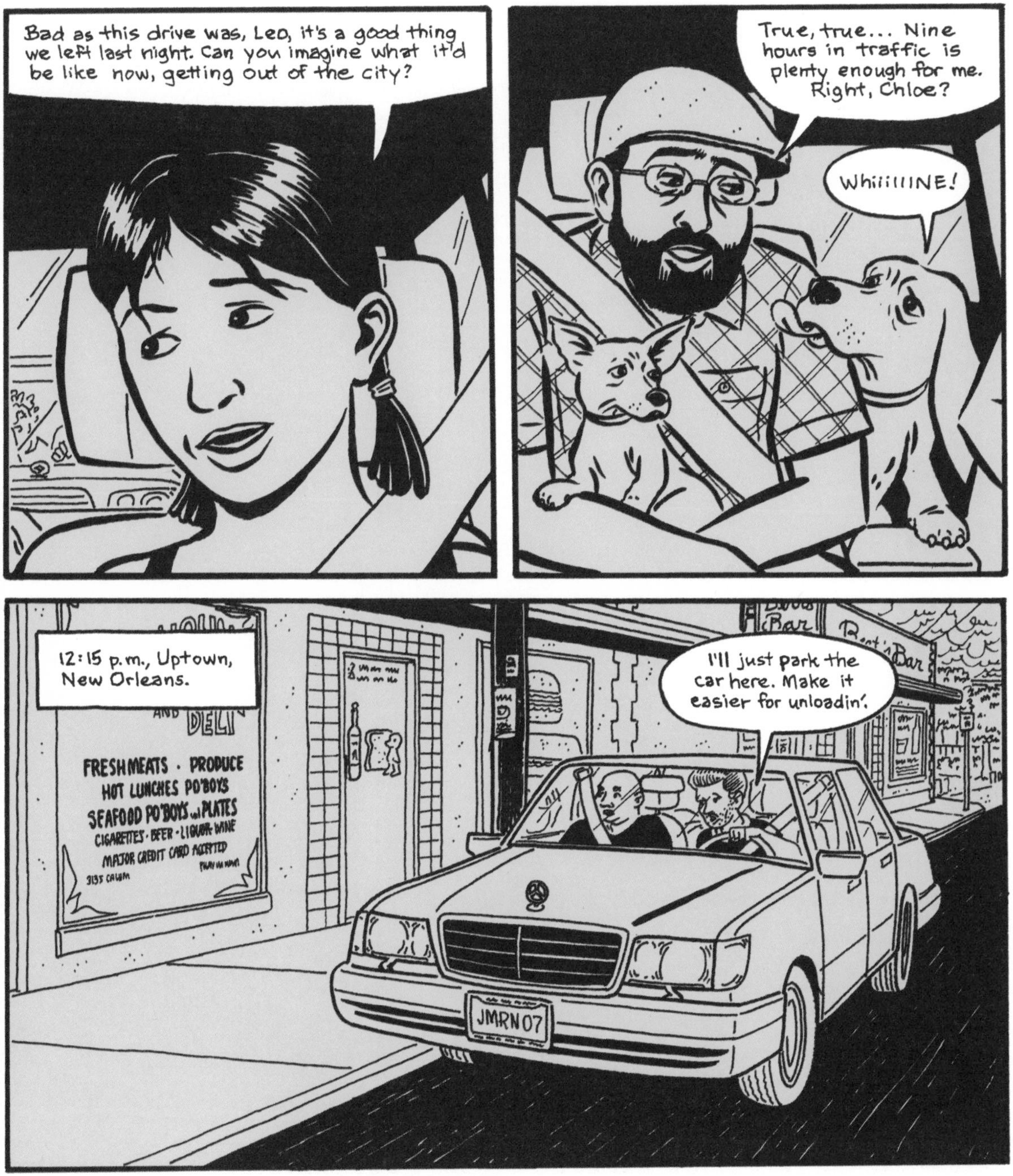
Bad as this drive was, Leo, it's a good thing we left last night. Can you imagine what it'd be like now, getting out of the city?
True, true... Nine hours in traffic is plenty enough for me. Right, Chloe?
WhiiiIIINE!
12:15 p.m., Uptown, New Orleans.
I'll just park the car here. Make it easier for unloadin'.
AND DELI
FRESHMEATS · PRODUCE
HOT LUNCHES PO'BOYS
SEAFOOD PO'BOYS
PLATES
CIGARETTES · BEER · LIQUOR · WINE
MAJOR CREDIT CARD ACCEPTED
Bar
Bert's Bar
JMRN 07

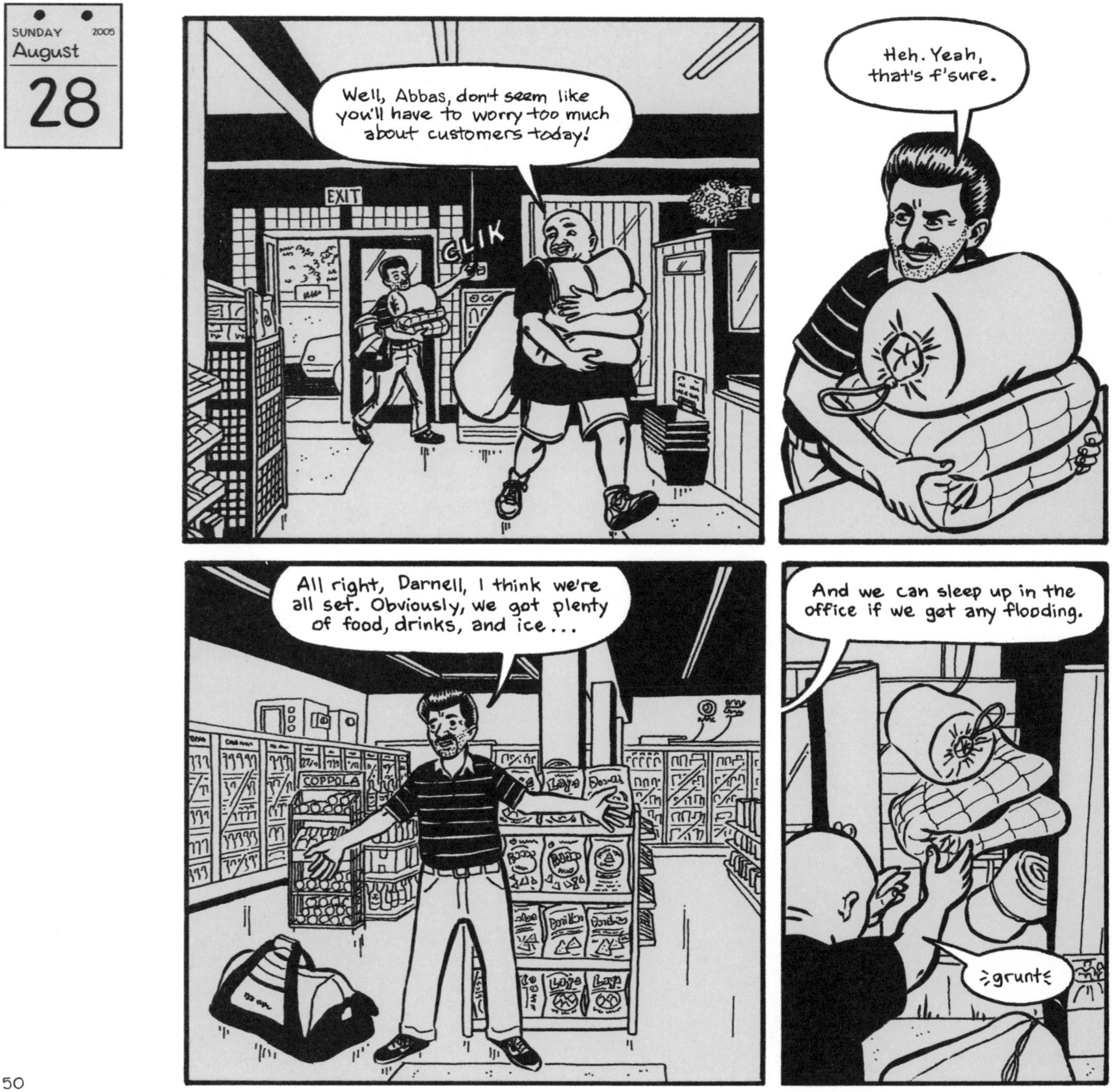
SUNDAY 2005
August
28
Well, Abbas, don't seem like you'll have to worry too much about customers today!
EXIT
CLIK
Heh. Yeah, that's f'sure.
All right, Darnell, I think we're all set. Obviously, we got plenty of food, drinks, and ice...
COPPOLA
And we can sleep up in the office if we get any flooding.
grunt

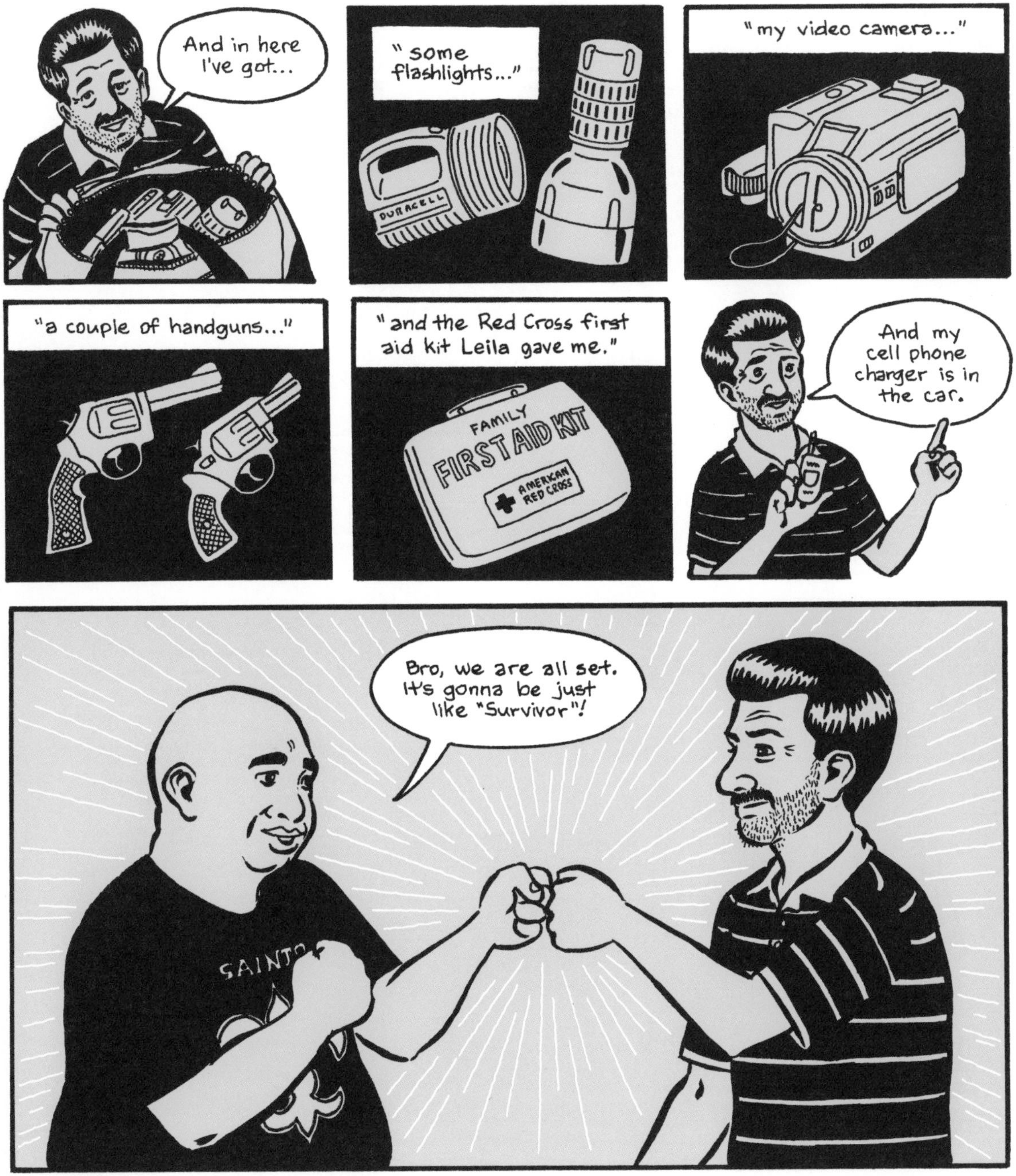
And in here I've got...
"some flashlights..."
DURACELL
"my video camera..."
"a couple of handguns..."
"and the Red Cross first aid kit Leila gave me."
FAMILY
FIRST AID KIT
AMERICAN RED CROSS
And my cell phone charger is in the car.
Bro, we are all set. It's gonna be just like "Survivor"!
SAINTS

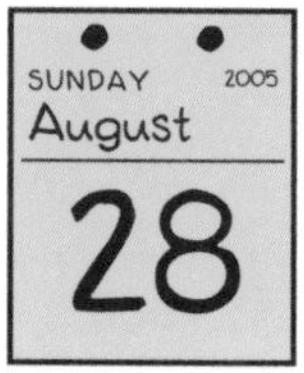
SUNDAY 2005
August
28

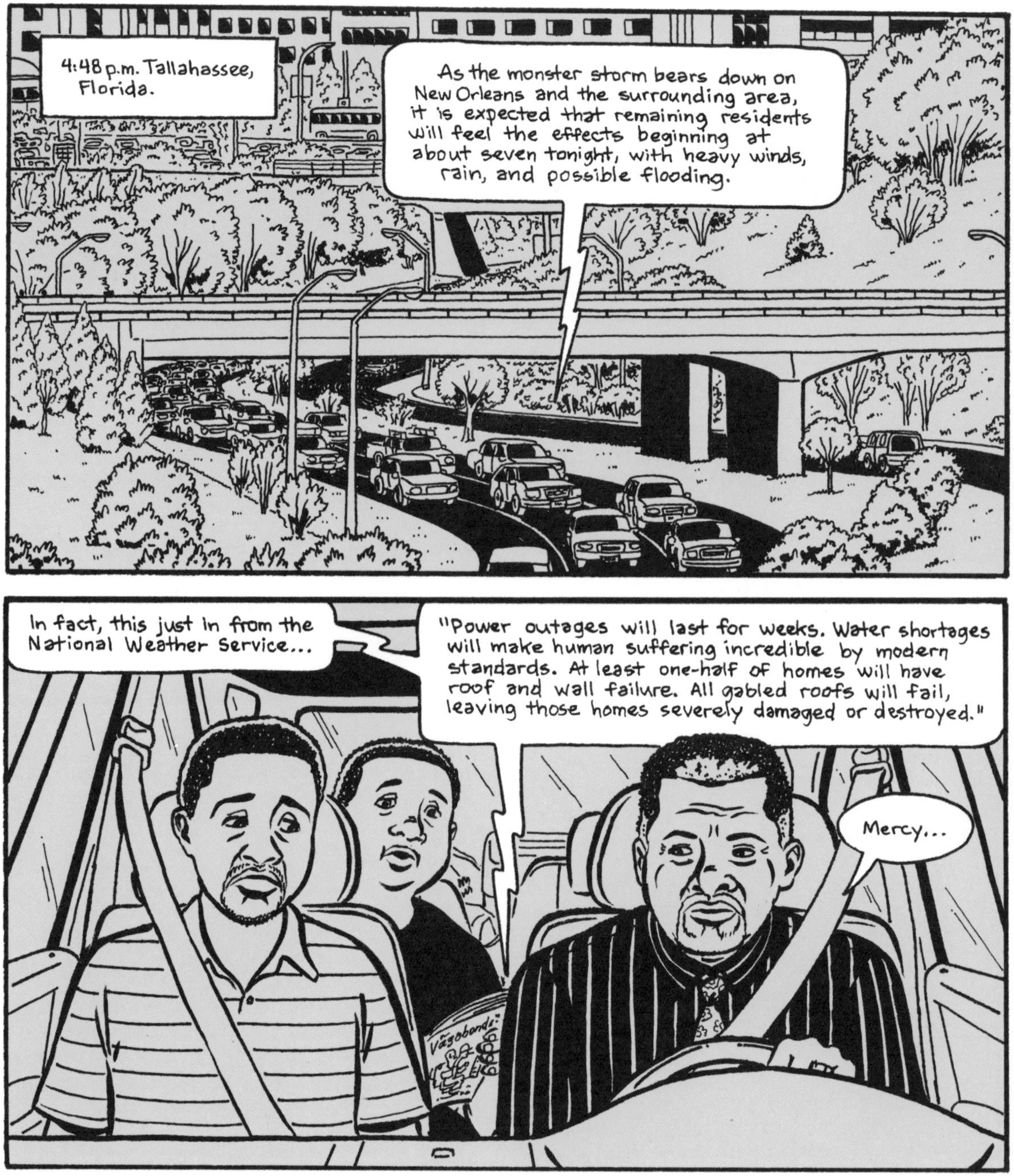
4:48 p.m. Tallahassee, Florida.
As the monster storm bears down on New Orleans and the surrounding area, it is expected that remaining residents will feel the effects beginning at about seven tonight, with heavy winds, rain, and possible flooding.
In fact, this just in from the National Weather Service...
"Power outages will last for weeks. Water shortages will make human suffering incredible by modern standards. At least one-half of homes will have roof and wall failure. All gabled roofs will fail, leaving those homes severely damaged or destroyed."
Mercy...
Vagabonds

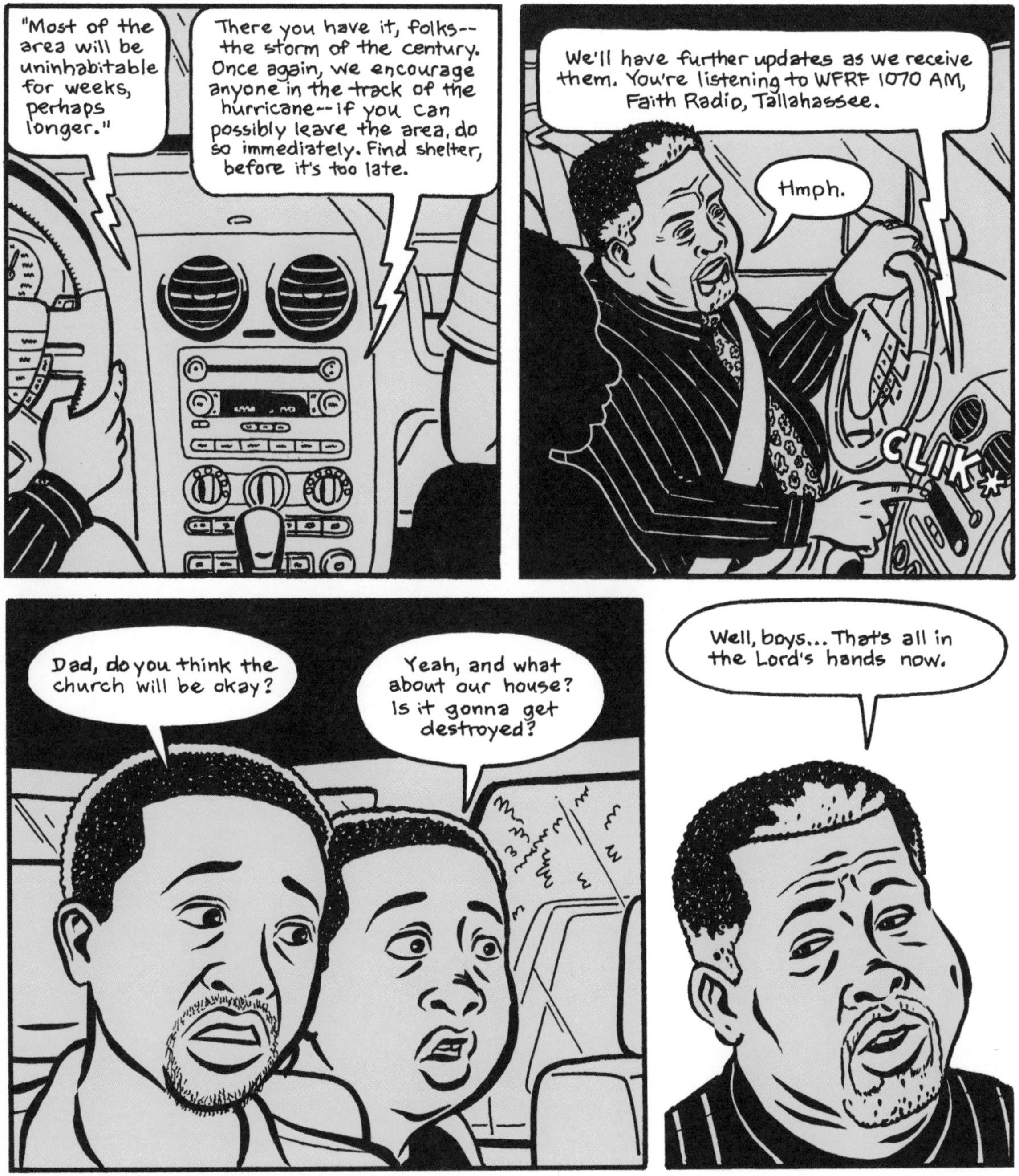
"Most of the area will be uninhabitable for weeks, perhaps longer."
There you have it, folks-- the storm of the century. Once again, we encourage anyone in the track of the hurricane--if you can possibly leave the area, do so immediately. Find shelter, before it's too late.
We'll have further updates as we receive them. You're listening to WFRF 1070 AM, Faith Radio, Tallahassee.
Hmph.
CLIK*
Dad, do you think the church will be okay?
Yeah, and what about our house? Is it gonna get destroyed?
Well, boys... That's all in the Lord's hands now.

SUNDAY 2005
August
28

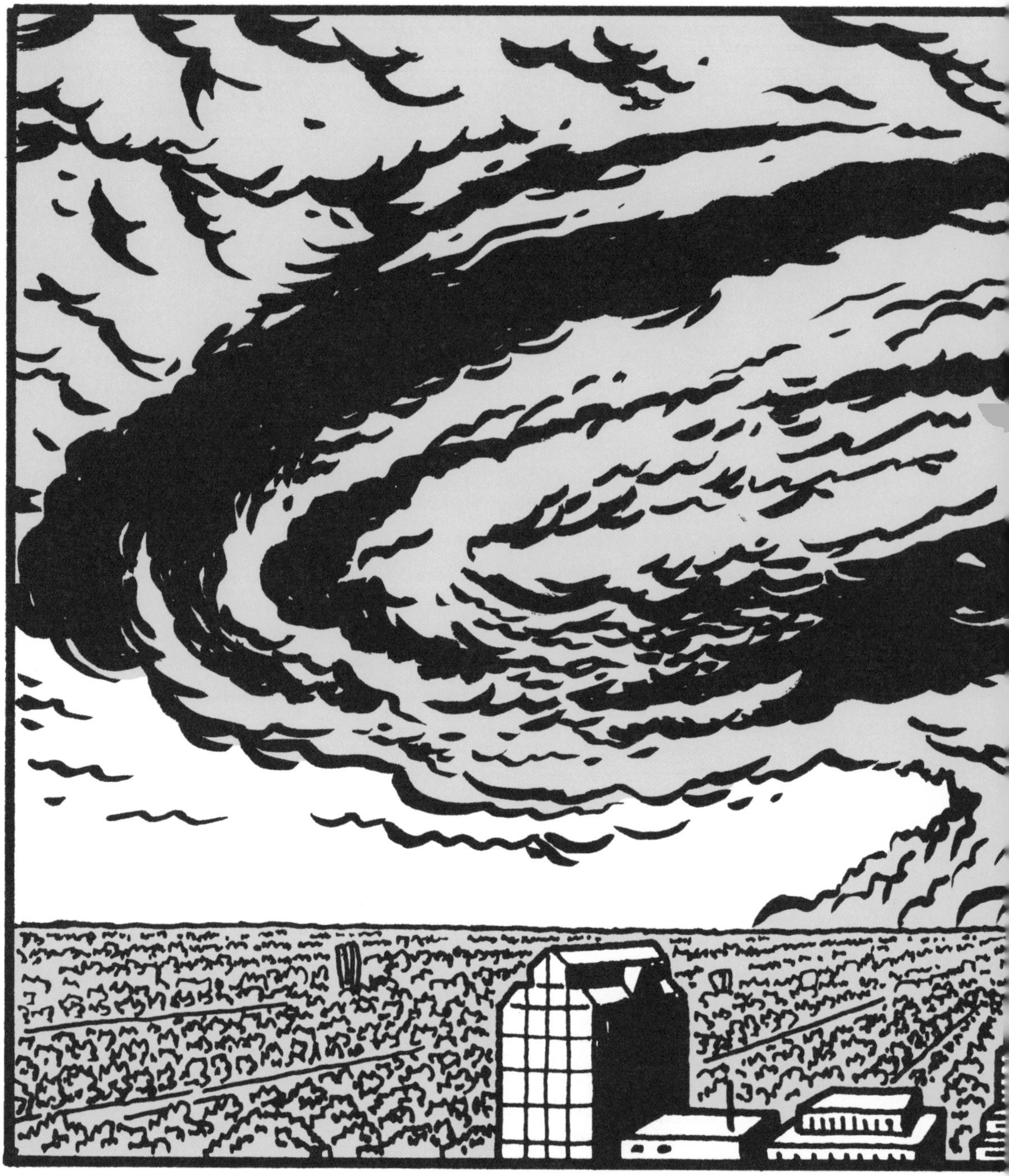

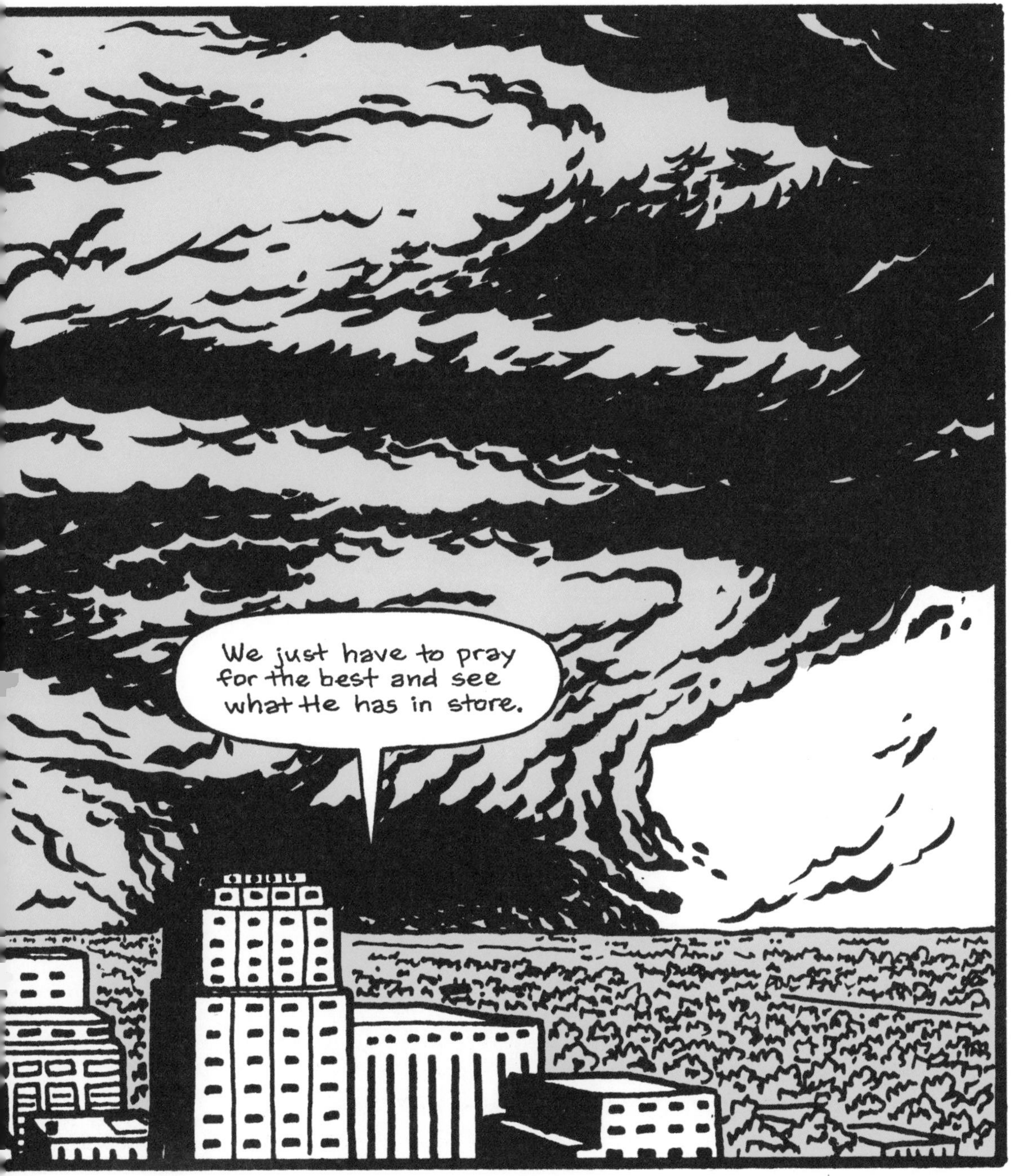
We just have to pray for the best and see what He has in store.

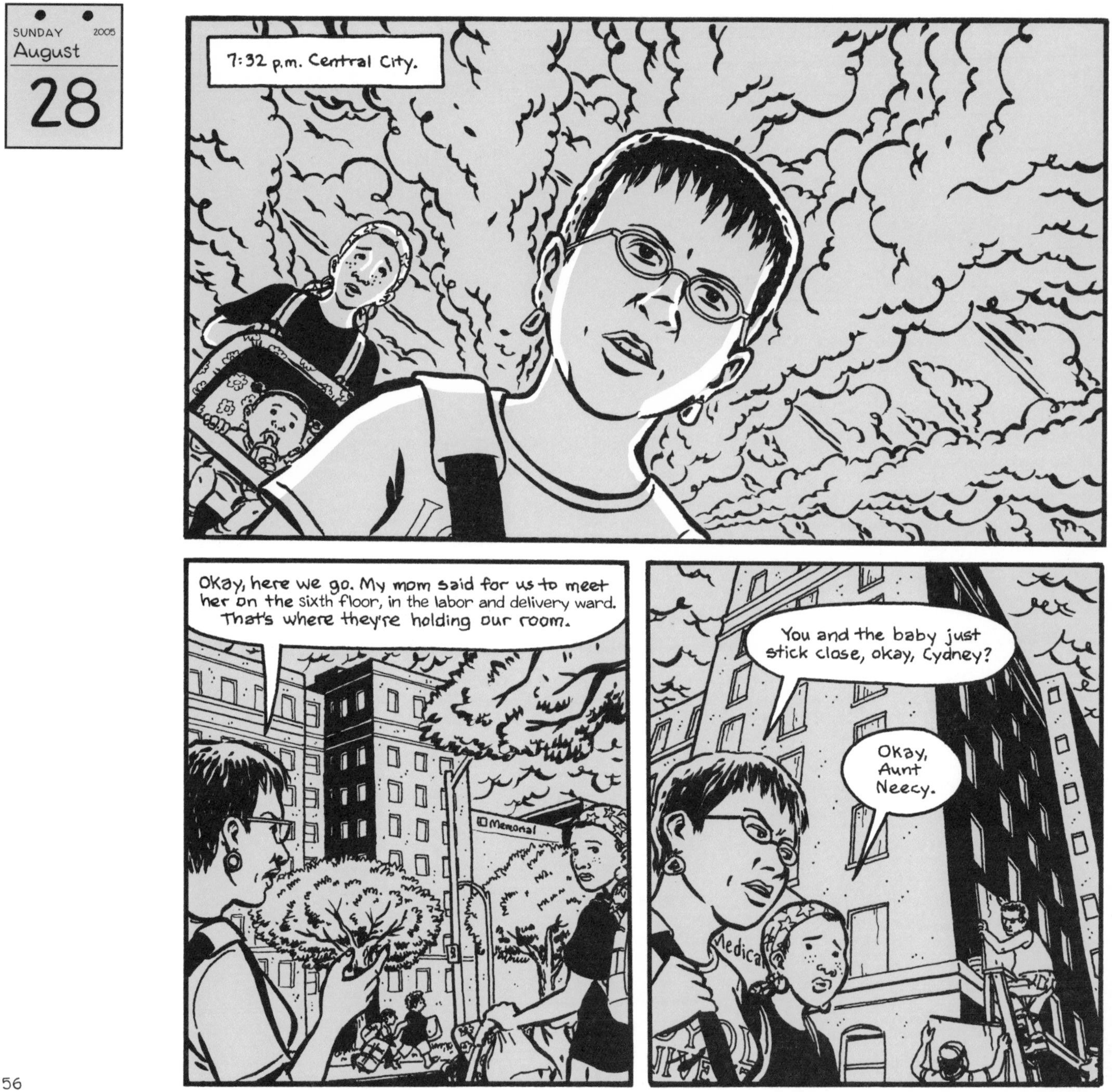
SUNDAY 2005
August
28
7:32 p.m. Central City.
Okay, here we go. My mom said for us to meet her on the sixth floor, in the labor and delivery ward. That's where they're holding our room.
Memorial
You and the baby just stick close, okay, Cydney?
Okay, Aunt Neecy.

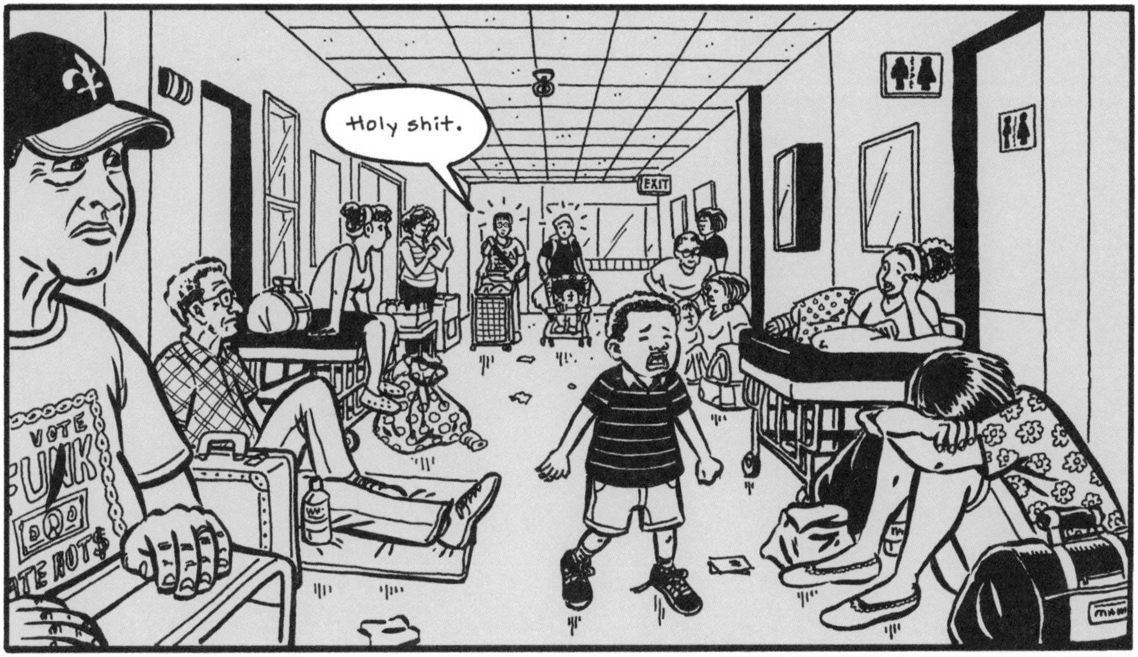
Holy shit.
EXIT
VOTE
FUNK

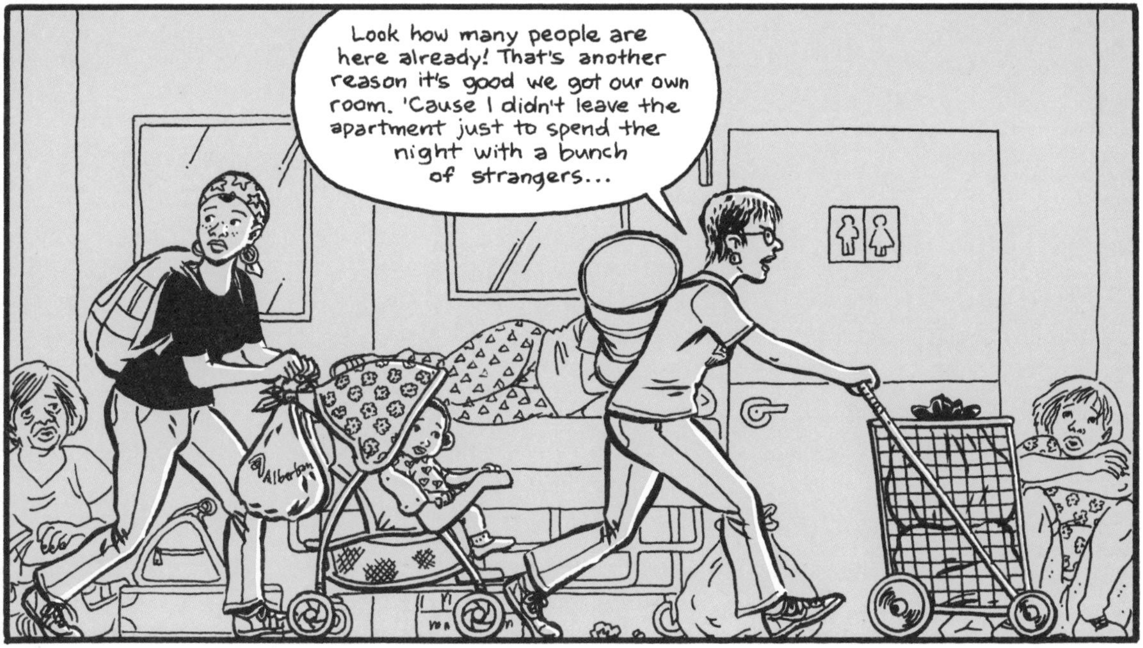
Look how many people are here already! That's another reason it's good we got our own room. 'Cause I didn't leave the apartment just to spend the night with a bunch of strangers...

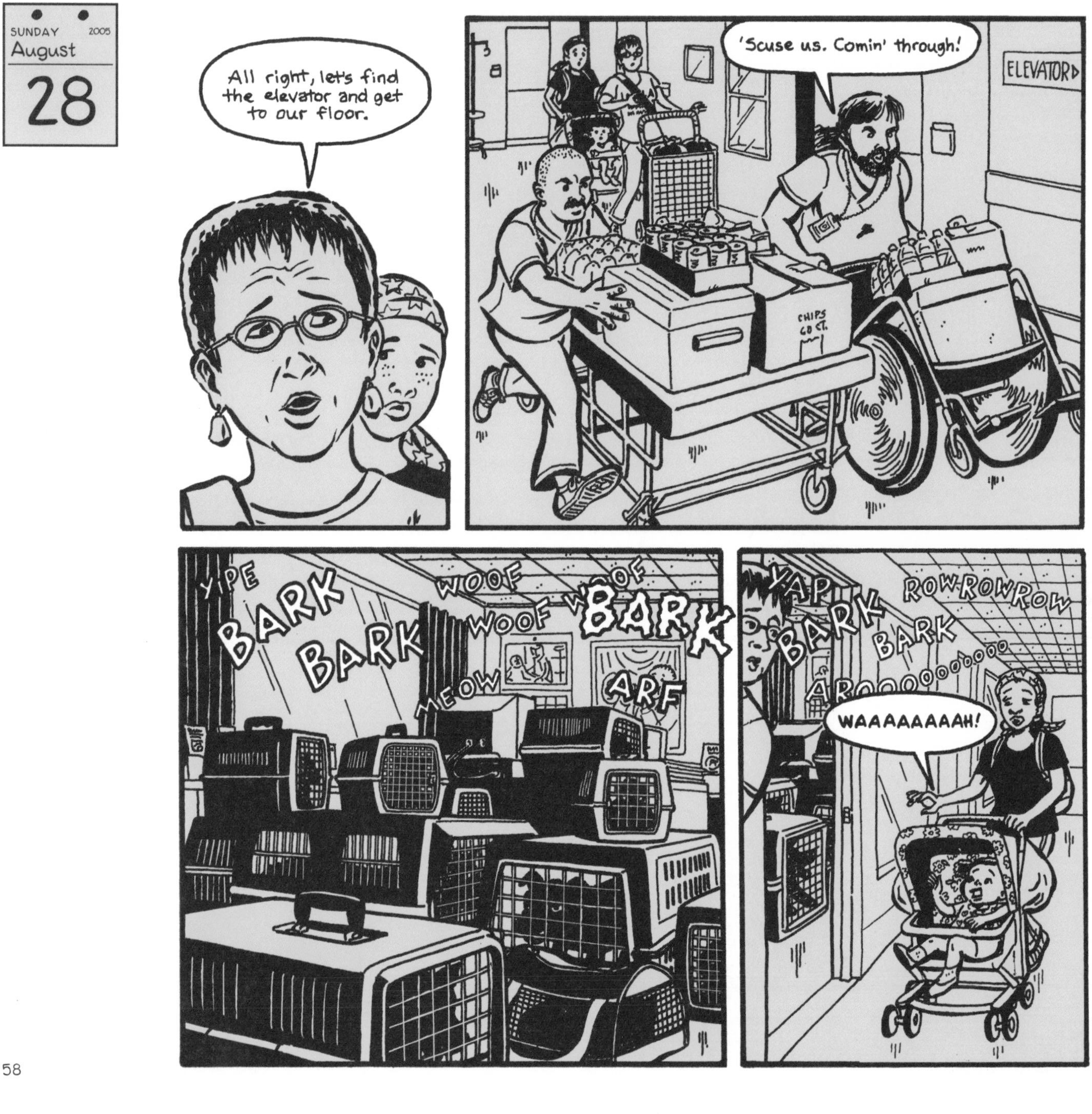
SUNDAY 2005
August
28
All right, let's find the elevator and get to our floor.
'Scuse us. Comin' through!
ELEVATOR
CHIPS
BARK
BARK
WOOF
WOOF
BARK
MEOW
ARF
YAP
BARK
ROWROWROW
BARK
WAAAAAAAAH!

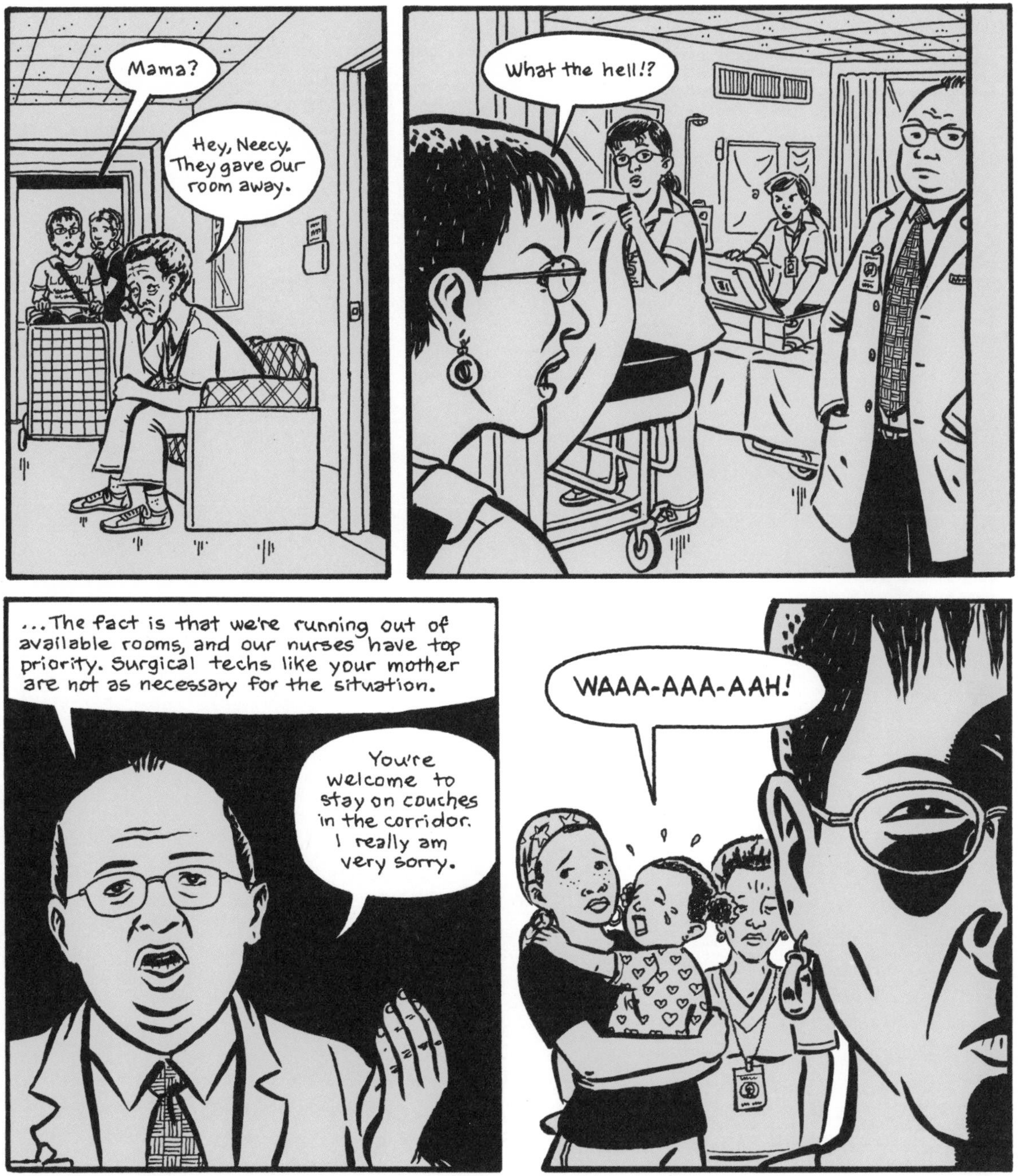
Mama?
Hey, Neecy. They gave our room away.
What the hell!?
...The fact is that we're running out of available rooms, and our nurses have top priority. Surgical techs like your mother are not as necessary for the situation.
You're welcome to stay on couches in the corridor. I really am very sorry.
WAAA-AAA-AAH!

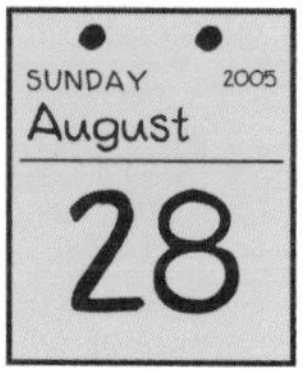
SUNDAY
2005
August
28

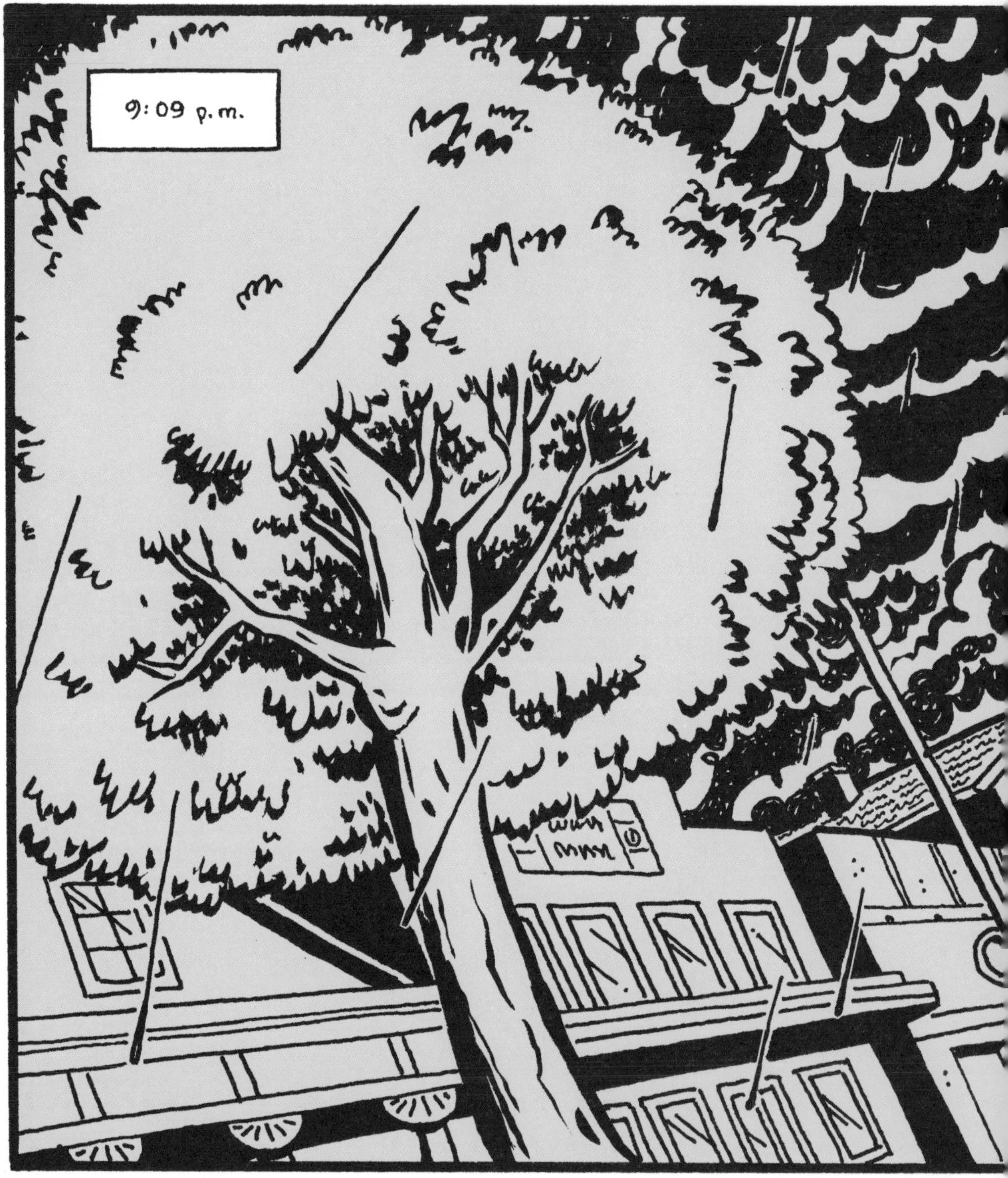
9:09 p.m.

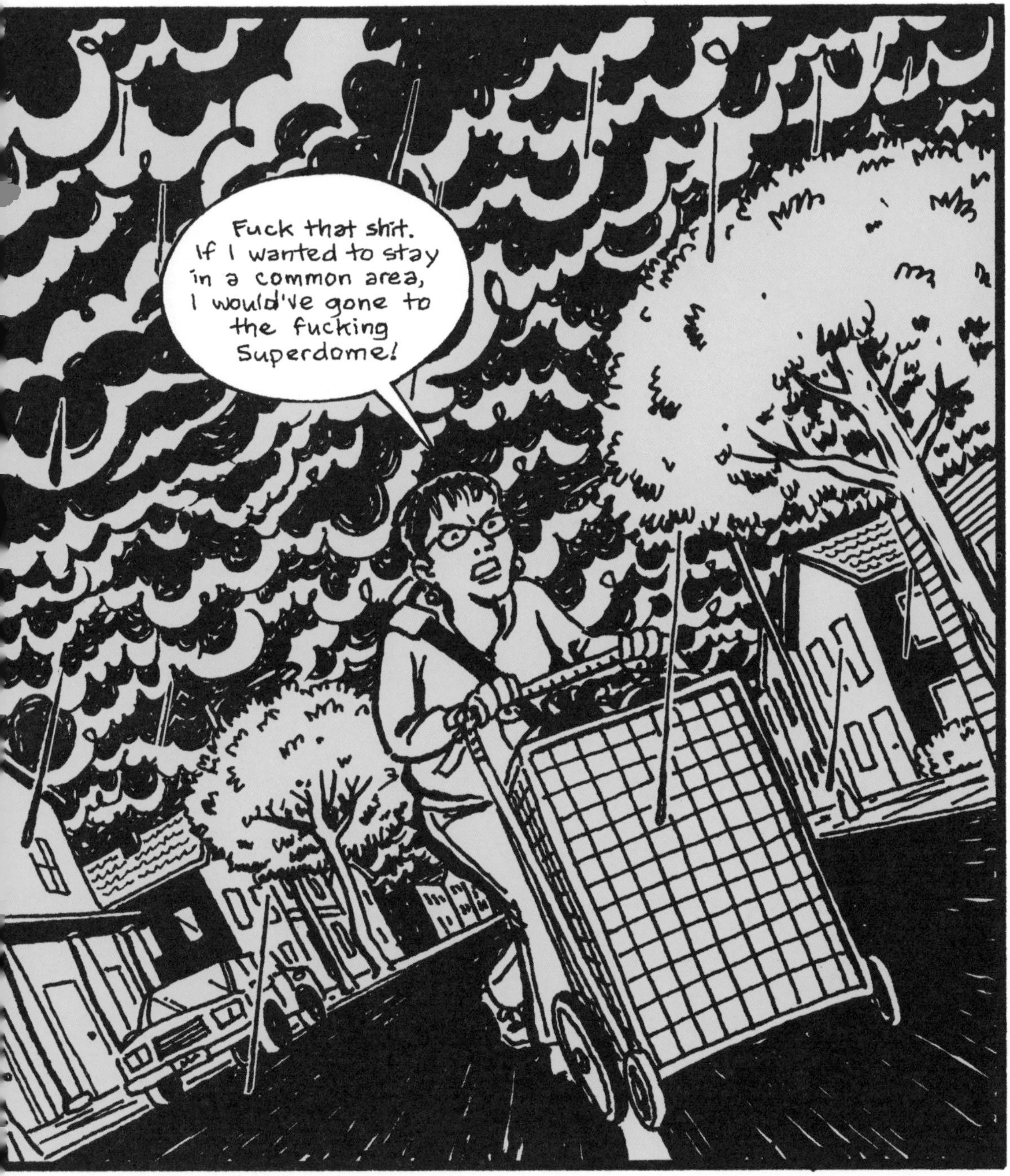
Fuck that shit. If I wanted to stay in a common area, I would've gone to the fucking Superdome!

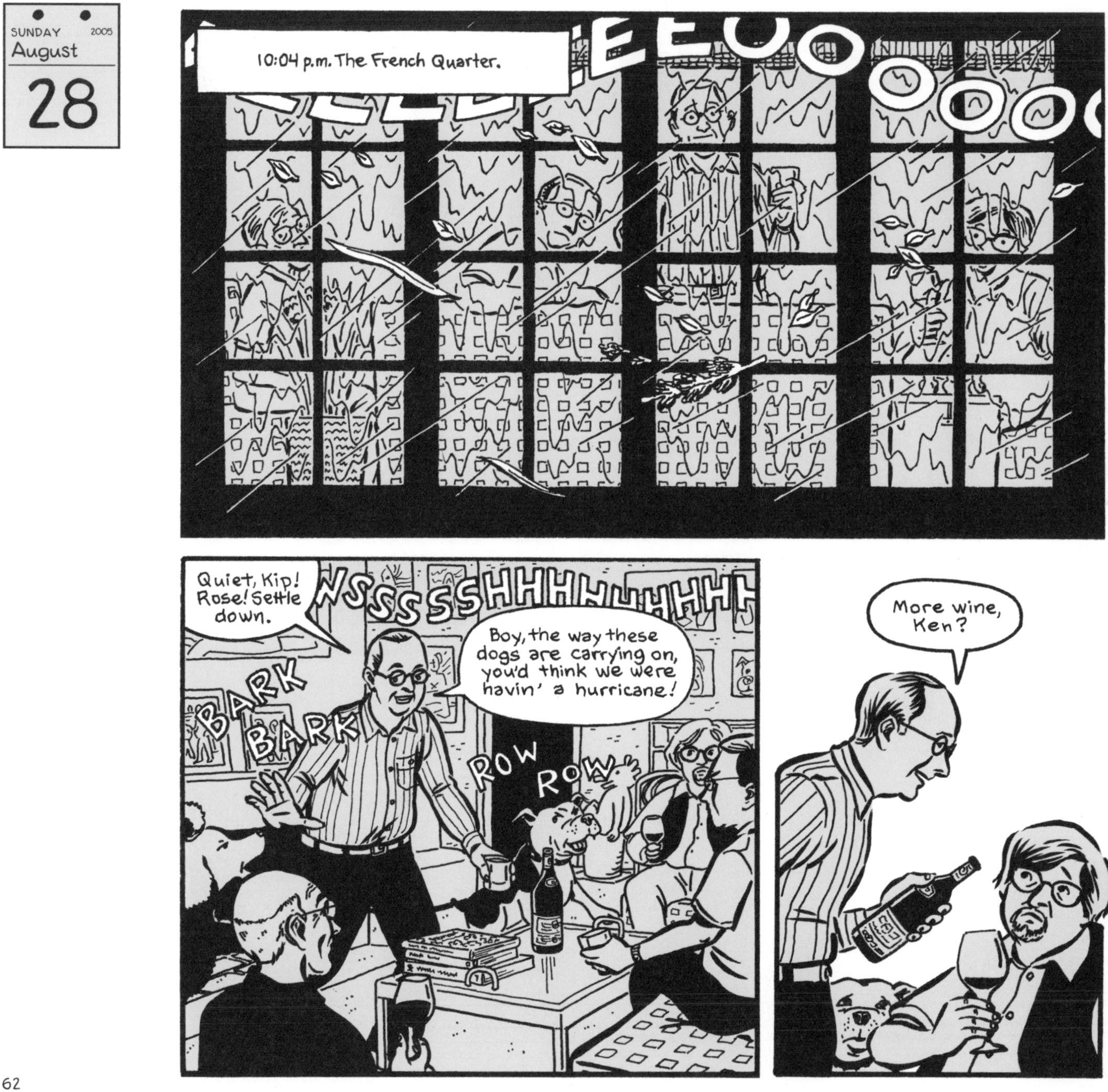
SUNDAY 2005
August
28
10:04 p.m. The French Quarter.
Quiet, Kip! Rose! Settle down.
BARK
BARK
Boy, the way these dogs are carrying on, you'd think we were havin' a hurricane!
ROW
ROW
More wine, Ken?

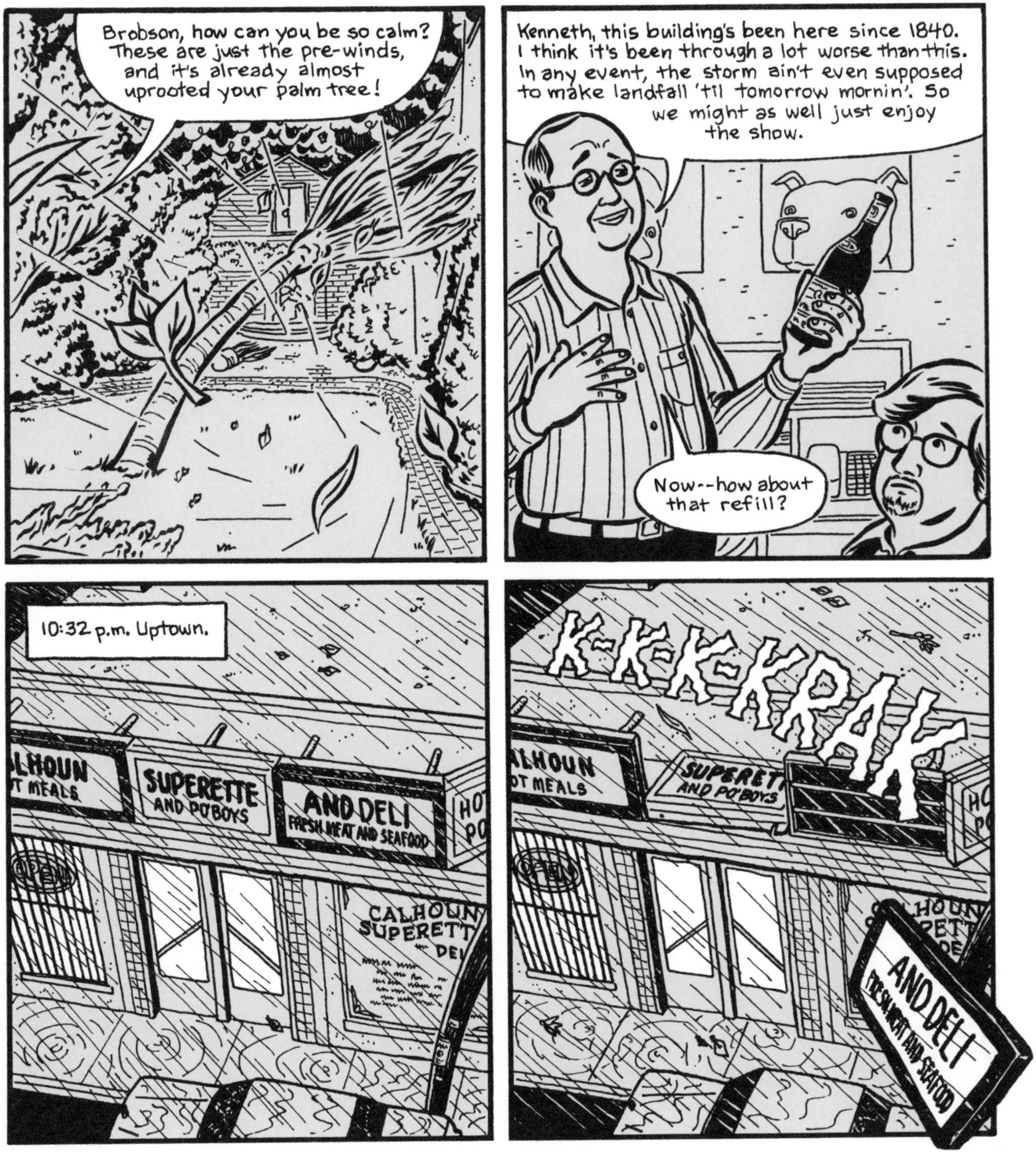
Brobson, how can you be so calm? These are just the pre-winds, and it's already almost uprooted your palm tree!
Kenneth, this building's been here since 1840. I think it's been through a lot worse than this. In any event, the storm ain't even supposed to make landfall 'til tomorrow mornin'. So we might as well just enjoy the show.
Now--how about that refill?
10:32 p.m. Uptown.
ALHOUN
OT MEALS
SUPERETTE
AND PO'BOYS
AND DELI
FRESH MEAT AND SEAFOOD
OPEN
CALHOUN
SUPERETT
DEL
K-K-K-KRAK
AND DELI
FRESH MEAT AND SEAFOOD

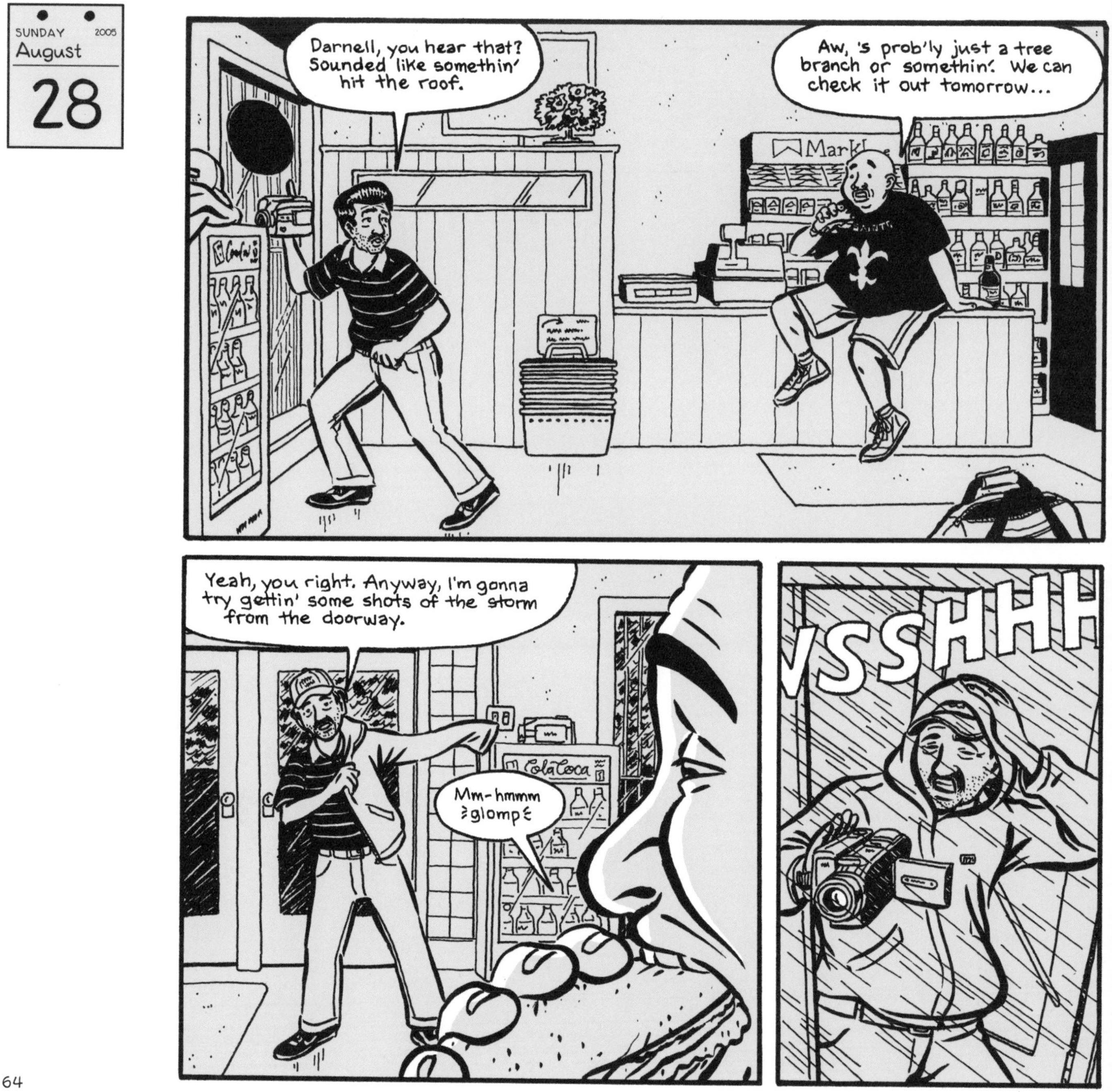
SUNDAY 2005
August
28
Darnell, you hear that? Sounded like somethin' hit the roof.
Aw, 's prob'ly just a tree branch or somethin'. We can check it out tomorrow...
Yeah, you right. Anyway, I'm gonna try gettin' some shots of the storm from the doorway.
ColaCoca
Mm-hmmm
glomp
VSSHHH

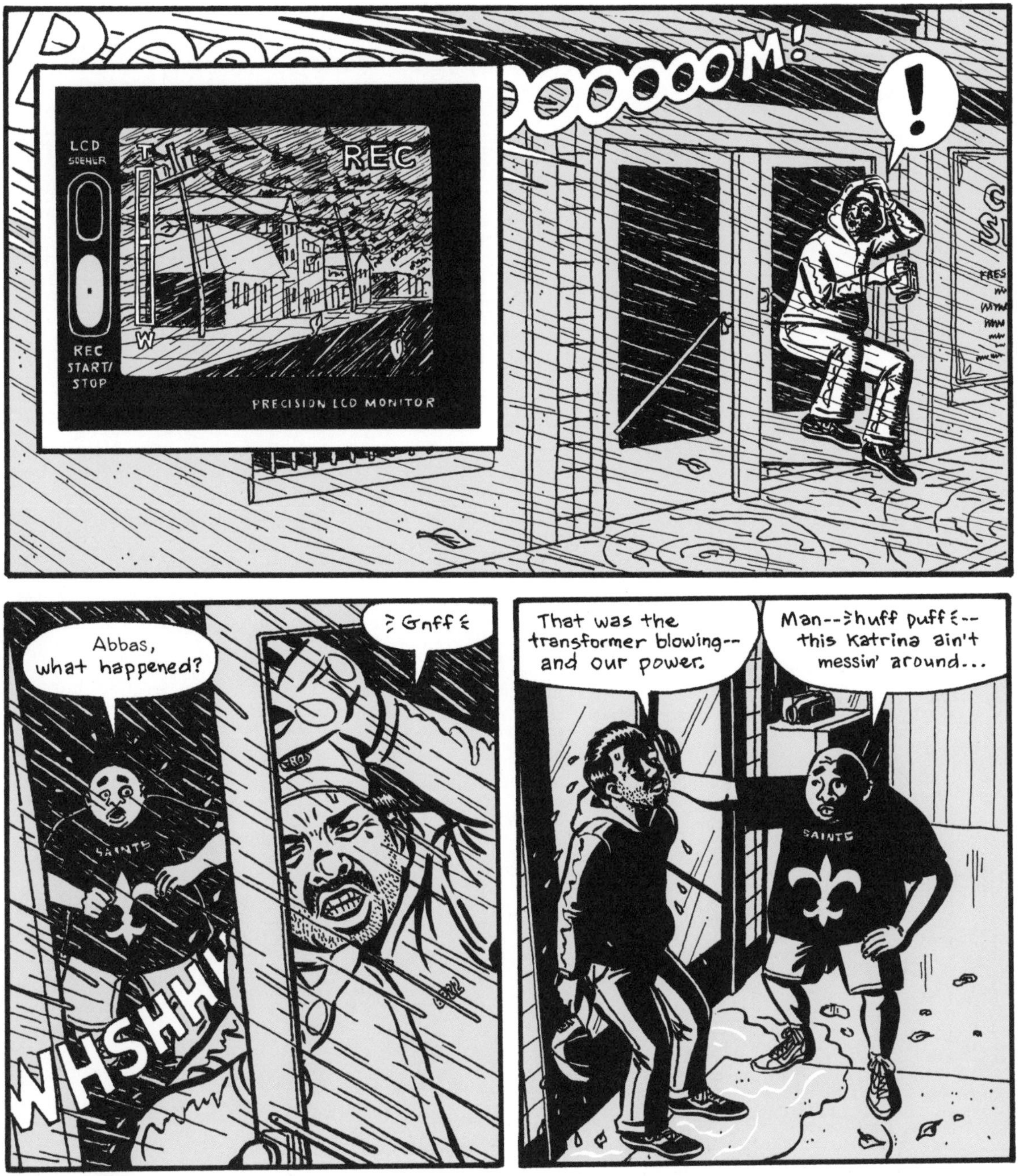

OOOOOOM!
!
LCD
REC
T
W
REC START/ STOP
PRECISION LCD MONITOR
Abbas, what happened?
≷ Gnff ≶
WHSHH
That was the transformer blowing-- and our power.
Man-- ≷ huff puff ≶ -- this Katrina ain't messin' around...

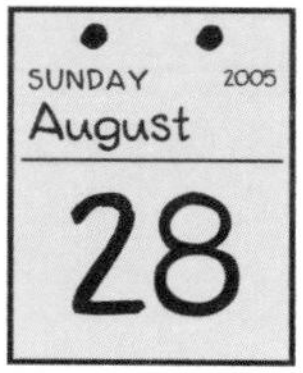
SUNDAY 2005
August
28

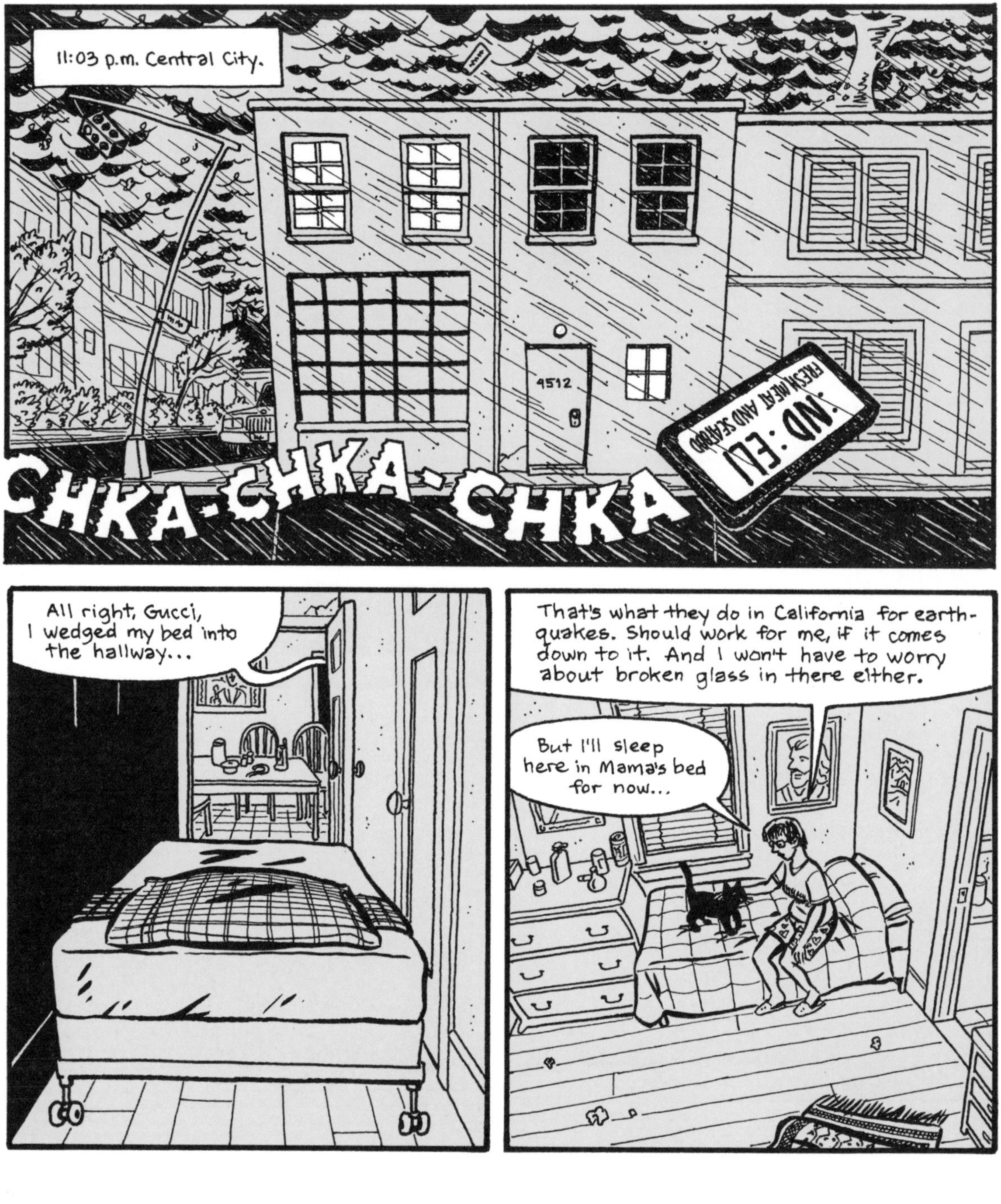
11:03 p.m. Central City.
CHKA-CHKA-CHKA
4512
All right, Gucci, I wedged my bed into the hallway...
That's what they do in California for earthquakes. Should work for me, if it comes down to it. And I won't have to worry about broken glass in there either.
But I'll sleep here in Mama's bed for now...

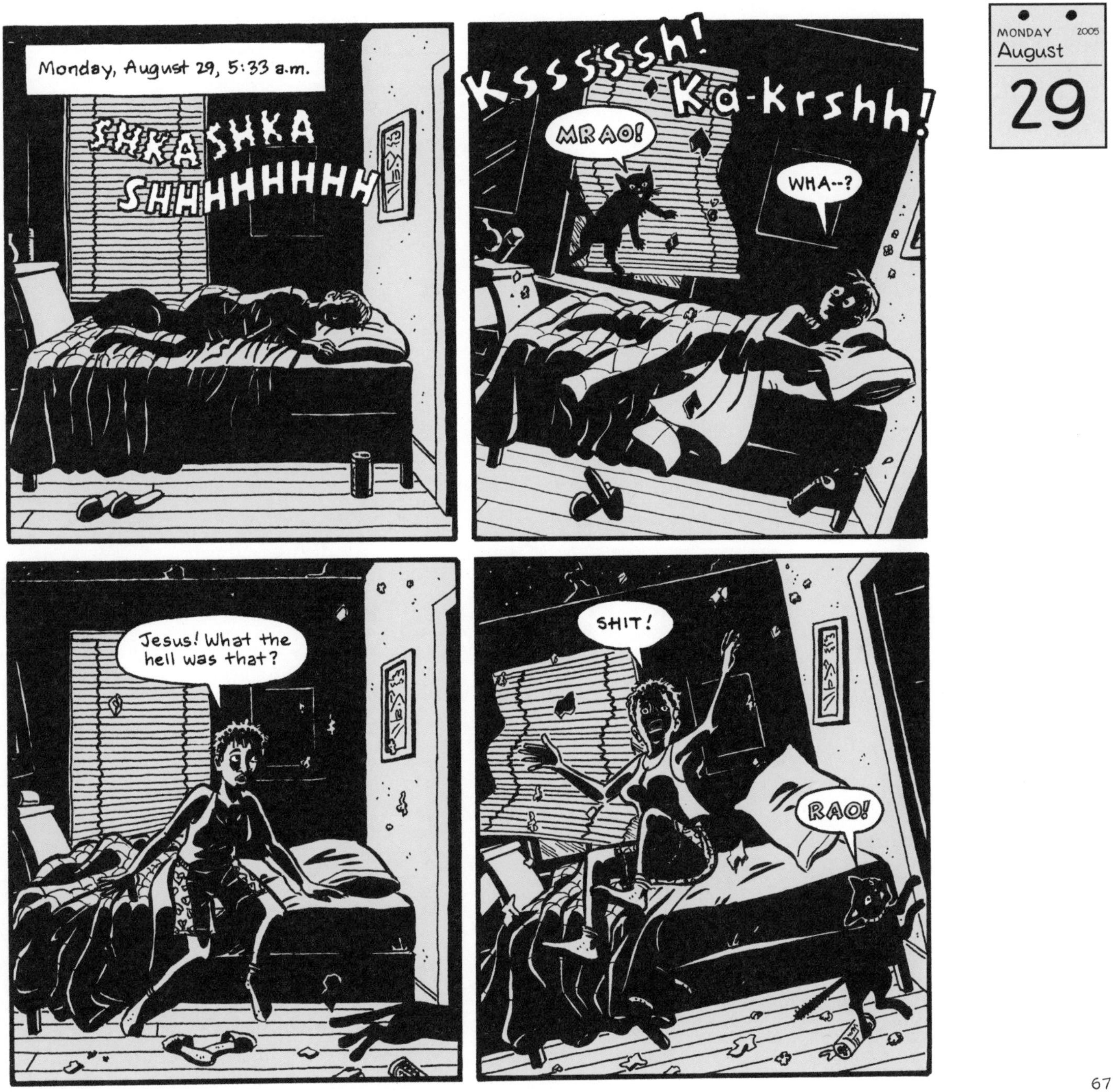
Monday, August 29, 5:33 a.m.
SHKASHKA
SHHHHHHHH
Ksssssh!
Ka-krshh!
MRAO!
WHA--?
Jesus! What the hell was that?
SHIT!
RAO!
MONDAY 2005
August
29

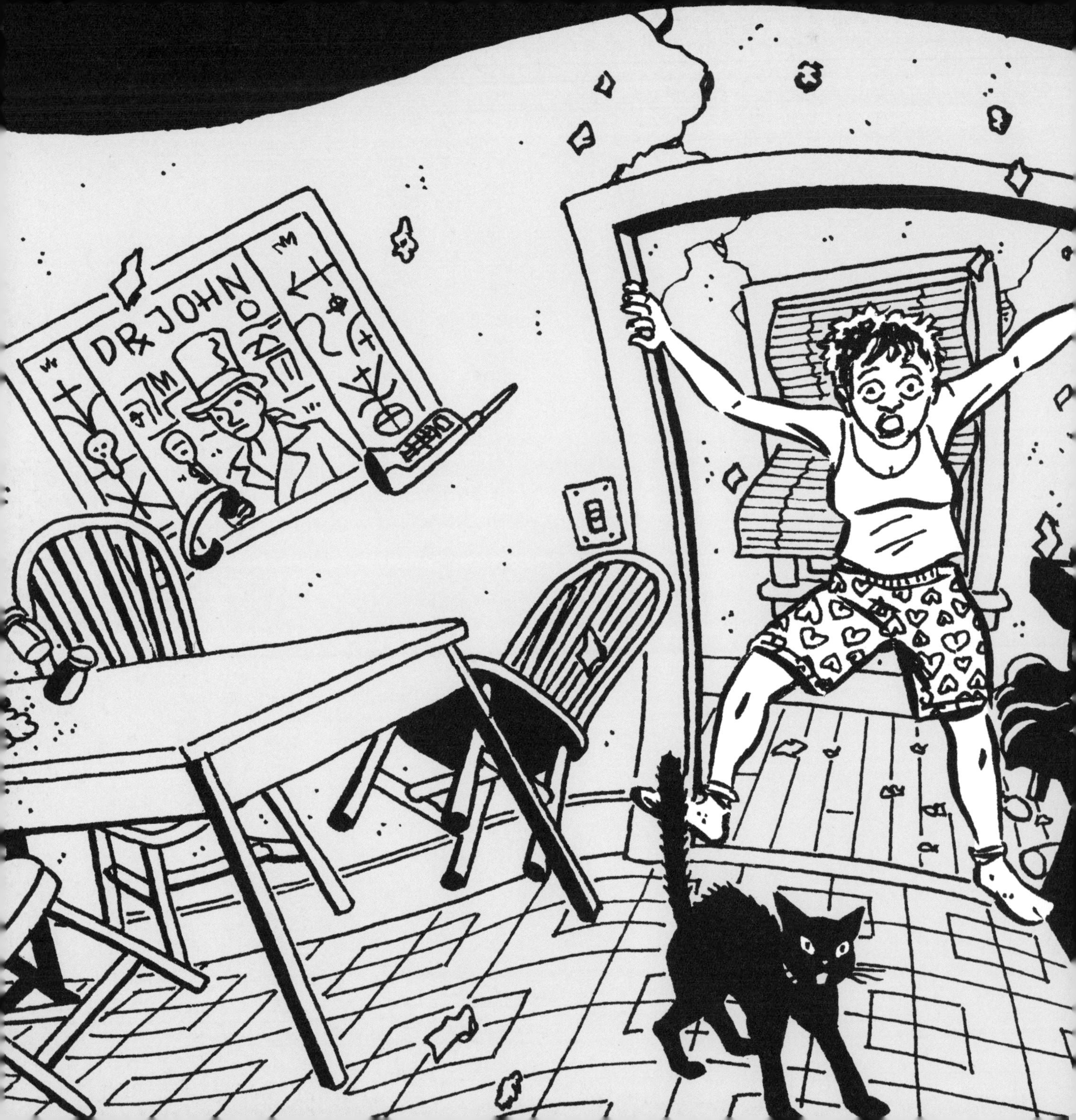
DR JOHN

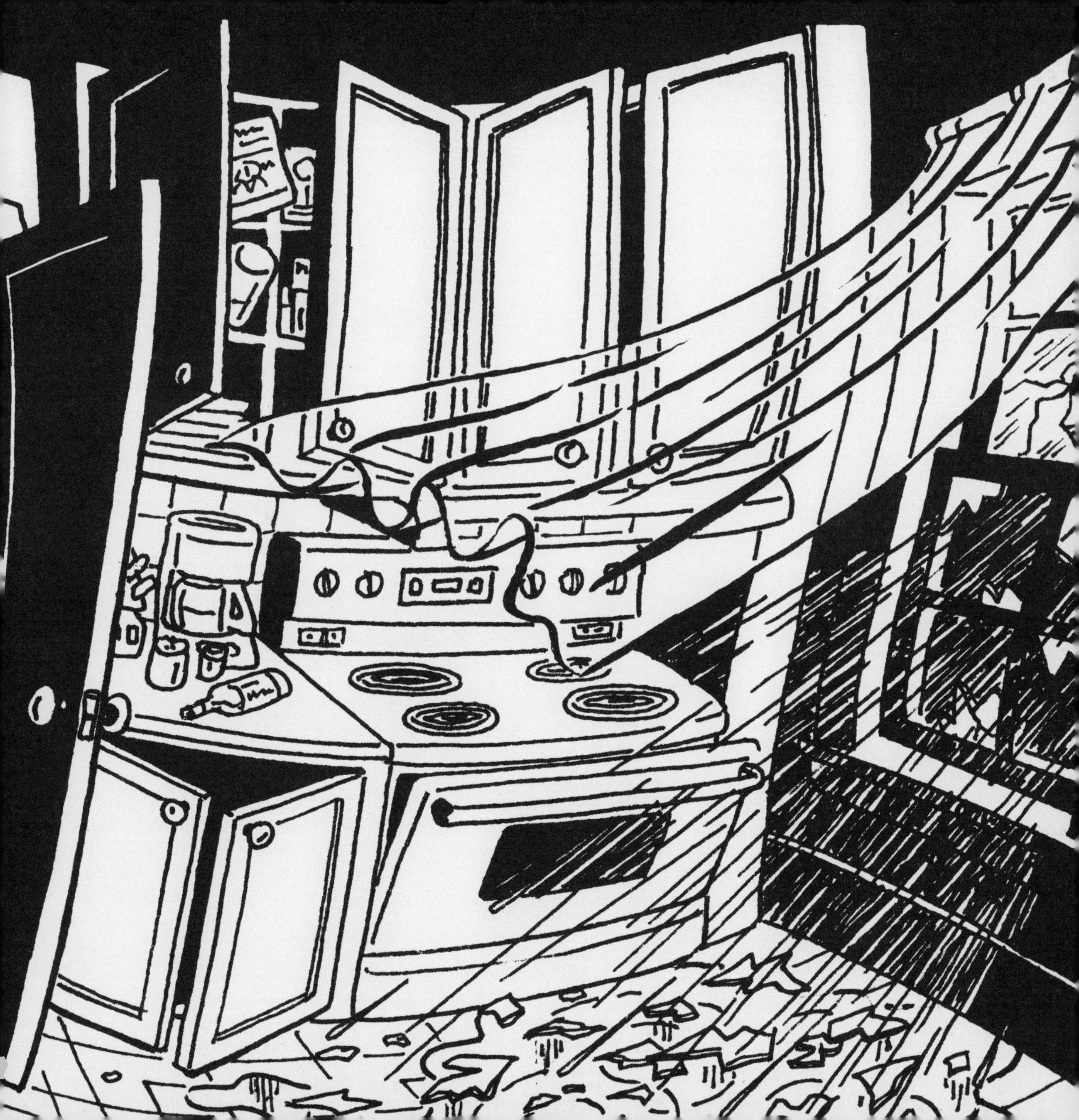

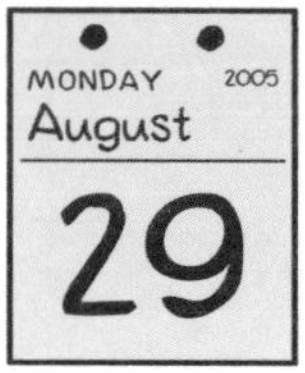
MONDAY 2005
August
29

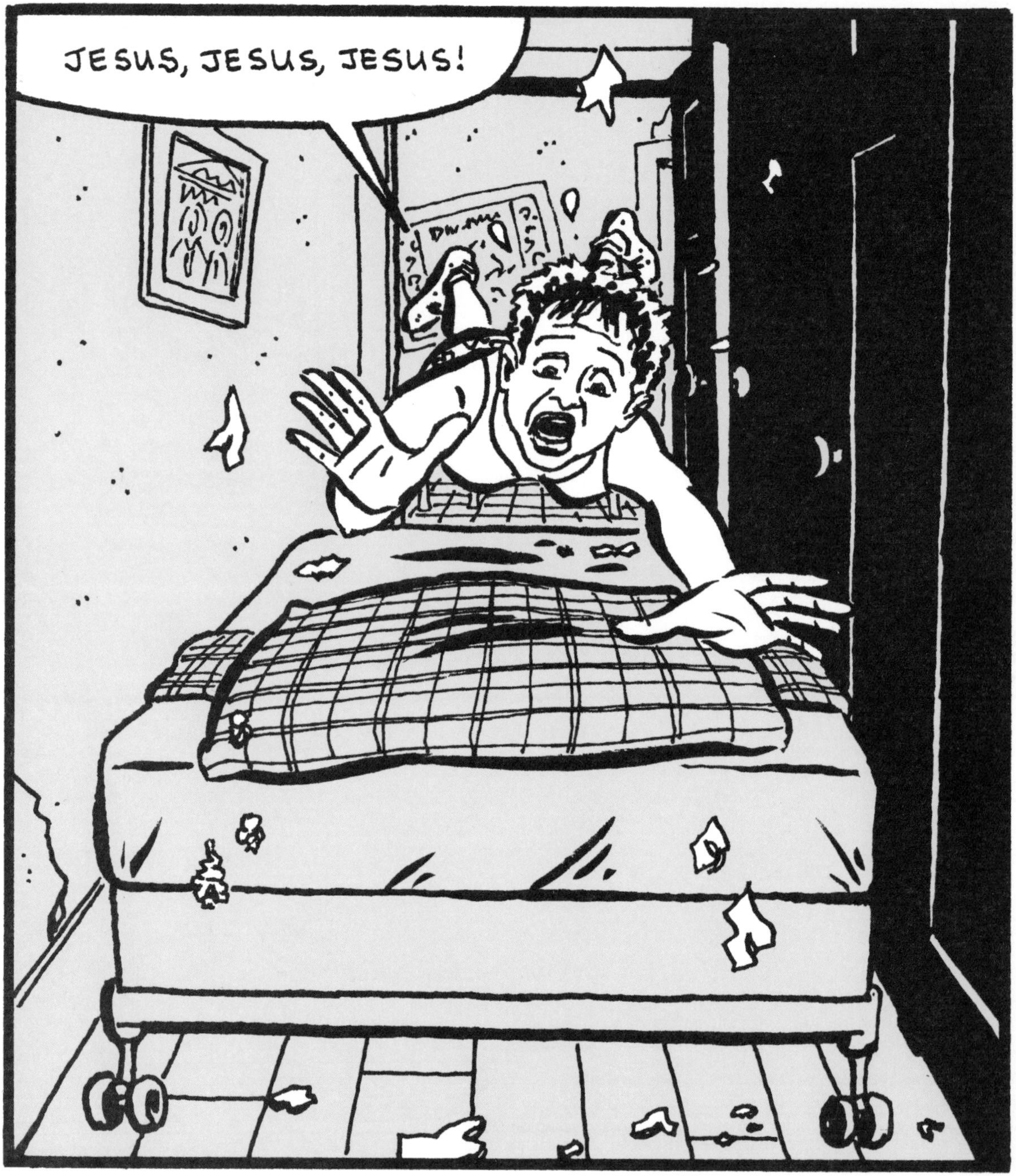
JESUS, JESUS, JESUS!

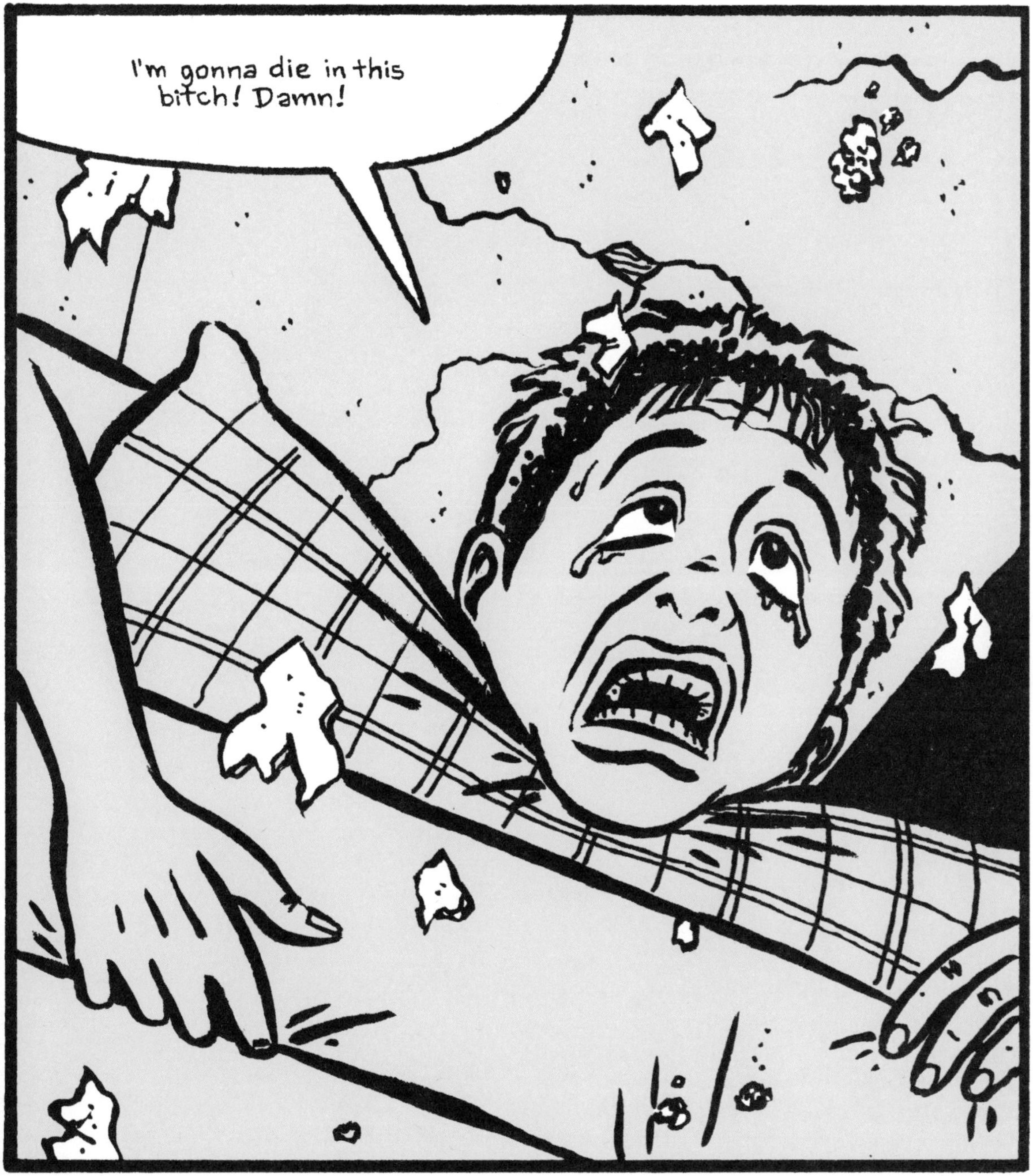
I'm gonna die in this bitch! Damn!

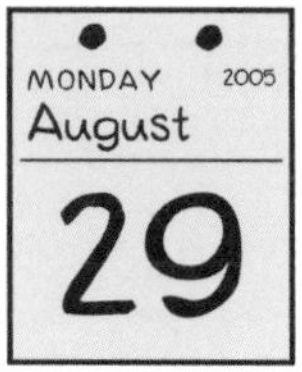
MONDAY
2005
August
29

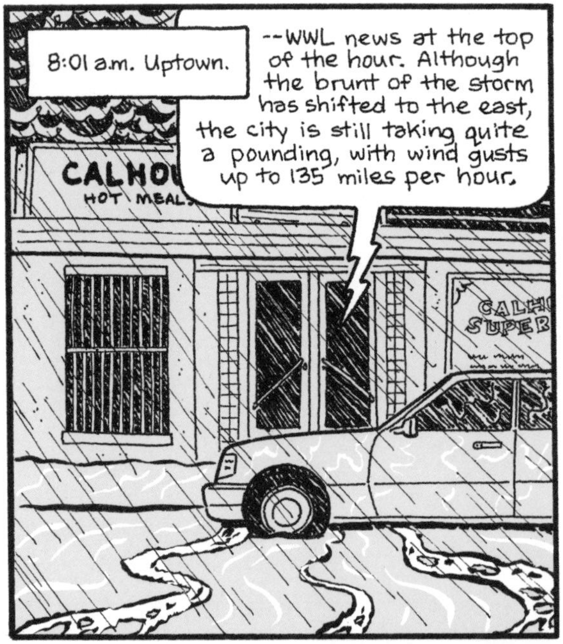
8:01 a.m. Uptown.
--WWL news at the top of the hour. Although the brunt of the storm has shifted to the east, the city is still taking quite a pounding, with wind gusts up to 135 miles per hour.
CALHOU
HOT MEALS

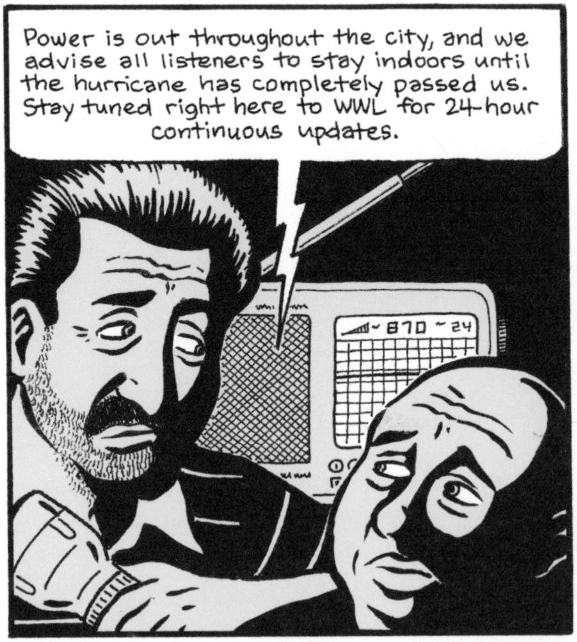
Power is out throughout the city, and we advise all listeners to stay indoors until the hurricane has completely passed us. Stay tuned right here to WWL for 24-hour continuous updates.

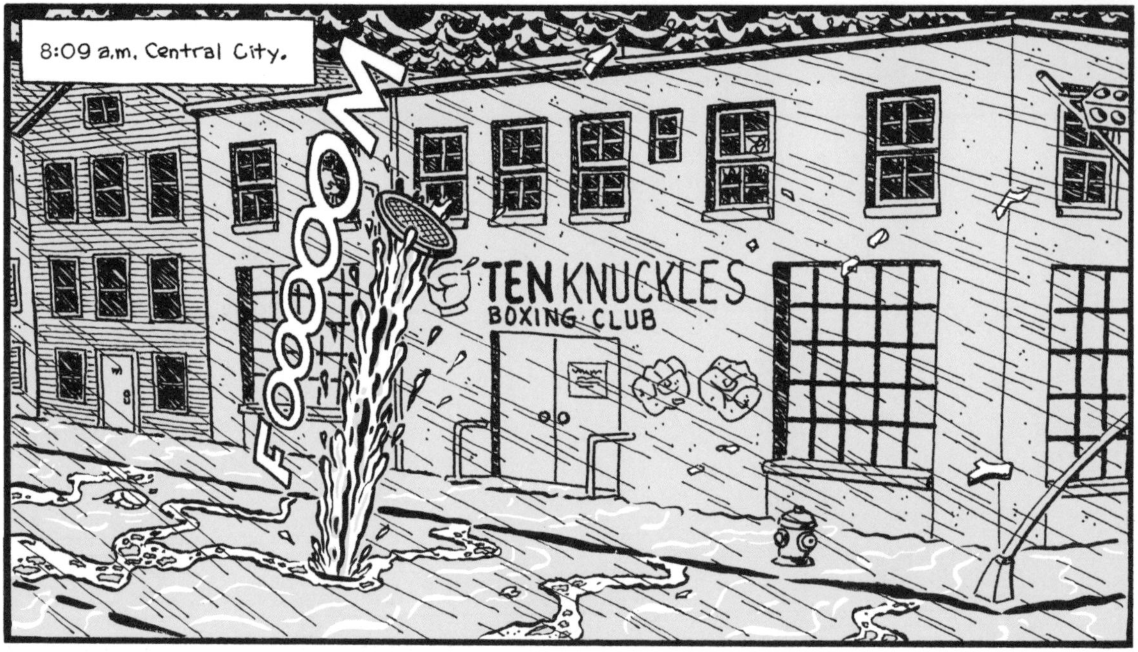
8:09 a.m. Central City.
FOOOOOM
TEN KNUCKLES
BOXING CLUB

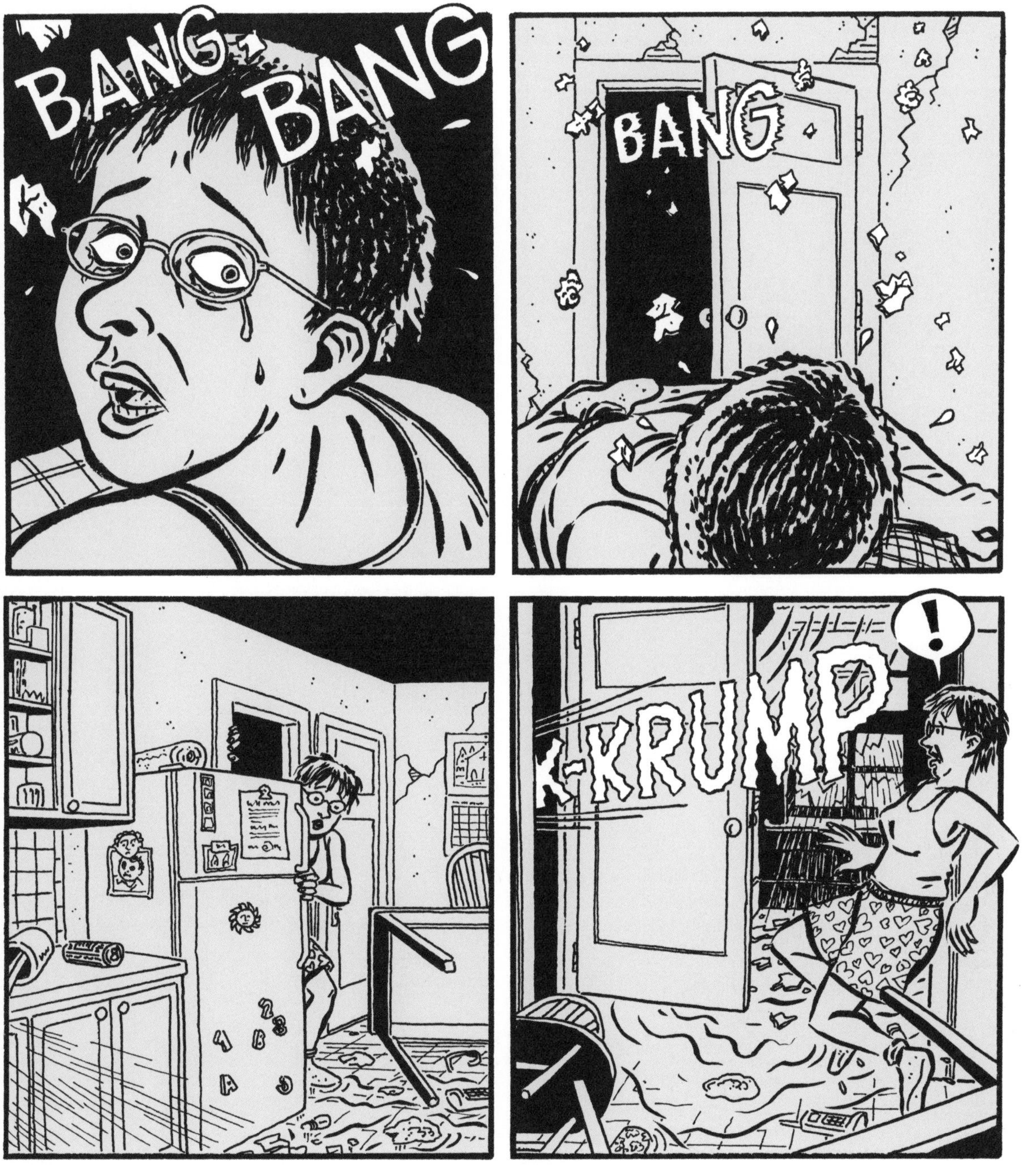
BANG BANG
BANG
K-KRUMP
!

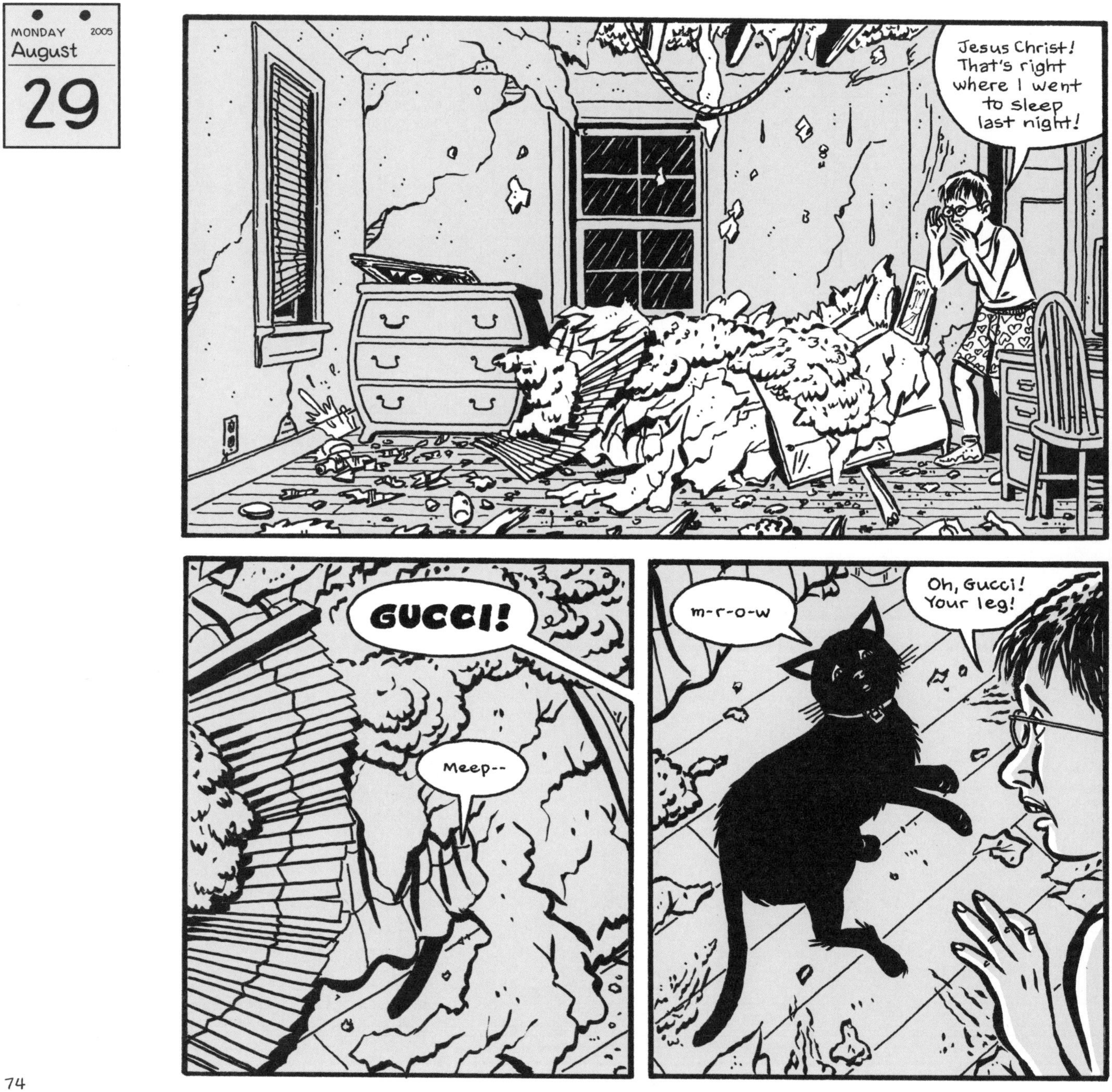
MONDAY
2005
August
29
Jesus Christ! That's right where I went to sleep last night!
GUCCI!
Meep--
m-r-o-w
Oh, Gucci! Your leg!

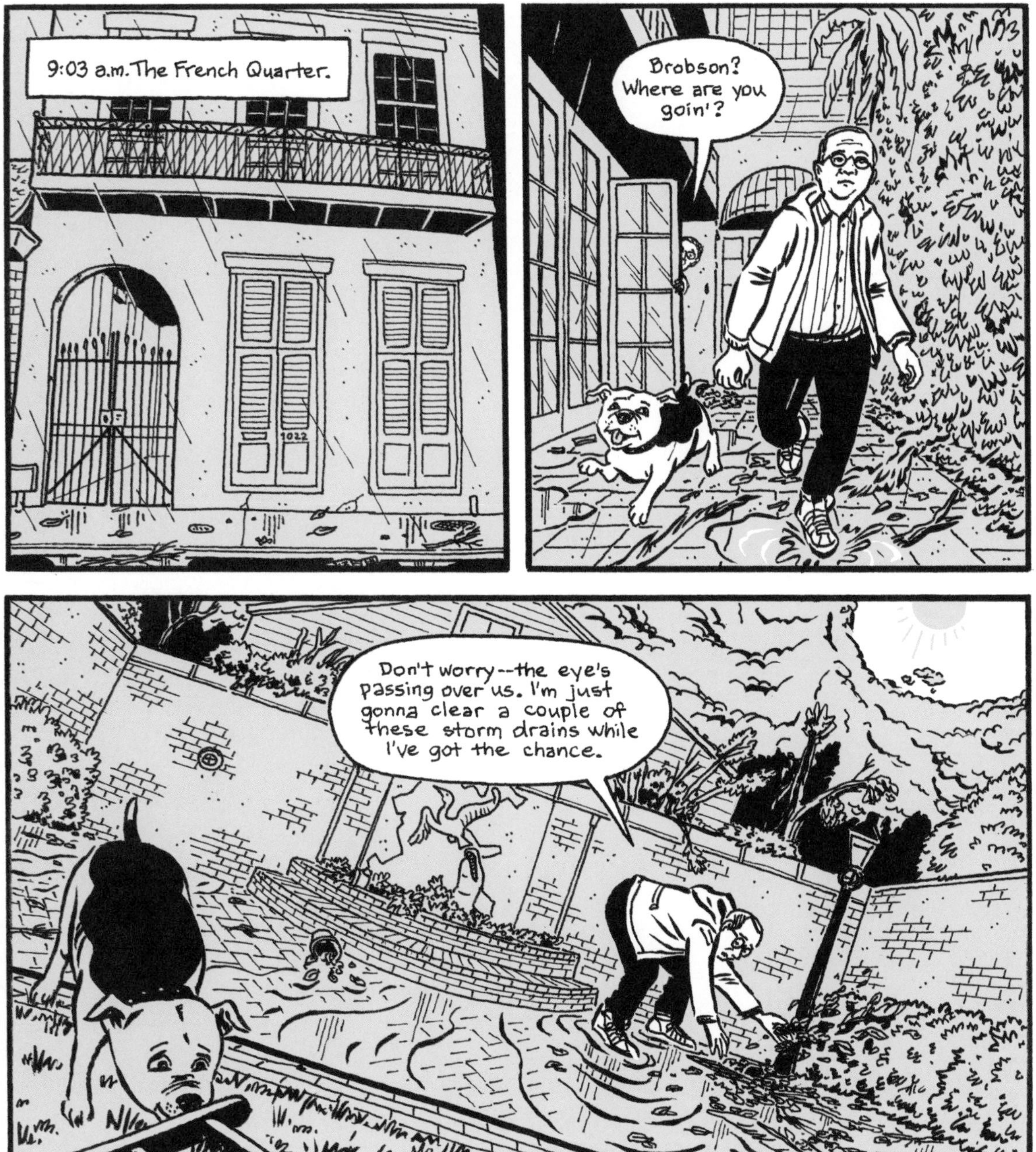
9:03 a.m. The French Quarter.
Brobson? Where are you goin'?
Don't worry--the eye's passing over us. I'm just gonna clear a couple of these storm drains while I've got the chance.

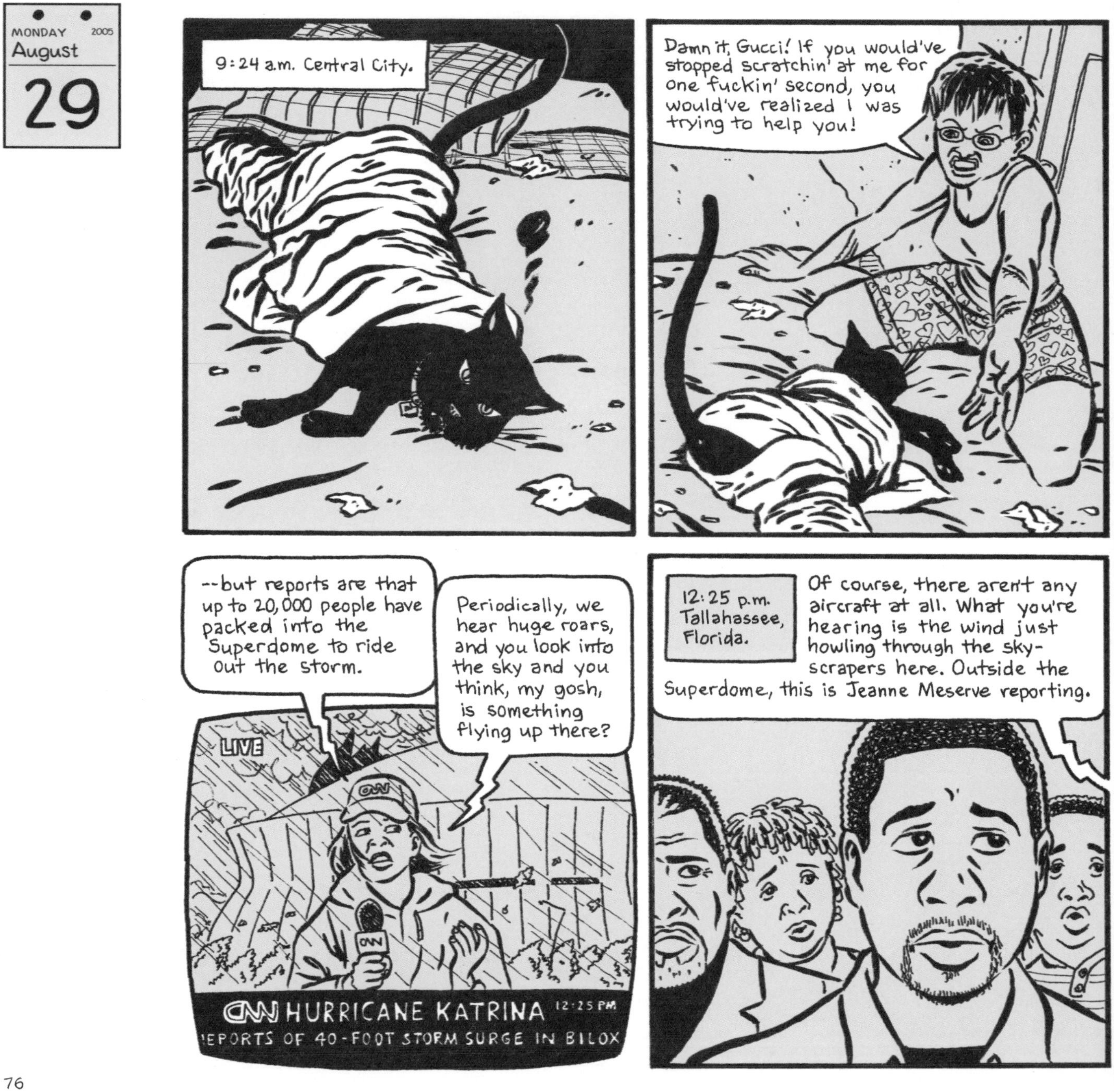
MONDAY 2005
August
29
9:24 a.m. Central City.
Damn it, Gucci! If you would've stopped scratchin' at me for one fuckin' second, you would've realized I was trying to help you!
--but reports are that up to 20,000 people have packed into the Superdome to ride out the storm.
Periodically, we hear huge roars, and you look into the sky and you think, my gosh, is something flying up there?
LIVE
CNN
CNN
CNN HURRICANE KATRINA 12:25 PM
EPORTS OF 40-FOOT STORM SURGE IN BILOX
12:25 p.m. Tallahassee, Florida.
Of course, there aren't any aircraft at all. What you're hearing is the wind just howling through the sky-scrapers here. Outside the Superdome, this is Jeanne Meserve reporting.

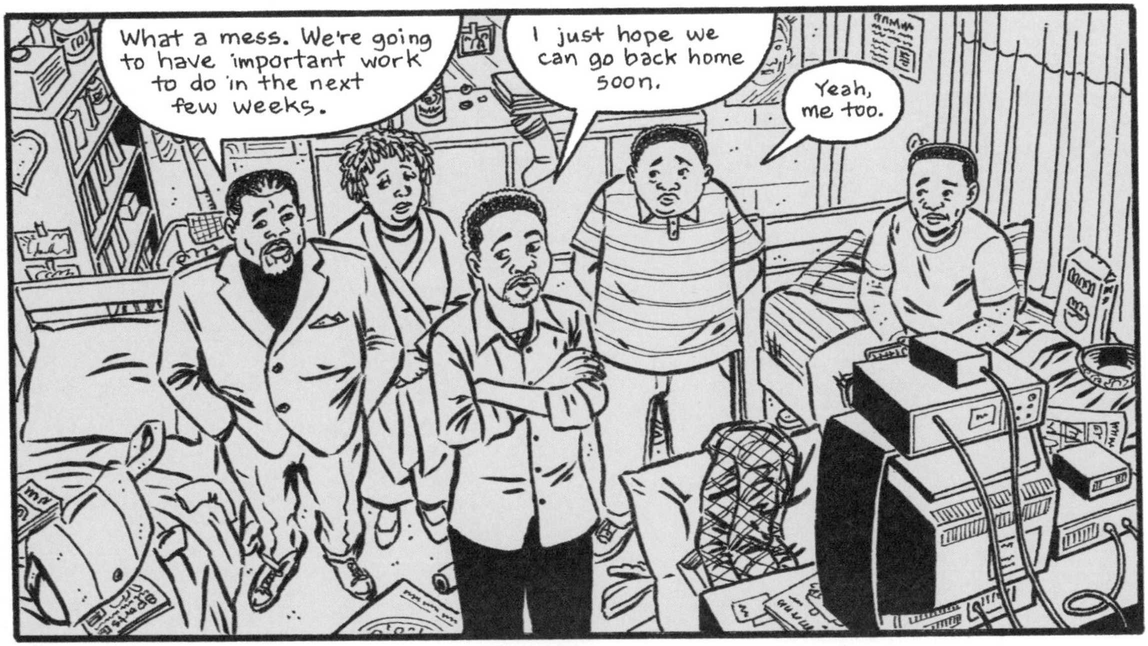
What a mess. We're going to have important work to do in the next few weeks.
I just hope we can go back home soon.
Yeah, me too.

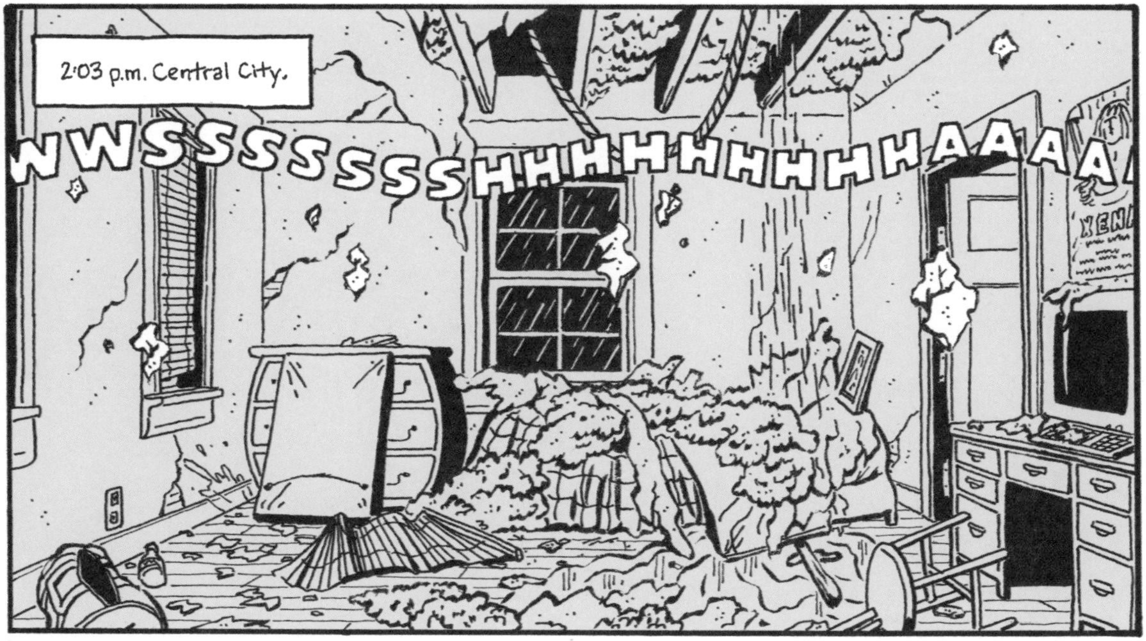
2:03 p.m. Central City.
WWSSSSSSSHHHHHHHHHAAAA

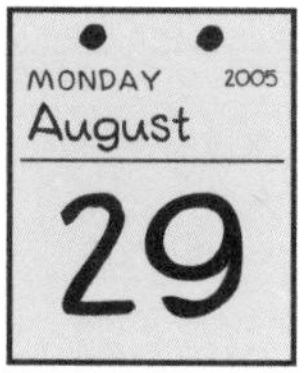
MONDAY 2005
August
29

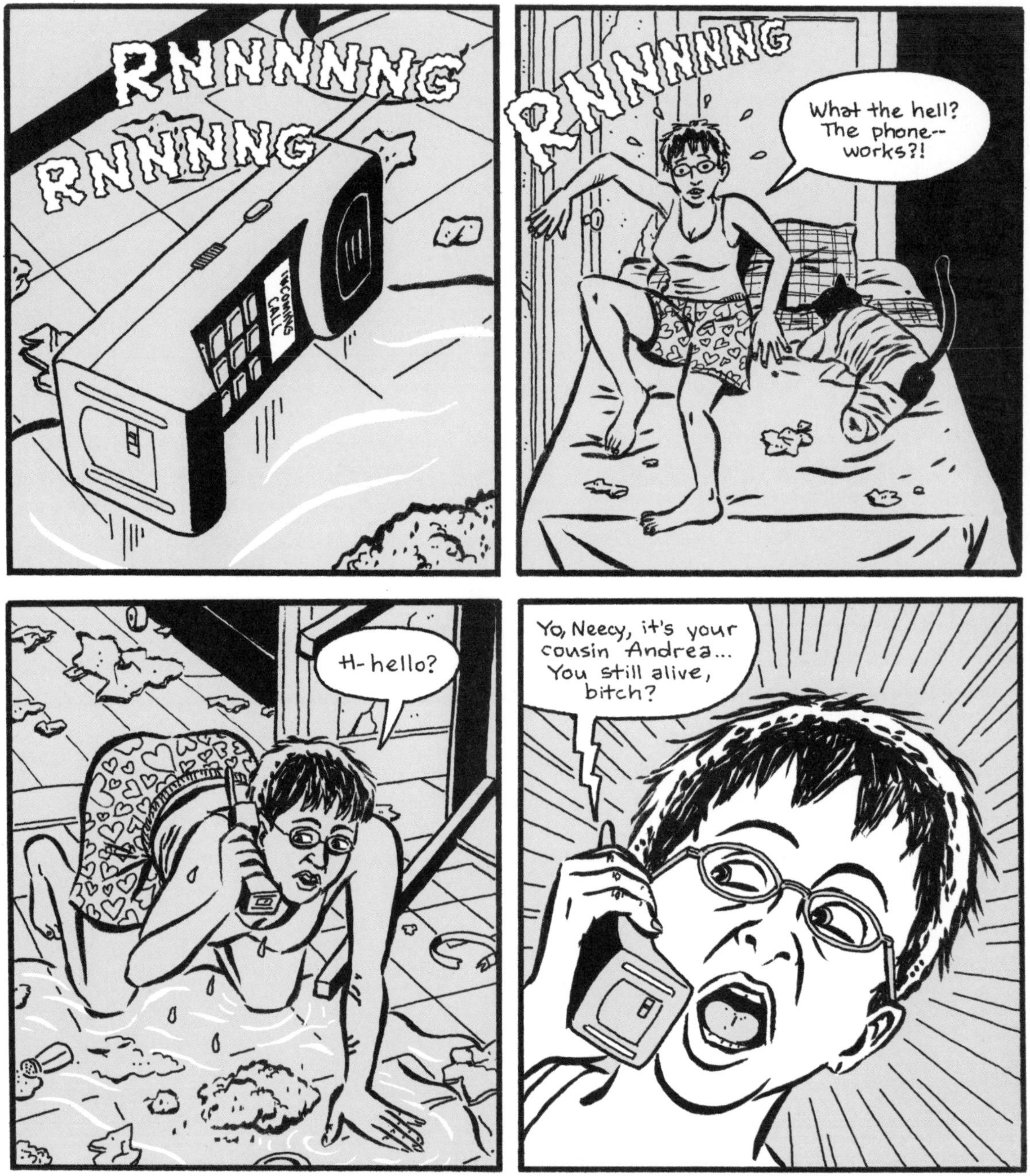
RNNNNNG
RNNNNG
INCOMING CALL
RNNNNNG
What the hell? The phone-- works?!
H-hello?
Yo, Neecy, it's your cousin Andrea... You still alive, bitch?

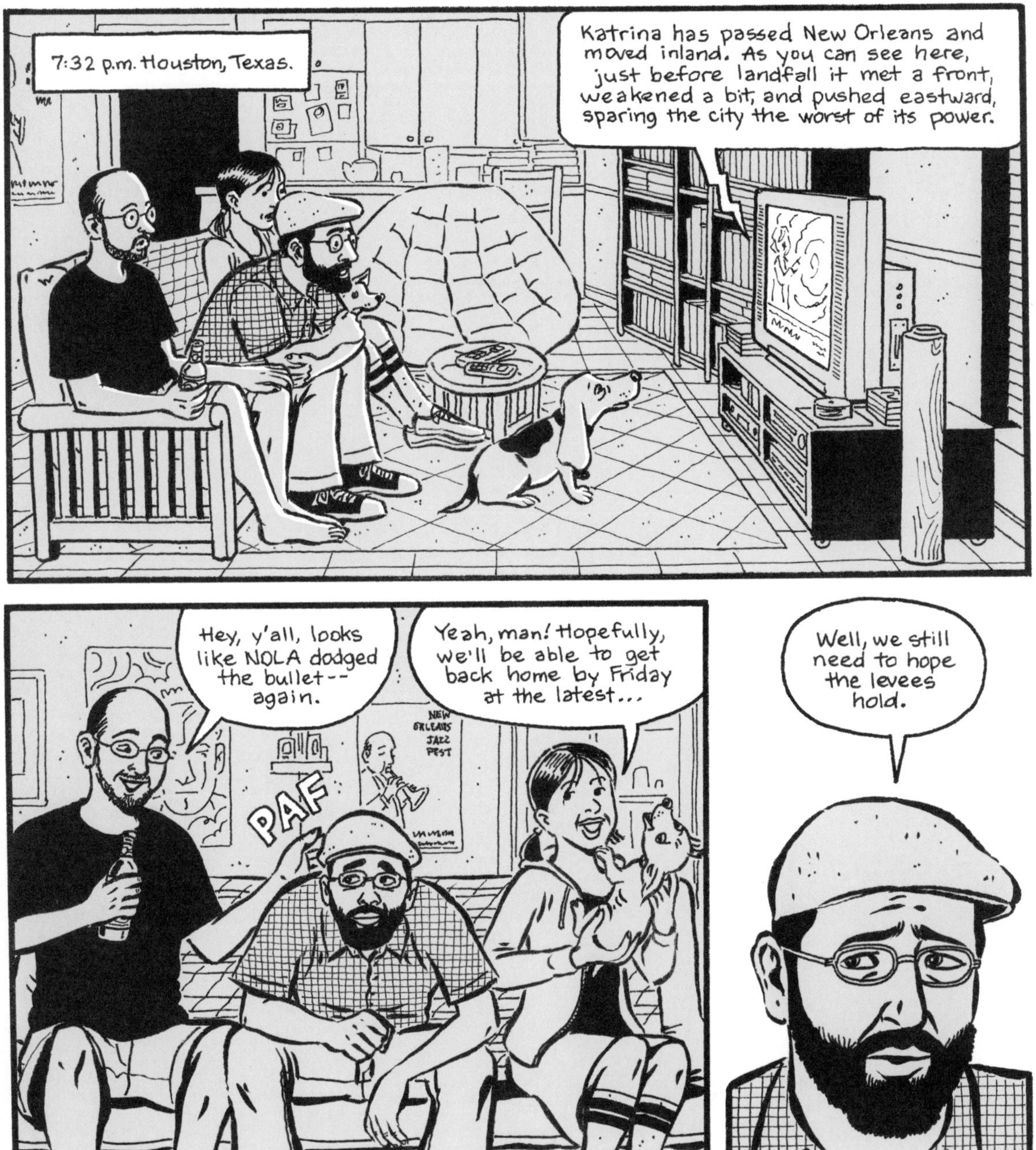
7:32 p.m. Houston, Texas.
Katrina has passed New Orleans and moved inland. As you can see here, just before landfall it met a front, weakened a bit, and pushed eastward, sparing the city the worst of its power.
Hey, y'all, looks like NOLA dodged the bullet--again.
PAF
NEW ORLEANS JAZZ FEST
Yeah, man! Hopefully, we'll be able to get back home by Friday at the latest...
Well, we still need to hope the levees hold.

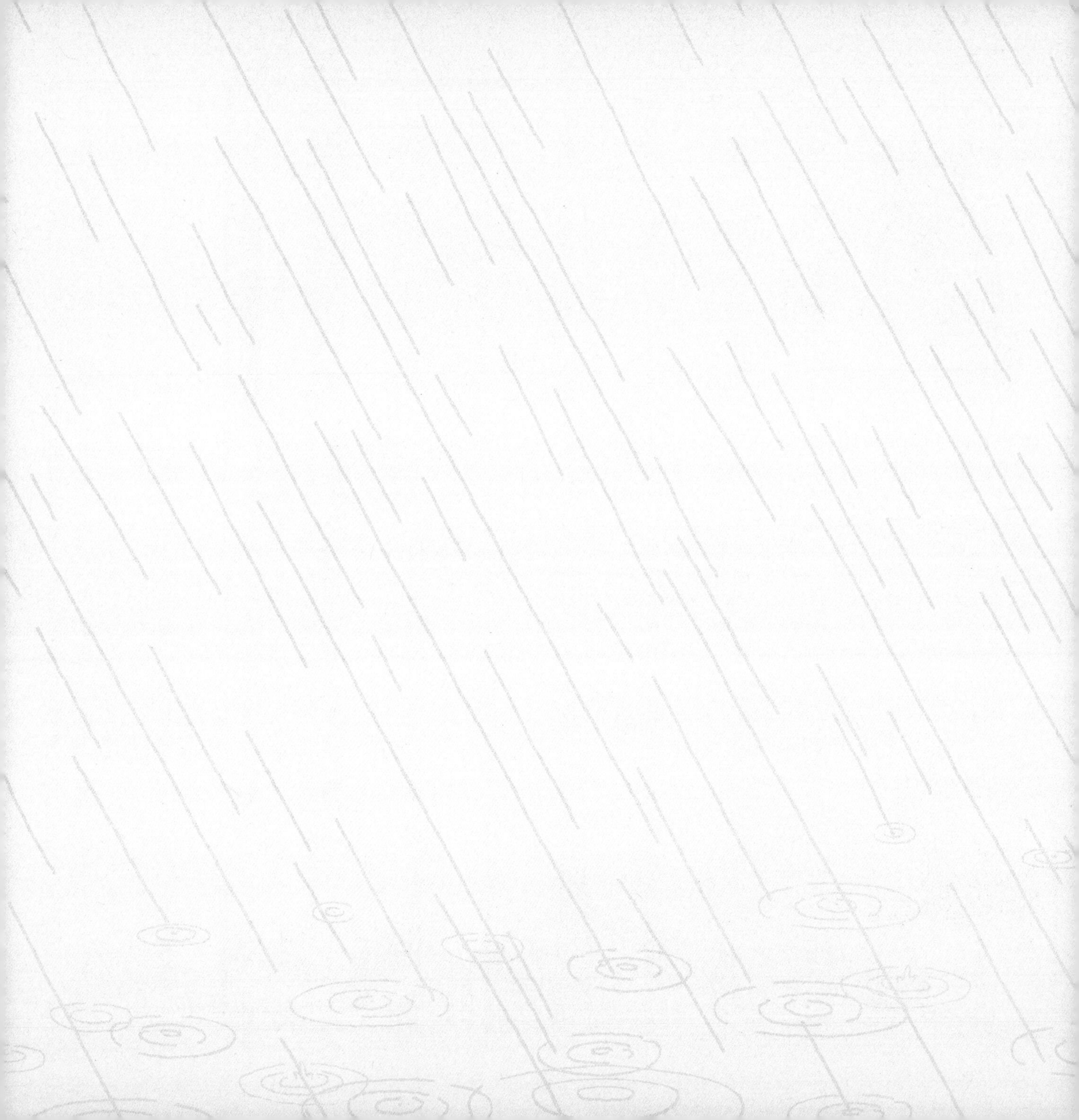

THE FLOOD

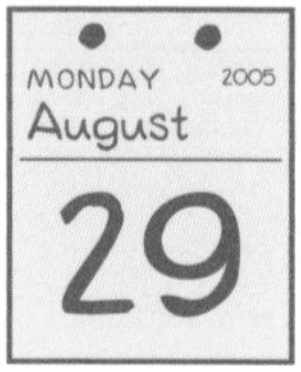
MONDAY 2005
August
29

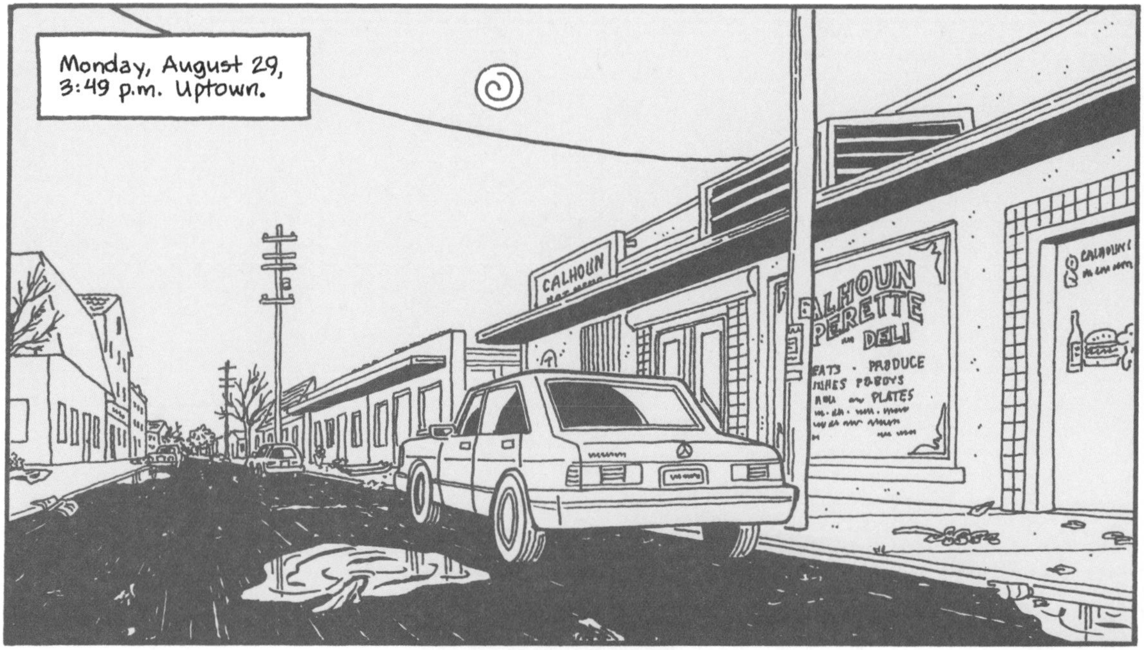
Monday, August 29, 3:49 p.m. Uptown.
CALHOUN
CALHOUN SUPERETTE DELI
PRODUCE
PLATES

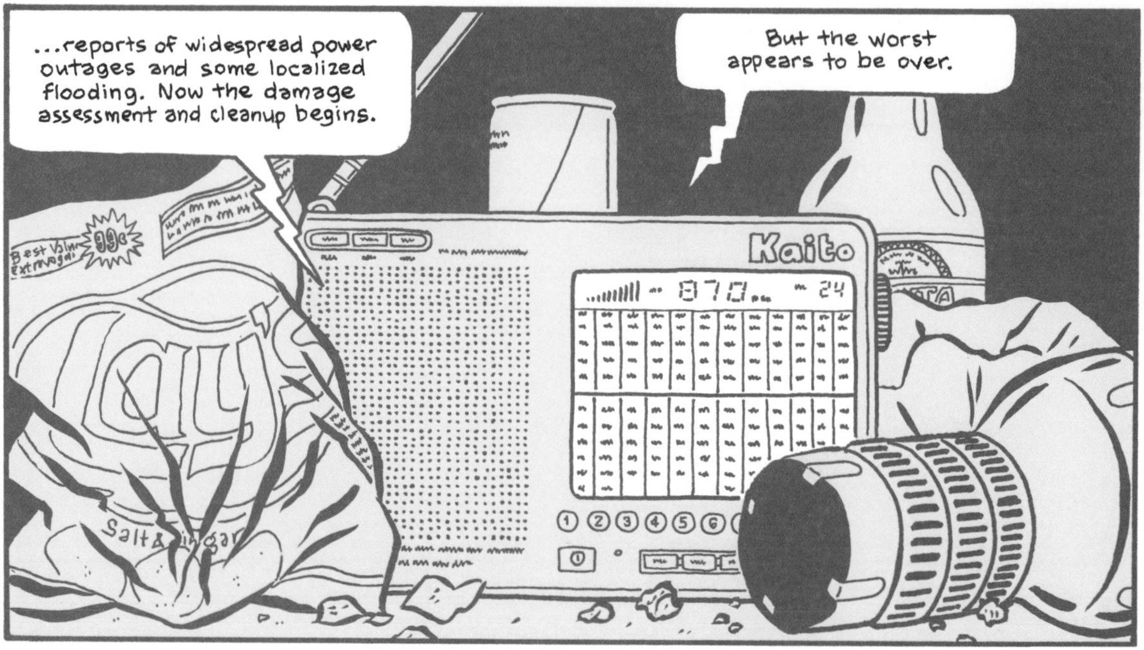
...reports of widespread power outages and some localized flooding. Now the damage assessment and cleanup begins.
But the worst appears to be over.
Kaito

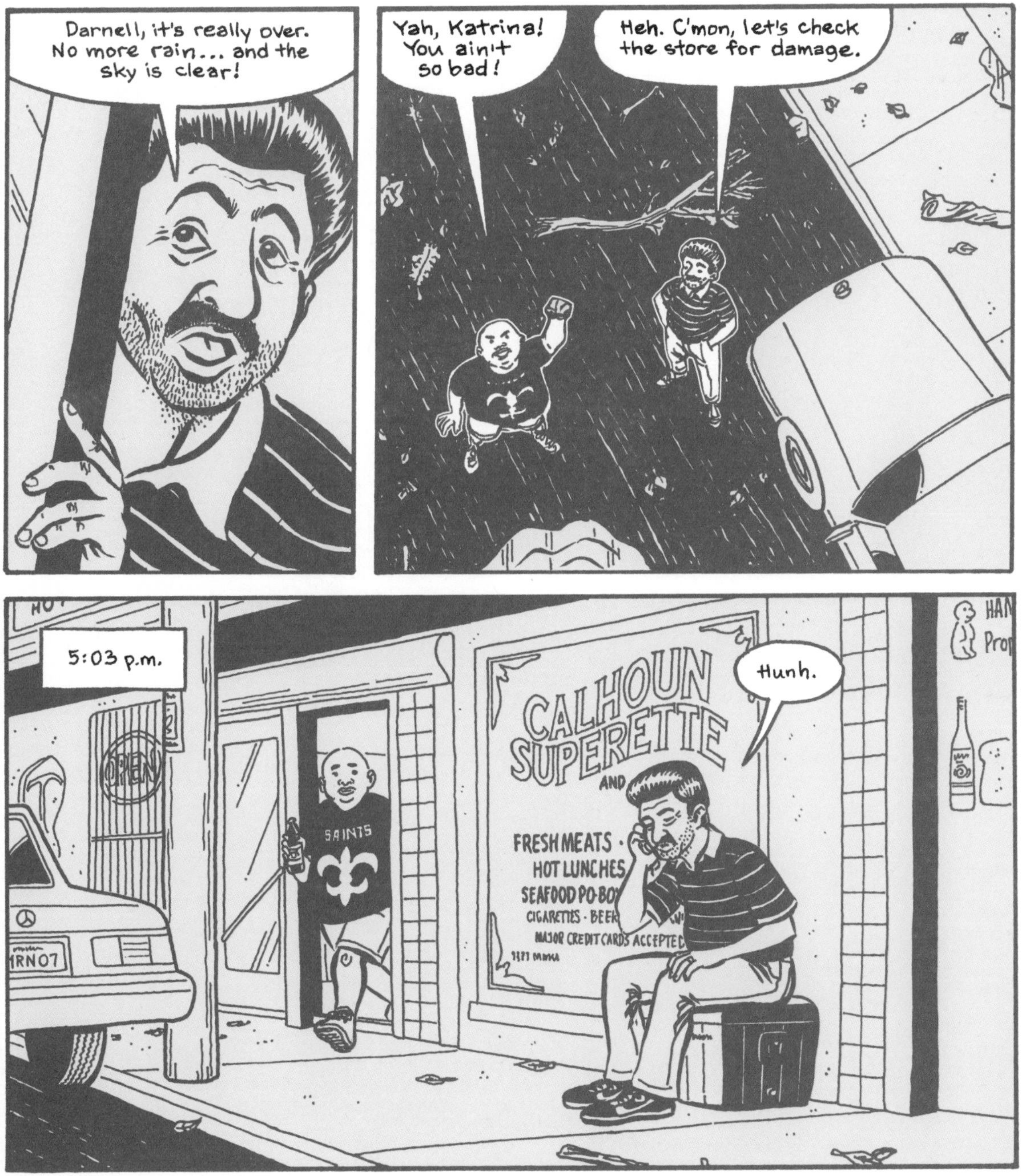
Darnell, it's really over. No more rain... and the sky is clear!
Yah, Katrina! You ain't so bad!
Heh. C'mon, let's check the store for damage.
5:03 p.m.
OPEN
SAINTS
CALHOUN SUPERETTE
AND
FRESH MEATS
HOT LUNCHES
Hunh.

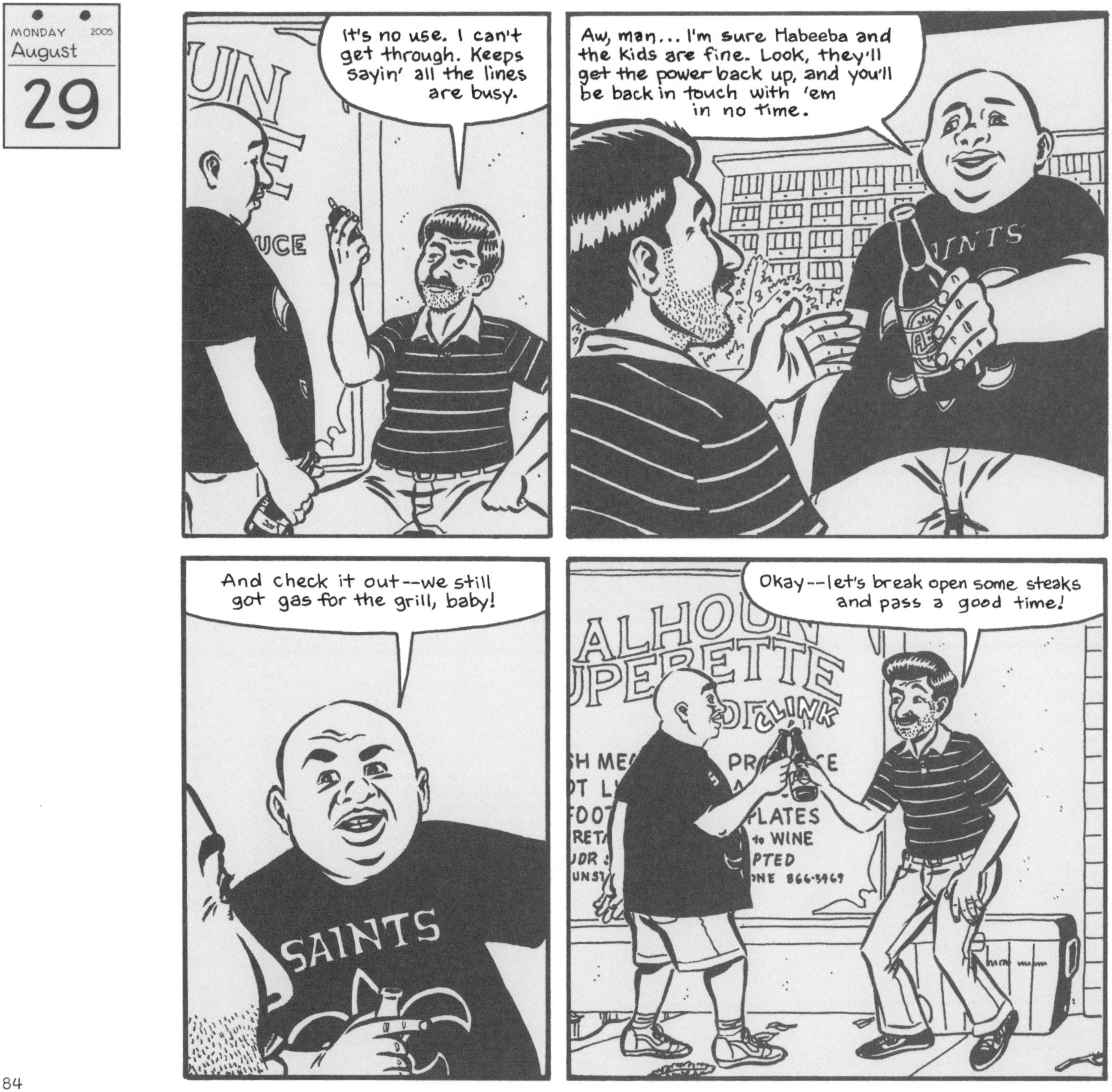
MONDAY 2005
August
29
It's no use. I can't get through. Keeps sayin' all the lines are busy.
Aw, man... I'm sure Habeeba and the kids are fine. Look, they'll get the power back up, and you'll be back in touch with 'em in no time.
And check it out--we still got gas for the grill, baby!
SAINTS
Okay--let's break open some steaks and pass a good time!
CLINK

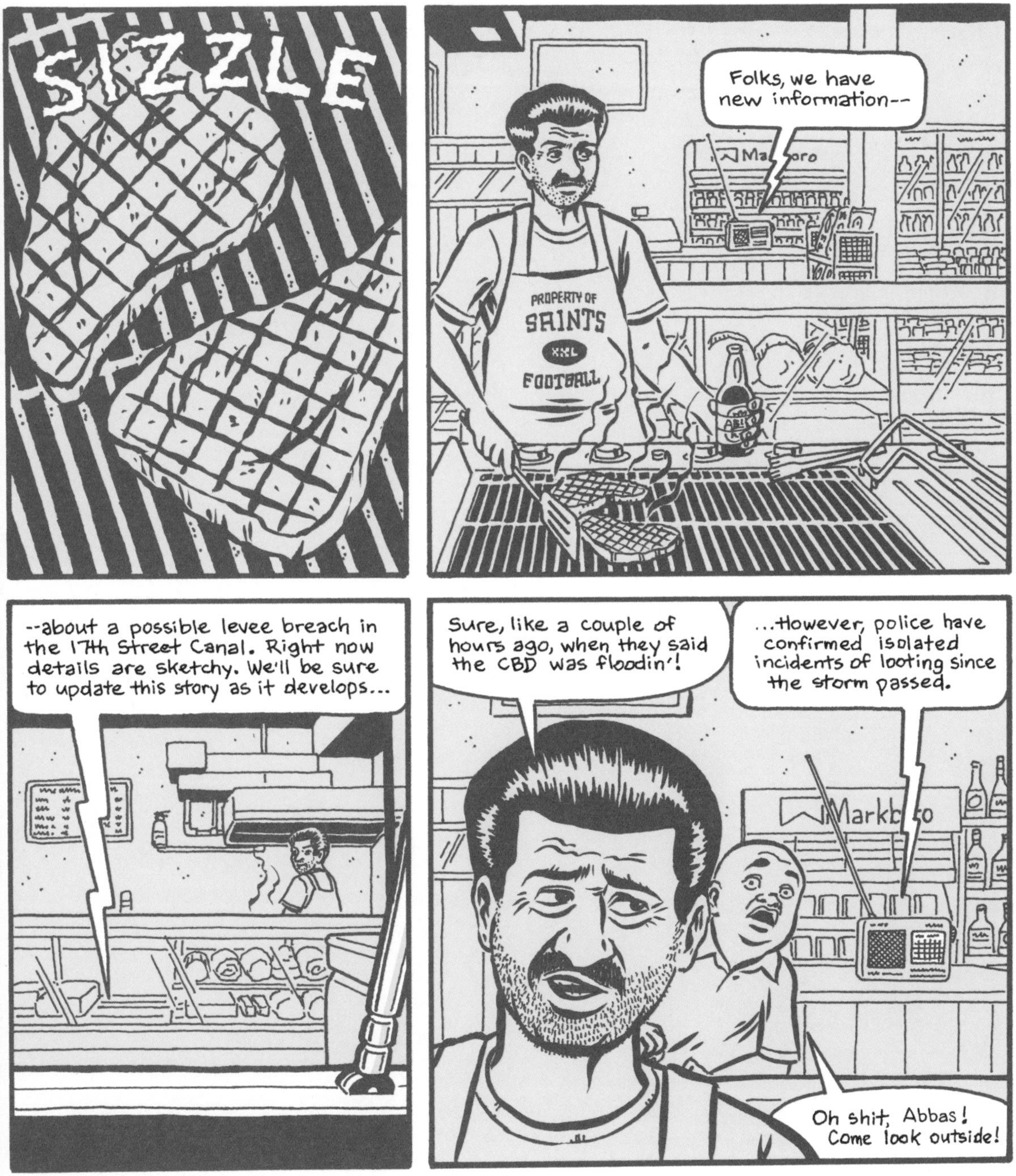
SIZZLE
Folks, we have new information--
PROPERTY OF SAINTS XXL FOOTBALL
Marlboro
--about a possible levee breach in the 17th Street Canal. Right now details are sketchy. We'll be sure to update this story as it develops...
Sure, like a couple of hours ago, when they said the CBD was floodin'!
...However, police have confirmed isolated incidents of looting since the storm passed.
Oh shit, Abbas! Come look outside!

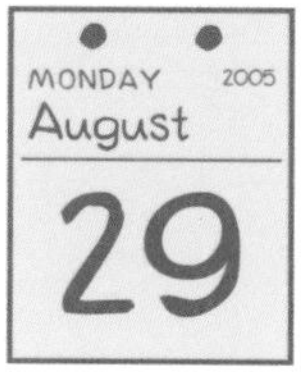
MONDAY 2005
August
29

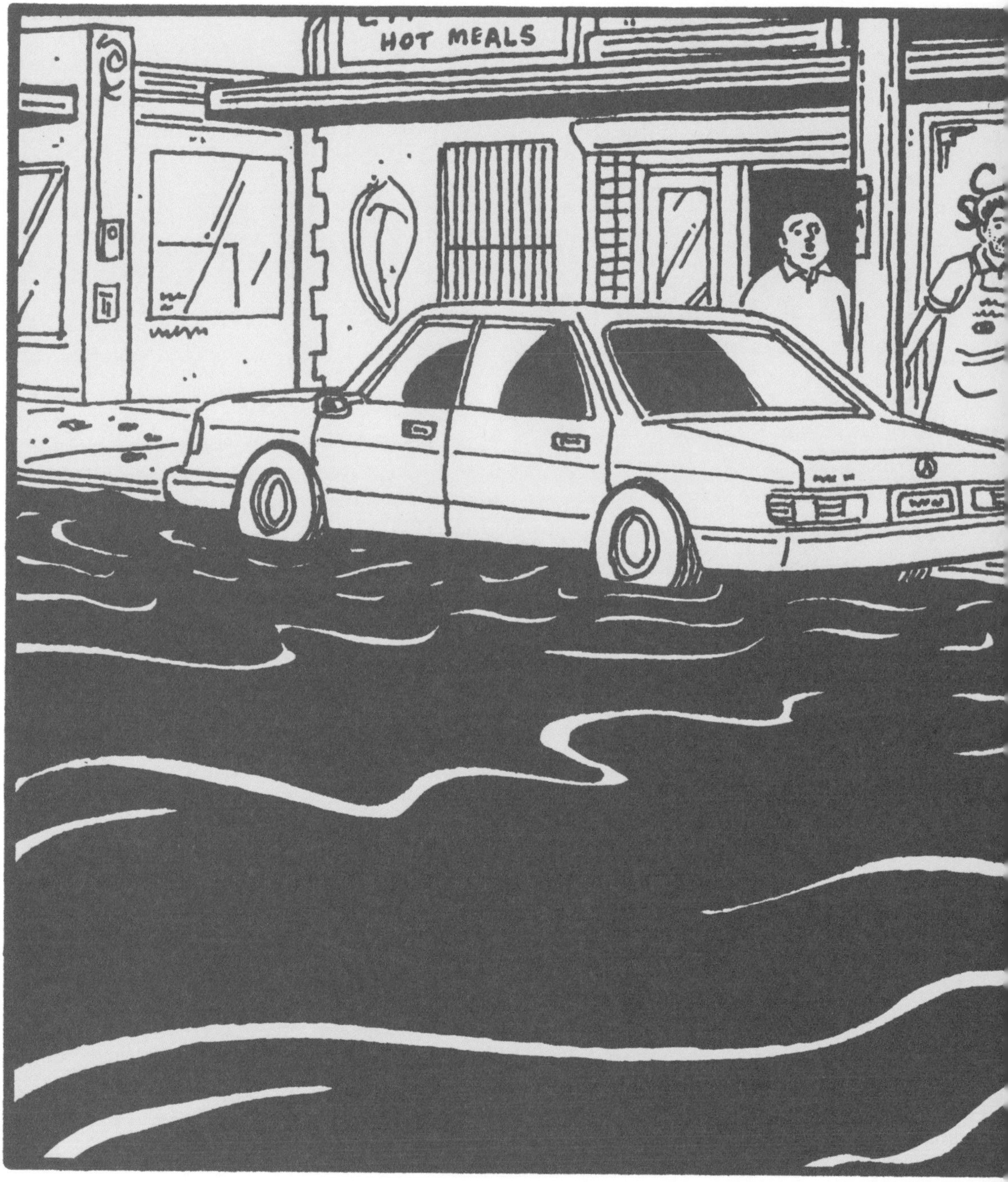
HOT MEALS

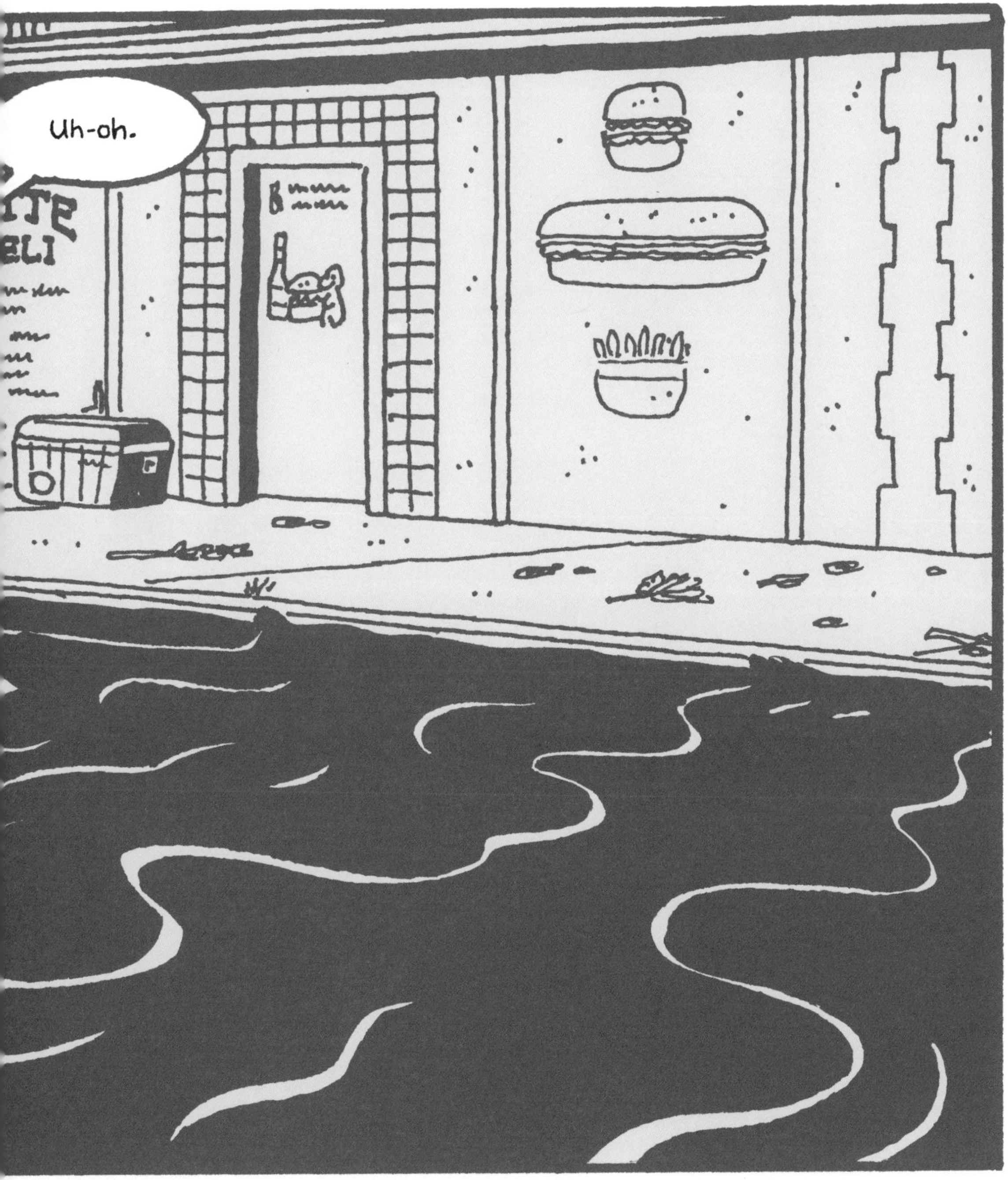
Uh-oh.
TTE
ELI

MONDAY 2005
August
29

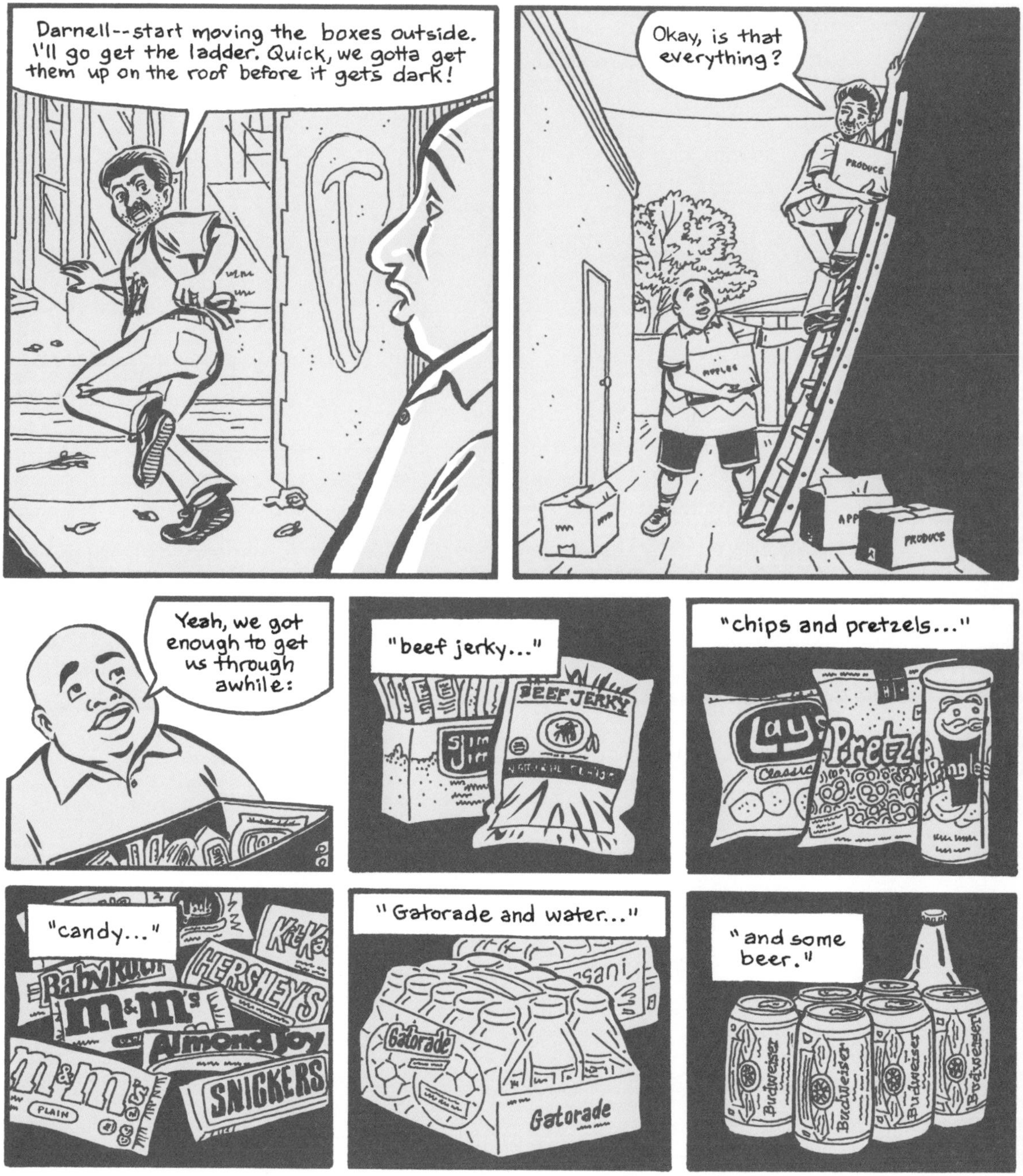

Darnell--start moving the boxes outside. I'll go get the ladder. Quick, we gotta get them up on the roof before it gets dark!
Okay, is that everything?
PRODUCE
APPLES
PRODUCE
Yeah, we got enough to get us through awhile:
"beef jerky..."
BEEF JERKY
"chips and pretzels..."
Lay's
Classic
"candy..."
Baby Ruth
m&m's
HERSHEY'S
Almond Joy
m&m's
PLAIN
SNICKERS
"Gatorade and water..."
Gatorade
Gatorade
"and some beer."
Budweiser
Budweiser
Budweiser
Budweiser

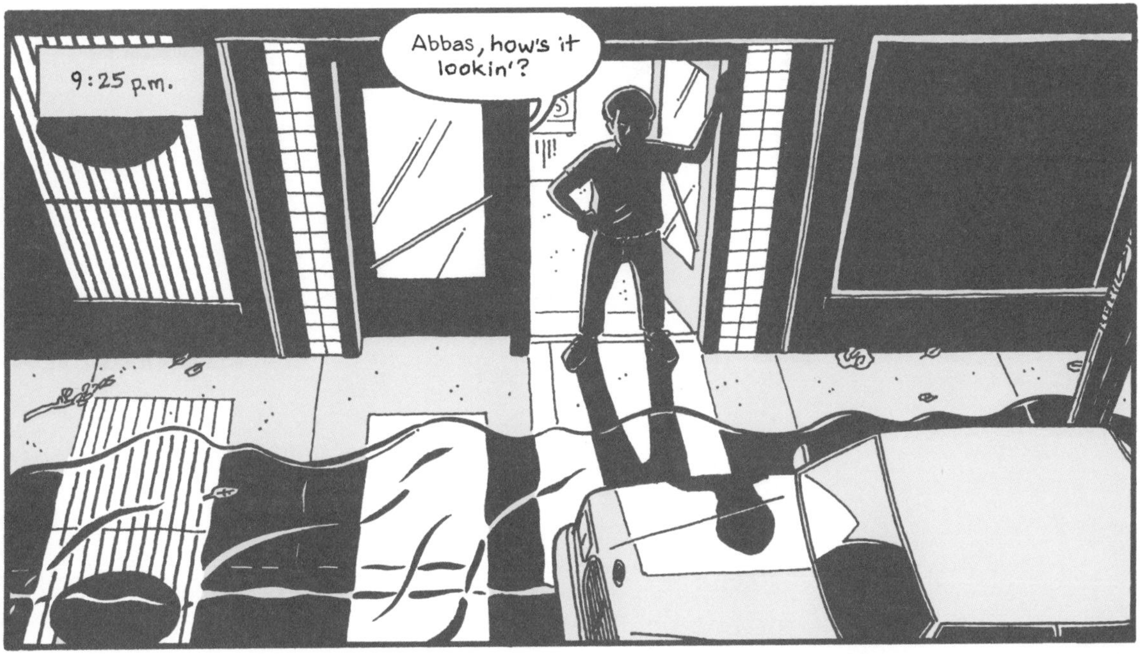
9:25 p.m.
Abbas, how's it lookin'?

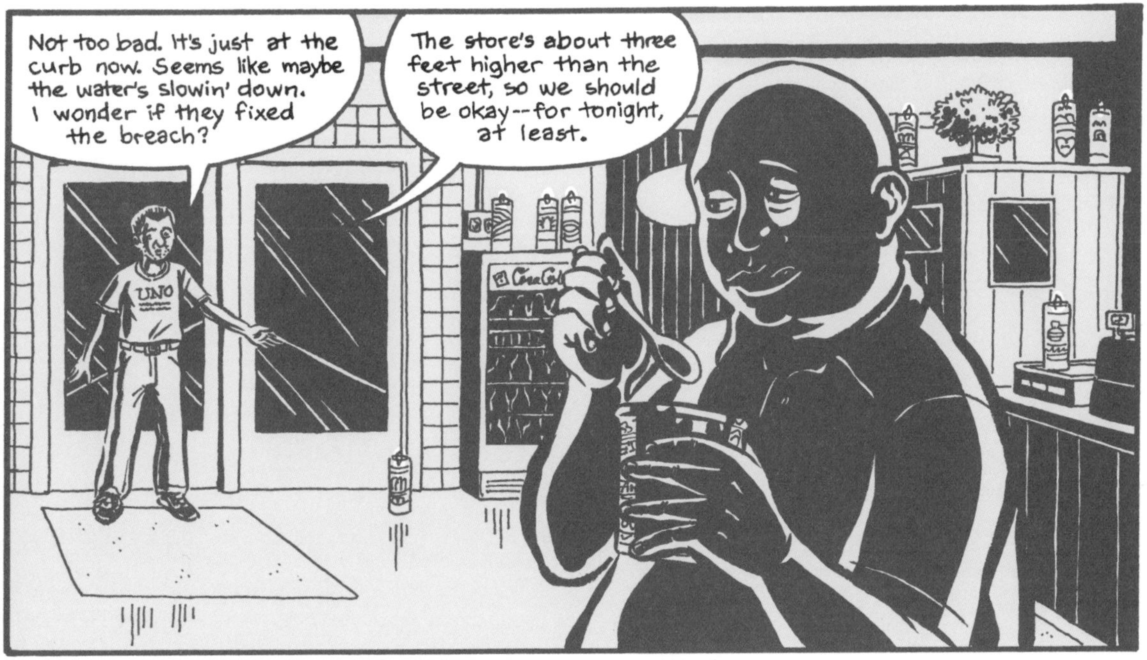
Not too bad. It's just at the curb now. Seems like maybe the water's slowin' down. I wonder if they fixed the breach?
The store's about three feet higher than the street, so we should be okay--for tonight, at least.
UNO

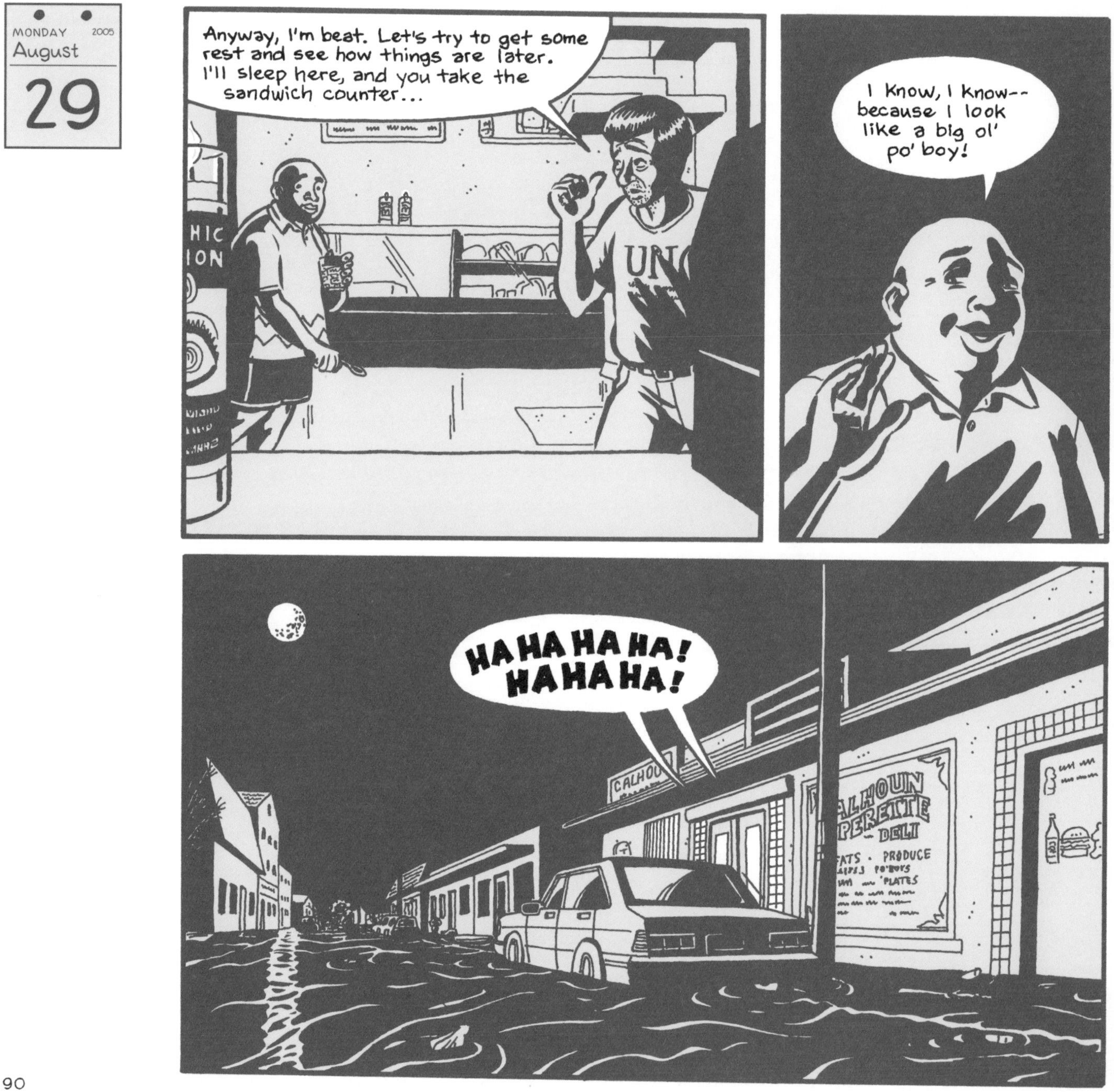
MONDAY 2005
August
29
Anyway, I'm beat. Let's try to get some rest and see how things are later. I'll sleep here, and you take the sandwich counter...
I know, I know-- because I look like a big ol' po' boy!
HAHAHAHA! HAHAHA!
DELI
PRODUCE
PLATES

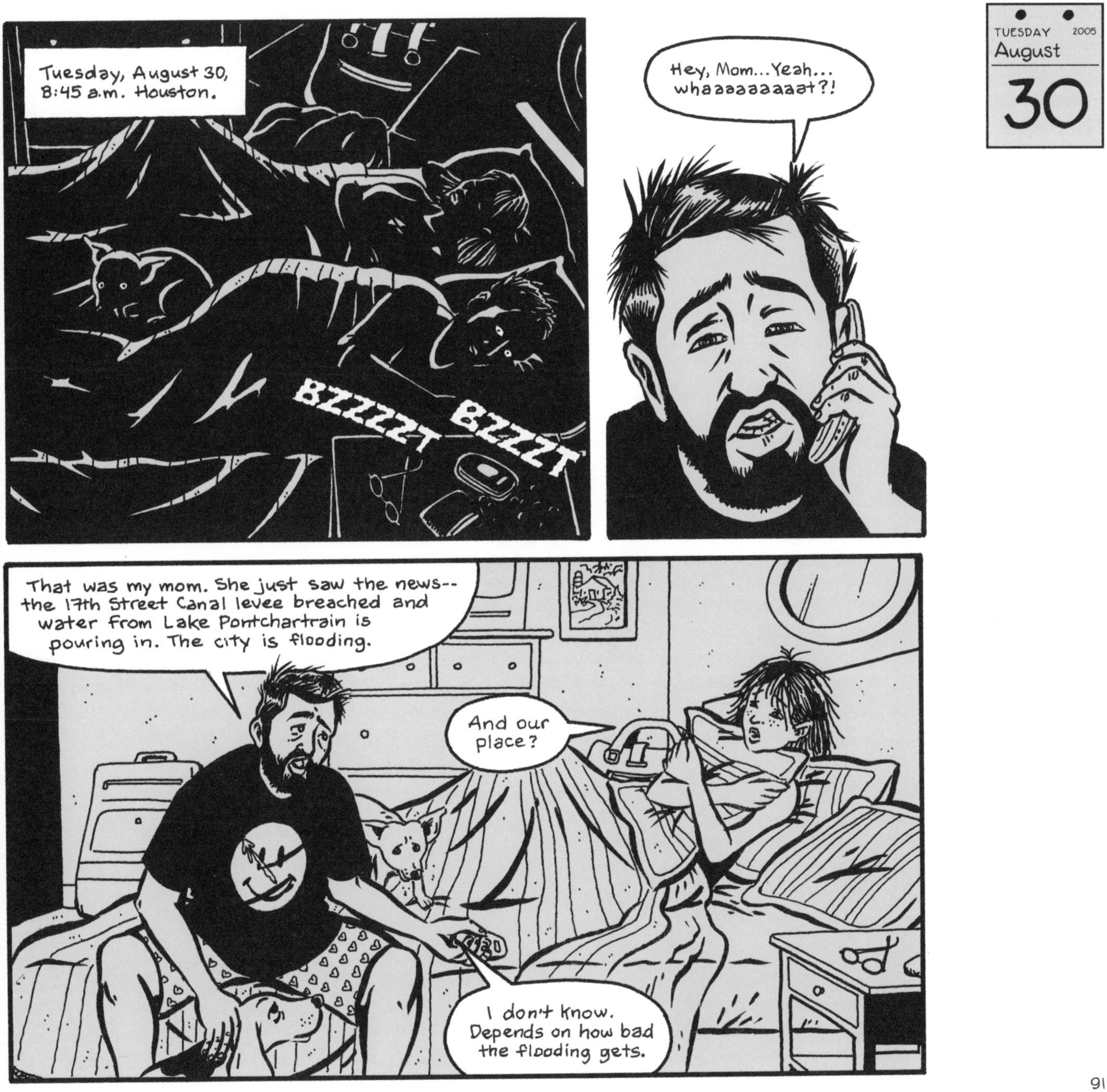
TUESDAY 2005
August
30
Tuesday, August 30, 8:45 a.m. Houston.
BZZZZT BZZZZT
Hey, Mom...Yeah... whaaaaaaaaat?!
That was my mom. She just saw the news--the 17th Street Canal levee breached and water from Lake Pontchartrain is pouring in. The city is flooding.
And our place?
I don't know. Depends on how bad the flooding gets.

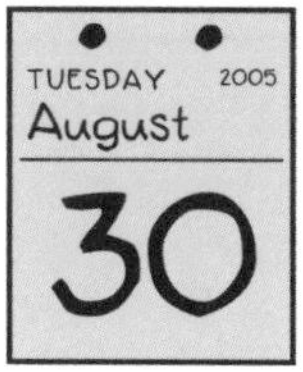
TUESDAY 2005
August
30

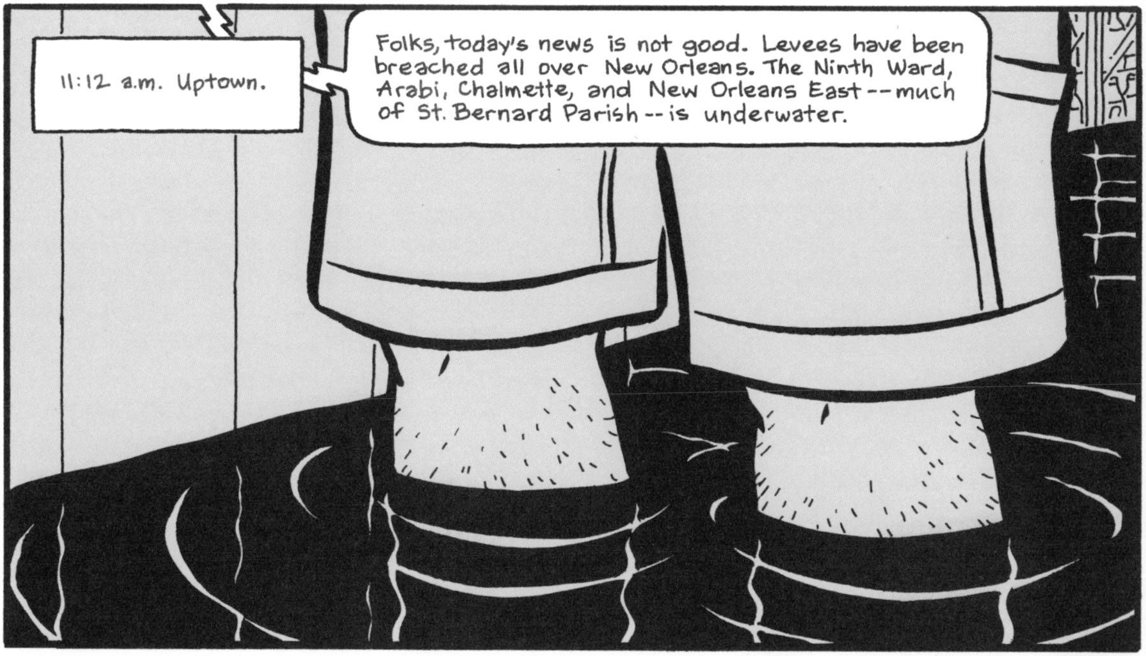
11:12 a.m. Uptown.
Folks, today's news is not good. Levees have been breached all over New Orleans. The Ninth Ward, Arabi, Chalmette, and New Orleans East -- much of St. Bernard Parish -- is underwater.

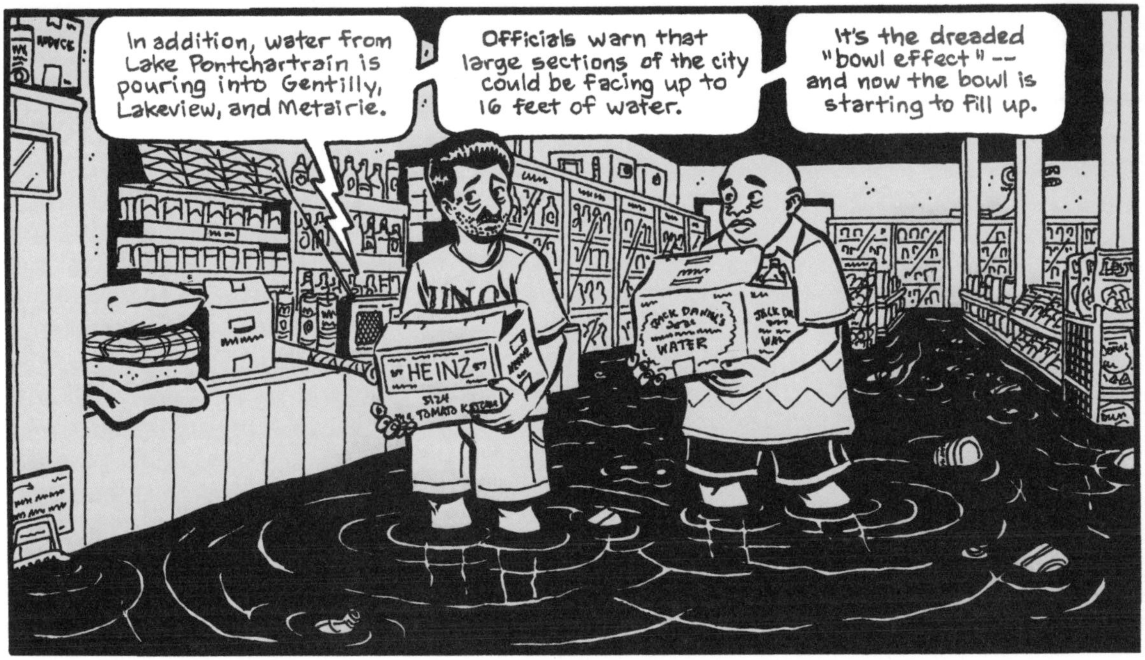
In addition, water from Lake Pontchartrain is pouring into Gentilly, Lakeview, and Metairie.
Officials warn that large sections of the city could be facing up to 16 feet of water.
It's the dreaded "bowl effect" -- and now the bowl is starting to fill up.
HEINZ
WATER

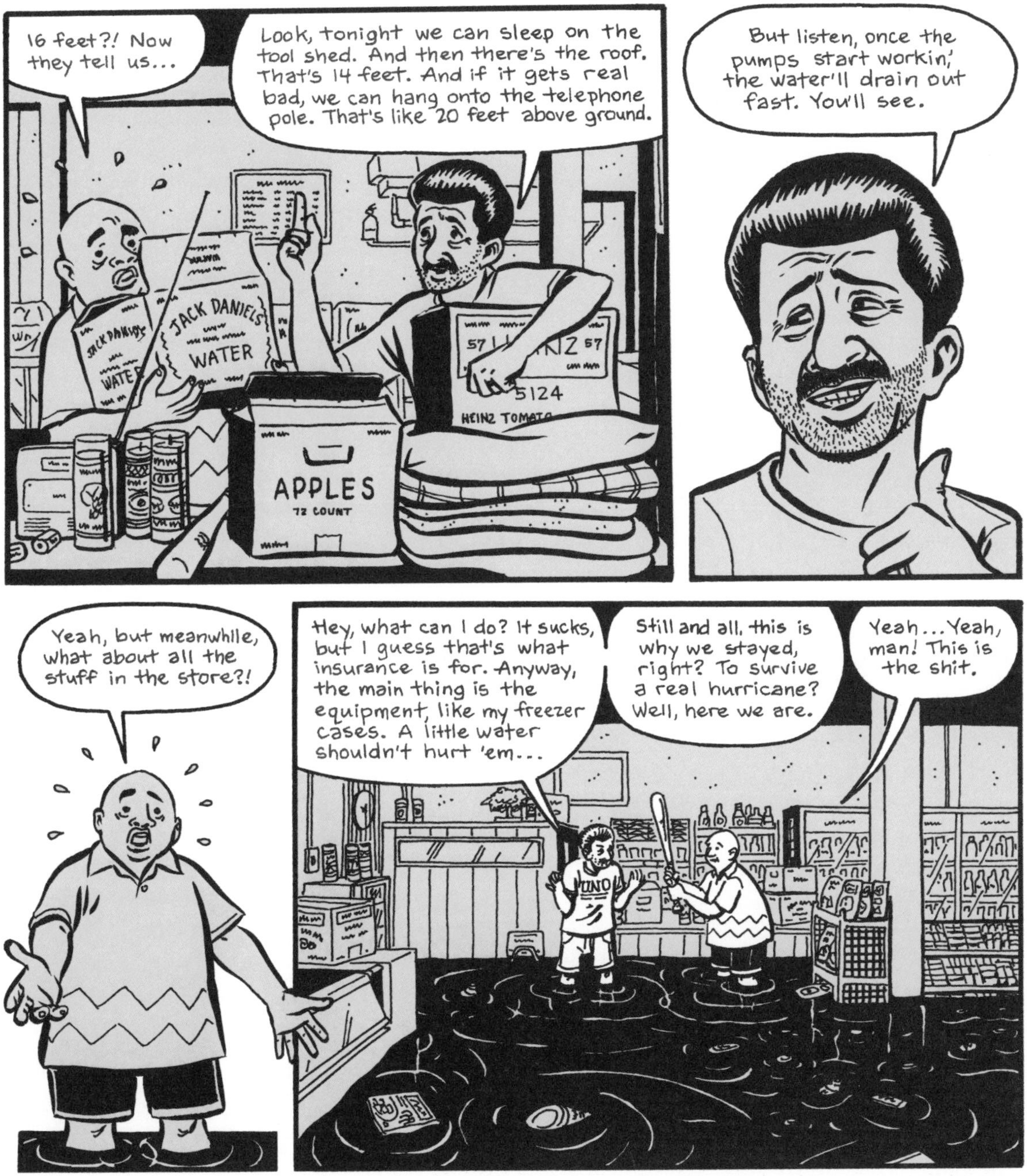
16 feet?! Now they tell us...
Look, tonight we can sleep on the tool shed. And then there's the roof. That's 14 feet. And if it gets real bad, we can hang onto the telephone pole. That's like 20 feet above ground.
JACK DANIELS
WATER
57
57
5124
HEINZ TOMATO
APPLES
72 COUNT
But listen, once the pumps start workin,' the water'll drain out fast. You'll see.
Yeah, but meanwhile, what about all the stuff in the store?!
Hey, what can I do? It sucks, but I guess that's what insurance is for. Anyway, the main thing is the equipment, like my freezer cases. A little water shouldn't hurt 'em...
Still and all, this is why we stayed, right? To survive a real hurricane? Well, here we are.
Yeah... Yeah, man! This is the shit.

TUESDAY 2005
August
30

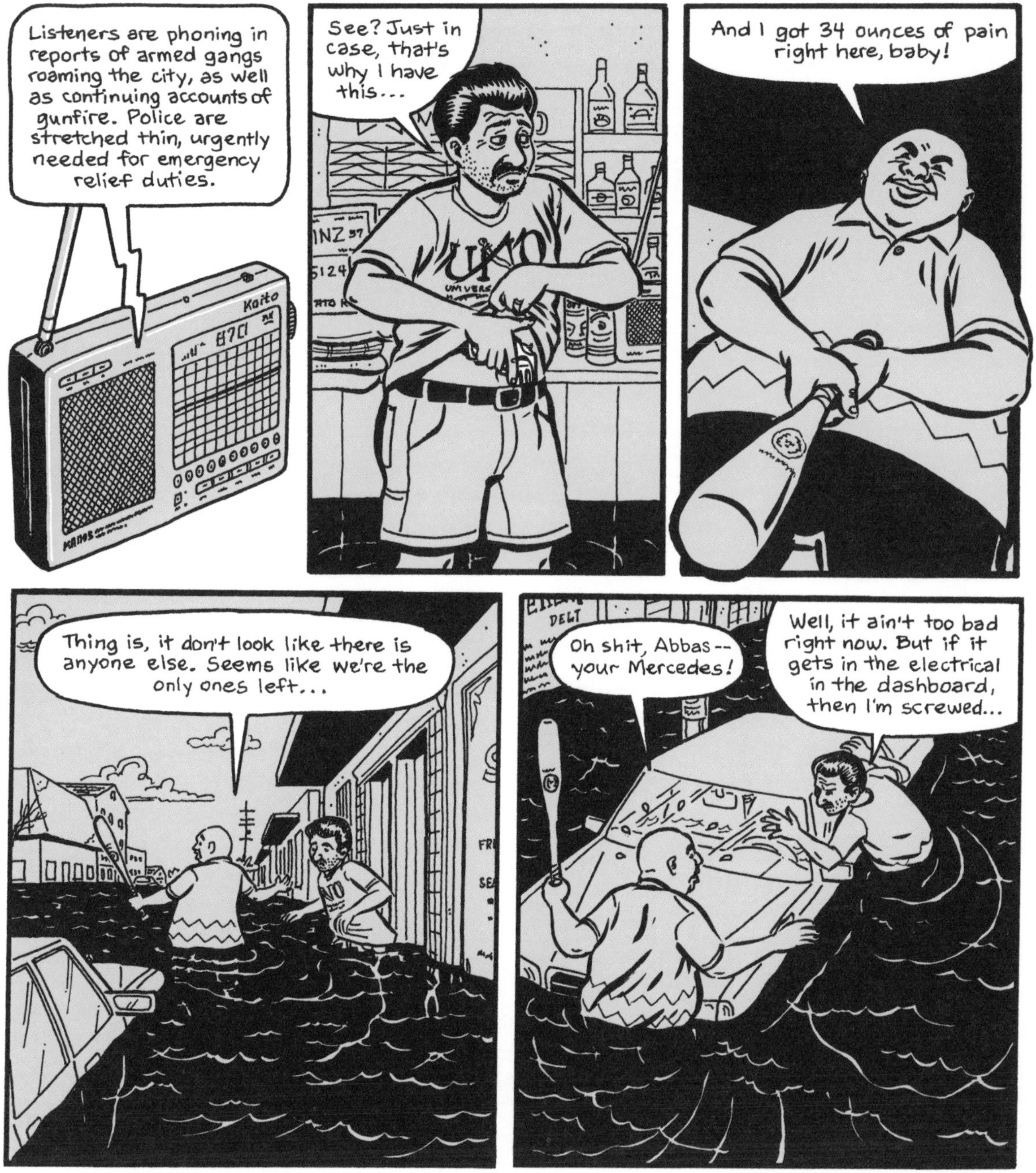
Listeners are phoning in reports of armed gangs roaming the city, as well as continuing accounts of gunfire. Police are stretched thin, urgently needed for emergency relief duties.
Koito
See? Just in case, that's why I have this...
And I got 34 ounces of pain right here, baby!
Thing is, it don't look like there is anyone else. Seems like we're the only ones left...
Oh shit, Abbas -- your Mercedes!
Well, it ain't too bad right now. But if it gets in the electrical in the dashboard, then I'm screwed...

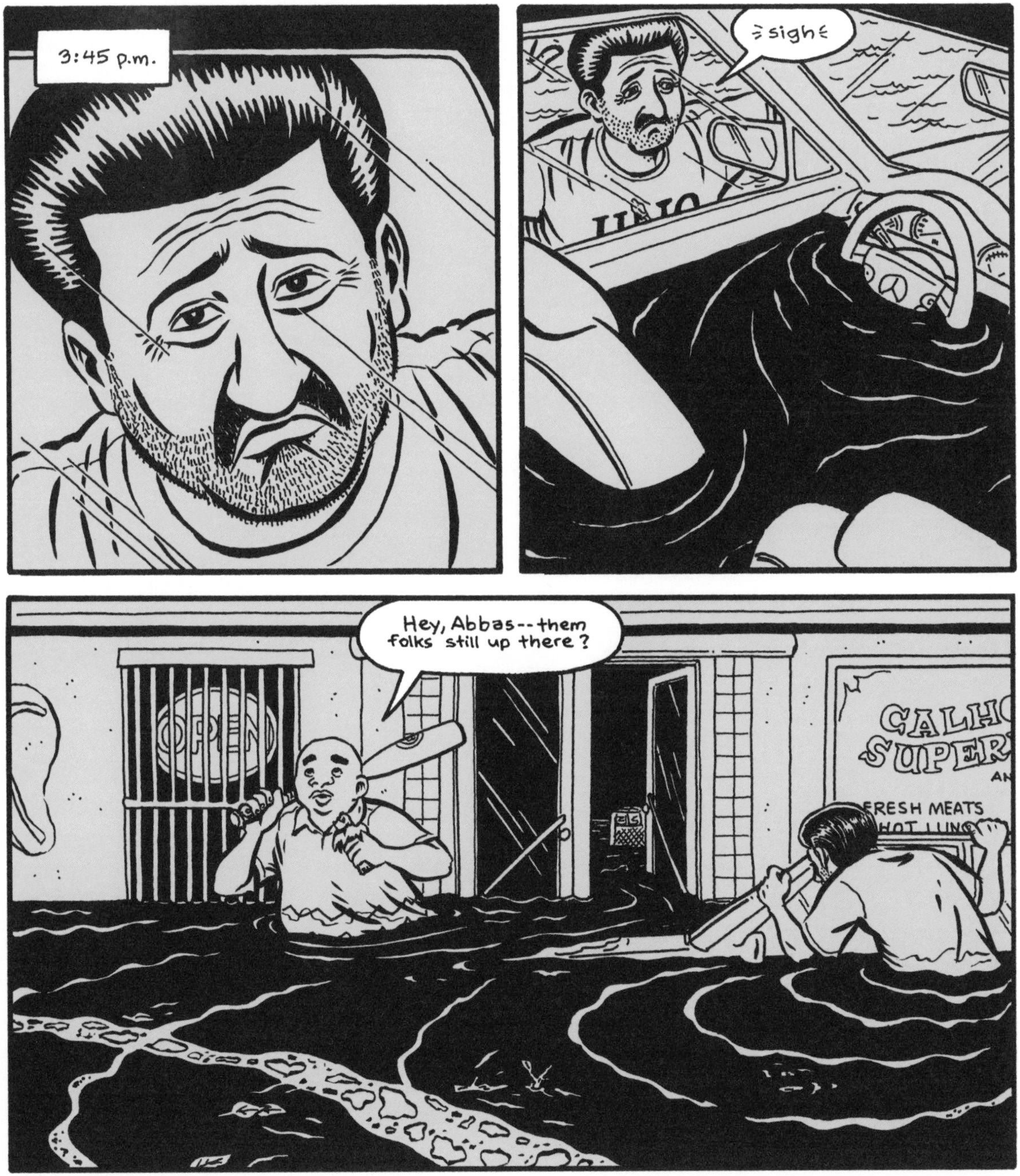
3:45 p.m.
sigh
Hey, Abbas--them folks still up there?
OPEN
FRESH MEATS

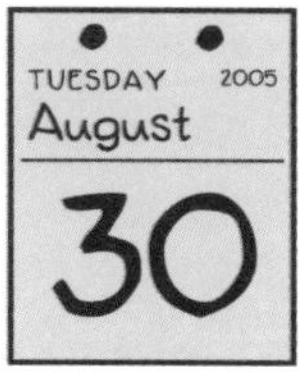
TUESDAY 2005
August
30

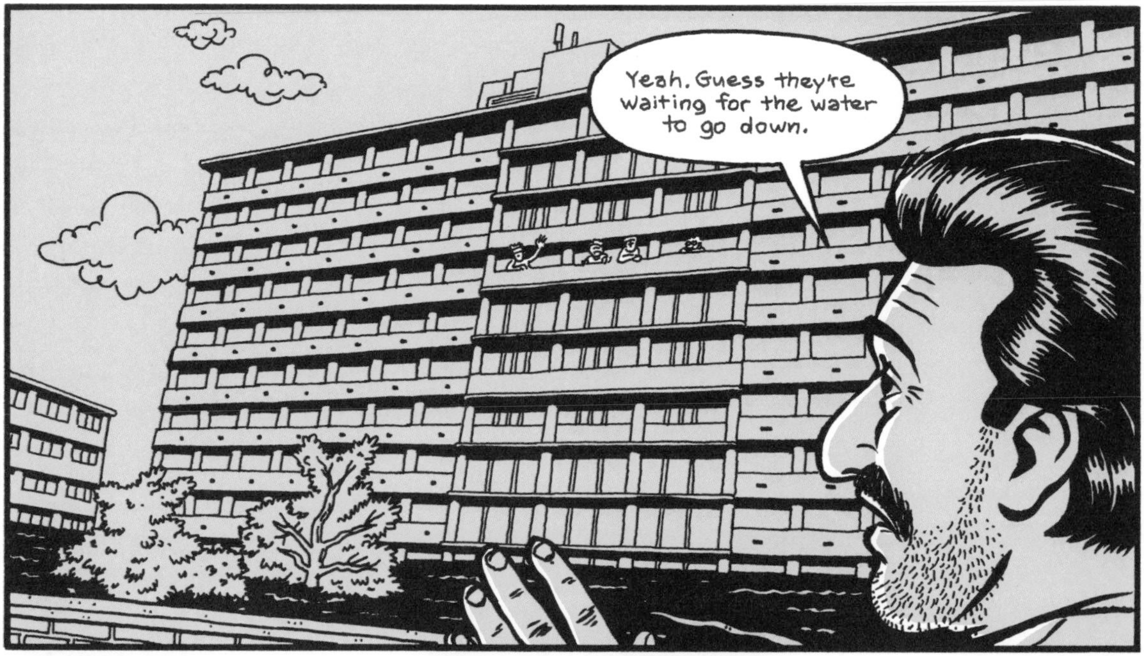
Yeah. Guess they're waiting for the water to go down.

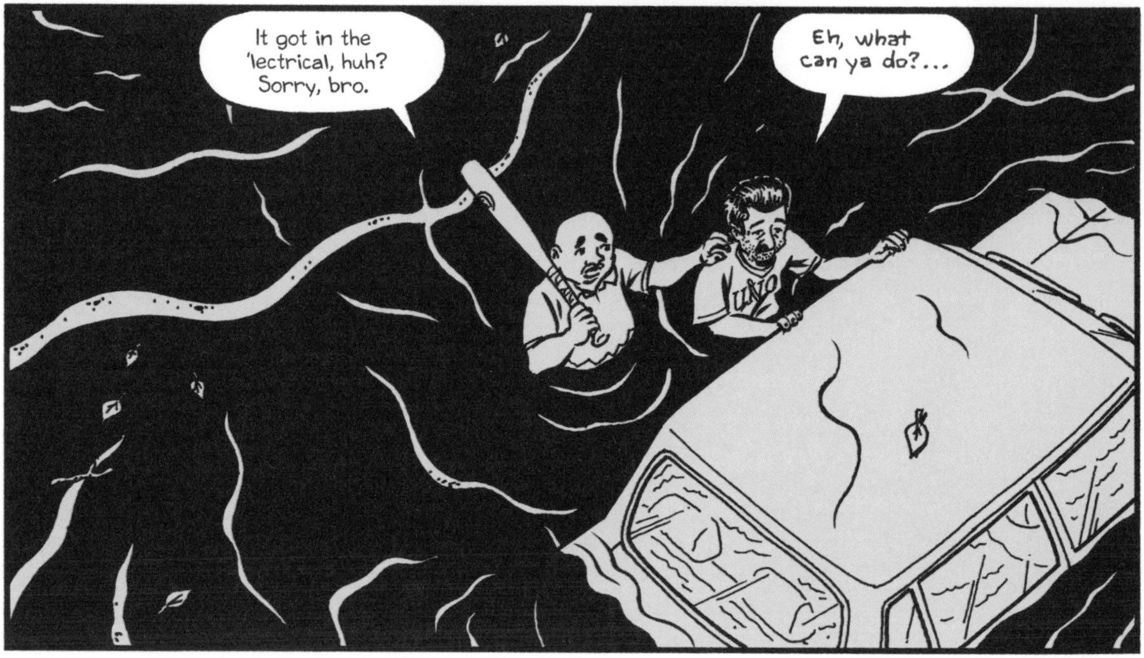
It got in the 'lectrical, huh? Sorry, bro.
Eh, what can ya do?...
UNO

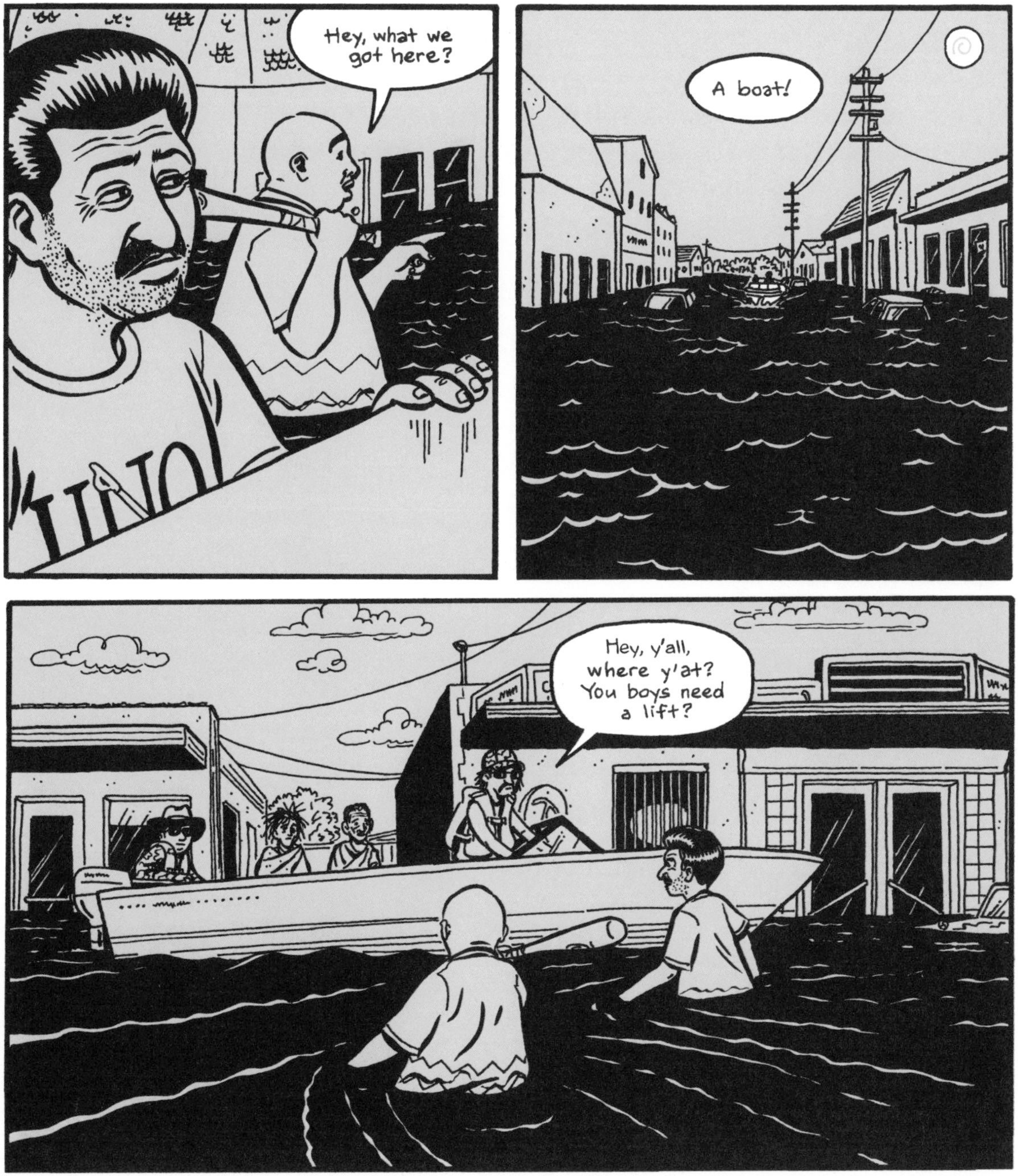

Hey, what we got here?
A boat!
Hey, y'all, where y'at? You boys need a lift?

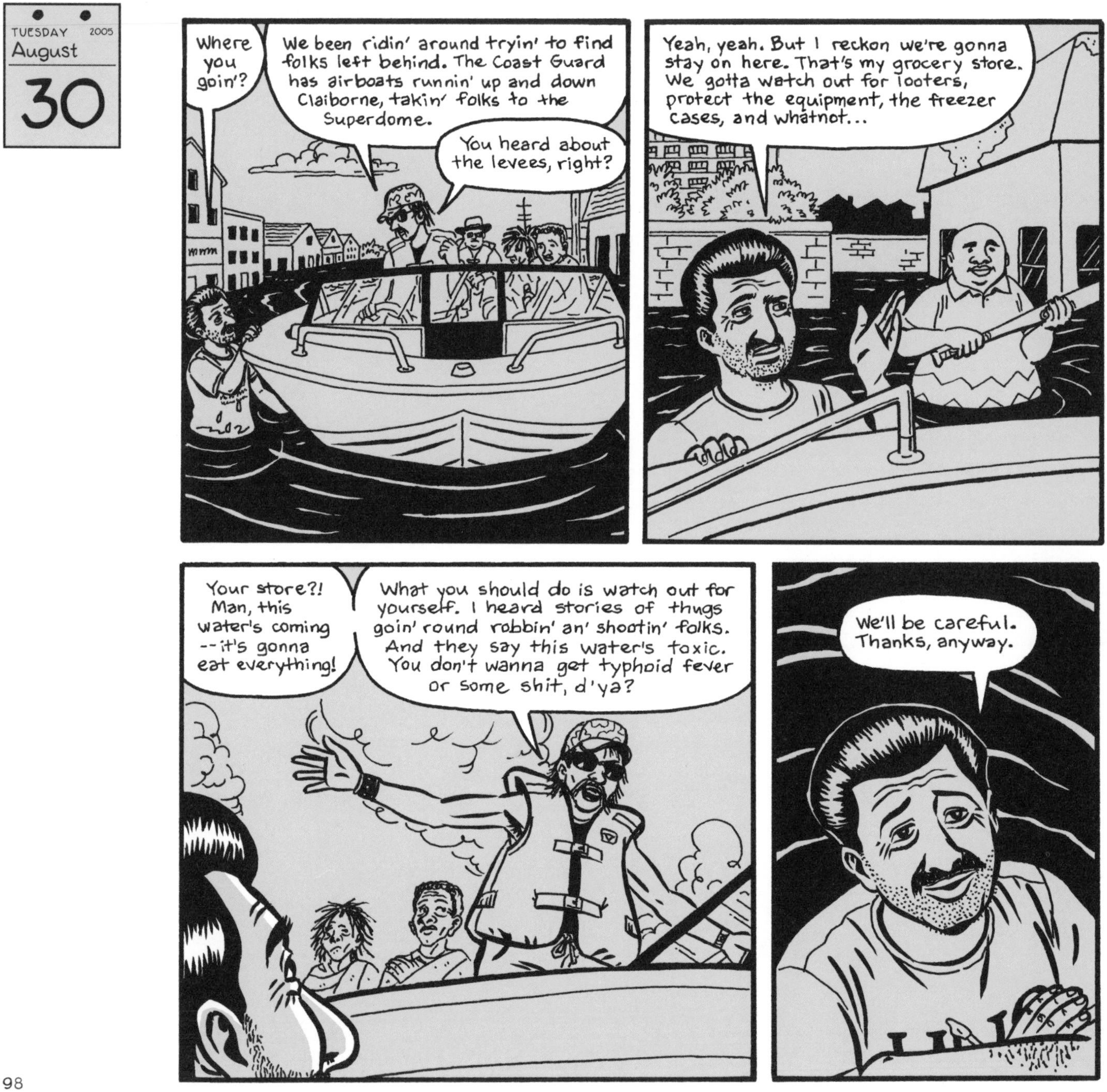
TUESDAY 2005
August
30
Where you goin'?
We been ridin' around tryin' to find folks left behind. The Coast Guard has airboats runnin' up and down Claiborne, takin' folks to the Superdome.
You heard about the levees, right?
Yeah, yeah. But I reckon we're gonna stay on here. That's my grocery store. We gotta watch out for looters, protect the equipment, the freezer cases, and whatnot...
Your store?! Man, this water's coming --it's gonna eat everything!
What you should do is watch out for yourself. I heard stories of thugs goin' round robbin' an' shootin' folks. And they say this water's toxic. You don't wanna get typhoid fever or some shit, d'ya?
We'll be careful. Thanks, anyway.

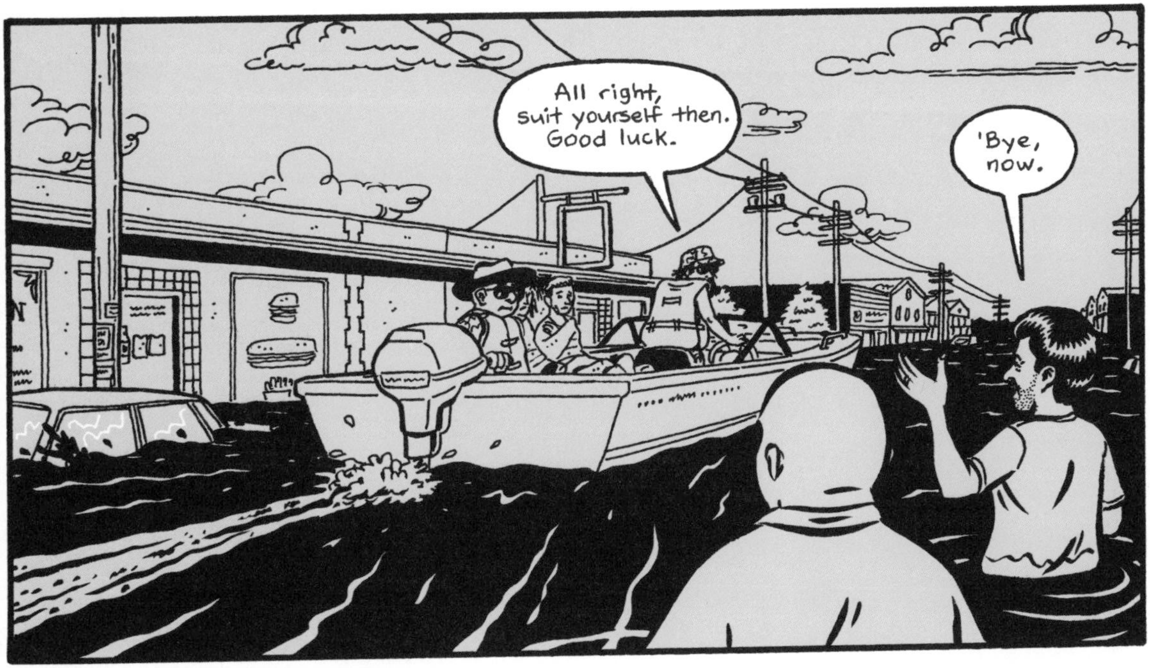
All right, suit yourself then. Good luck.
'Bye, now.

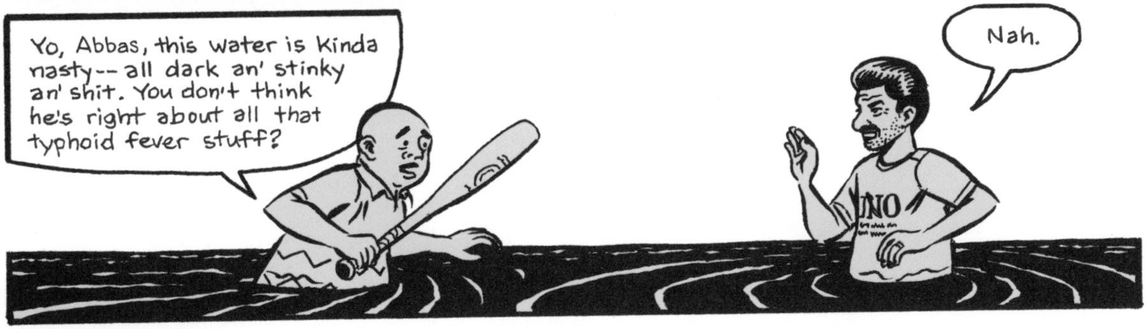
Yo, Abbas, this water is kinda nasty-- all dark an' stinky an' shit. You don't think he's right about all that typhoid fever stuff?
Nah.
UNO

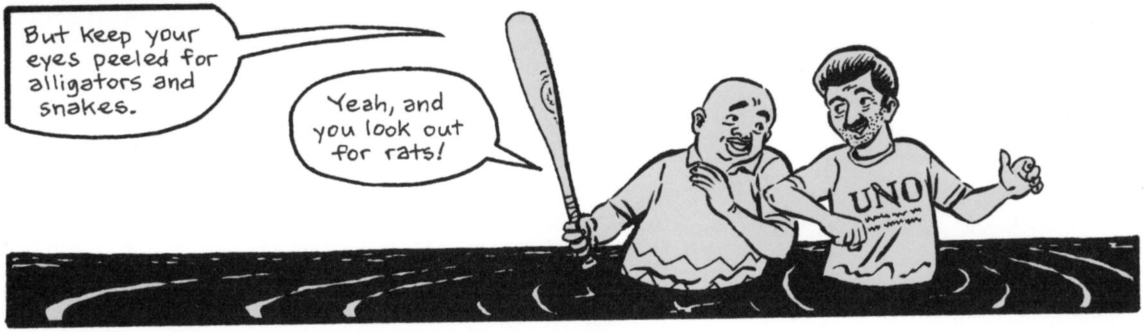
But keep your eyes peeled for alligators and snakes.
Yeah, and you look out for rats!
UNO

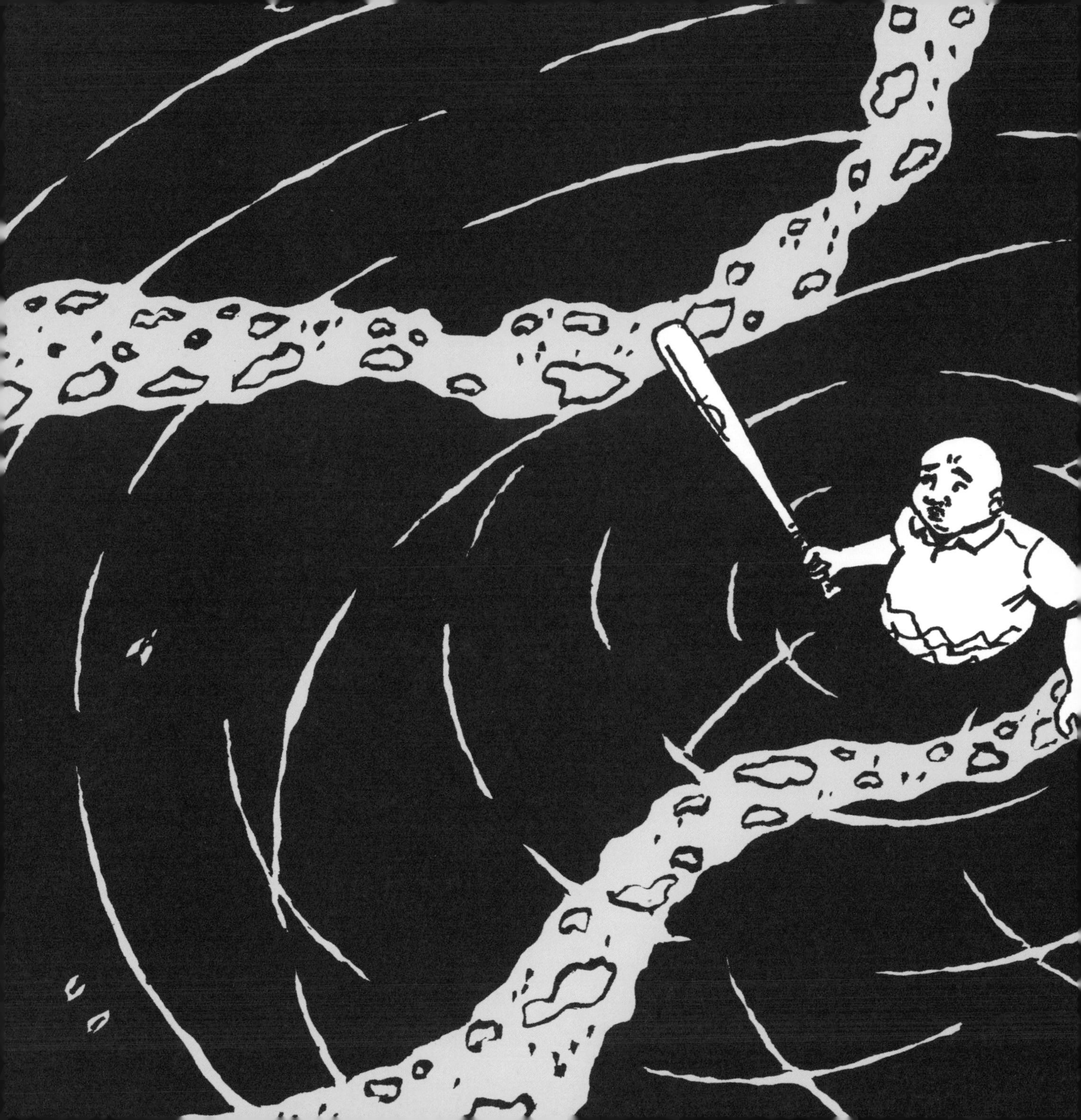

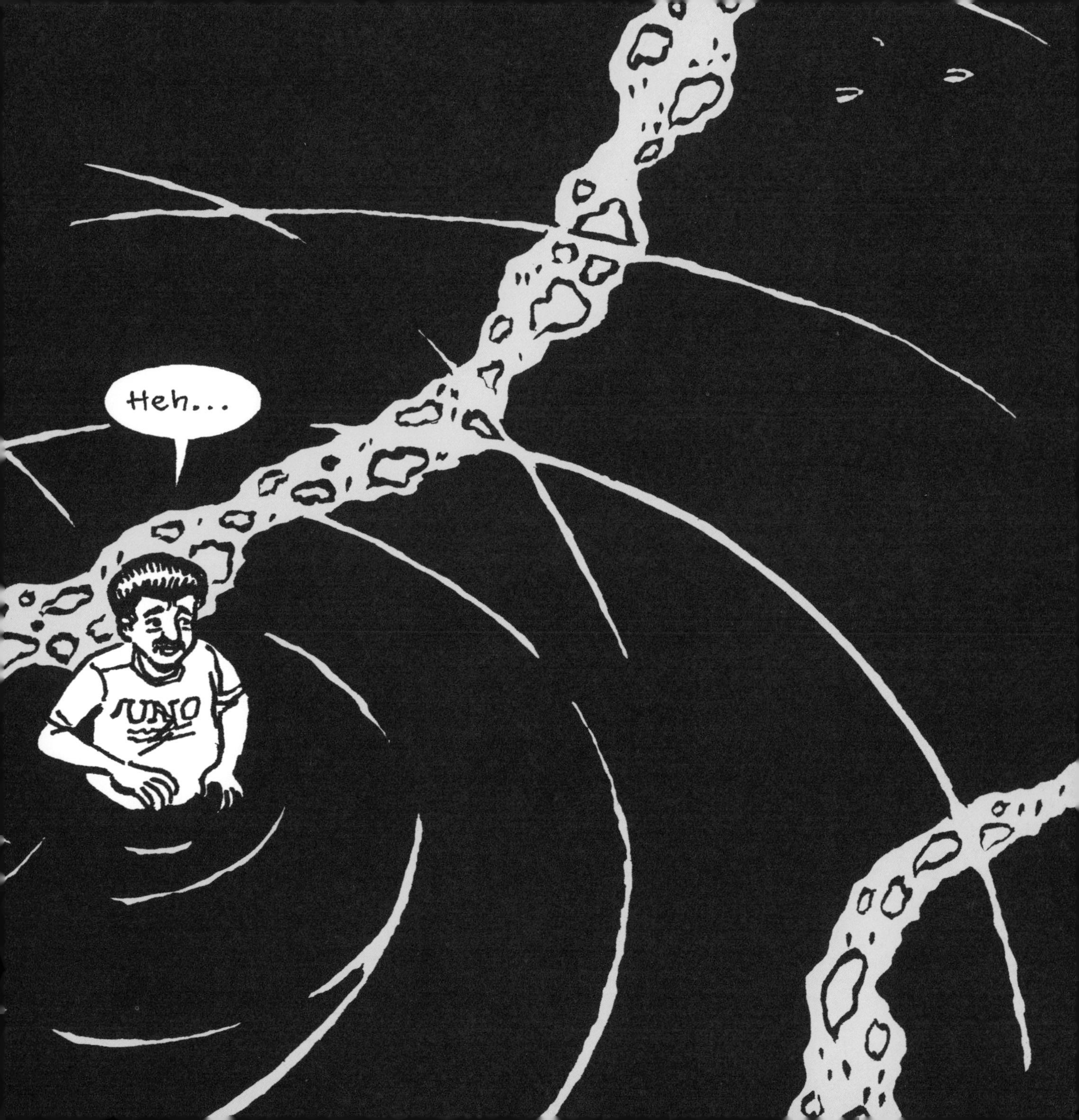
Heh...

TUESDAY 2005
August
30

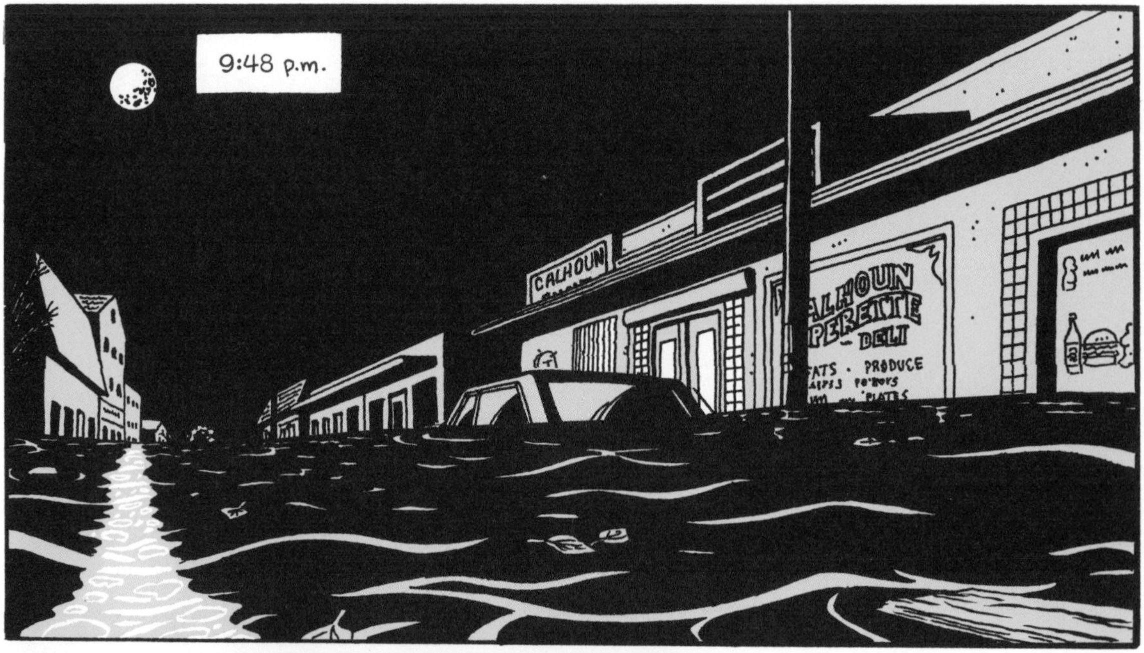
9:48 p.m.
CALHOUN

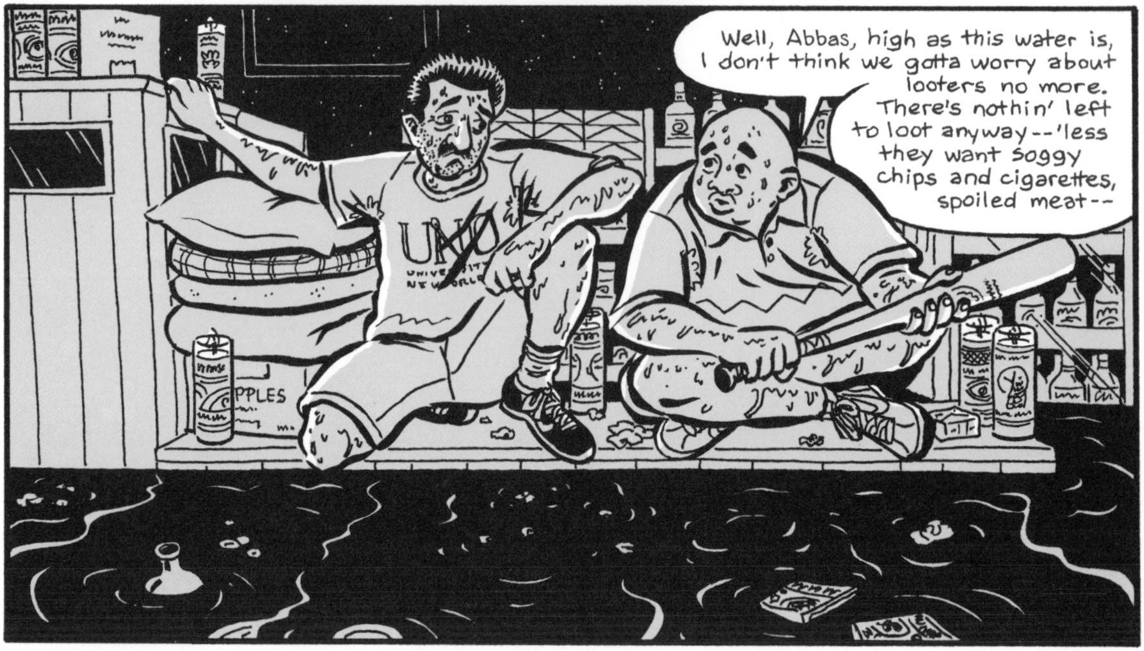
Well, Abbas, high as this water is, I don't think we gotta worry about looters no more. There's nothin' left to loot anyway--'less they want soggy chips and cigarettes, spoiled meat--

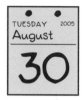

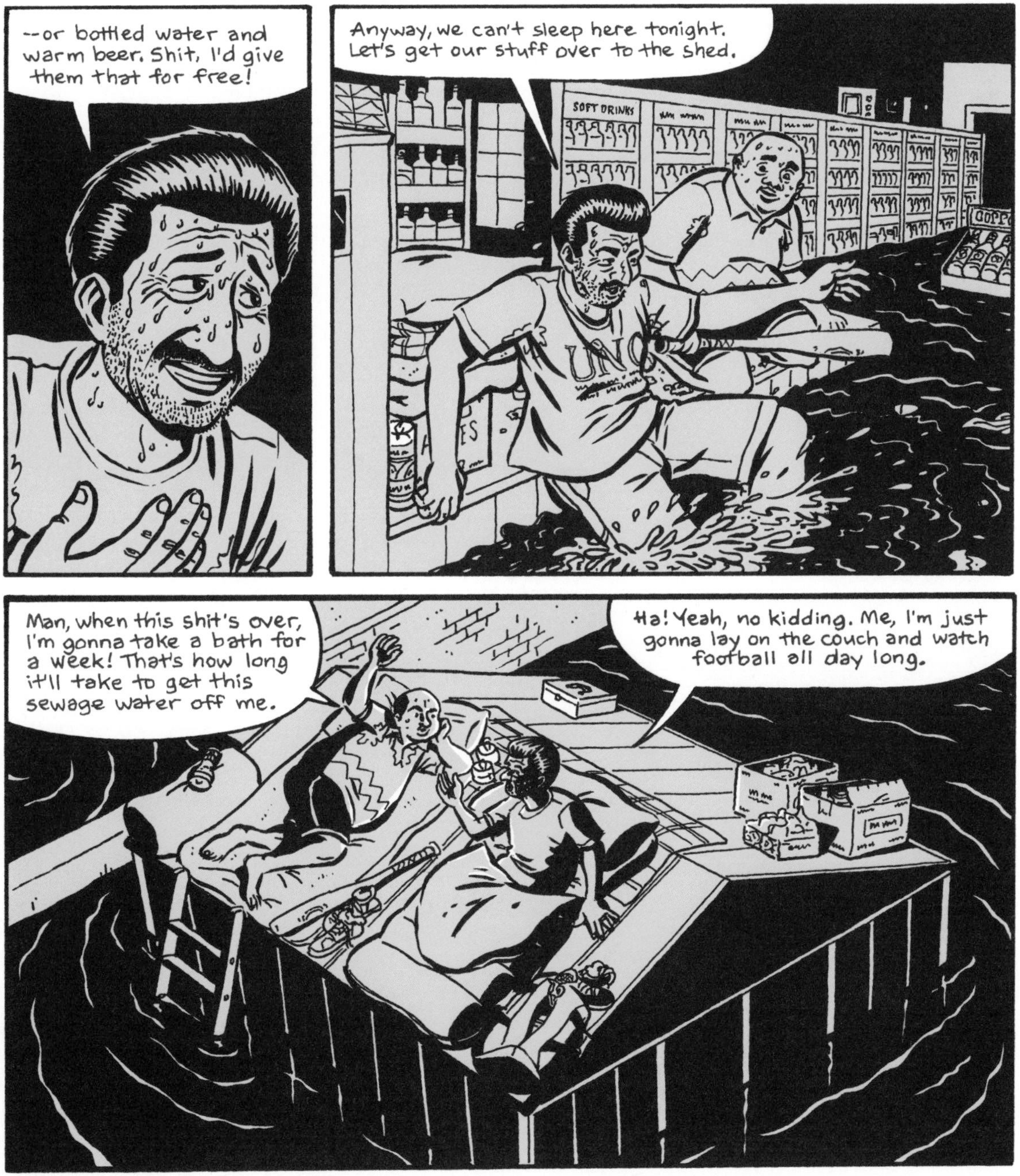
--or bottled water and warm beer. Shit, I'd give them that for free!
Anyway, we can't sleep here tonight. Let's get our stuff over to the shed.
SOFT DRINKS
Man, when this shit's over, I'm gonna take a bath for a week! That's how long it'll take to get this sewage water off me.
Ha! Yeah, no kidding. Me, I'm just gonna lay on the couch and watch football all day long.

TUESDAY 2005
August
30

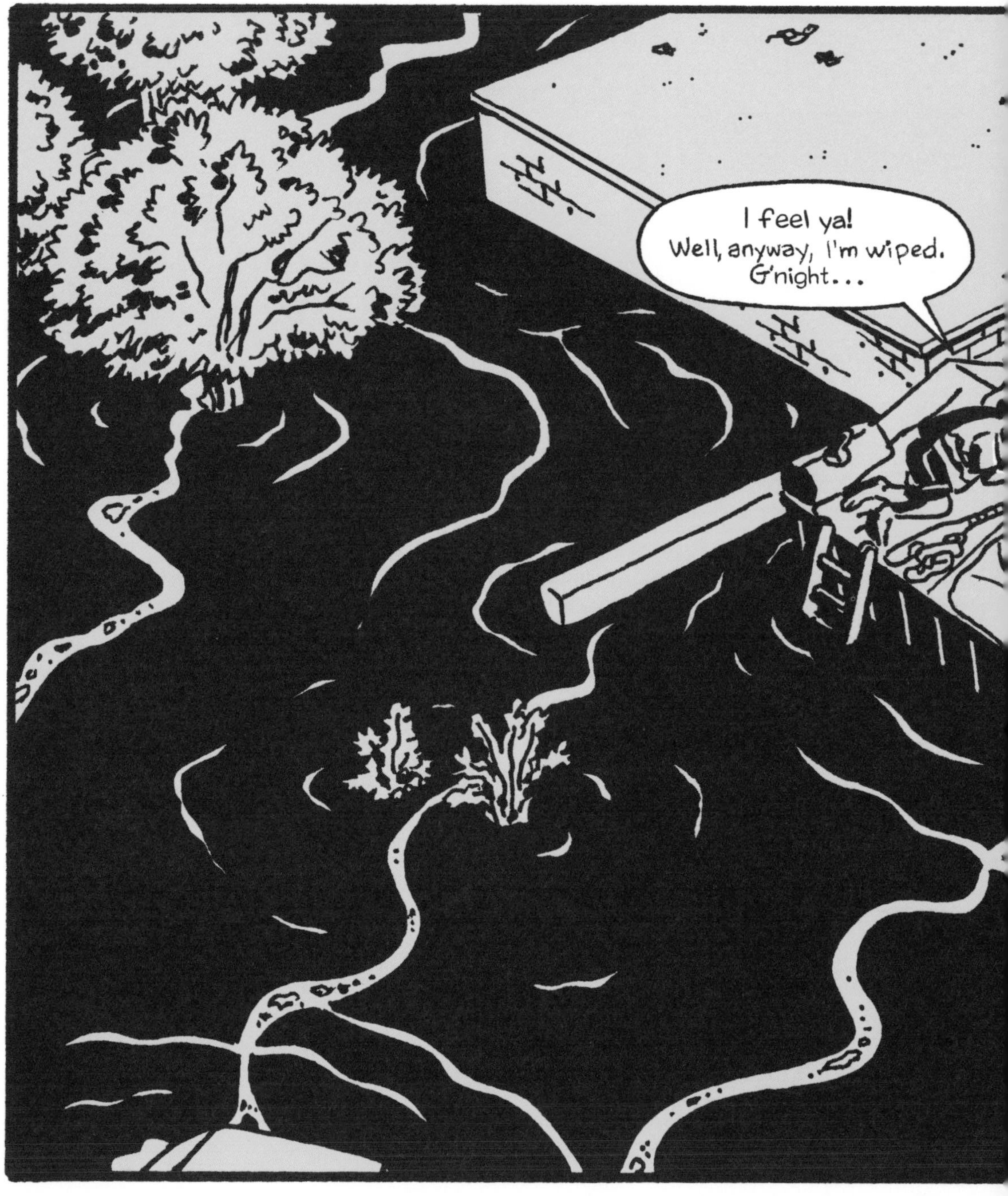
I feel ya!
Well, anyway, I'm wiped.
G'night...

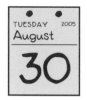

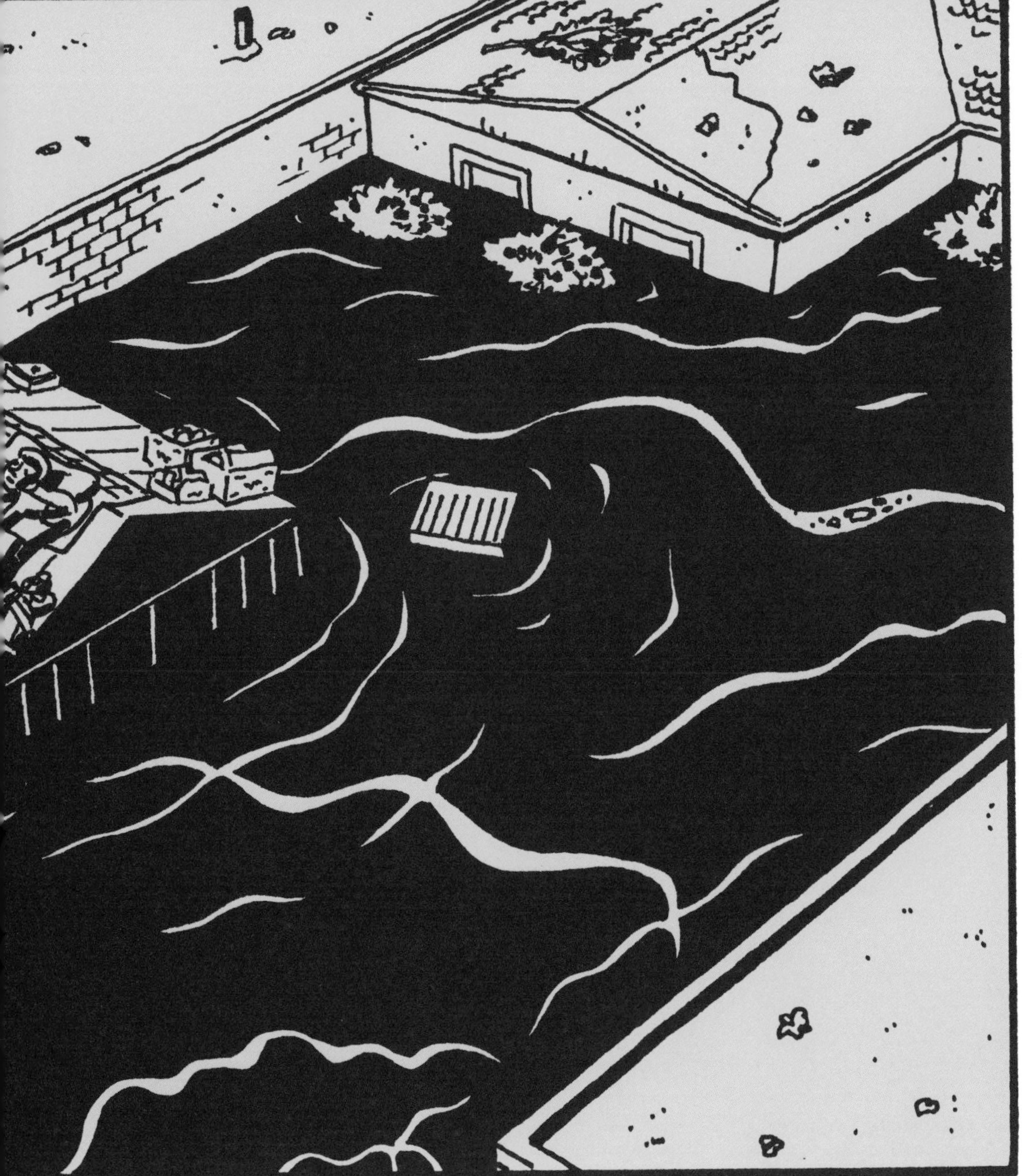

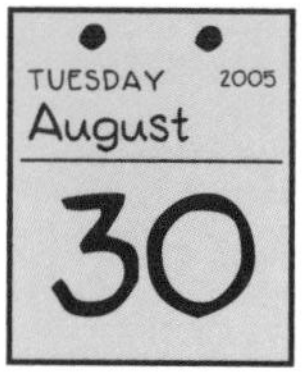
TUESDAY 2005
August
30

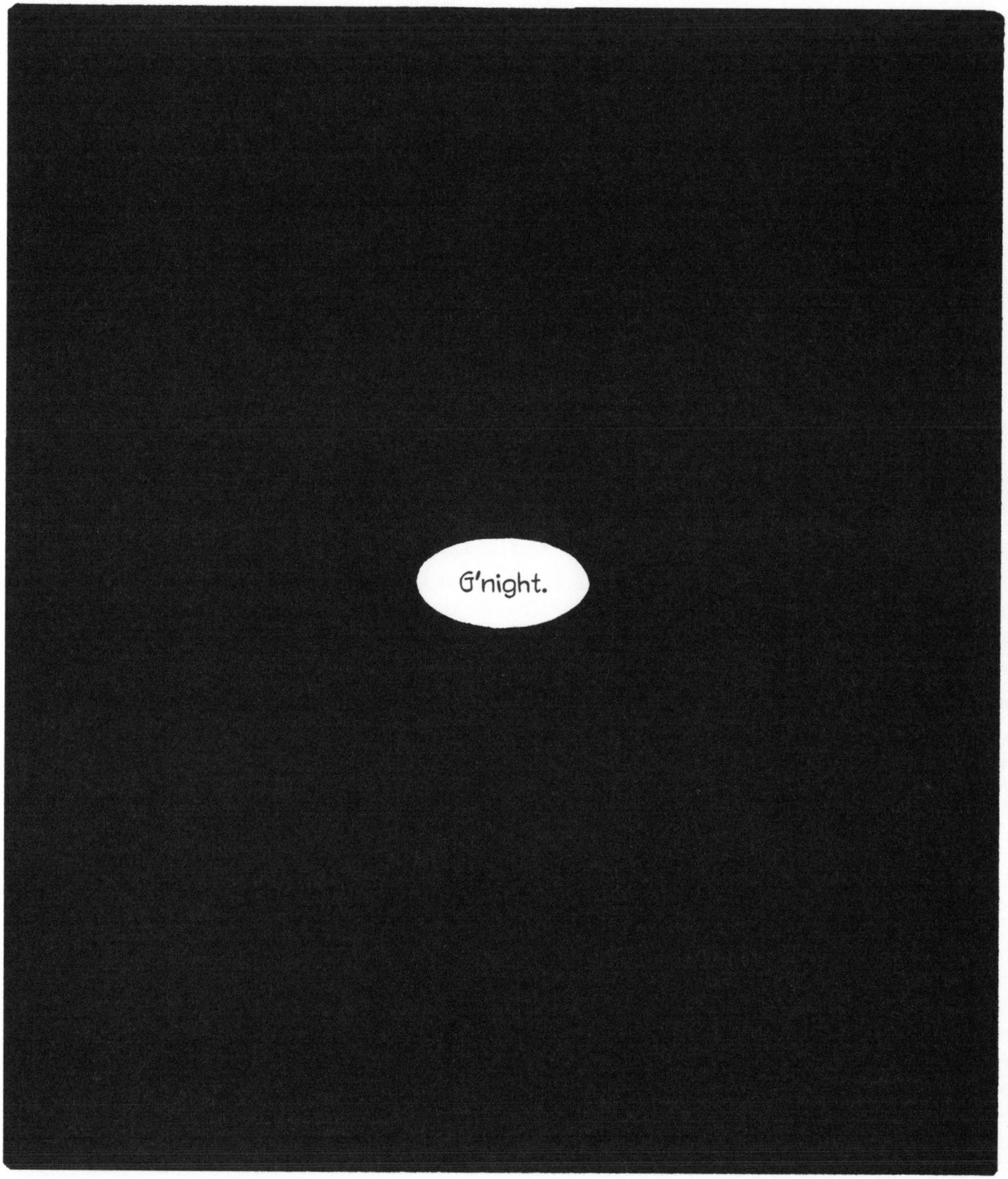
G'night.

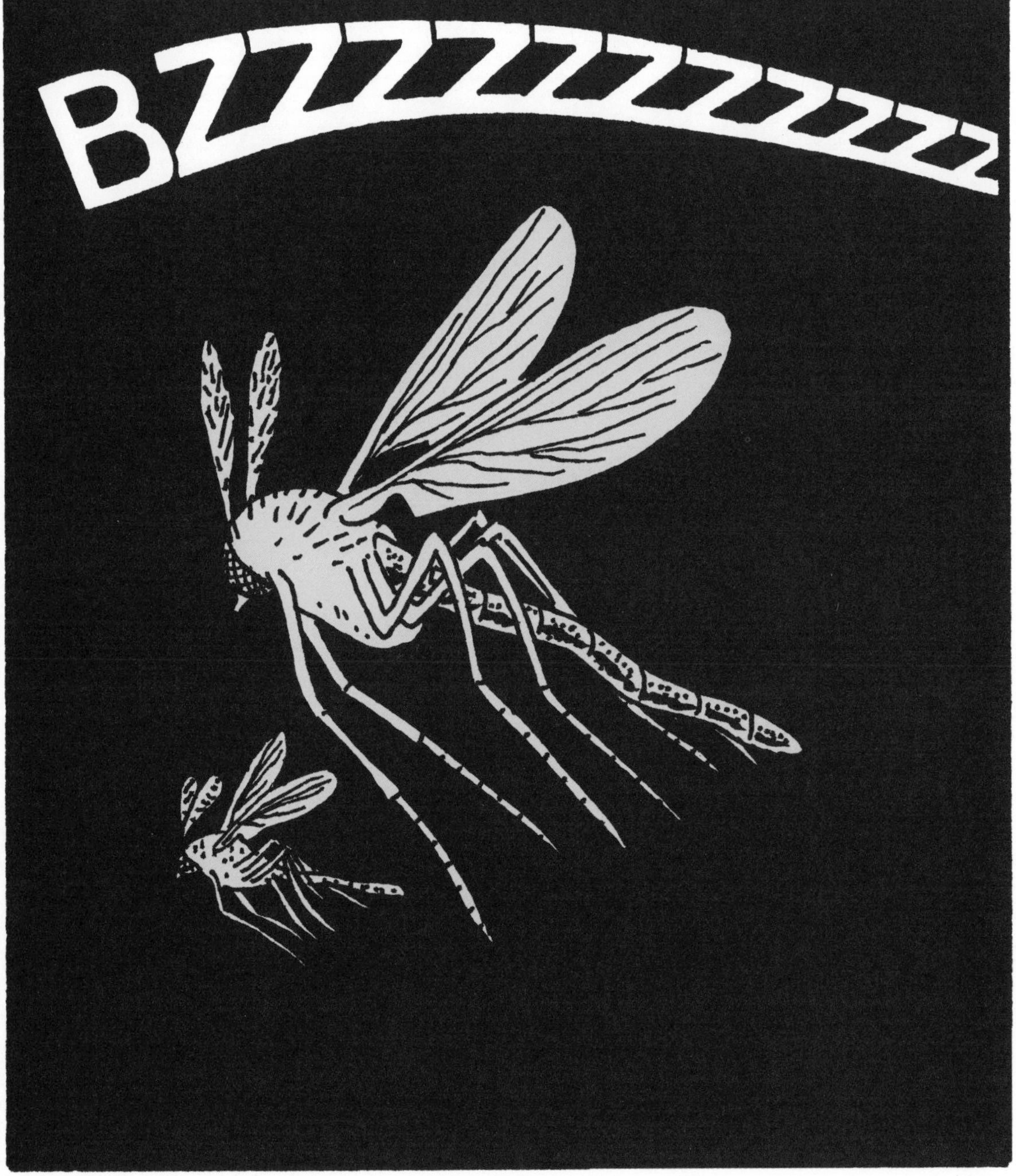
BZZZZZZZZZZZZ

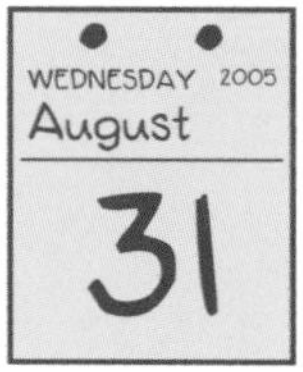
WEDNESDAY 2005
August
31

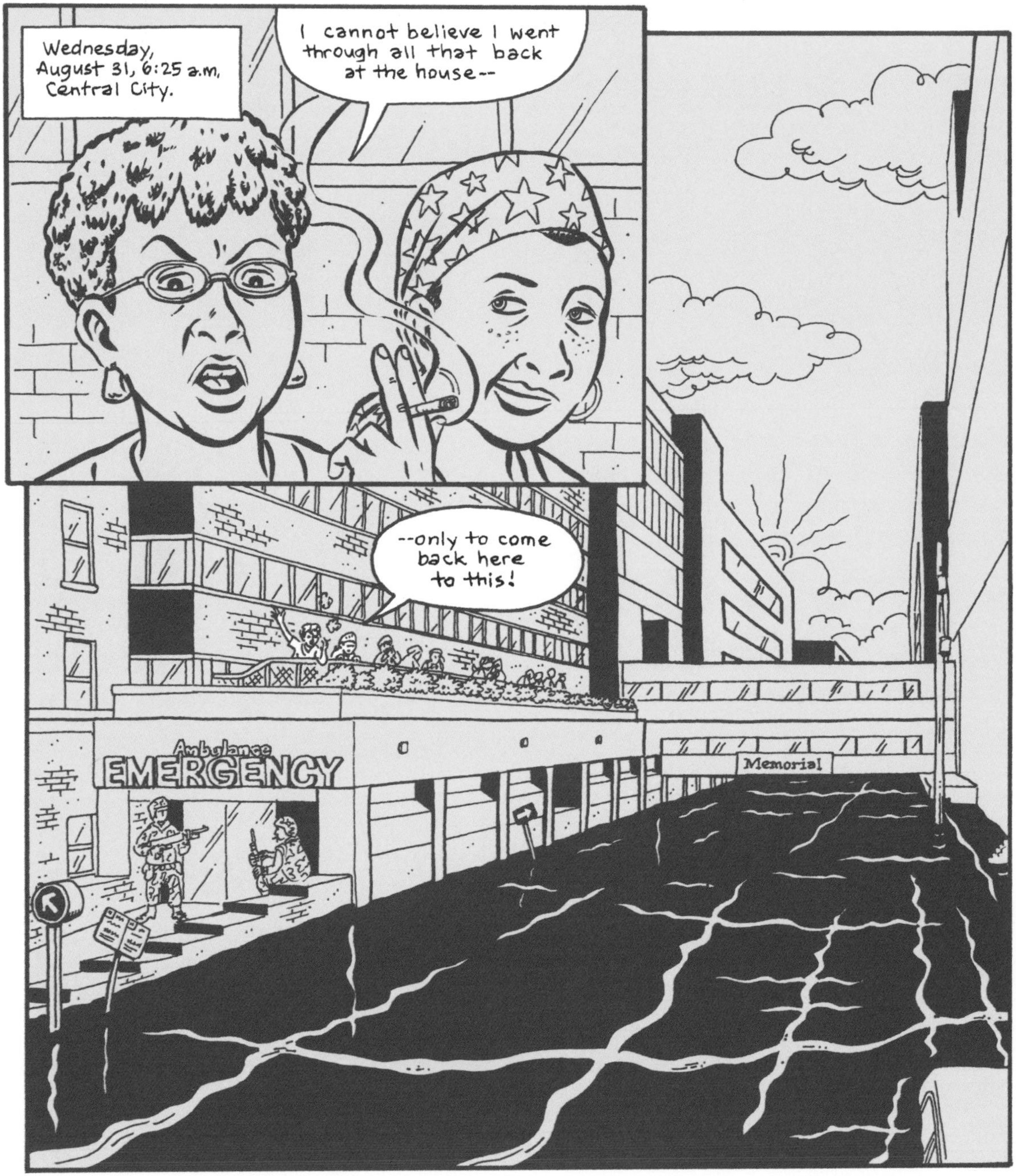
Wednesday, August 31, 6:25 a.m. Central City.
I cannot believe I went through all that back at the house--
--only to come back here to this!
Ambulance
EMERGENCY
Memorial

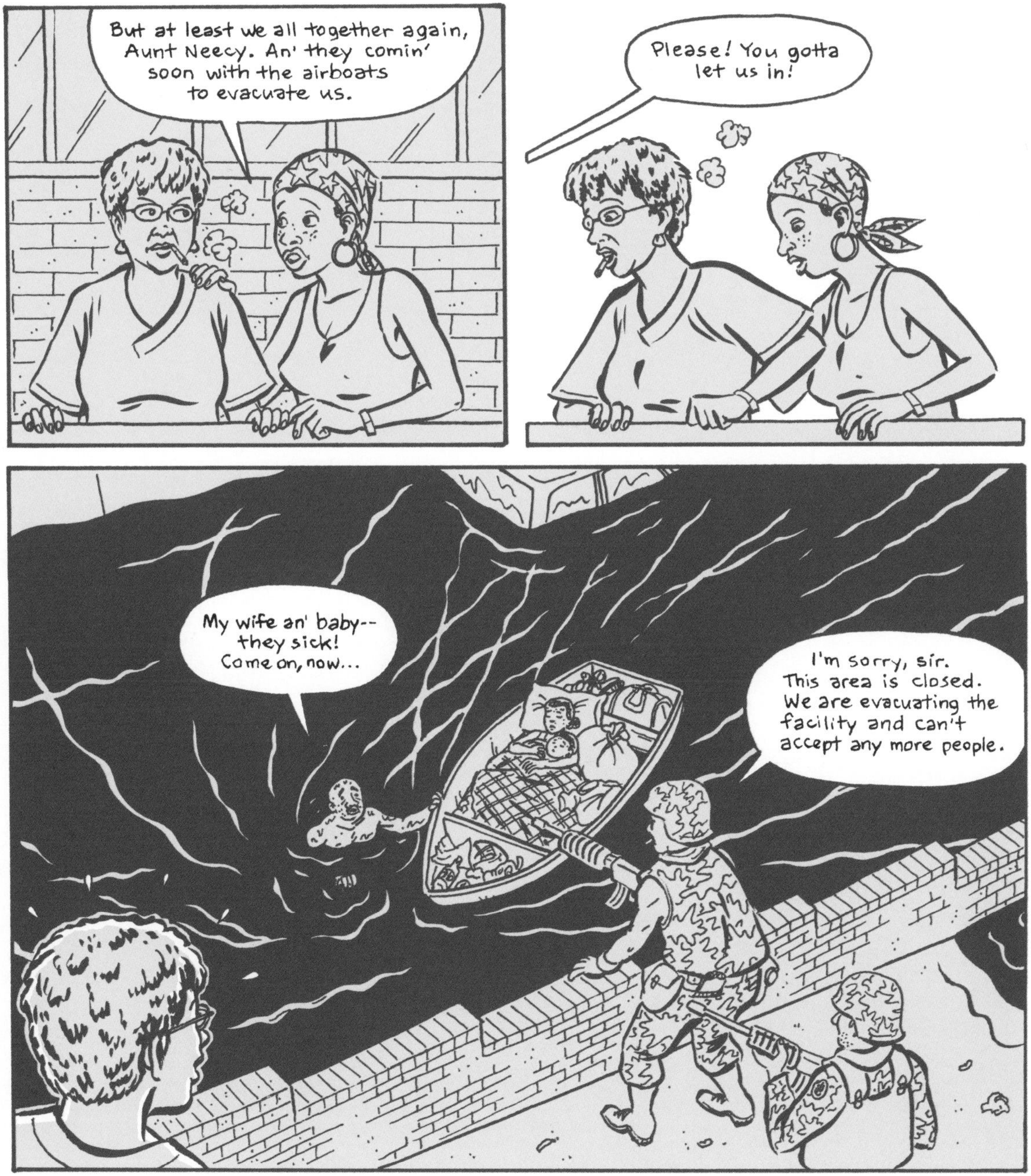
But at least we all together again, Aunt Neecy. An' they comin' soon with the airboats to evacuate us.
Please! You gotta let us in!
My wife an' baby-- they sick! Come on, now...
I'm sorry, sir. This area is closed. We are evacuating the facility and can't accept any more people.

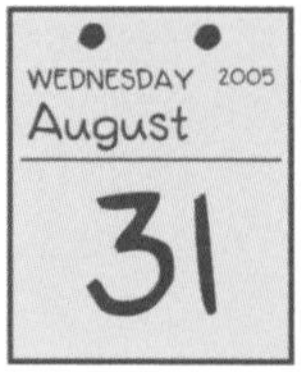
WEDNESDAY 2005
August
31

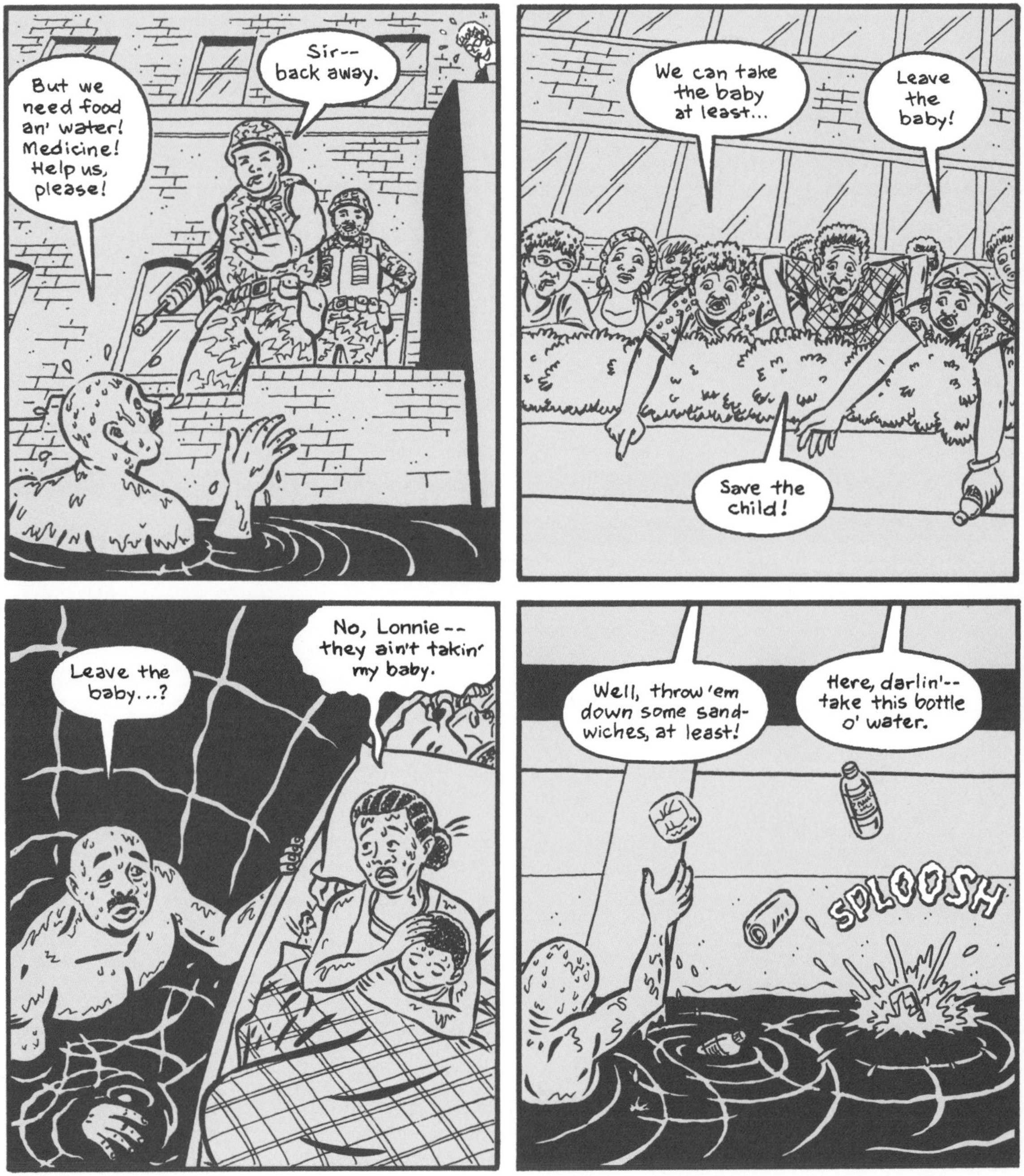
But we need food an' water! Medicine! Help us, please!
Sir-- back away.
We can take the baby at least...
Leave the baby!
Save the child!
Leave the baby...?
No, Lonnie -- they ain't takin' my baby.
Well, throw 'em down some sand-wiches, at least!
Here, darlin'-- take this bottle o' water.
SPLOOSH

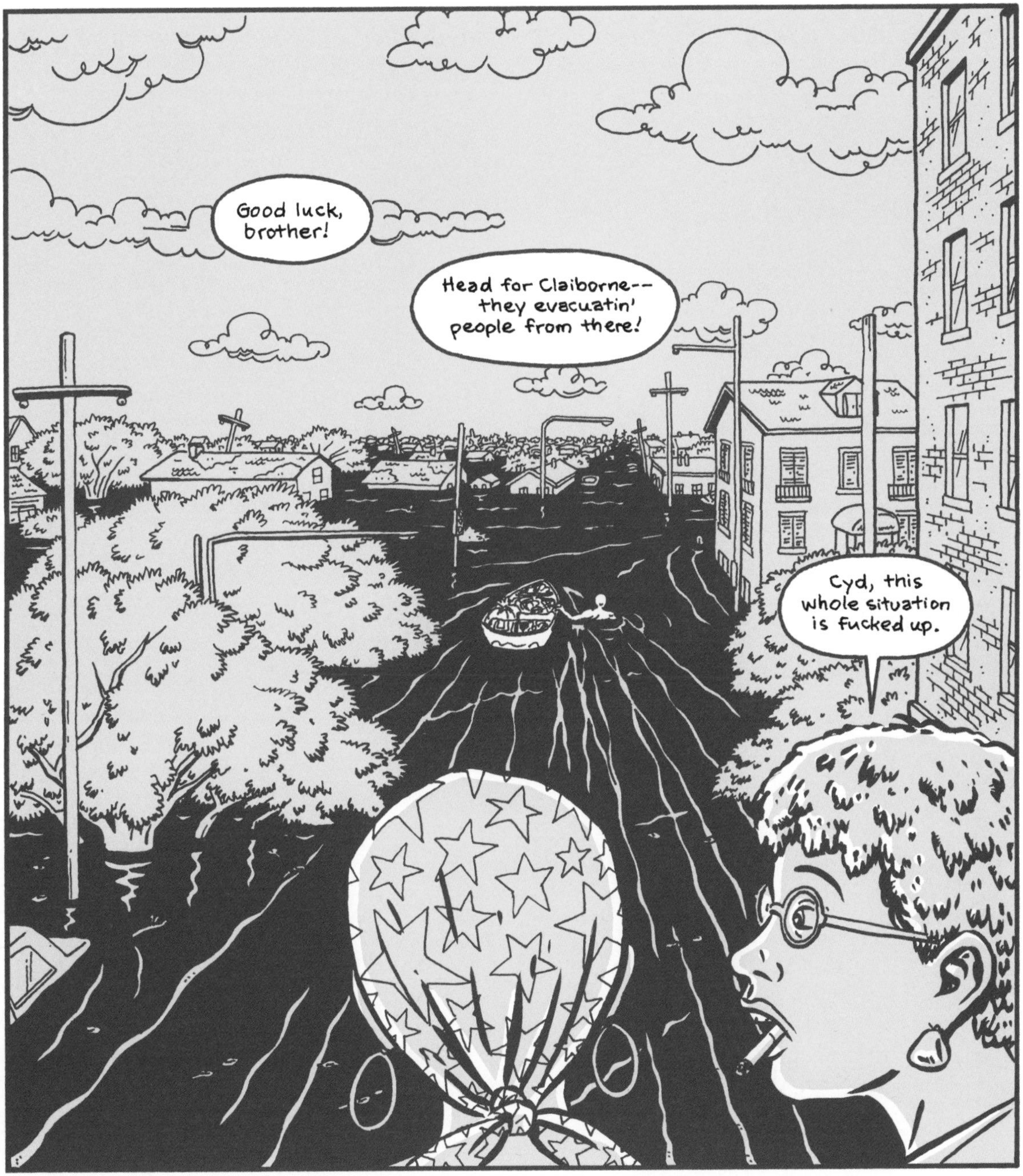
Good luck, brother!
Head for Claiborne-- they evacuatin' people from there!
Cyd, this whole situation is fucked up.

WEDNESDAY 2005
August
31

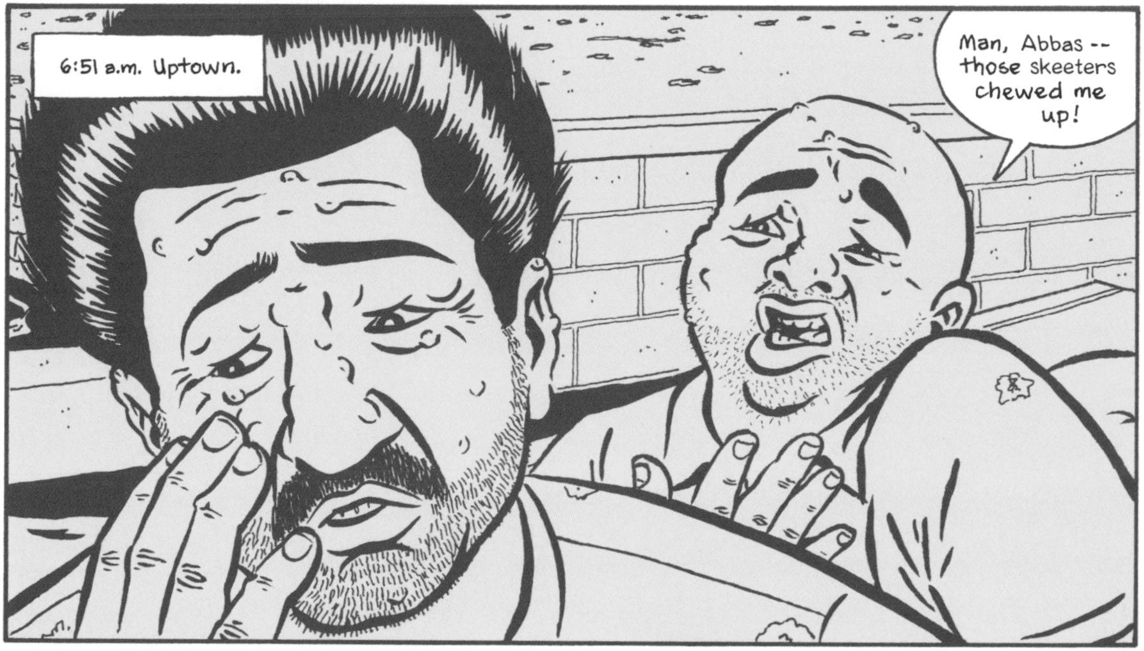
6:51 a.m. Uptown.
Man, Abbas -- those skeeters chewed me up!

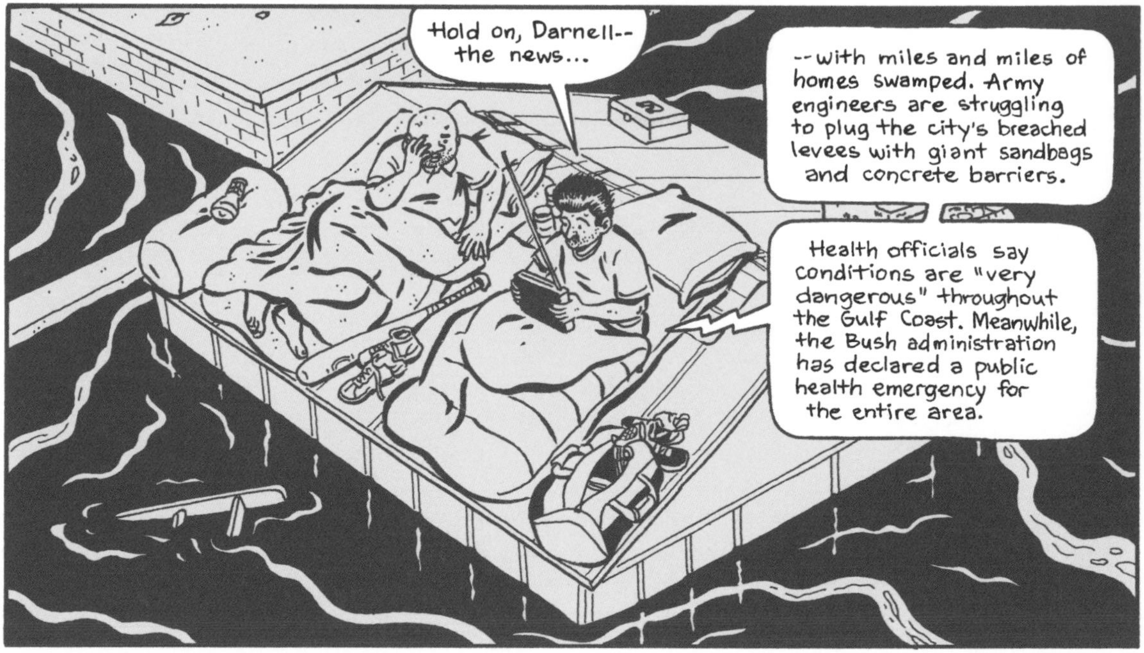
Hold on, Darnell-- the news...
--with miles and miles of homes swamped. Army engineers are struggling to plug the city's breached levees with giant sandbags and concrete barriers.
Health officials say conditions are "very dangerous" throughout the Gulf Coast. Meanwhile, the Bush administration has declared a public health emergency for the entire area.

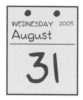

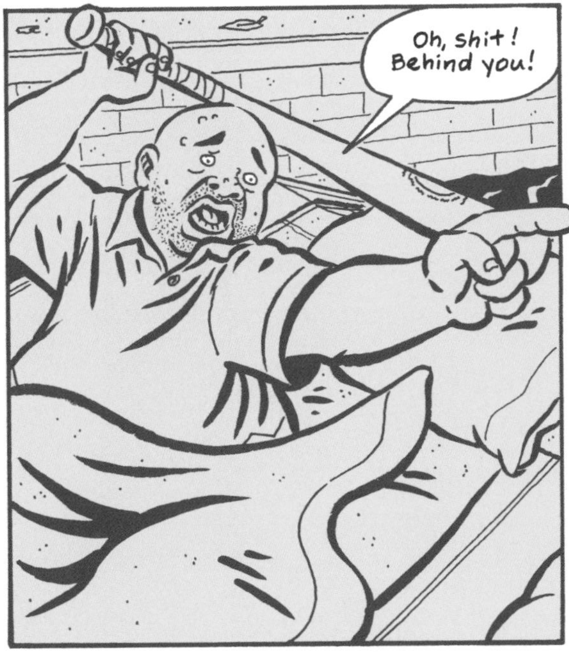
Oh, shit! Behind you!

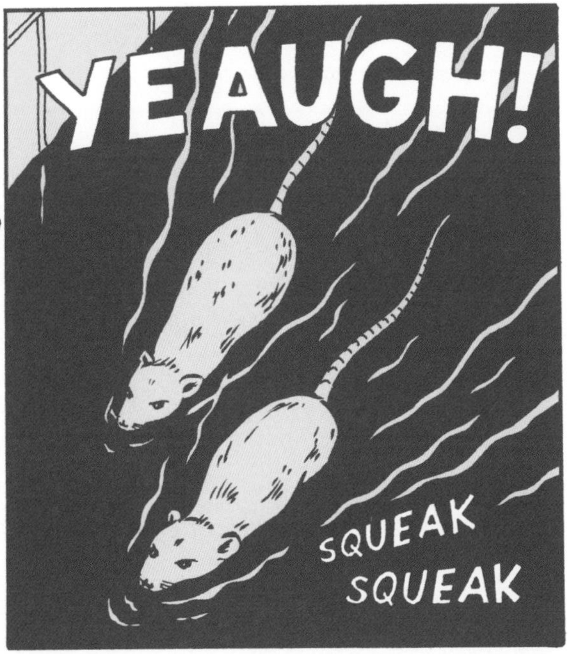
YEAUGH!
SQUEAK
SQUEAK

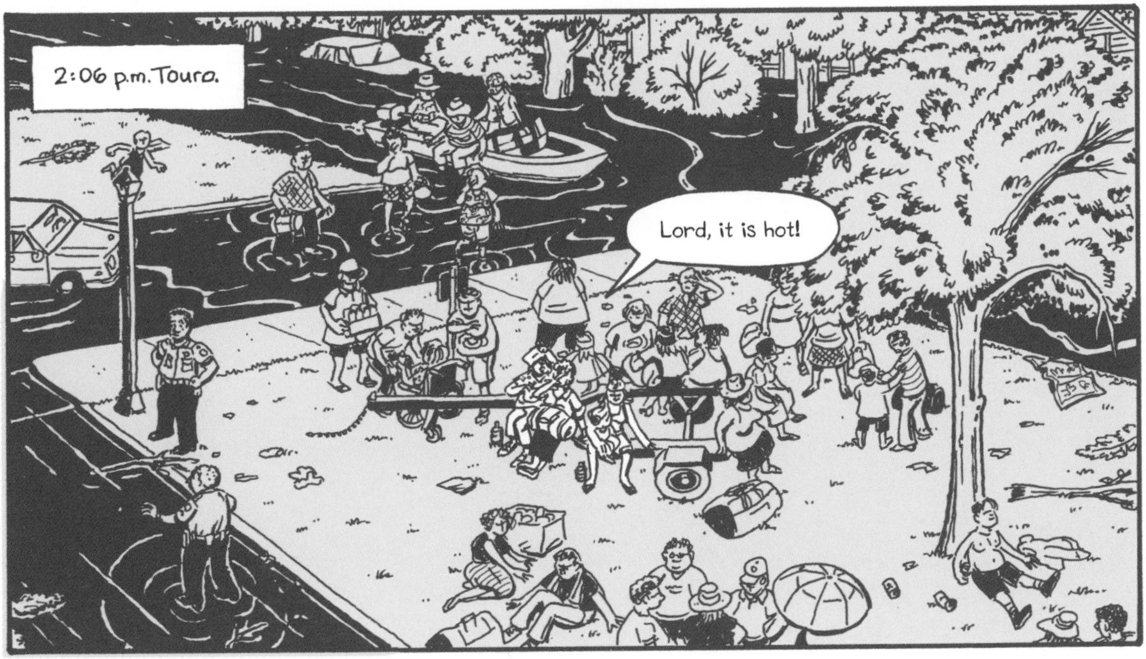
2:06 p.m. Touro.
Lord, it is hot!

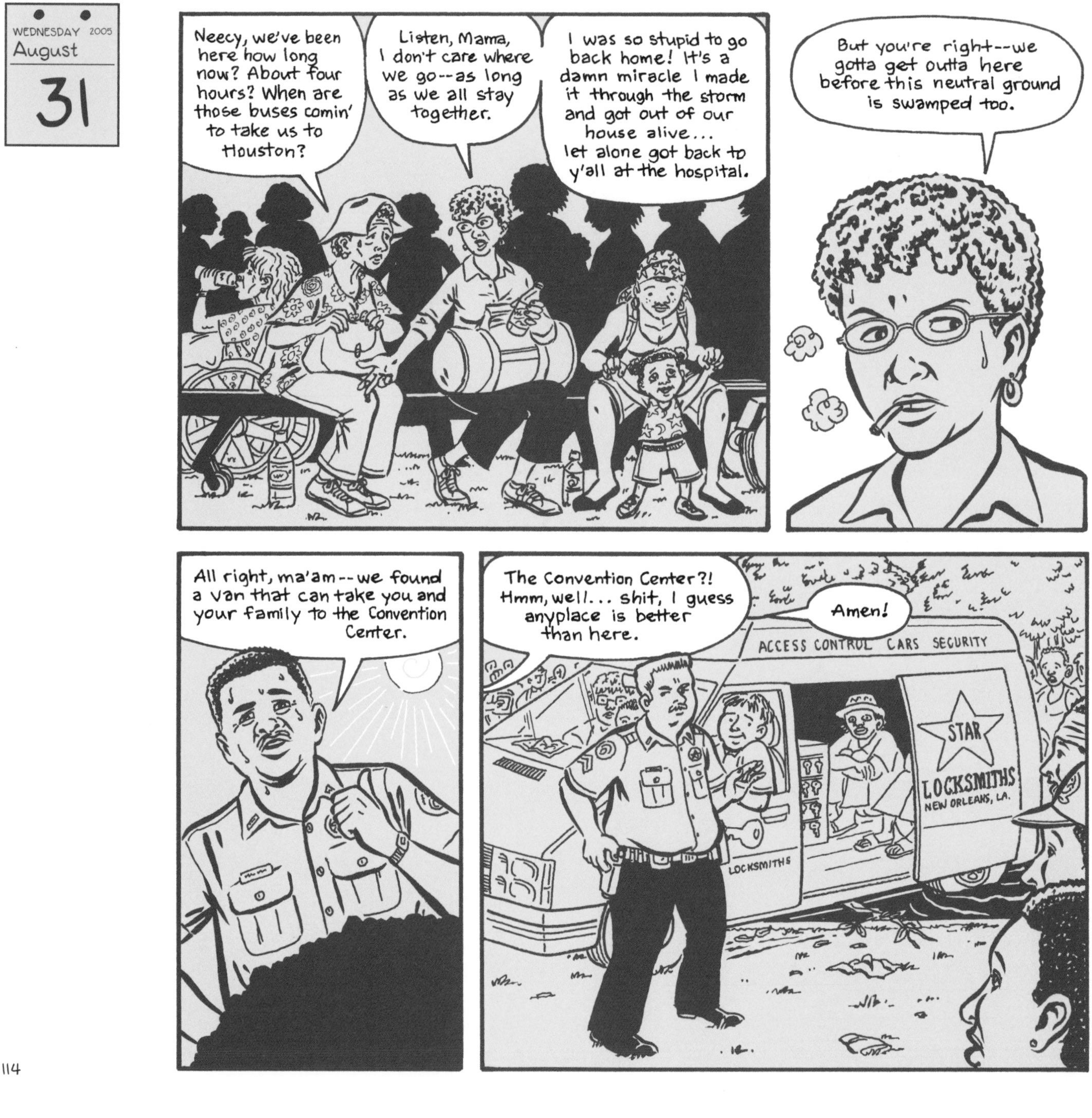
WEDNESDAY 2005
August
31
Neecy, we've been here how long now? About four hours? When are those buses comin' to take us to Houston?
Listen, Mama, I don't care where we go--as long as we all stay together.
I was so stupid to go back home! It's a damn miracle I made it through the storm and got out of our house alive... let alone got back to y'all at the hospital.
But you're right--we gotta get outta here before this neutral ground is swamped too.
All right, ma'am--we found a van that can take you and your family to the Convention Center.
The Convention Center?! Hmm, well... shit, I guess anyplace is better than here.
Amen!
ACCESS CONTROL CARS SECURITY
STAR
LOCKSMITHS
NEW ORLEANS, LA.
LOCKSMITHS

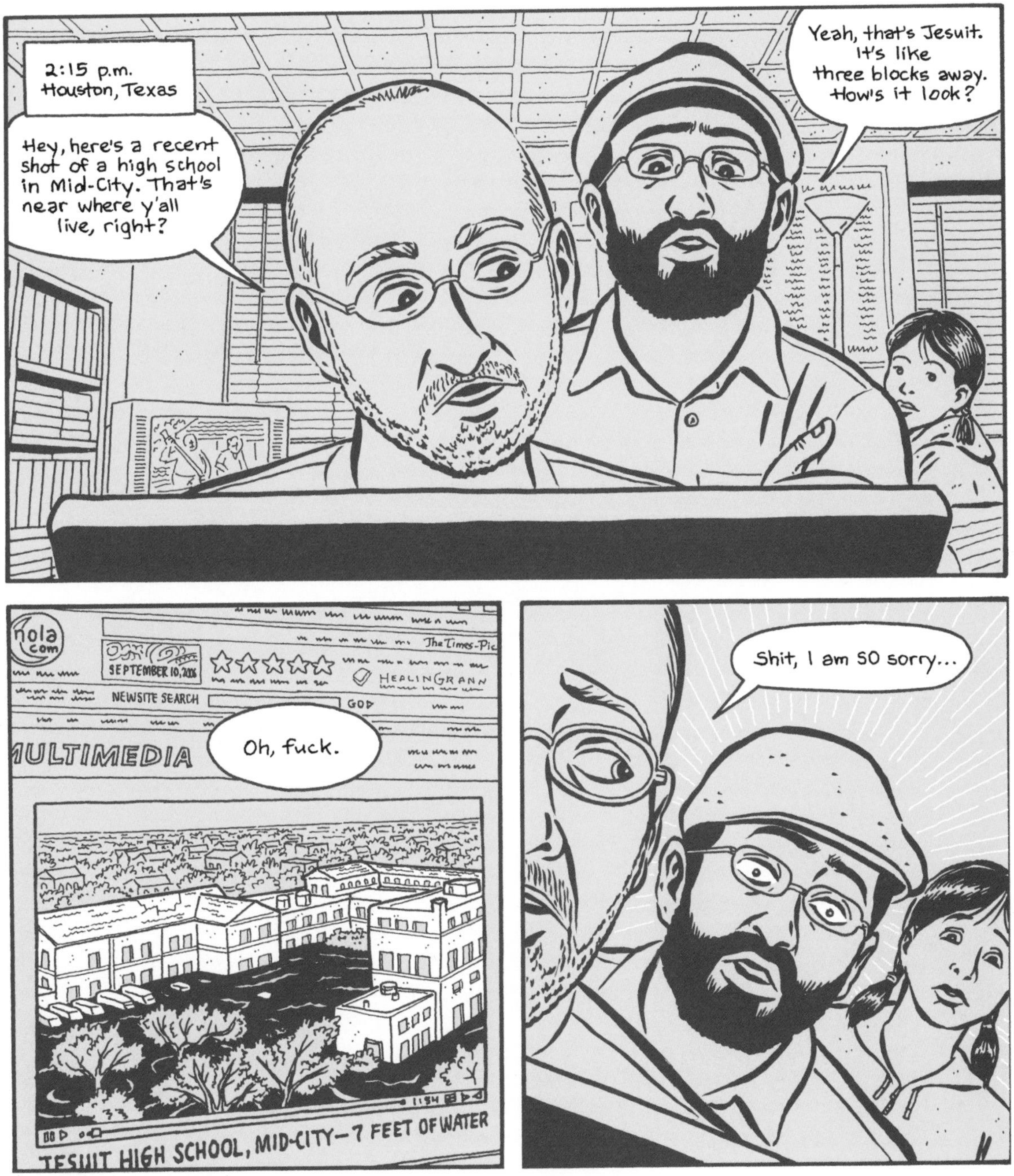
2:15 p.m.
Houston, Texas
Hey, here's a recent shot of a high school in Mid-City. That's near where y'all live, right?
Yeah, that's Jesuit. It's like three blocks away. How's it look?
nola.com
The Times-Pic
SEPTEMBER 10,
HEALINGGRANN
NEWSITE SEARCH
GO
MULTIMEDIA
Oh, fuck.
JESUIT HIGH SCHOOL, MID-CITY—7 FEET OF WATER
Shit, I am SO sorry...

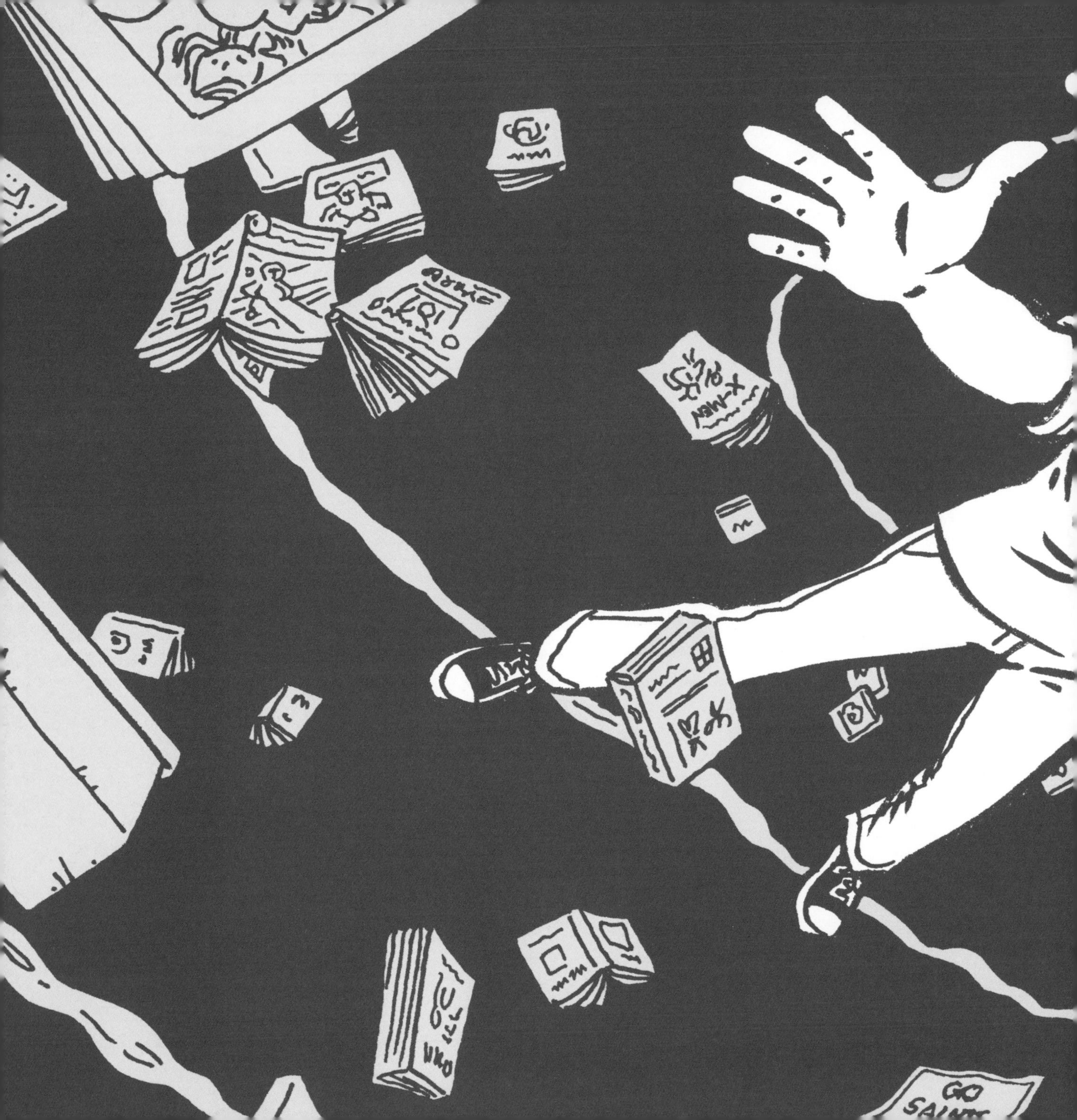
X-MEN
GO

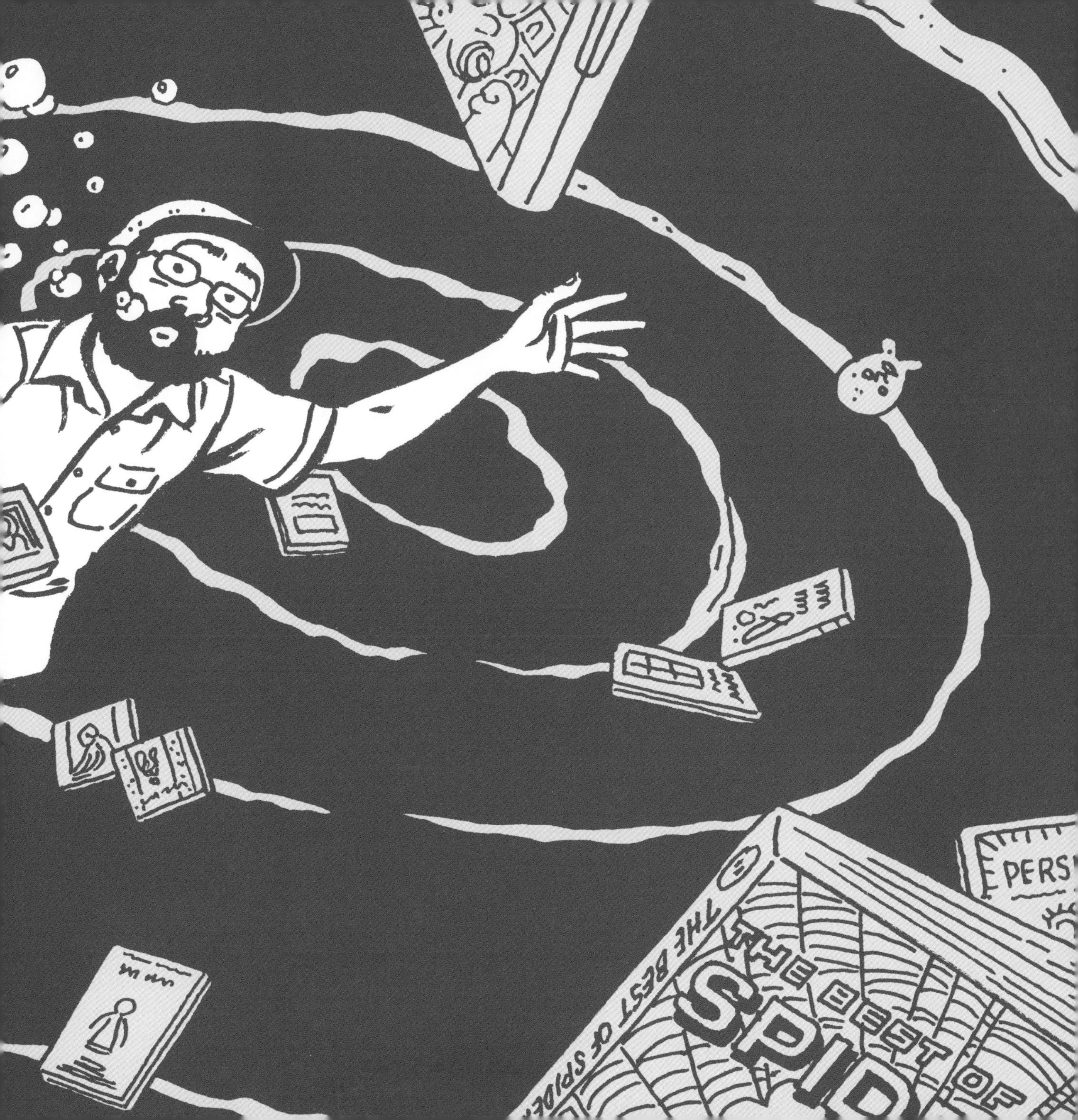

THE BEST OF
SPID
THE BEST OF SPIDE
PERS

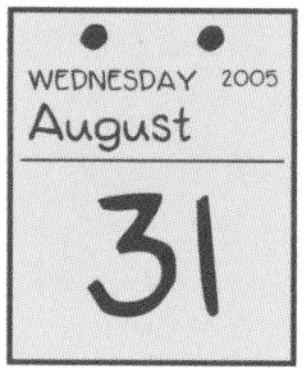
WEDNESDAY 2005
August
31

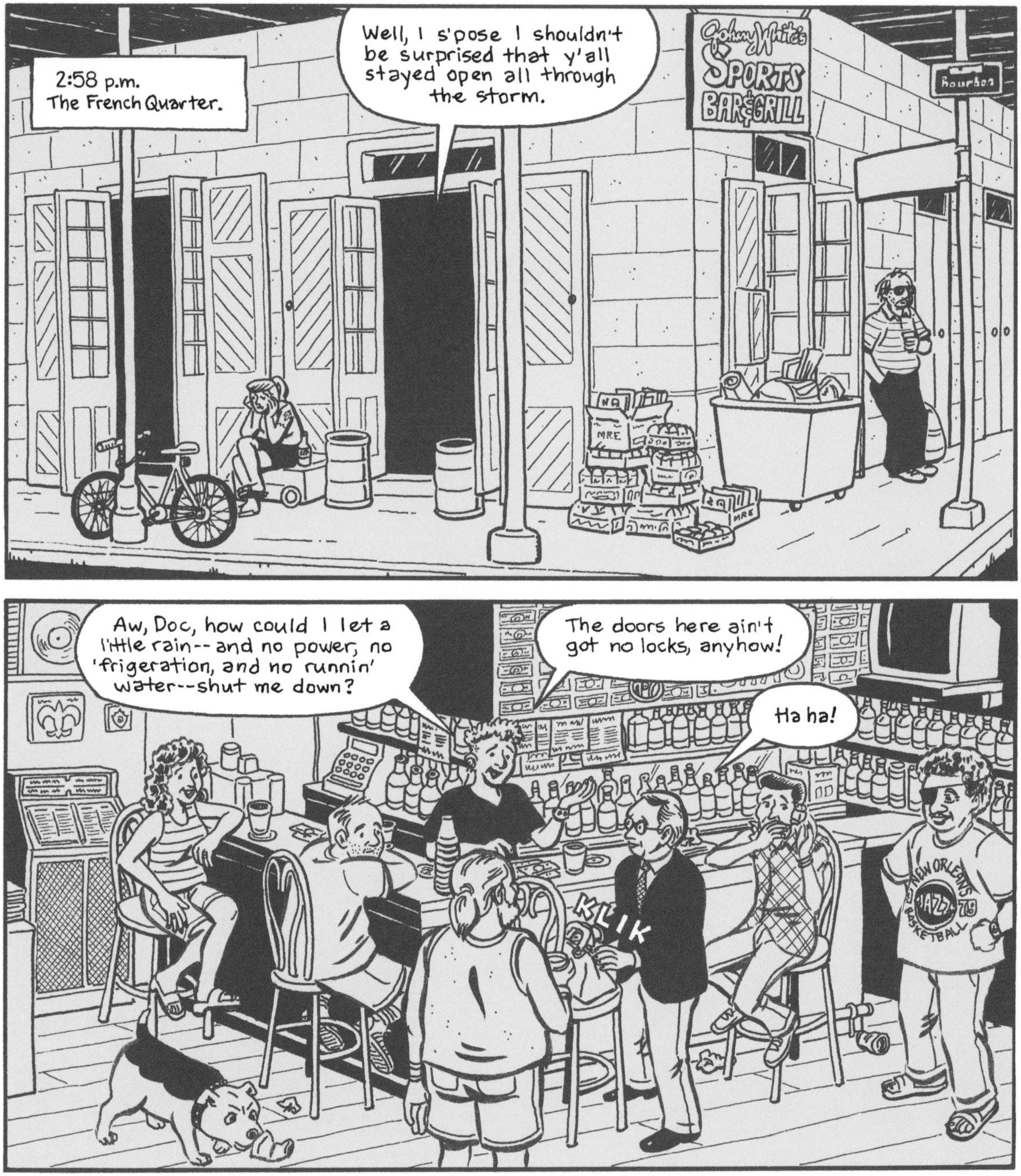
2:58 p.m.
The French Quarter.
Well, I s'pose I shouldn't be surprised that y'all stayed open all through the storm.
Johnny White's SPORTS BAR & GRILL
Bourbon
Aw, Doc, how could I let a little rain-- and no power, no 'frigeration, and no runnin' water--shut me down?
The doors here ain't got no locks, anyhow!
Ha ha!
KLIK
NEW ORLEANS JAZZ 78 BASKETBALL

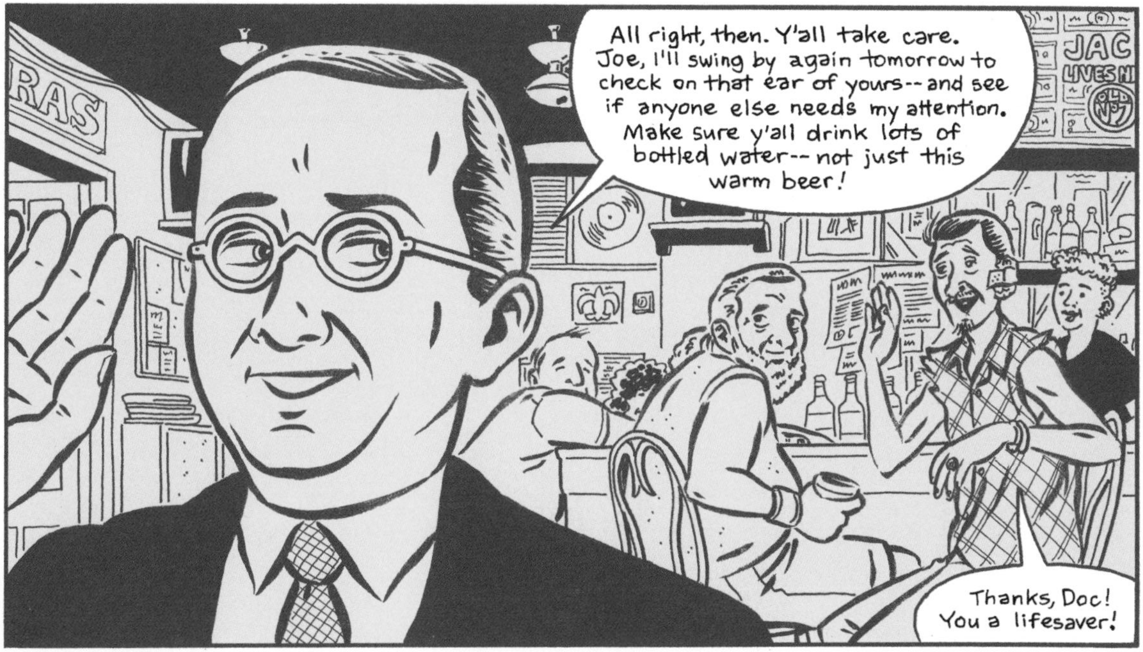
All right, then. Y'all take care. Joe, I'll swing by again tomorrow to check on that ear of yours-- and see if anyone else needs my attention. Make sure y'all drink lots of bottled water-- not just this warm beer!
Thanks, Doc! You a lifesaver!

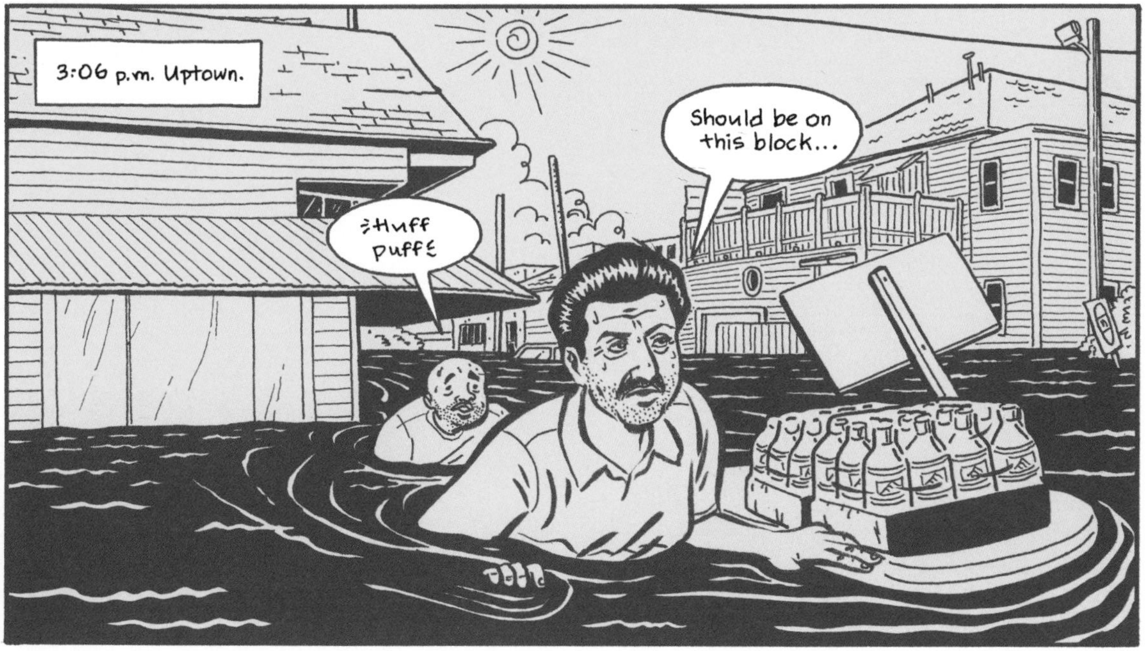
3:06 p.m. Uptown.
Should be on this block...
≷Huff puff≷

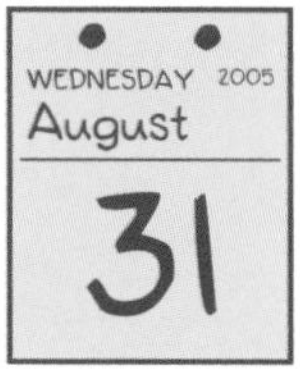
WEDNESDAY 2005
August
31

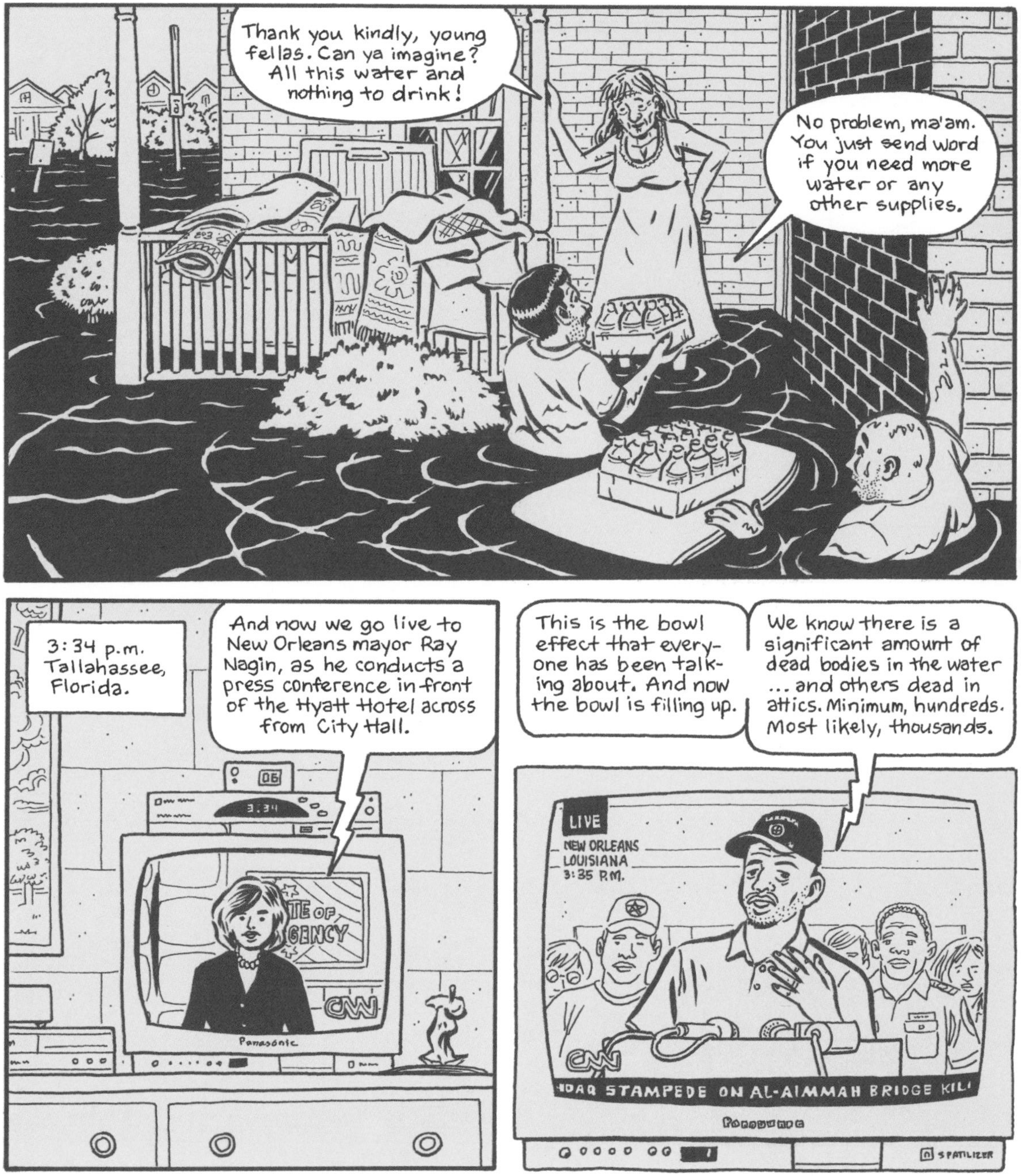
Thank you kindly, young fellas. Can ya imagine? All this water and nothing to drink!
No problem, ma'am. You just send word if you need more water or any other supplies.
3:34 p.m. Tallahassee, Florida.
And now we go live to New Orleans mayor Ray Nagin, as he conducts a press conference in front of the Hyatt Hotel across from City Hall.
CNN
Panasonic
This is the bowl effect that everyone has been talking about. And now the bowl is filling up.
We know there is a significant amount of dead bodies in the water ... and others dead in attics. Minimum, hundreds. Most likely, thousands.
LIVE
NEW ORLEANS
LOUISIANA
3:35 P.M.
CNN
STAMPEDE ON AL-AIMMAH BRIDGE
SPATILIZER

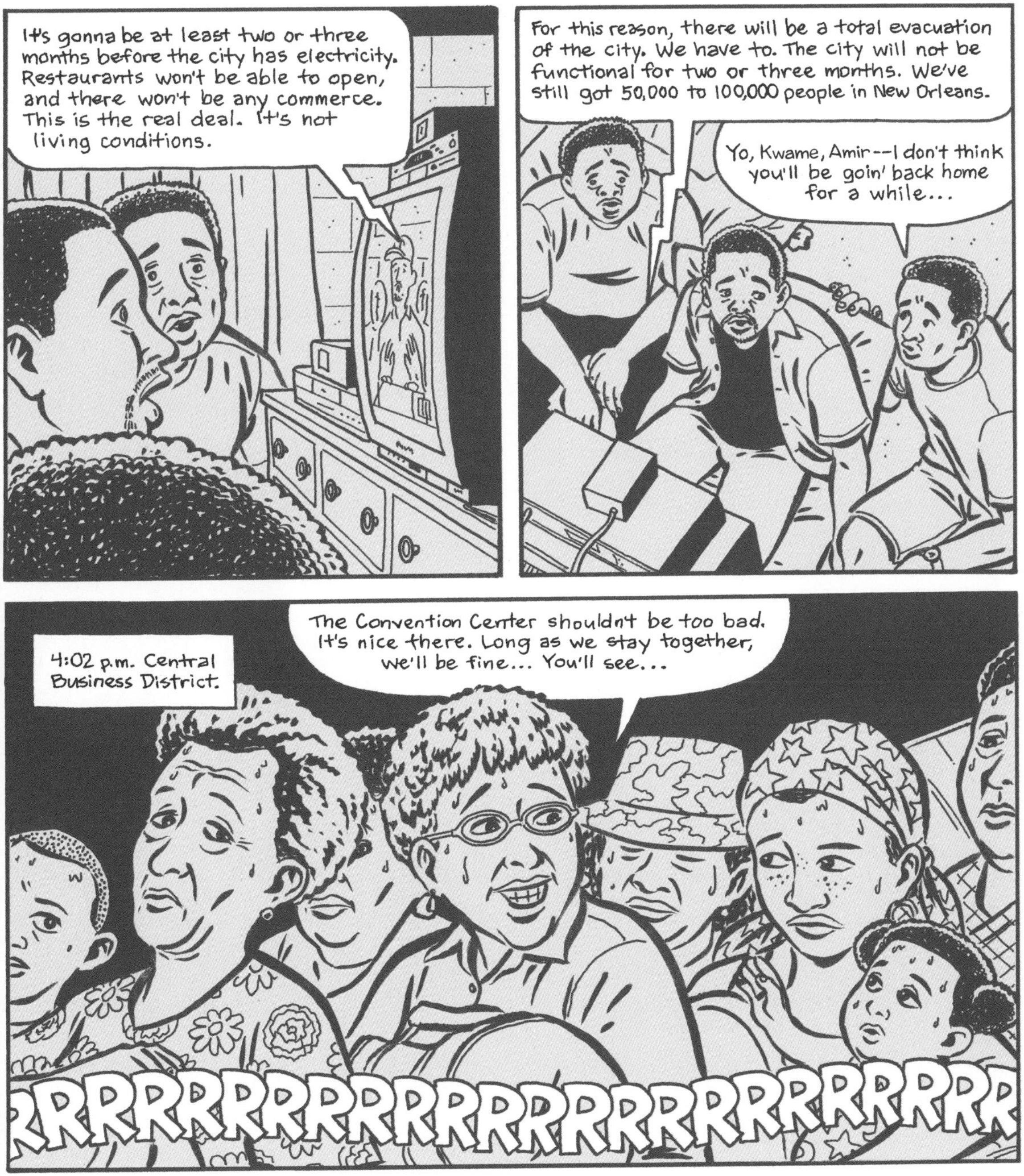
It's gonna be at least two or three months before the city has electricity. Restaurants won't be able to open, and there won't be any commerce. This is the real deal. It's not living conditions.
For this reason, there will be a total evacuation of the city. We have to. The city will not be functional for two or three months. We've still got 50,000 to 100,000 people in New Orleans.
Yo, Kwame, Amir--I don't think you'll be goin' back home for a while...
4:02 p.m. Central Business District.
The Convention Center shouldn't be too bad. It's nice there. Long as we stay together, we'll be fine... You'll see...
RRRRRRRRRRRRRRRRRRRRRRRRRR

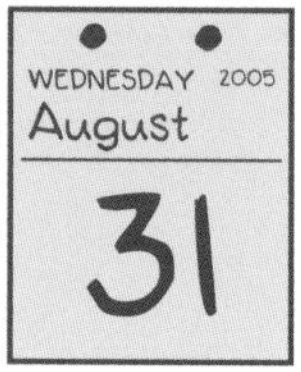
WEDNESDAY 2005
August
31

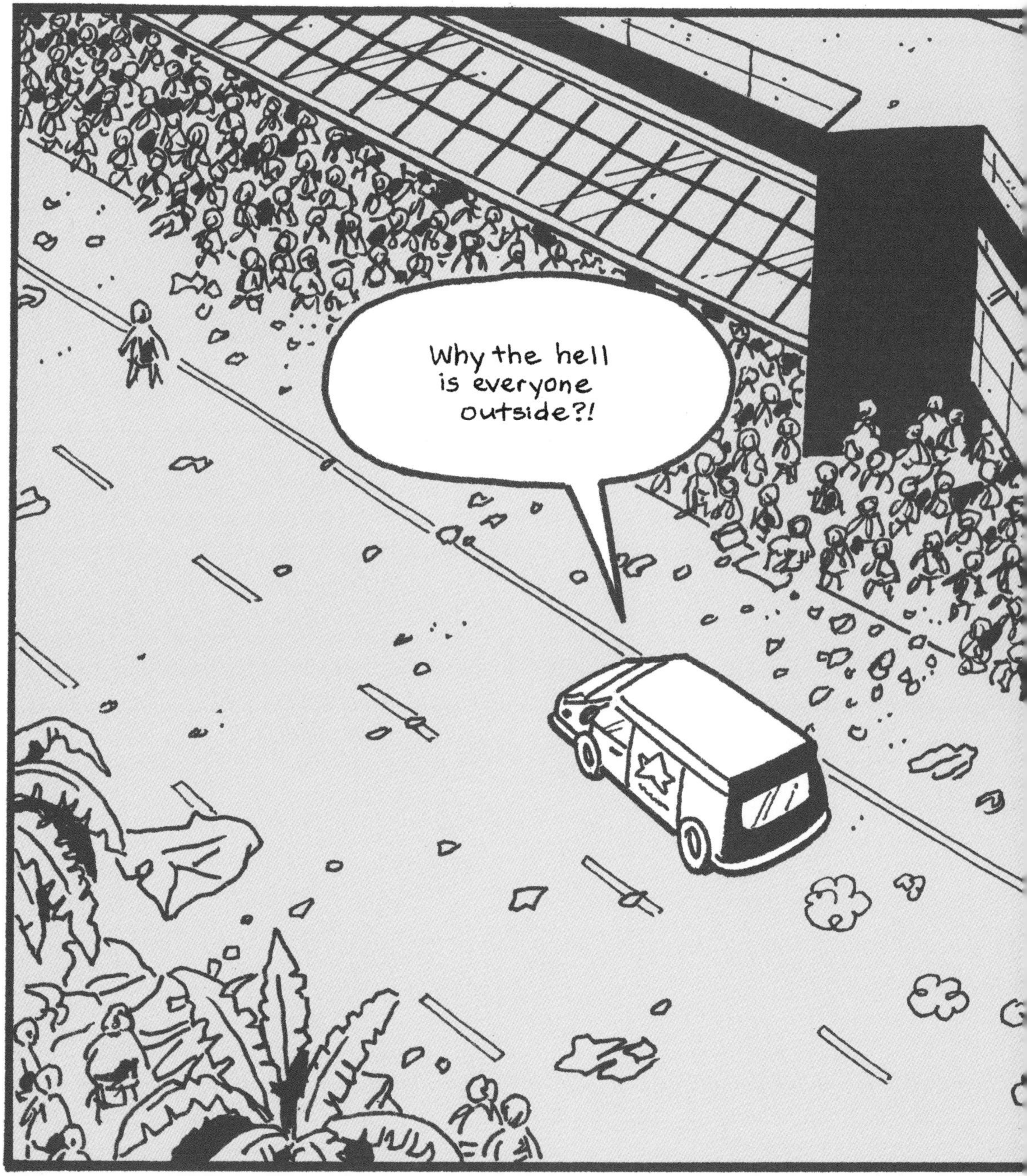
Why the hell is everyone outside?!

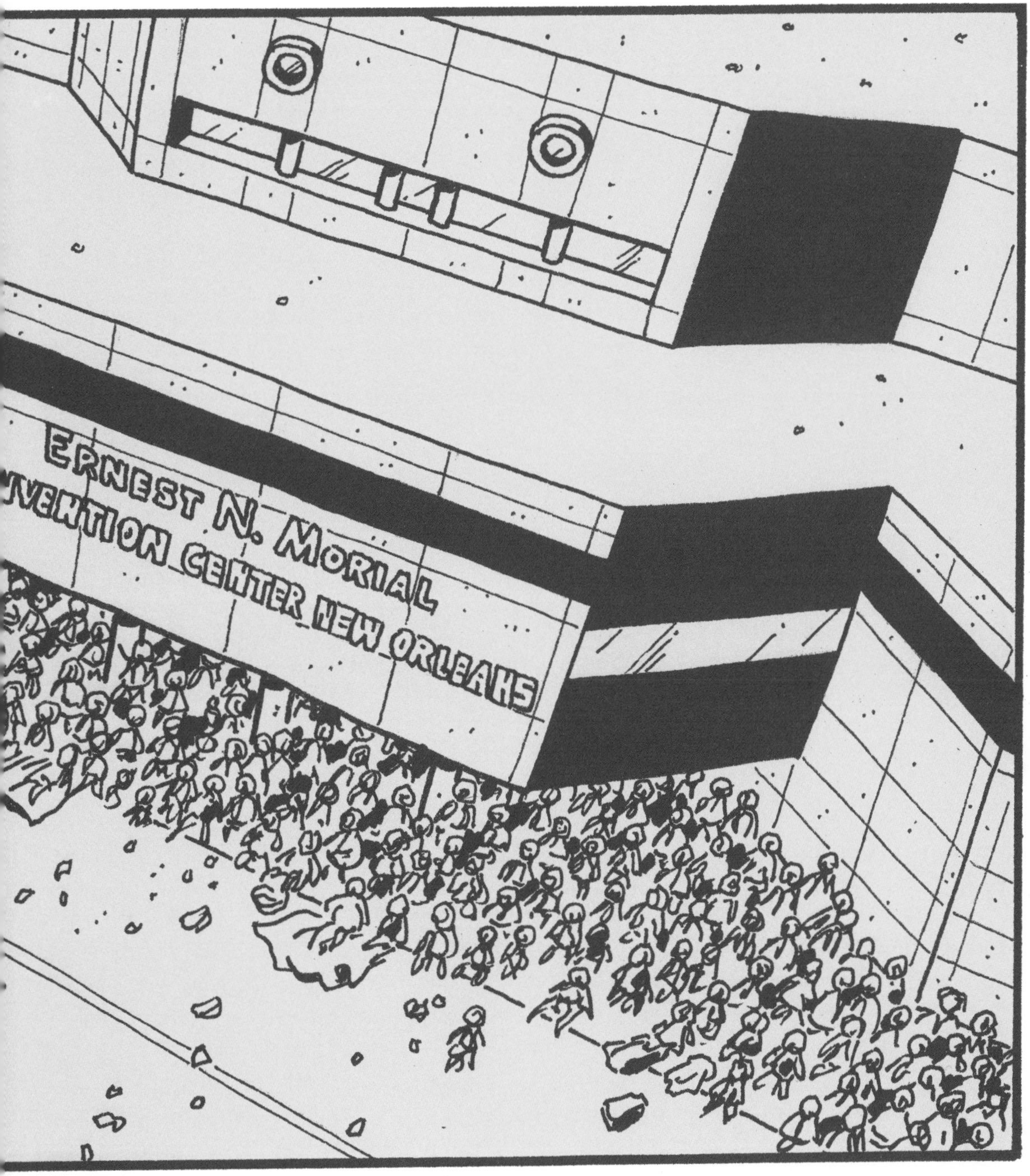
ERNEST N. MORIAL
VENTION CENTER NEW ORLEANS

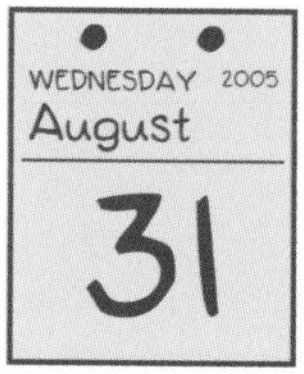
WEDNESDAY 2005
August
31

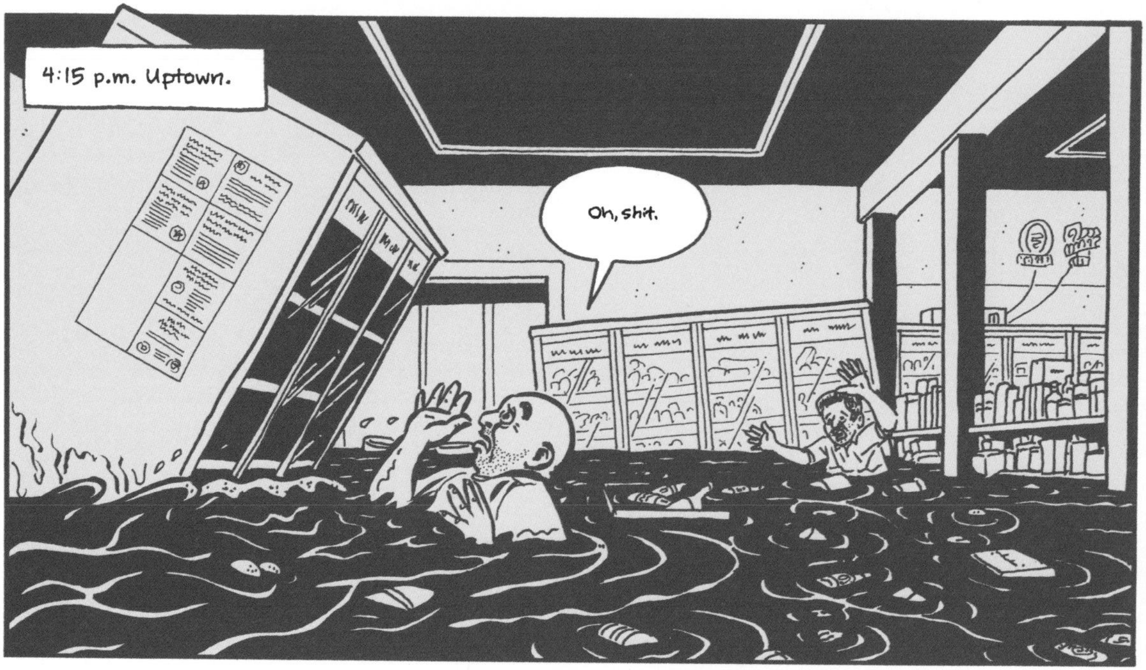
4:15 p.m. Uptown.
Oh, shit.

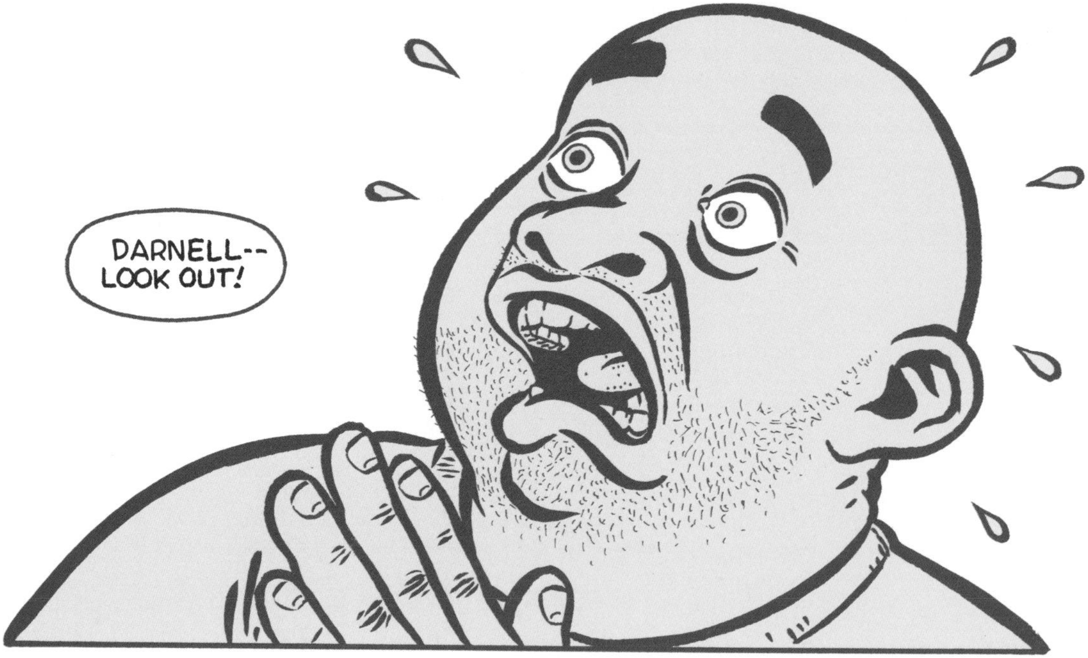
DARNELL--
LOOK OUT!

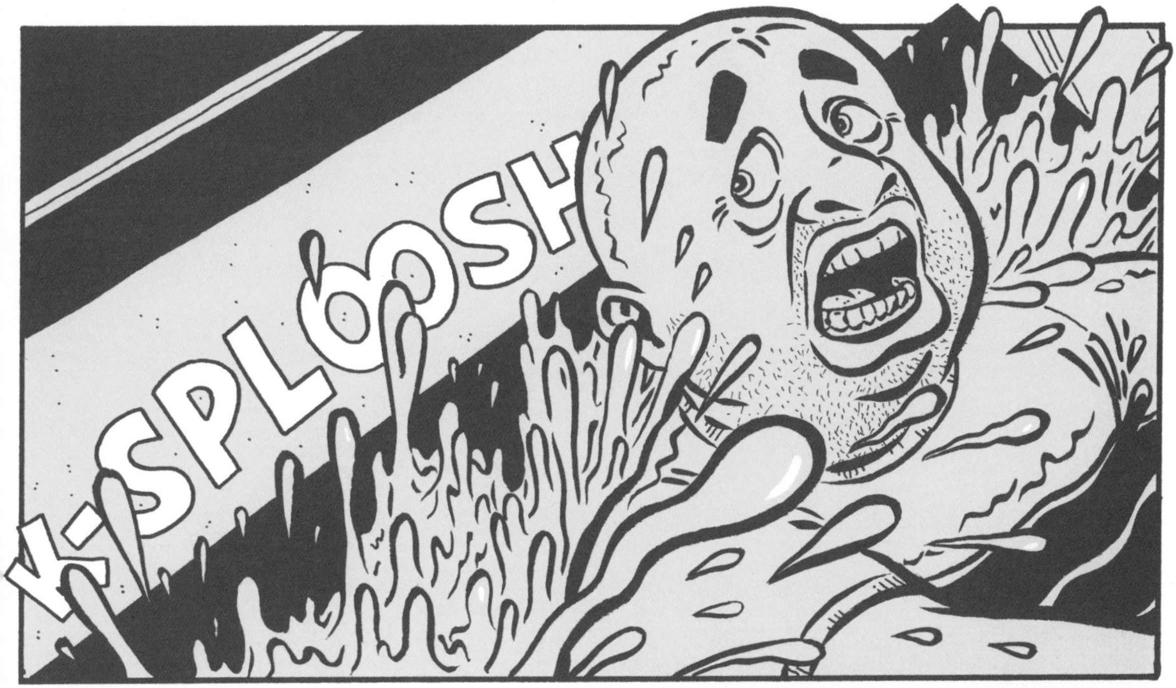
K-SPLOOSH

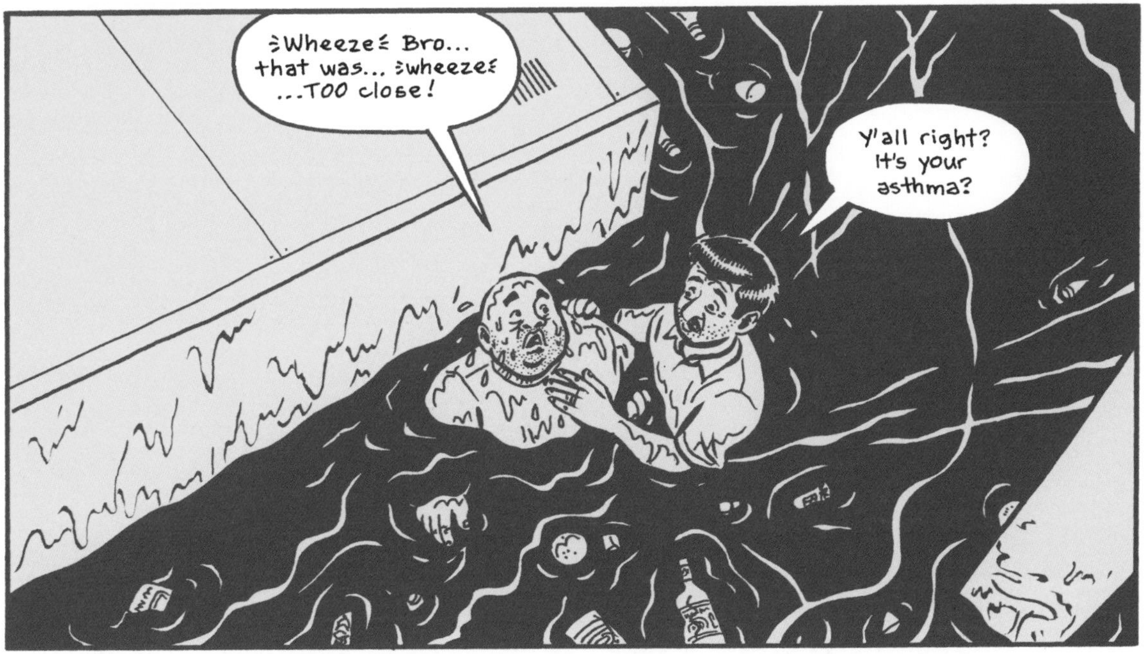
:Wheeze: Bro... that was... :wheeze: ...TOO close!
Y'all right? It's your asthma?

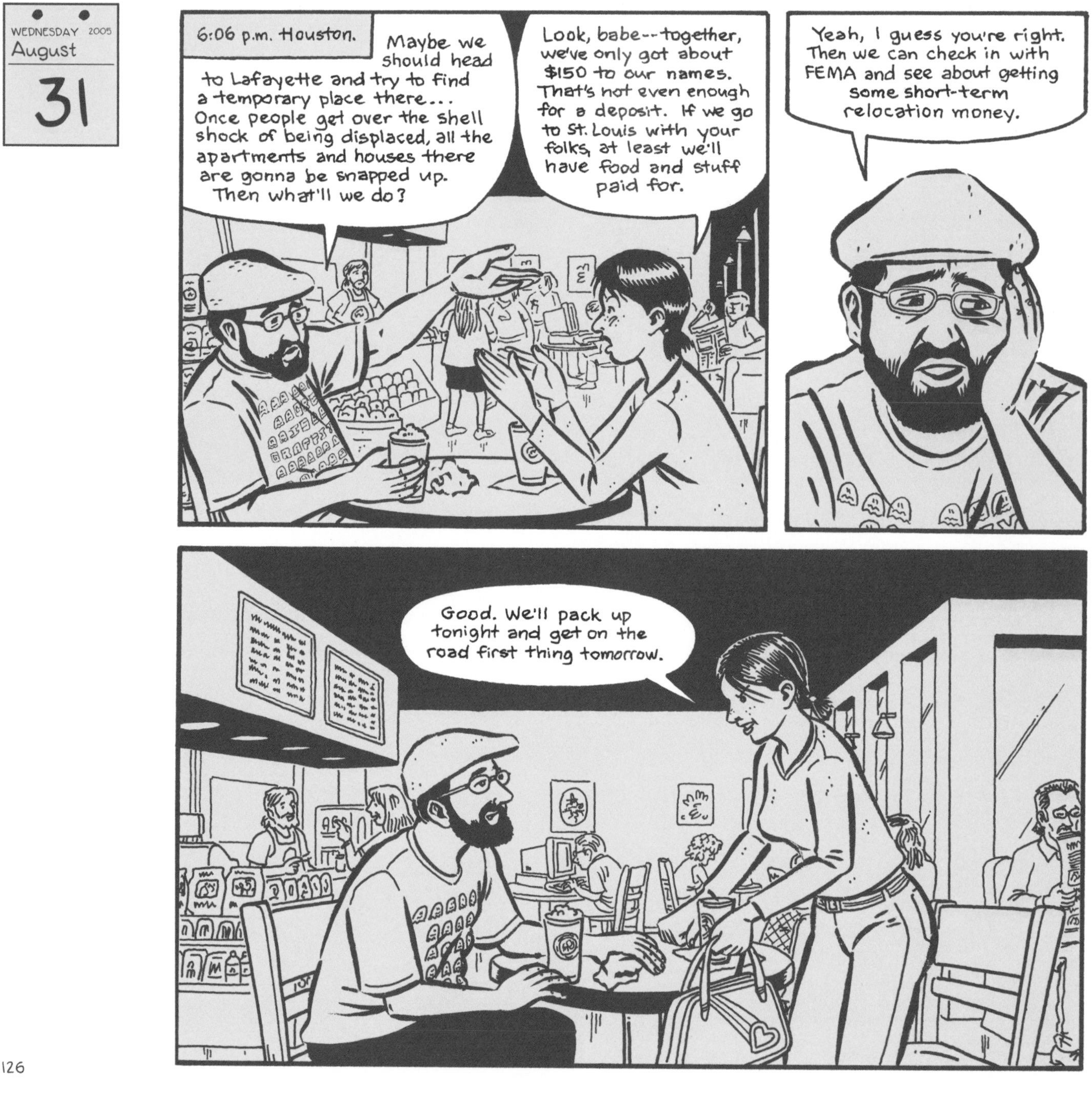

WEDNESDAY 2005
August
31
6:06 p.m. Houston.
Maybe we should head to Lafayette and try to find a temporary place there... Once people get over the shell shock of being displaced, all the apartments and houses there are gonna be snapped up. Then what'll we do?
Look, babe--together, we've only got about $150 to our names. That's not even enough for a deposit. If we go to St. Louis with your folks, at least we'll have food and stuff paid for.
Yeah, I guess you're right. Then we can check in with FEMA and see about getting some short-term relocation money.
Good. We'll pack up tonight and get on the road first thing tomorrow.

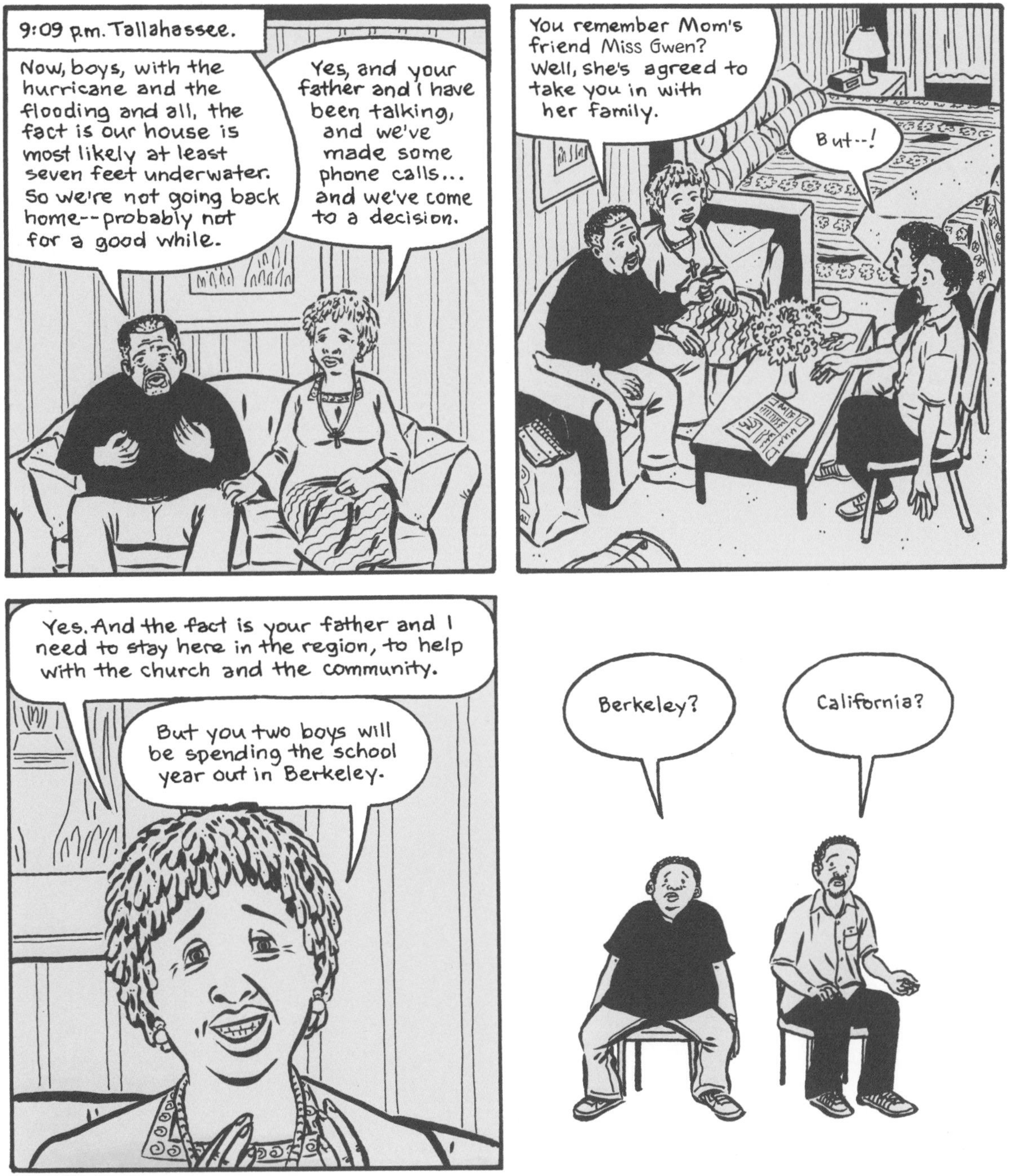
9:09 p.m. Tallahassee.
Now, boys, with the hurricane and the flooding and all, the fact is our house is most likely at least seven feet underwater. So we're not going back home--probably not for a good while.
Yes, and your father and I have been talking, and we've made some phone calls... and we've come to a decision.
You remember Mom's friend Miss Gwen? Well, she's agreed to take you in with her family.
But--!
Yes. And the fact is your father and I need to stay here in the region, to help with the church and the community.
But you two boys will be spending the school year out in Berkeley.
Berkeley?
California?

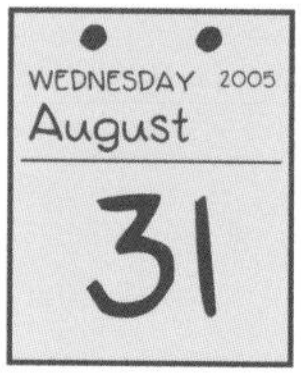
WEDNESDAY 2005
August
31

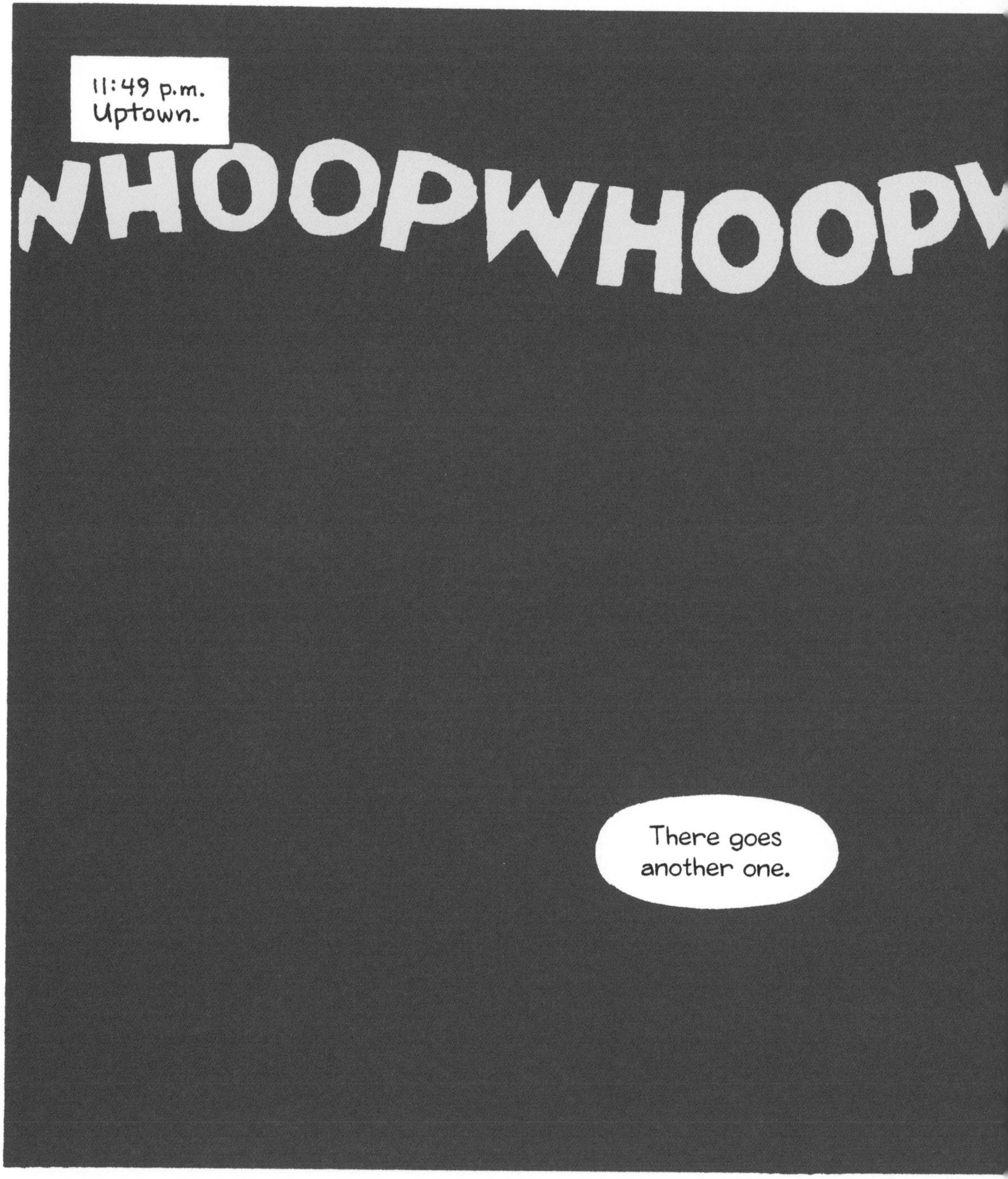
11:49 p.m.
Uptown.
WHOOPWHOOP
There goes another one.

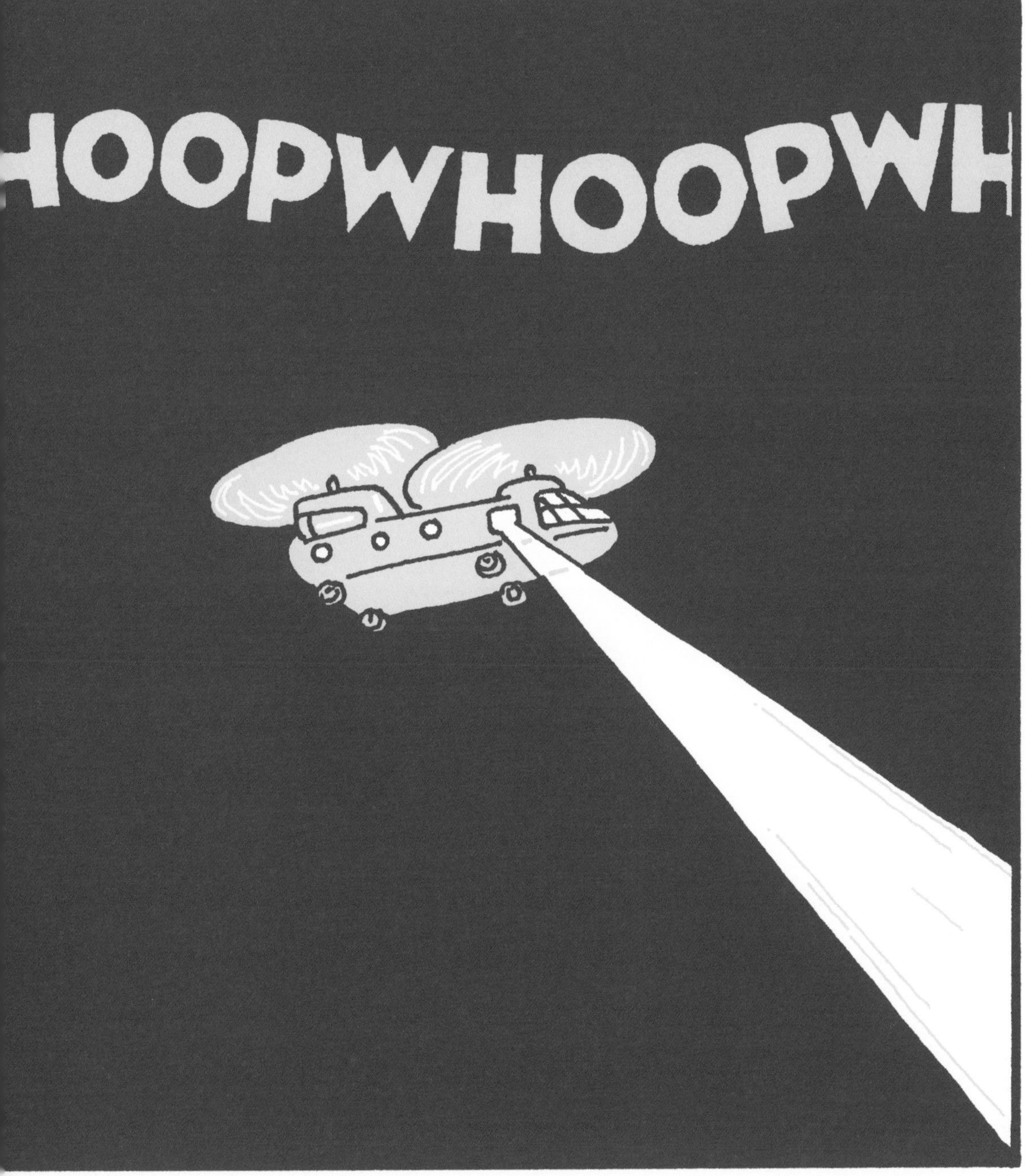
HOOPWHOOPWH

WEDNESDAY 2005
August
31

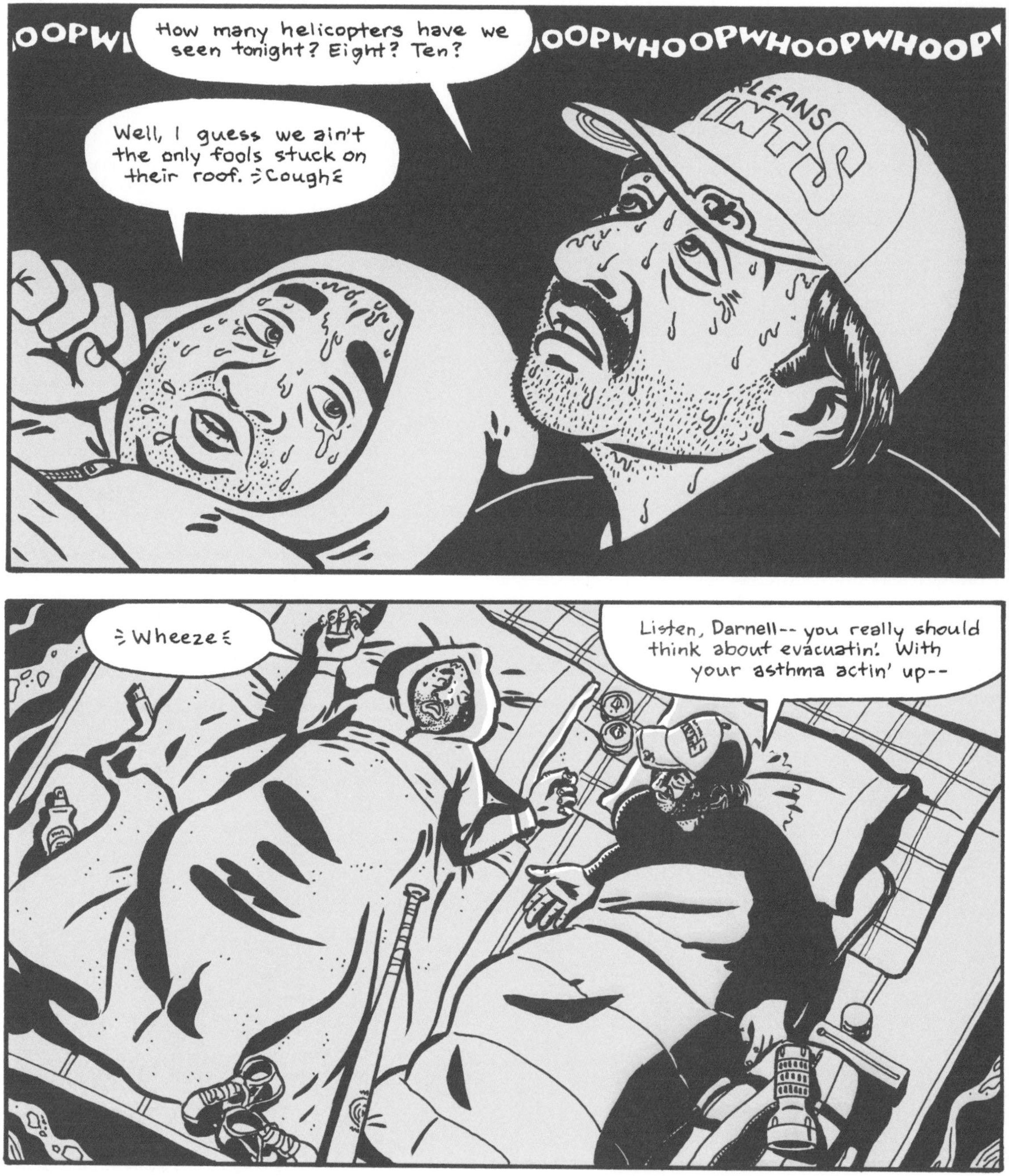
OOPWHOOPWHOOPWHOOP
How many helicopters have we seen tonight? Eight? Ten?
Well, I guess we ain't the only fools stuck on their roof. ≈Cough≈
≈Wheeze≈
Listen, Darnell-- you really should think about evacuatin'. With your asthma actin' up--

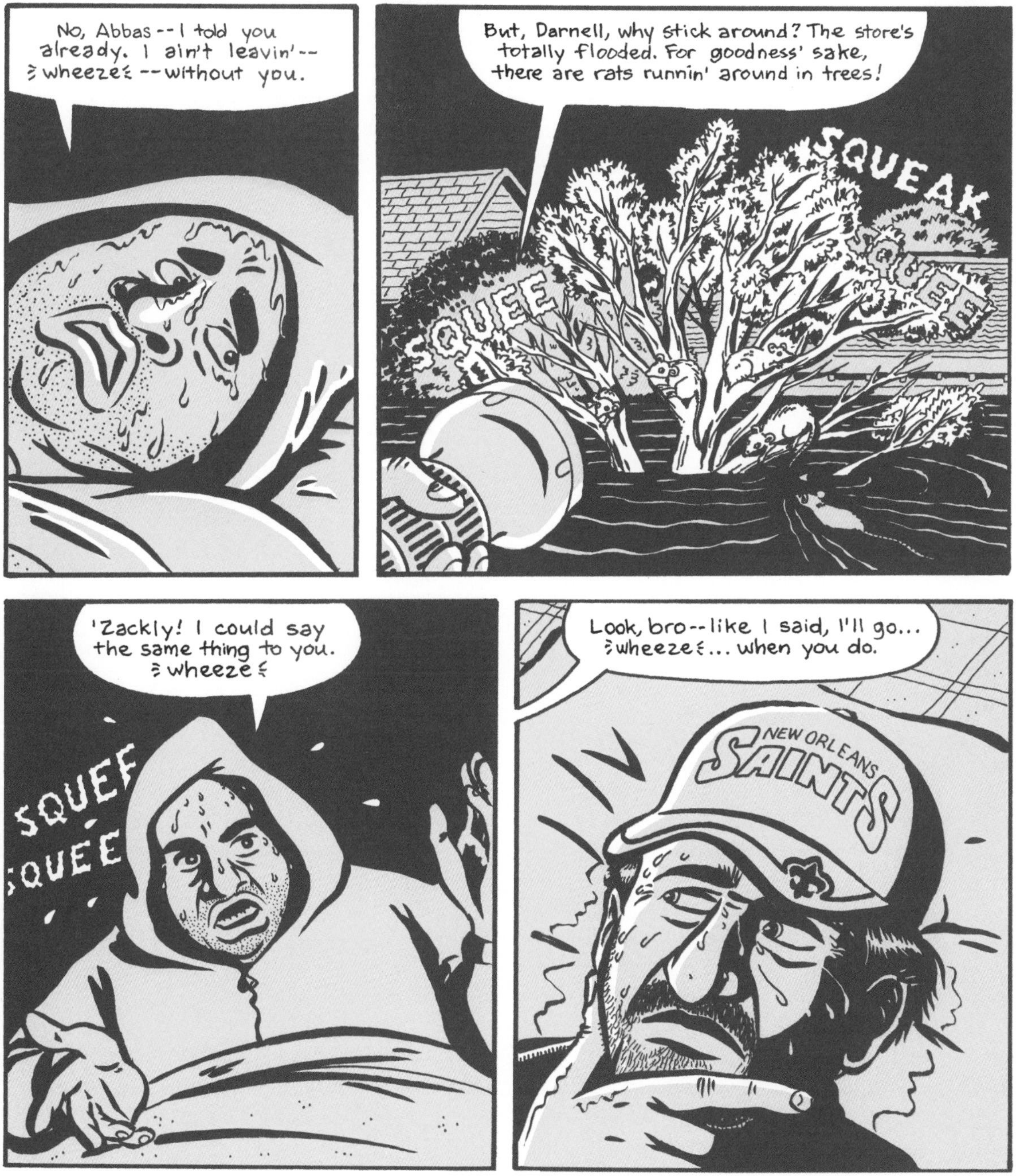
No, Abbas -- I told you already. I ain't leavin' -- ≷wheeze≶ -- without you.
But, Darnell, why stick around? The store's totally flooded. For goodness' sake, there are rats runnin' around in trees!
SQUEAK
SQUEE
SQUEE
'Zackly! I could say the same thing to you. ≷wheeze≶
SQUEE
SQUEE
Look, bro -- like I said, I'll go... ≷wheeze≶... when you do.
NEW ORLEANS SAINTS

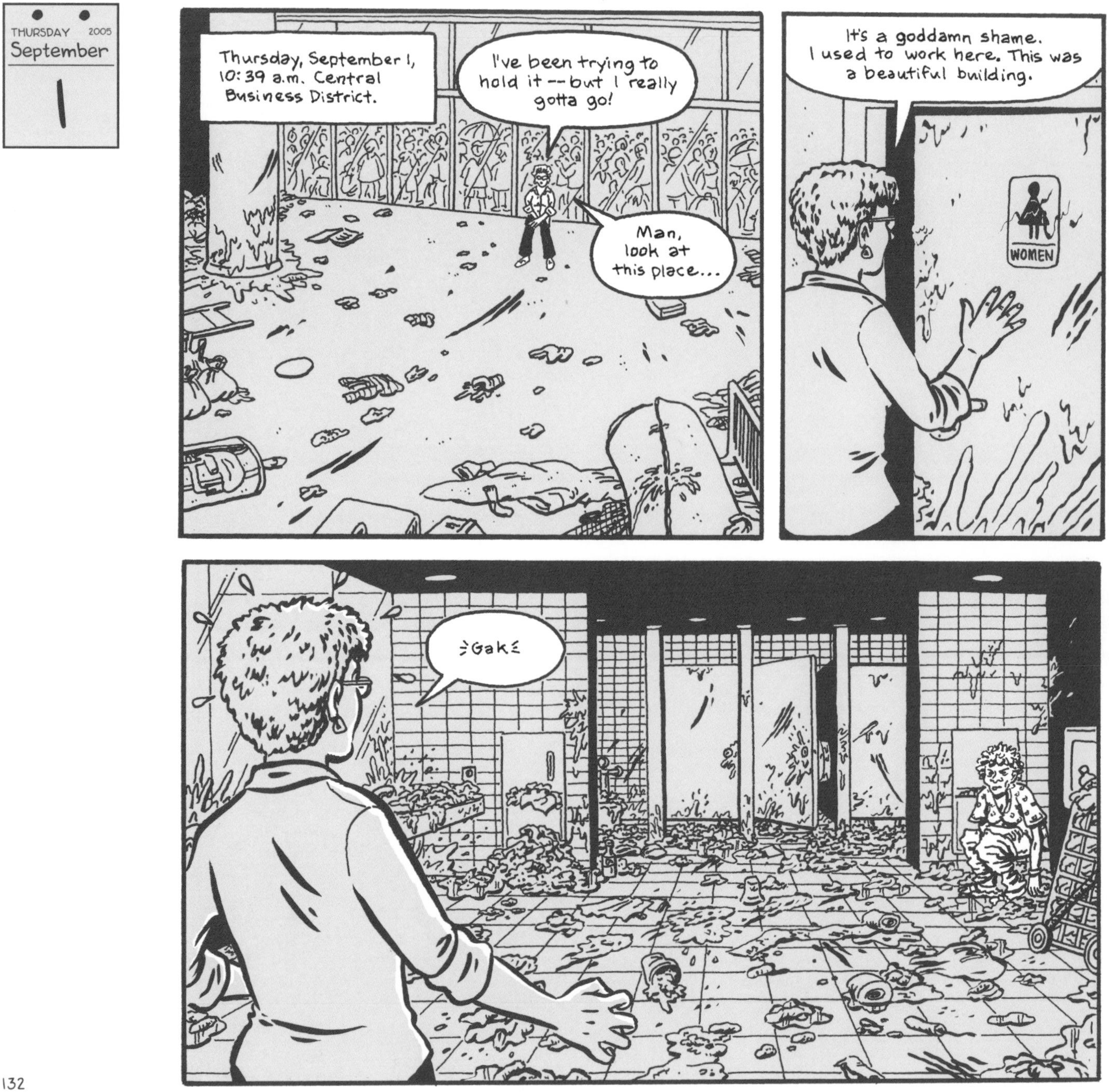
THURSDAY 2005
September
1
Thursday, September 1, 10:39 a.m. Central Business District.
I've been trying to hold it -- but I really gotta go!
Man, look at this place...
It's a goddamn shame. I used to work here. This was a beautiful building.
WOMEN
Gak

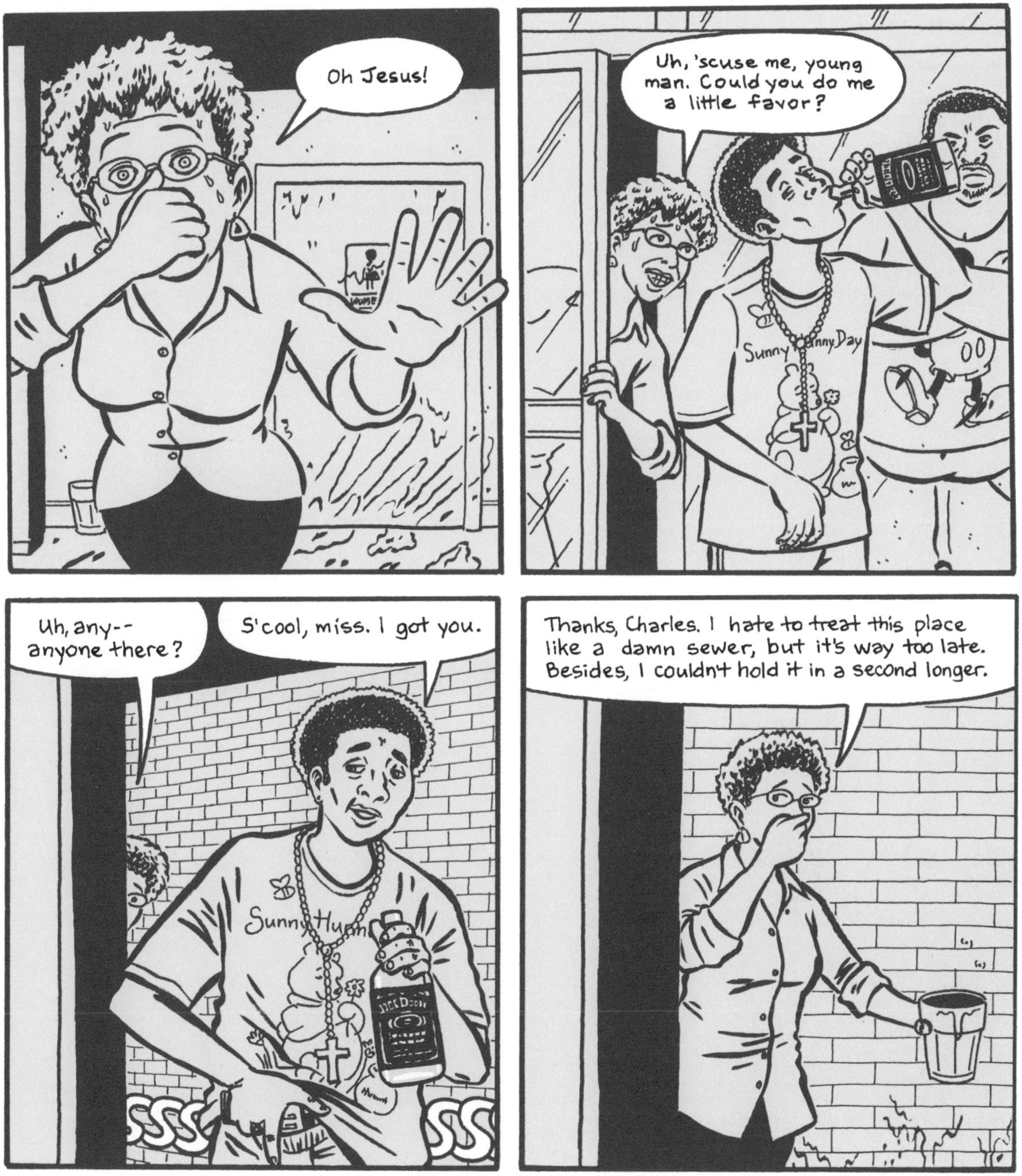
Oh Jesus!
Uh, 'scuse me, young man. Could you do me a little favor?
Sunny Sunny Day
Uh, any-- anyone there?
S'cool, miss. I got you.
Thanks, Charles. I hate to treat this place like a damn sewer, but it's way too late. Besides, I couldn't hold it in a second longer.

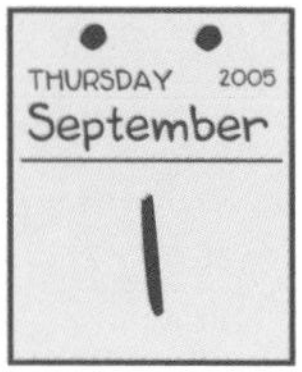
THURSDAY 2005
September
1

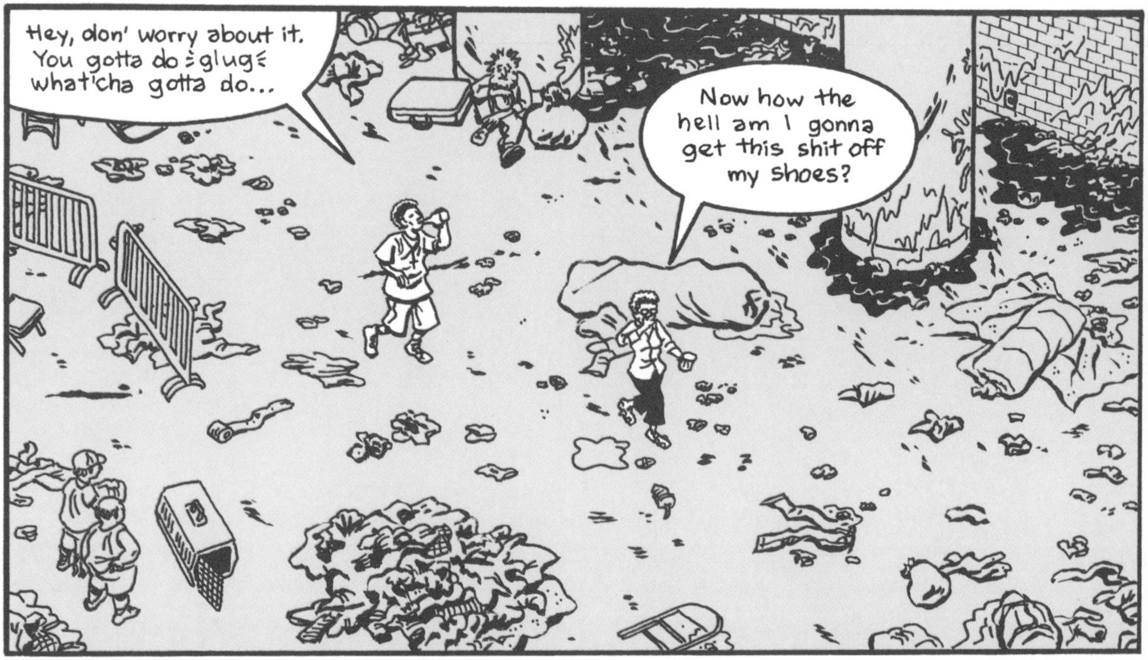
Hey, don' worry about it. You gotta do ≶glug≶ what'cha gotta do...
Now how the hell am I gonna get this shit off my shoes?

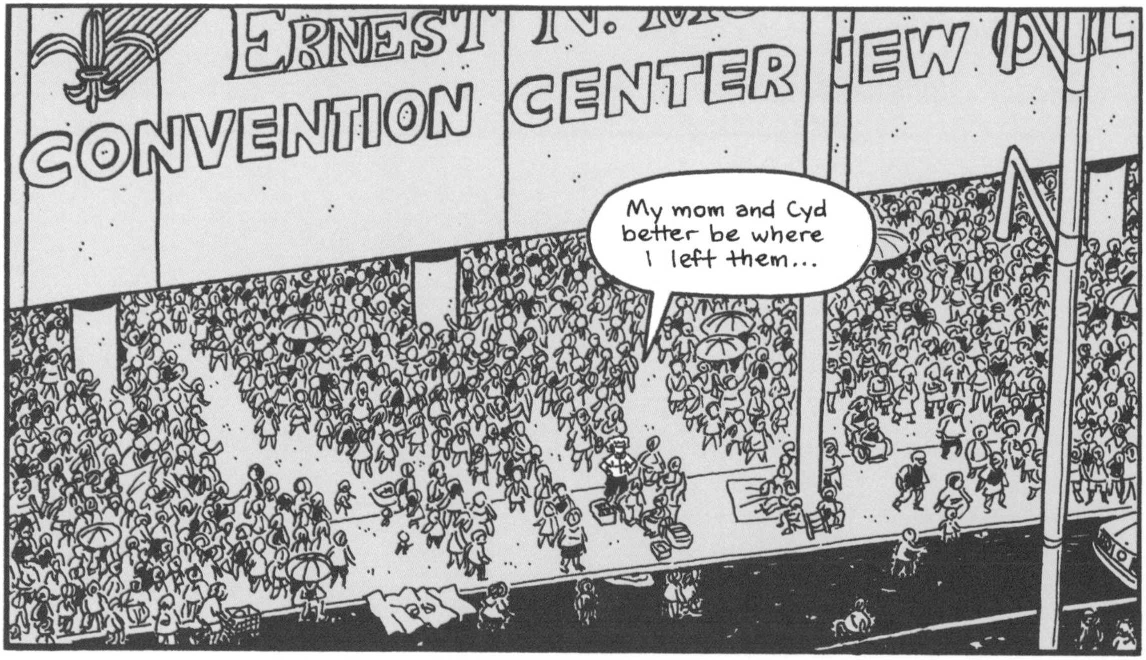
ERNEST N.
CONVENTION CENTER
My mom and Cyd better be where I left them...

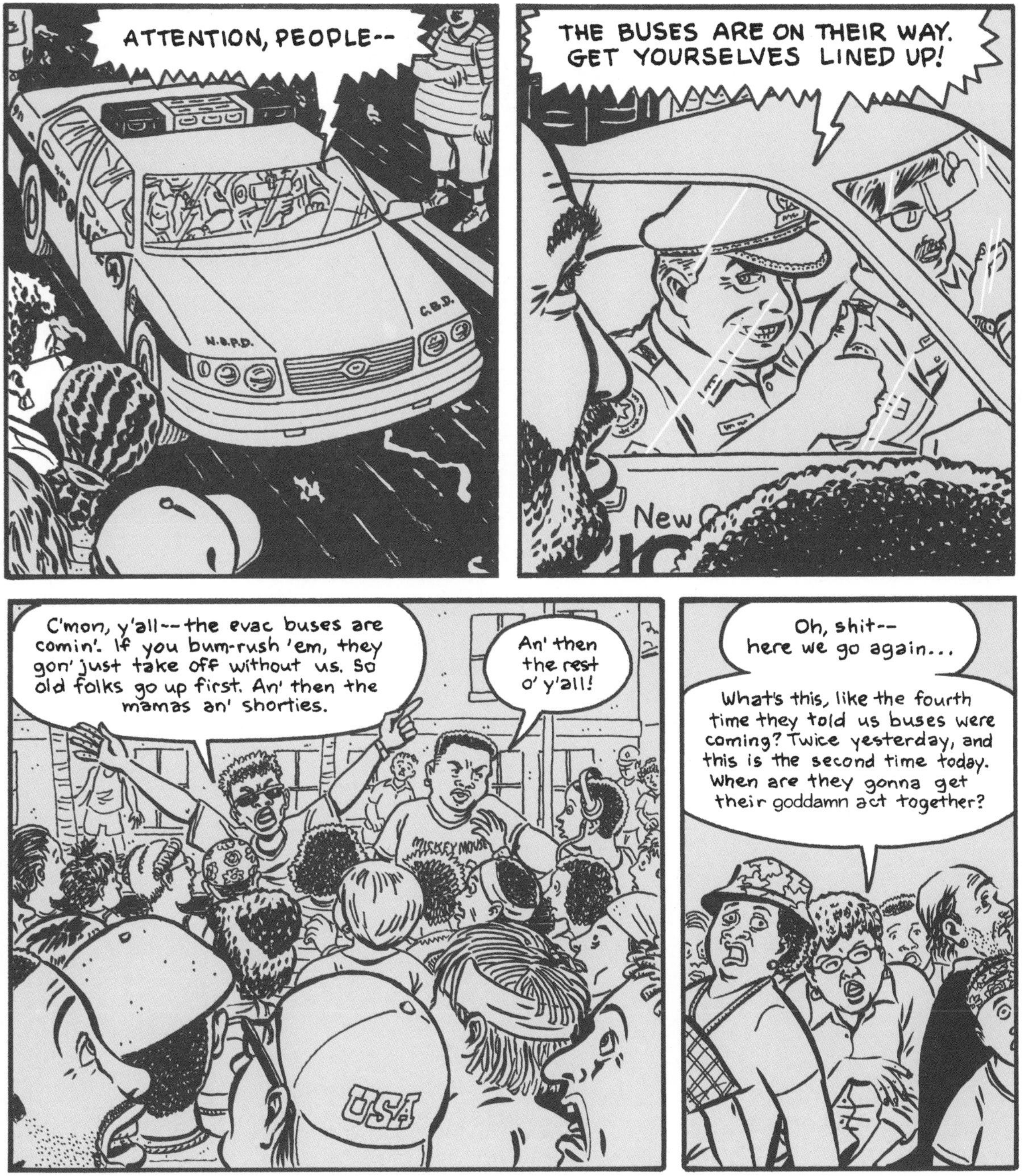
ATTENTION, PEOPLE--
N.O.P.D.
THE BUSES ARE ON THEIR WAY. GET YOURSELVES LINED UP!
New
C'mon, y'all--the evac buses are comin'. If you bum-rush 'em, they gon' just take off without us. So old folks go up first. An' then the mamas an' shorties.
An' then the rest o' y'all!
USA
Oh, shit-- here we go again...
What's this, like the fourth time they told us buses were coming? Twice yesterday, and this is the second time today. When are they gonna get their goddamn act together?

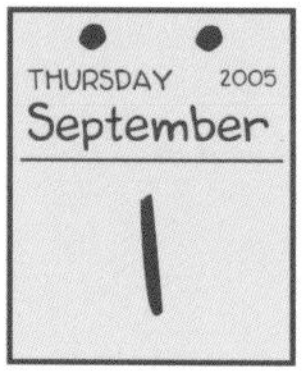
THURSDAY 2005
September
1

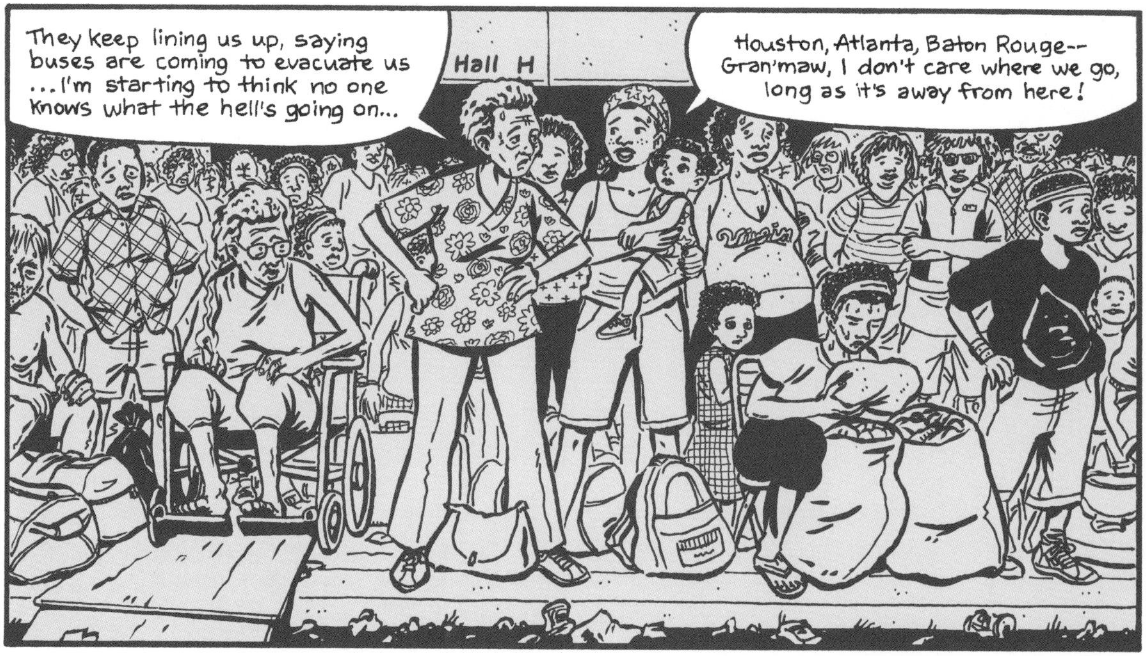
They keep lining us up, saying buses are coming to evacuate us ...I'm starting to think no one knows what the hell's going on...
Hall H
Houston, Atlanta, Baton Rouge-- Gran'maw, I don't care where we go, long as it's away from here!

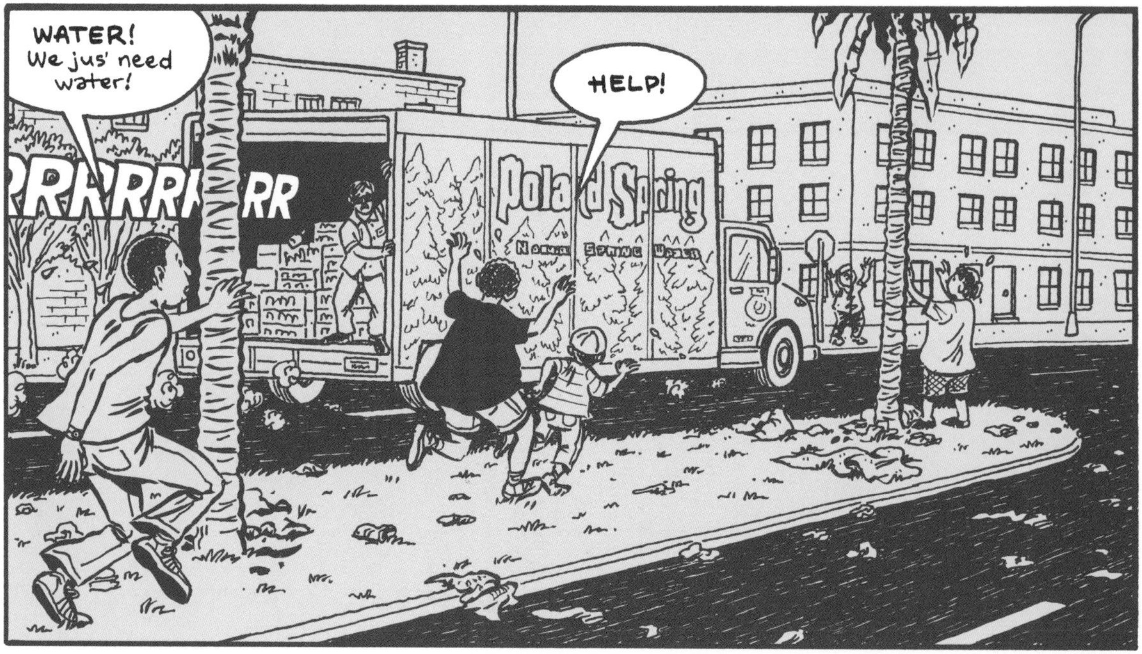
WATER! We jus' need water!
HELP!

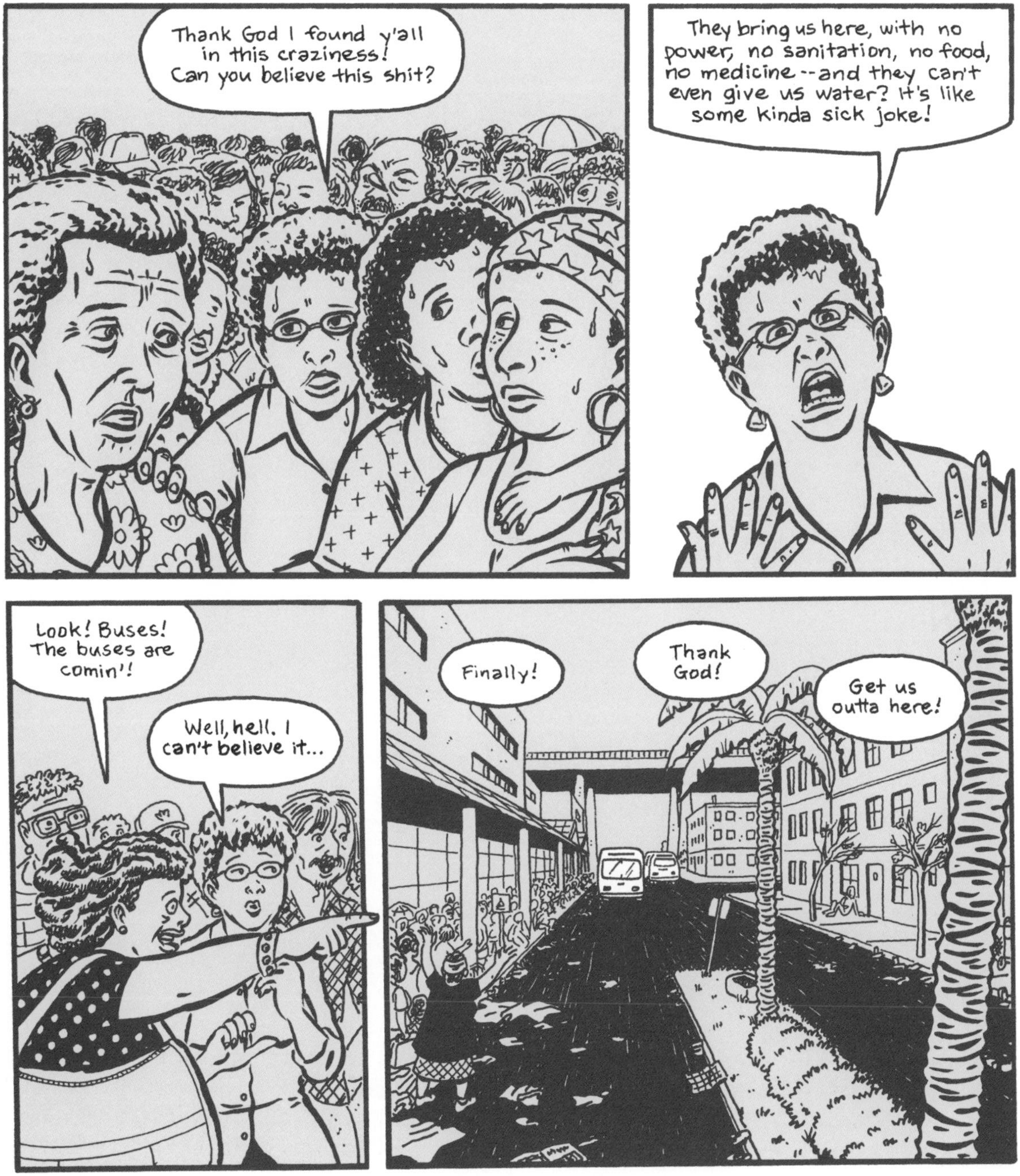
Thank God I found y'all in this craziness! Can you believe this shit?
They bring us here, with no power, no sanitation, no food, no medicine--and they can't even give us water? It's like some kinda sick joke!
Look! Buses! The buses are comin'!
Well, hell. I can't believe it...
Finally!
Thank God!
Get us outta here!

THURSDAY 2005
September
1

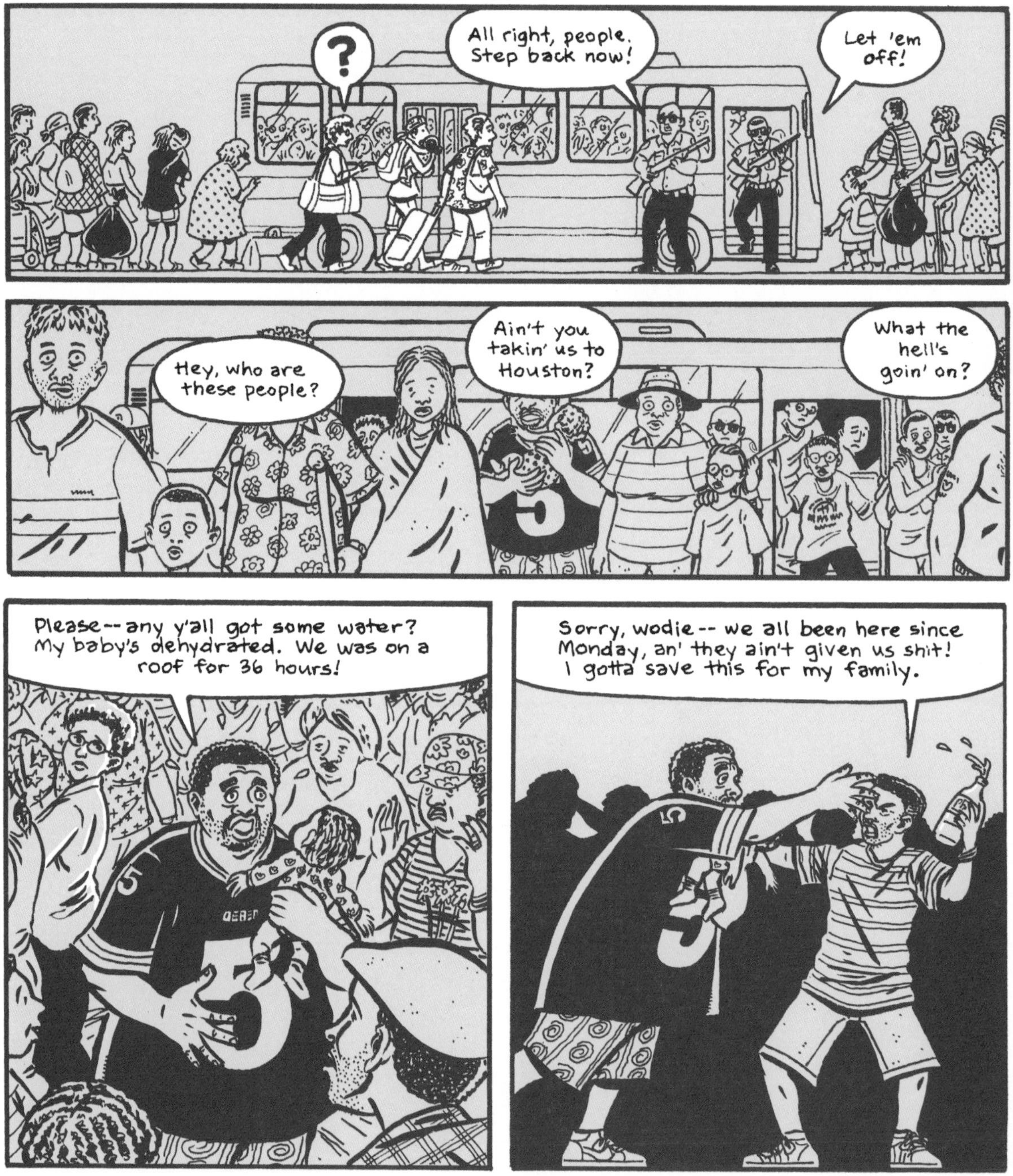
?
All right, people. Step back now!
Let 'em off!
Hey, who are these people?
Ain't you takin' us to Houston?
What the hell's goin' on?
Please--any y'all got some water? My baby's dehydrated. We was on a roof for 36 hours!
Sorry, wodie-- we all been here since Monday, an' they ain't given us shit! I gotta save this for my family.

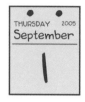

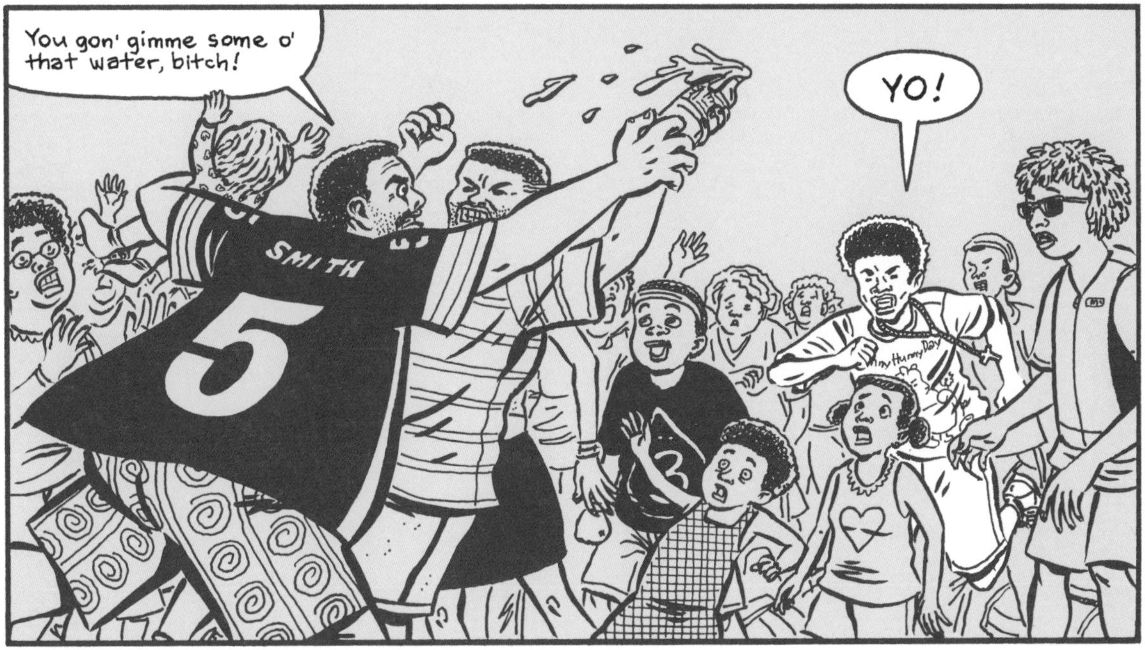
You gon' gimme some o' that water, bitch!
YO!
SMITH
5

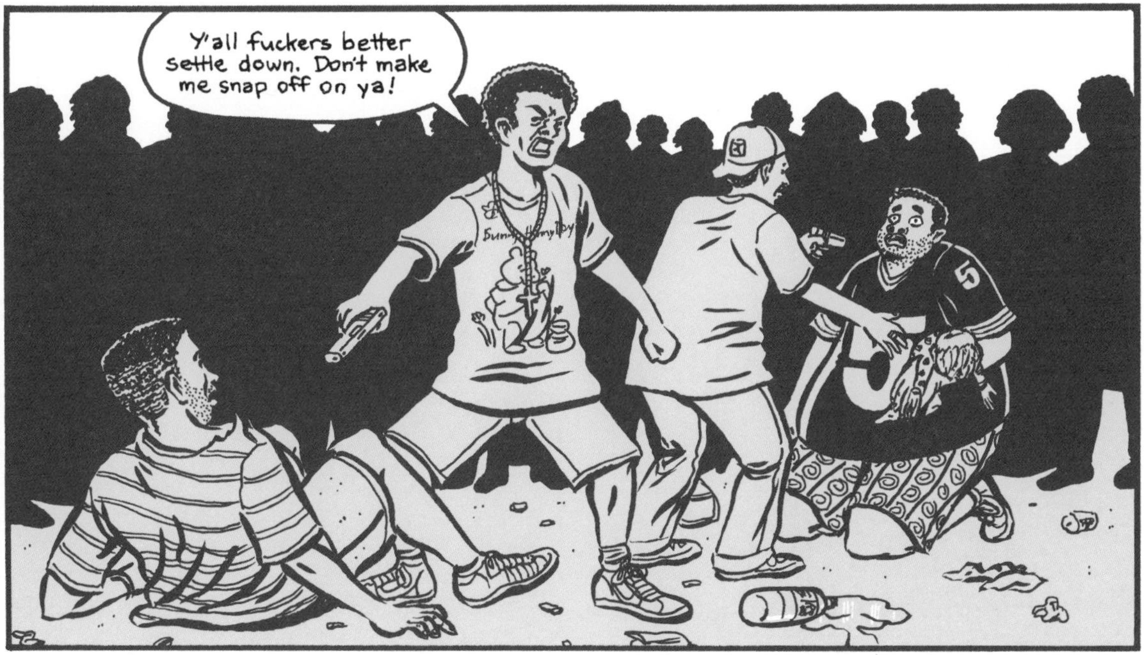
Y'all fuckers better settle down. Don't make me snap off on ya!

THURSDAY 2005
September
1
But... you gotta help me... What am I s'posed to do with her?

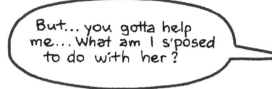

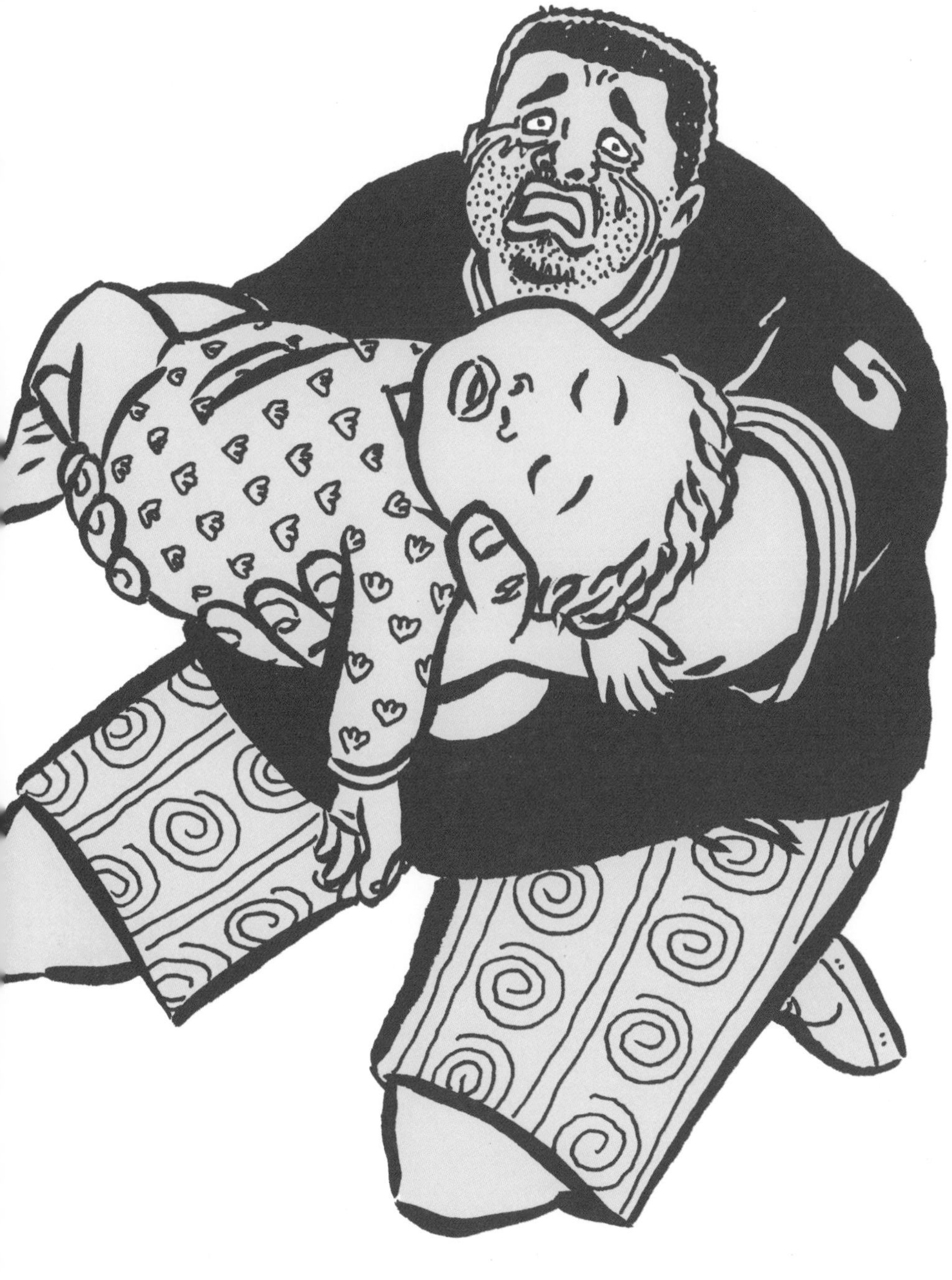

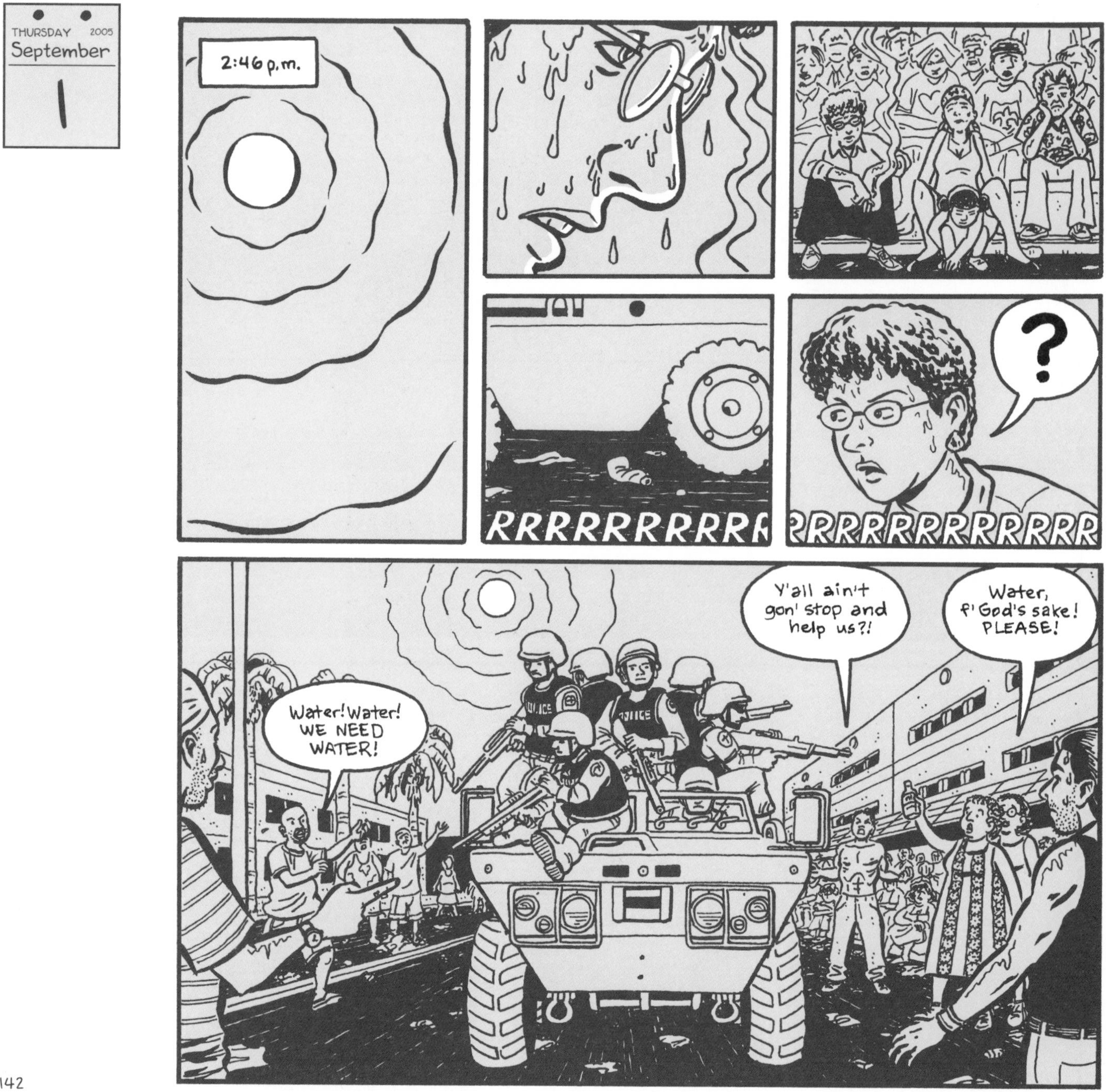
THURSDAY 2005
September
1
2:46 p.m.
RRRRRRRRR
?
RRRRRRRRRRRR
Water! Water! WE NEED WATER!
Y'all ain't gon' stop and help us?!
Water, f' God's sake! PLEASE!

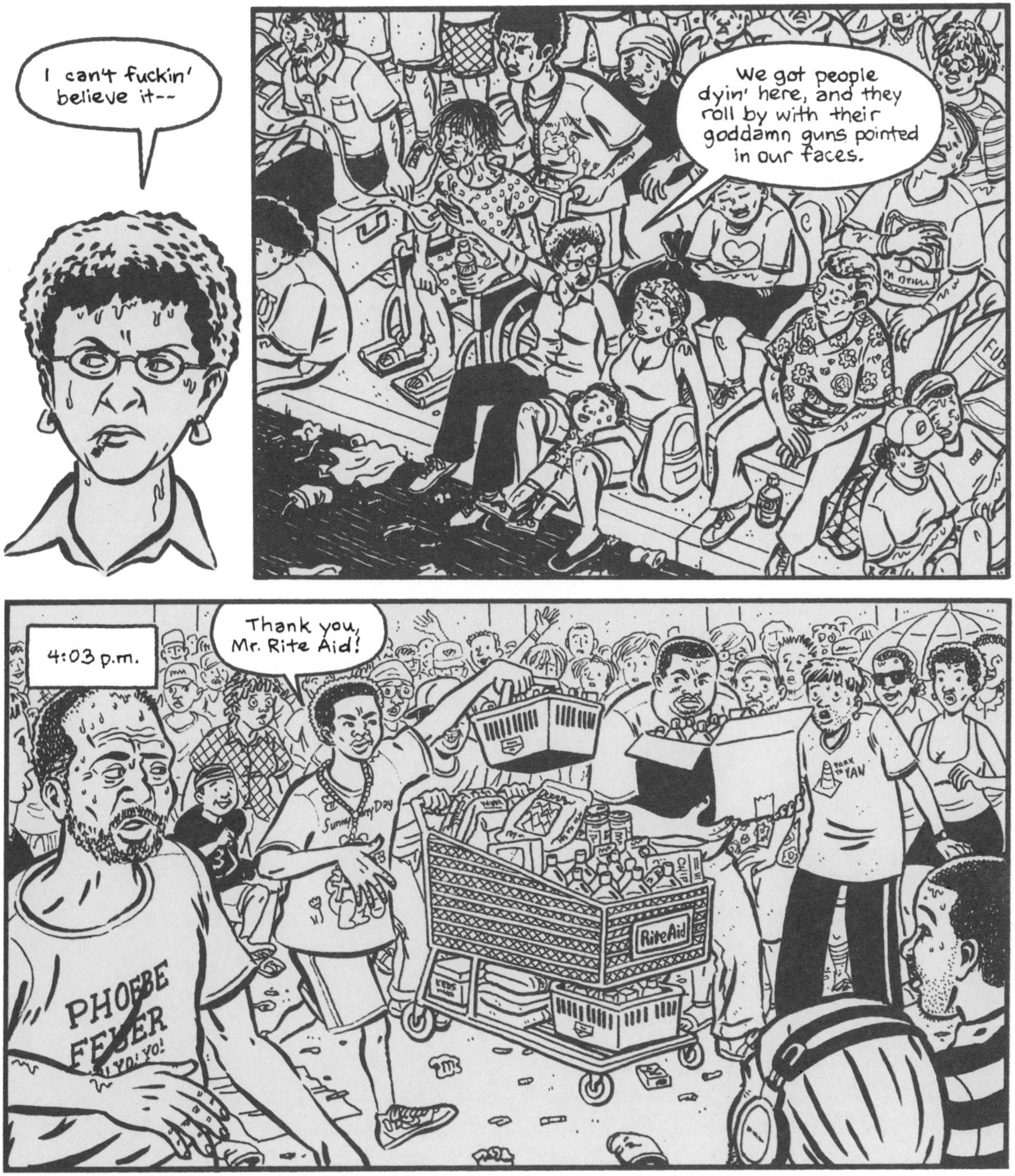
I can't fuckin' believe it--
We got people dyin' here, and they roll by with their goddamn guns pointed in our faces.
4:03 p.m.
Thank you, Mr. Rite Aid!
Rite Aid
PHOEBE FEVER
YO! YO!

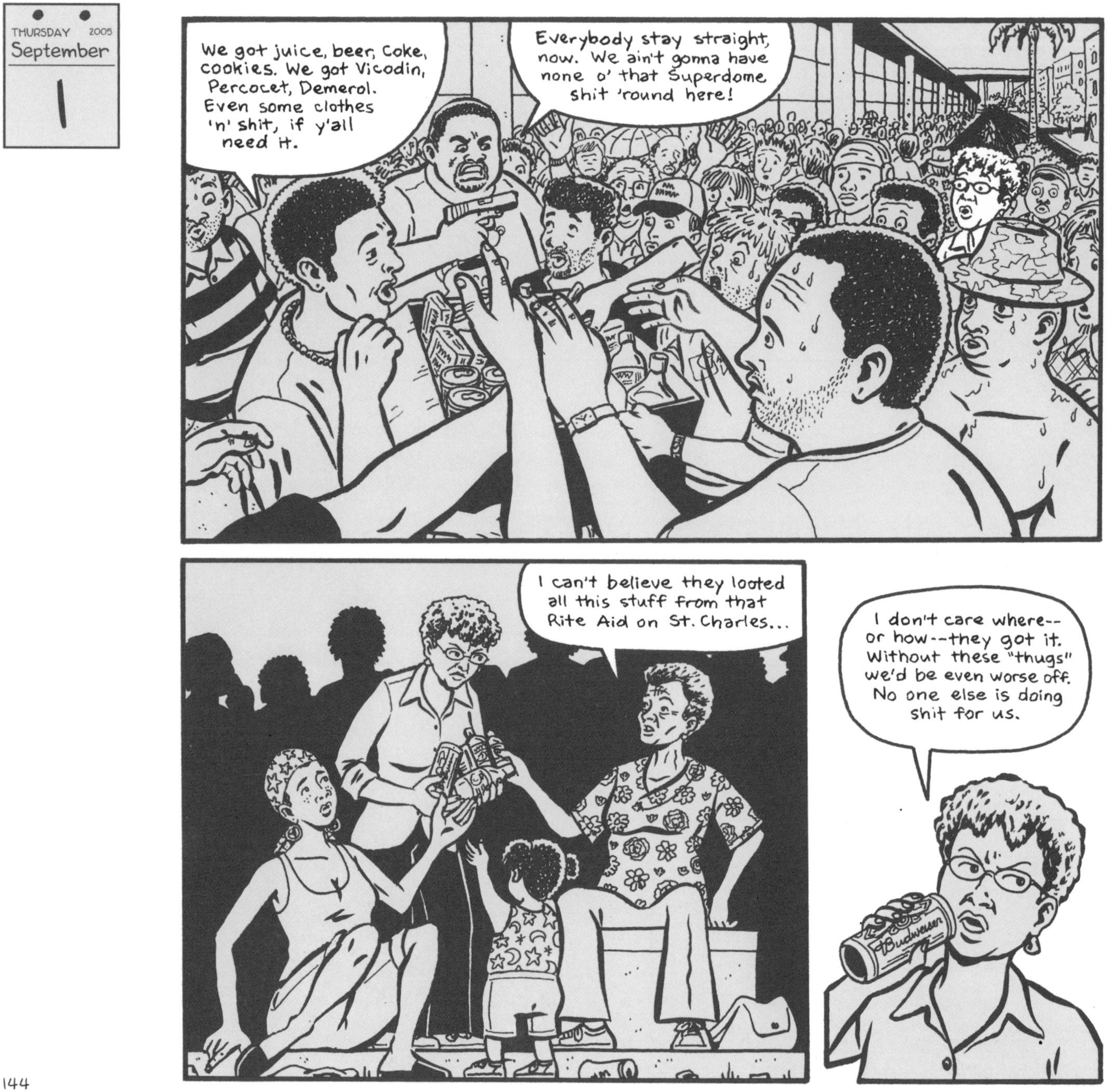
THURSDAY 2005
September
1
We got juice, beer, Coke, cookies. We got Vicodin, Percocet, Demerol. Even some clothes 'n' shit, if y'all need it.
Everybody stay straight, now. We ain't gonna have none o' that Superdome shit 'round here!
I can't believe they looted all this stuff from that Rite Aid on St. Charles...
I don't care where--or how--they got it. Without these "thugs" we'd be even worse off. No one else is doing shit for us.
Budweiser

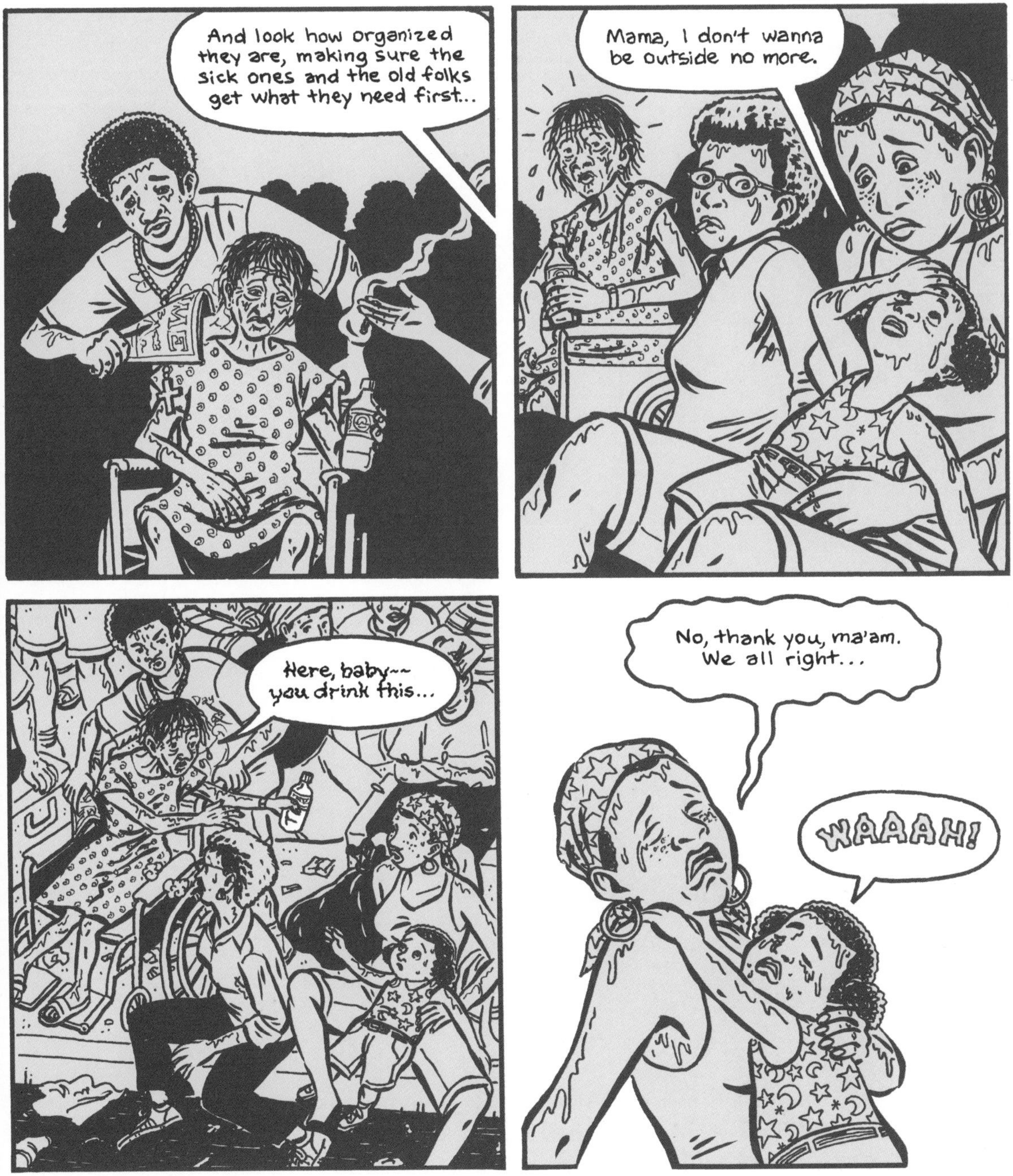
And look how organized they are, making sure the sick ones and the old folks get what they need first...
Mama, I don't wanna be outside no more.
Here, baby-- you drink this...
No, thank you, ma'am. We all right...
WAAAH!

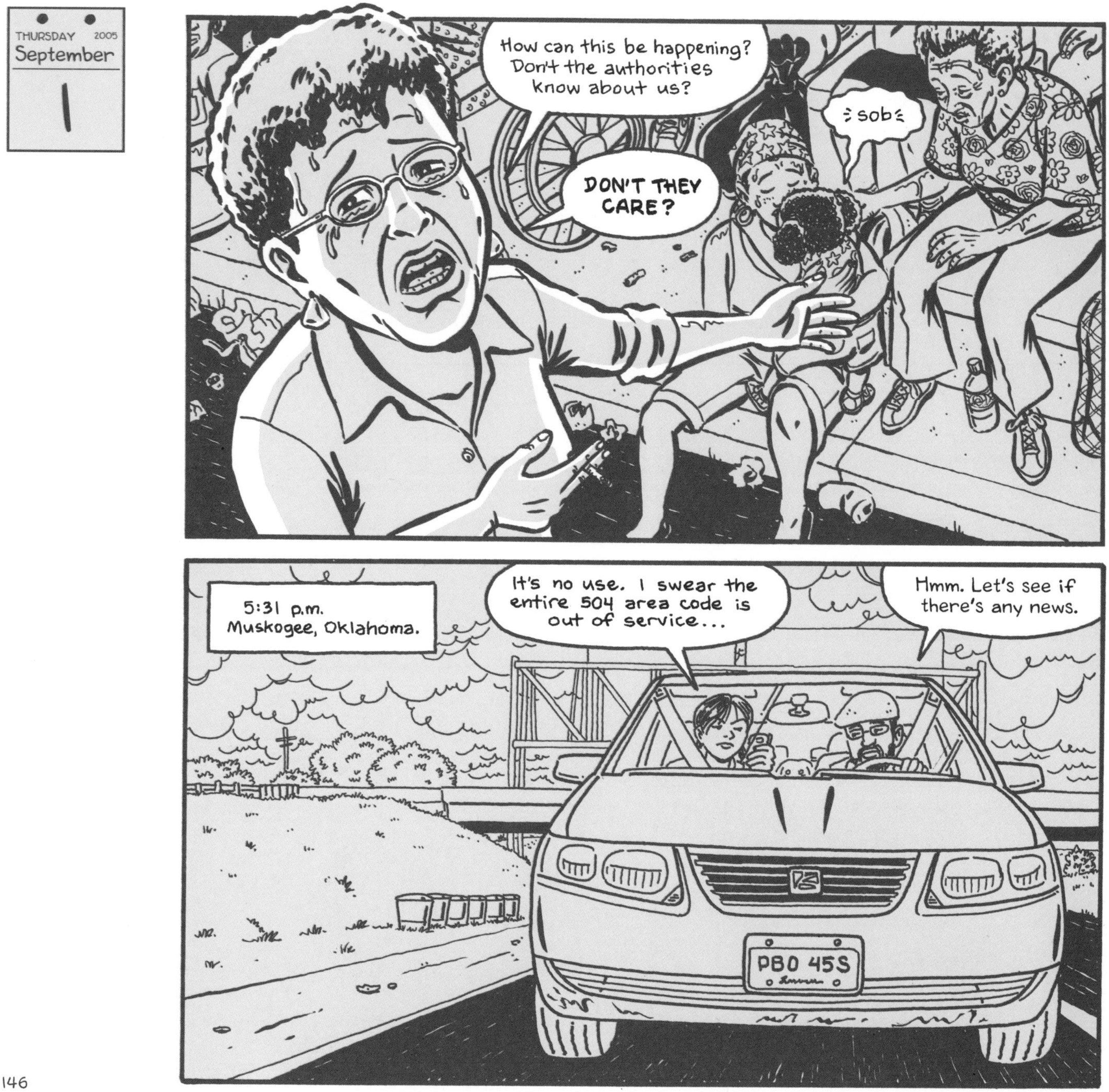
THURSDAY 2005
September
1
How can this be happening? Don't the authorities know about us?
DON'T THEY CARE?
sob
5:31 p.m. Muskogee, Oklahoma.
It's no use. I swear the entire 504 area code is out of service...
Hmm. Let's see if there's any news.
PBO 45S

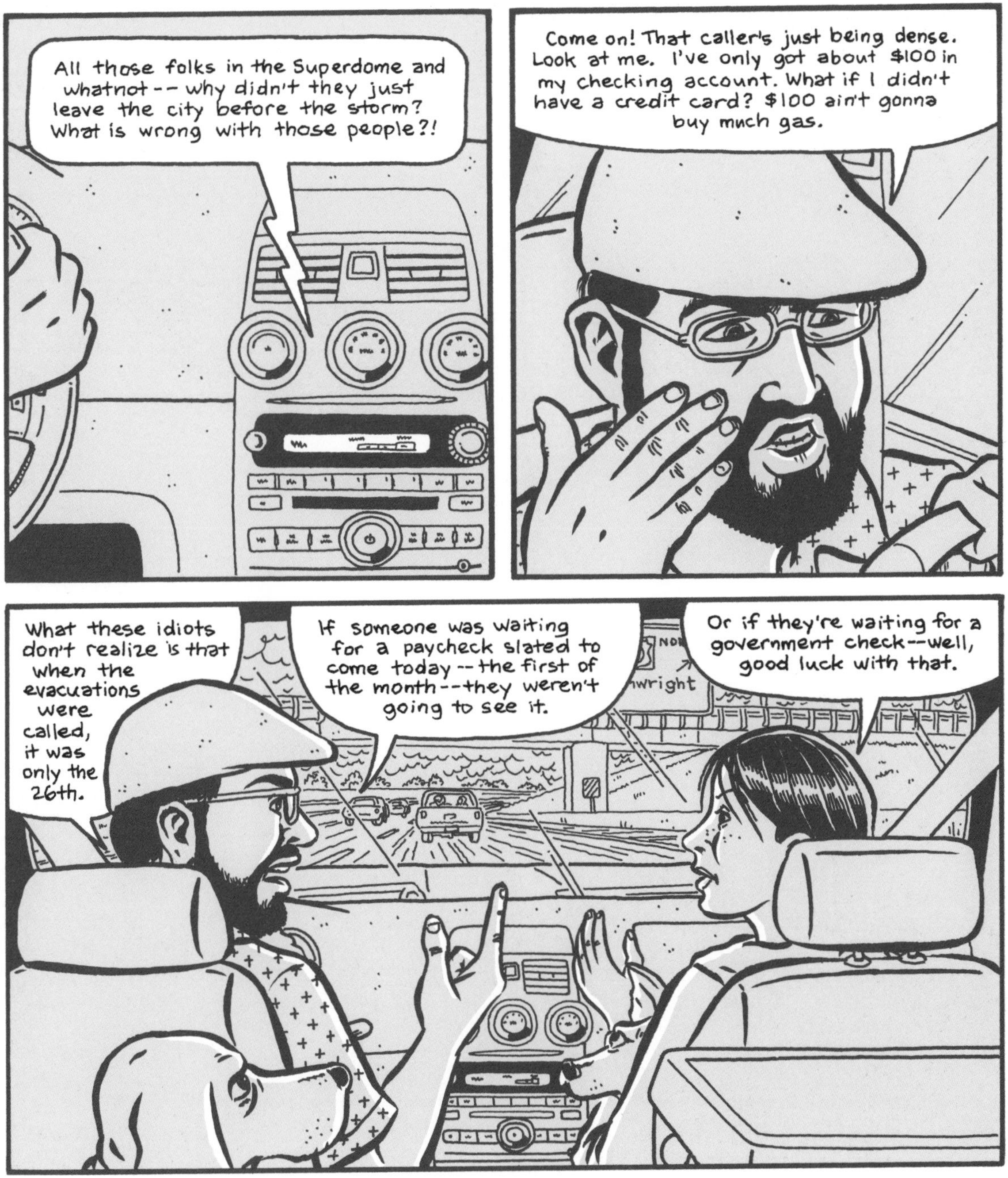
All those folks in the Superdome and whatnot -- why didn't they just leave the city before the storm? What is wrong with those people?!
Come on! That caller's just being dense. Look at me. I've only got about $100 in my checking account. What if I didn't have a credit card? $100 ain't gonna buy much gas.
What these idiots don't realize is that when the evacuations were called, it was only the 26th.
If someone was waiting for a paycheck slated to come today -- the first of the month -- they weren't going to see it.
Or if they're waiting for a government check--well, good luck with that.
nwright

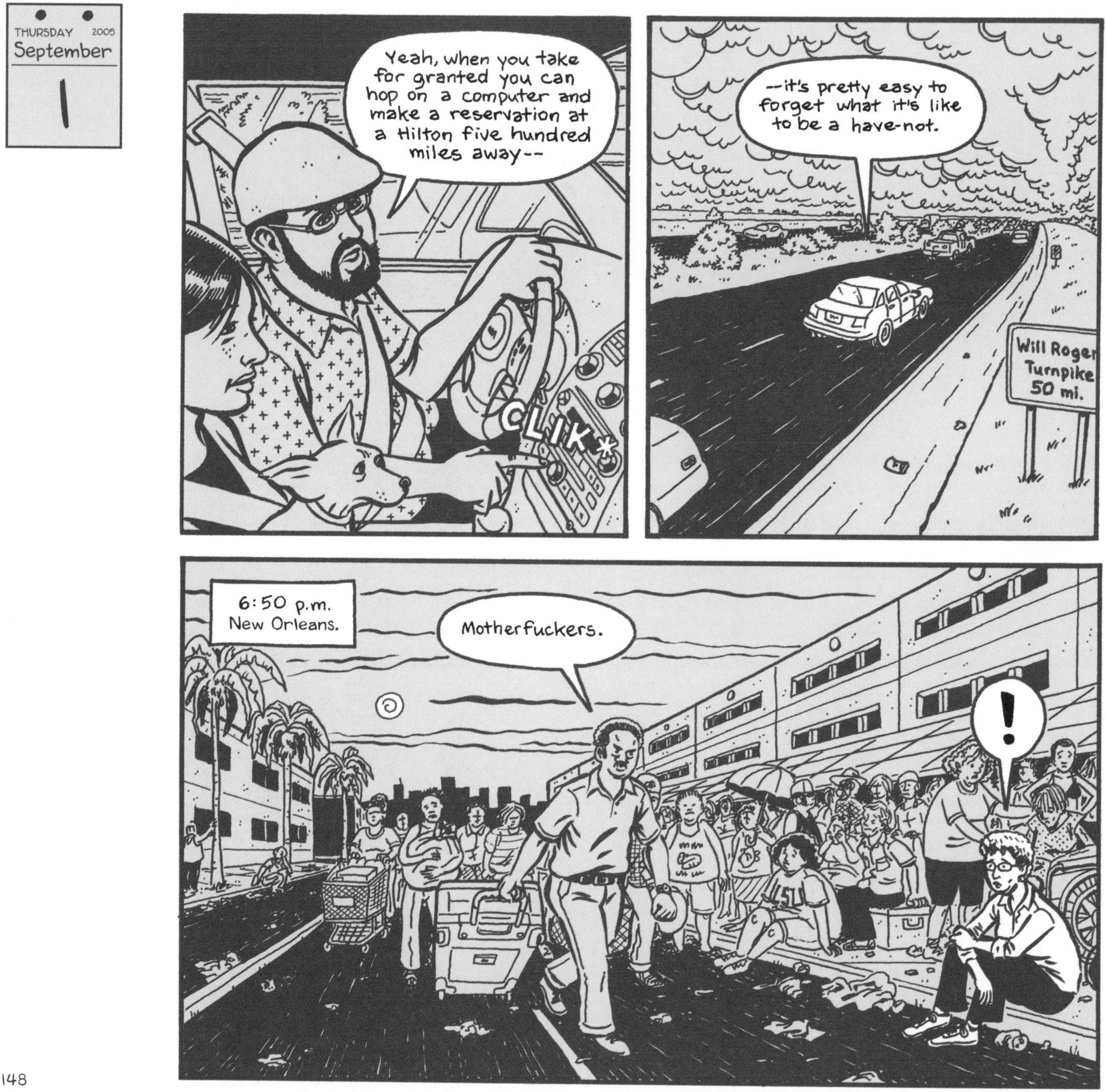
THURSDAY 2005
September
1
Yeah, when you take for granted you can hop on a computer and make a reservation at a Hilton five hundred miles away--
CLIK*
--it's pretty easy to forget what it's like to be a have-not.
Will Roger Turnpike 50 mi.
6:50 p.m. New Orleans.
Motherfuckers.
!

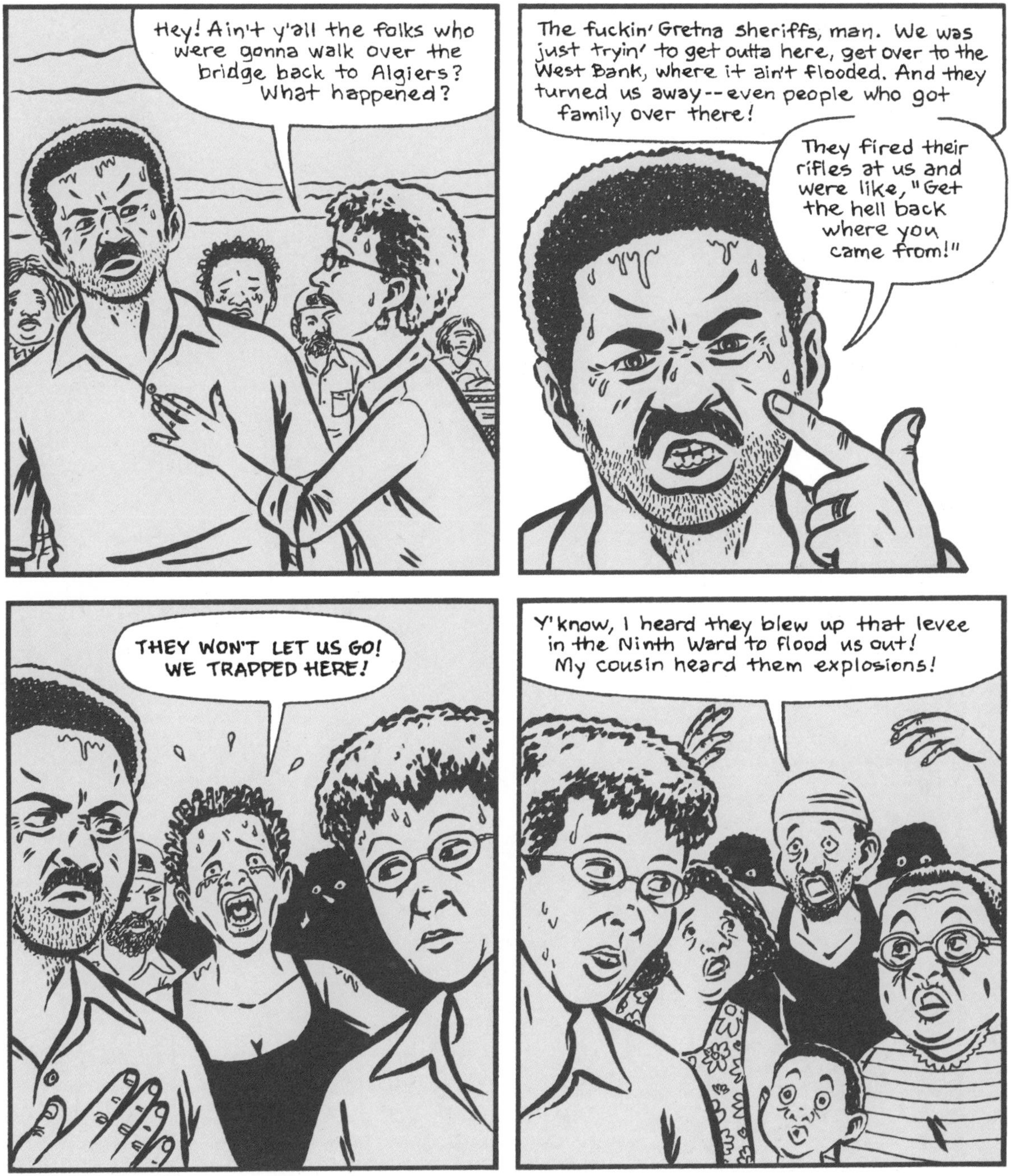
Hey! Ain't y'all the folks who were gonna walk over the bridge back to Algiers? What happened?
The fuckin' Gretna sheriffs, man. We was just tryin' to get outta here, get over to the West Bank, where it ain't flooded. And they turned us away--even people who got family over there!
They fired their rifles at us and were like, "Get the hell back where you came from!"
THEY WON'T LET US GO! WE TRAPPED HERE!
Y'know, I heard they blew up that levee in the Ninth Ward to flood us out! My cousin heard them explosions!

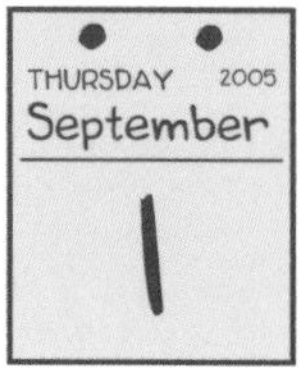
THURSDAY 2005
September
1

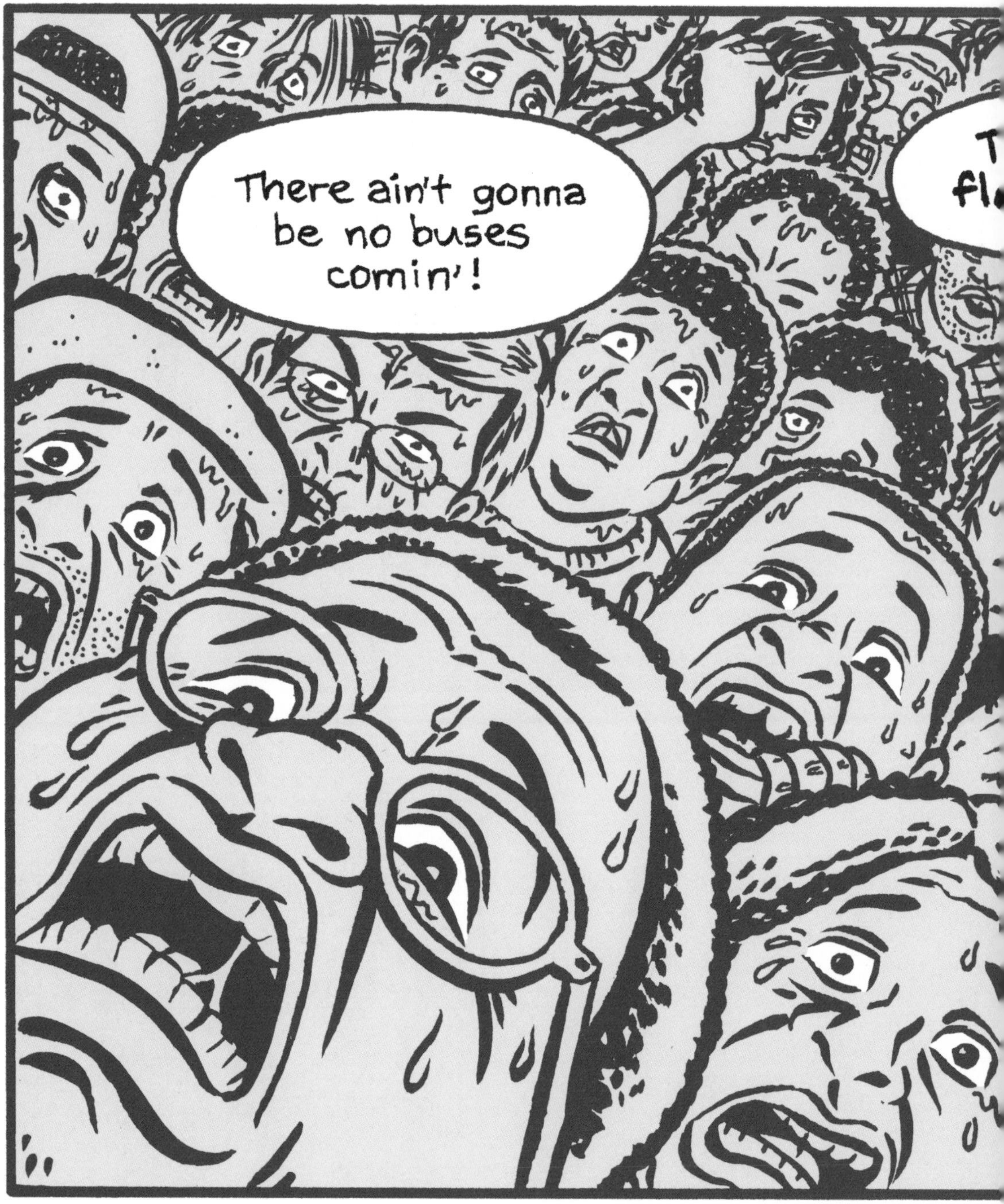
There ain't gonna be no buses comin'!

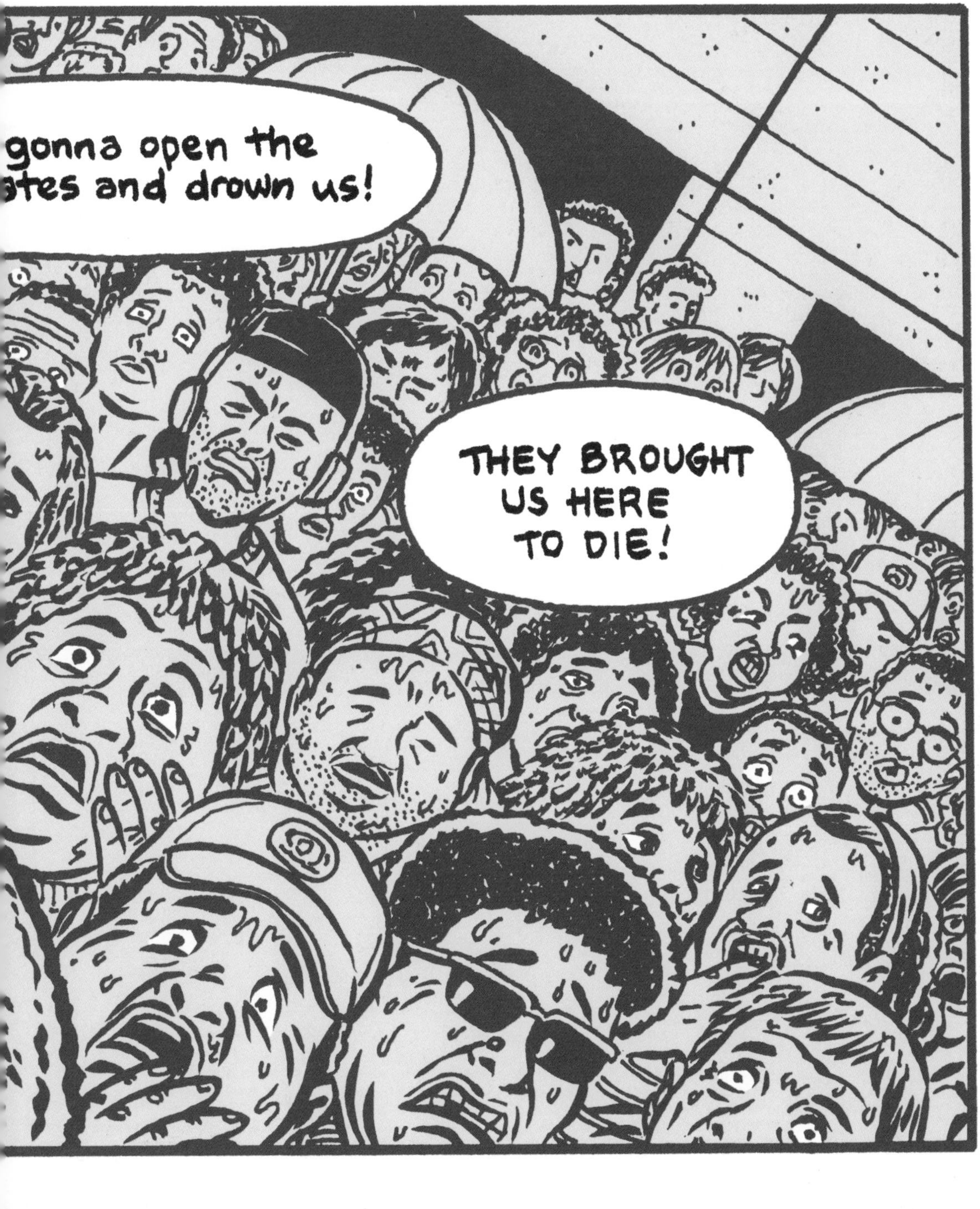
gonna open the
ates and drown us!
THEY BROUGHT US HERE TO DIE!

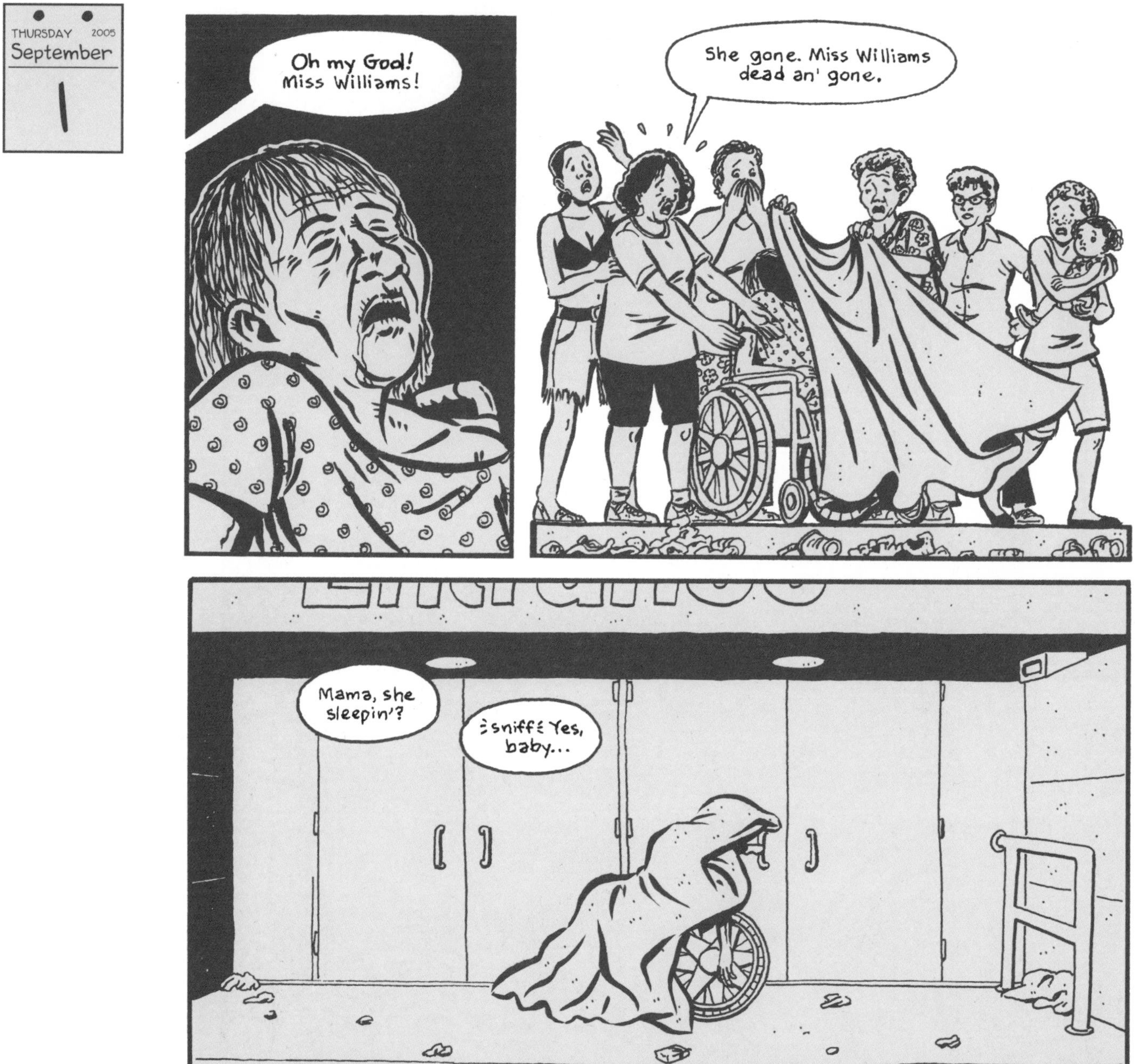

THURSDAY 2005
September
1
Oh my God! Miss Williams!
She gone. Miss Williams dead an' gone.
Mama, she sleepin'?
sniff Yes, baby...

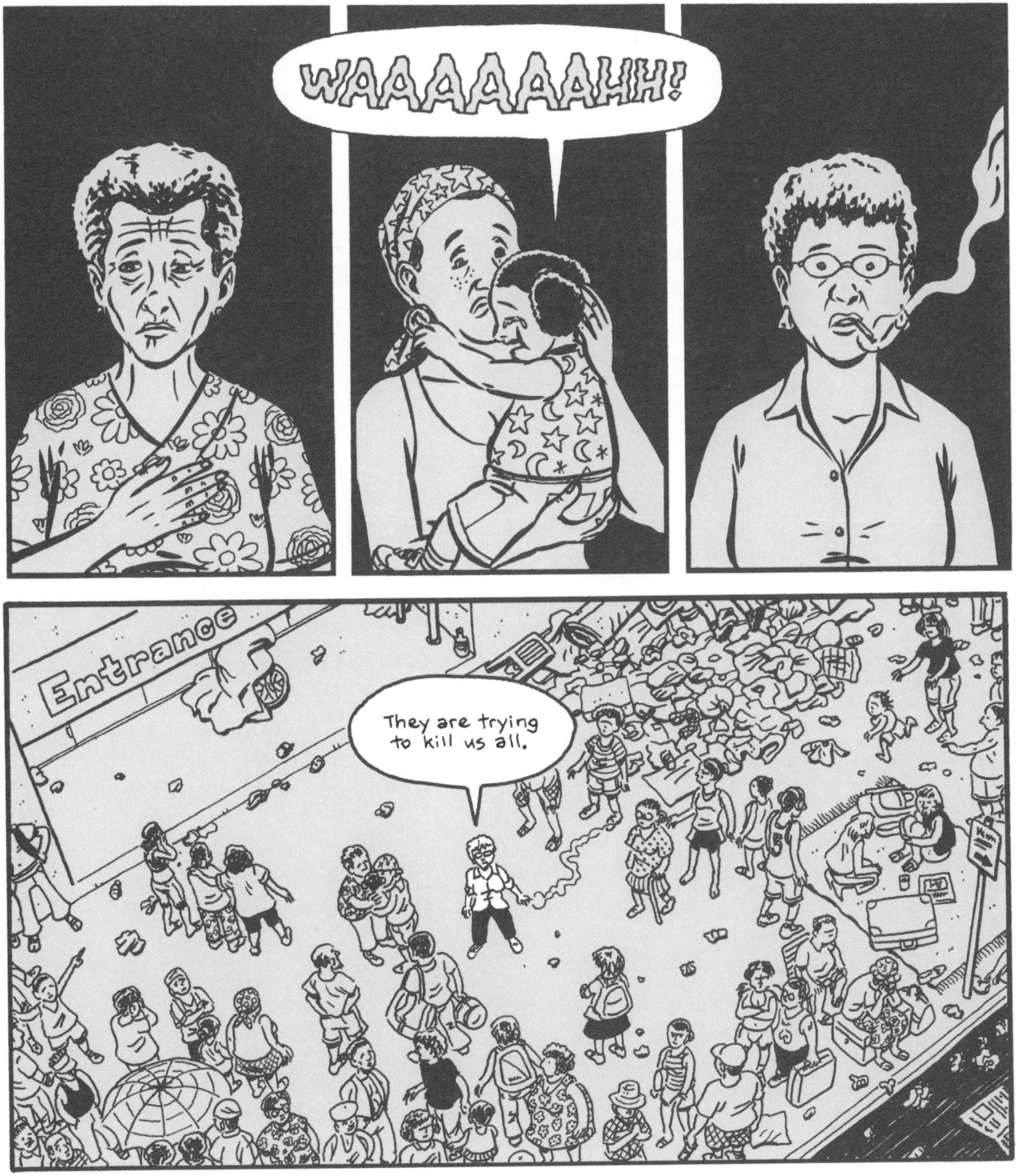
WAAAAAAHH!
Entrance
They are trying to kill us all.

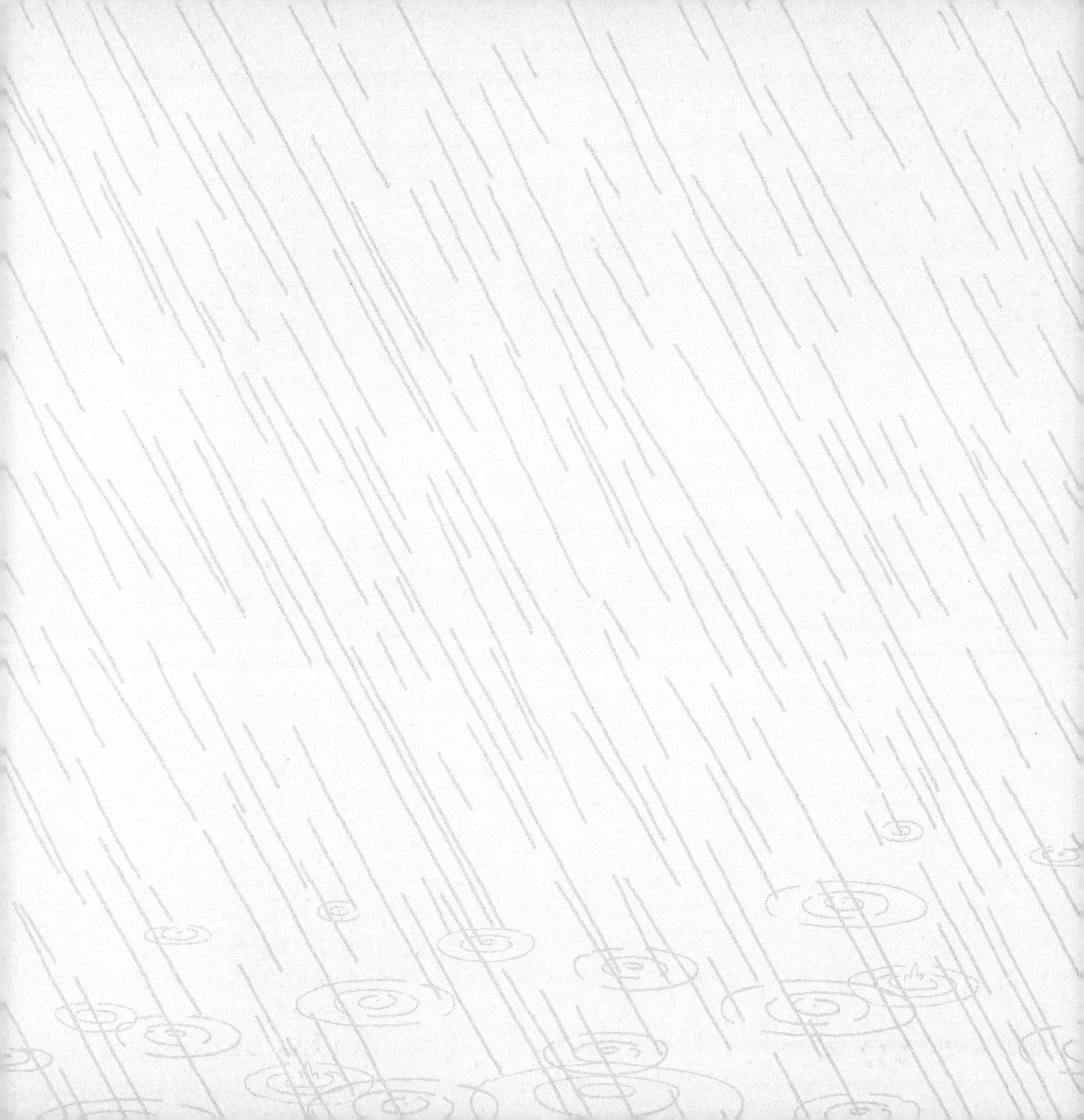

THE DIASPORA

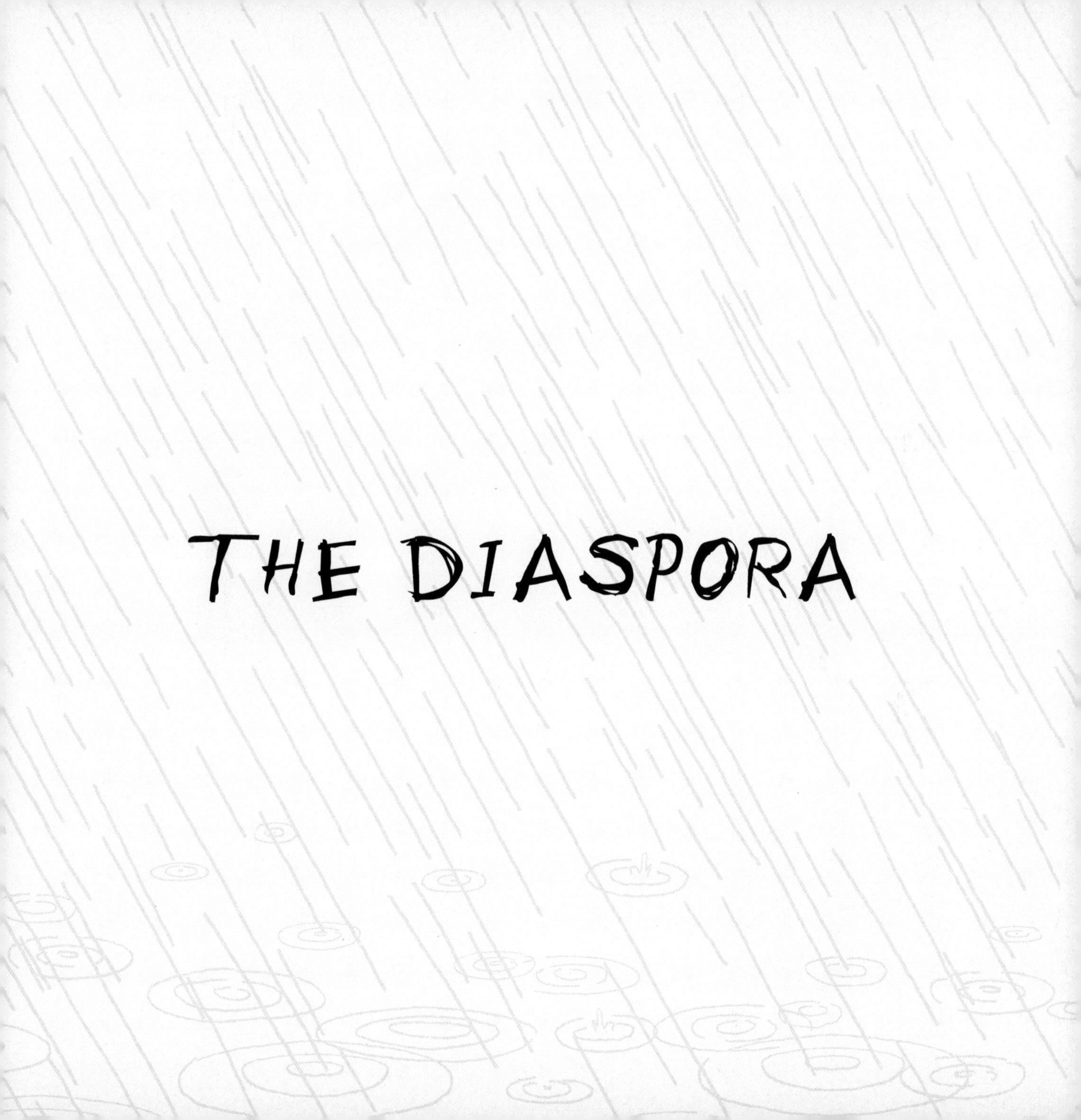

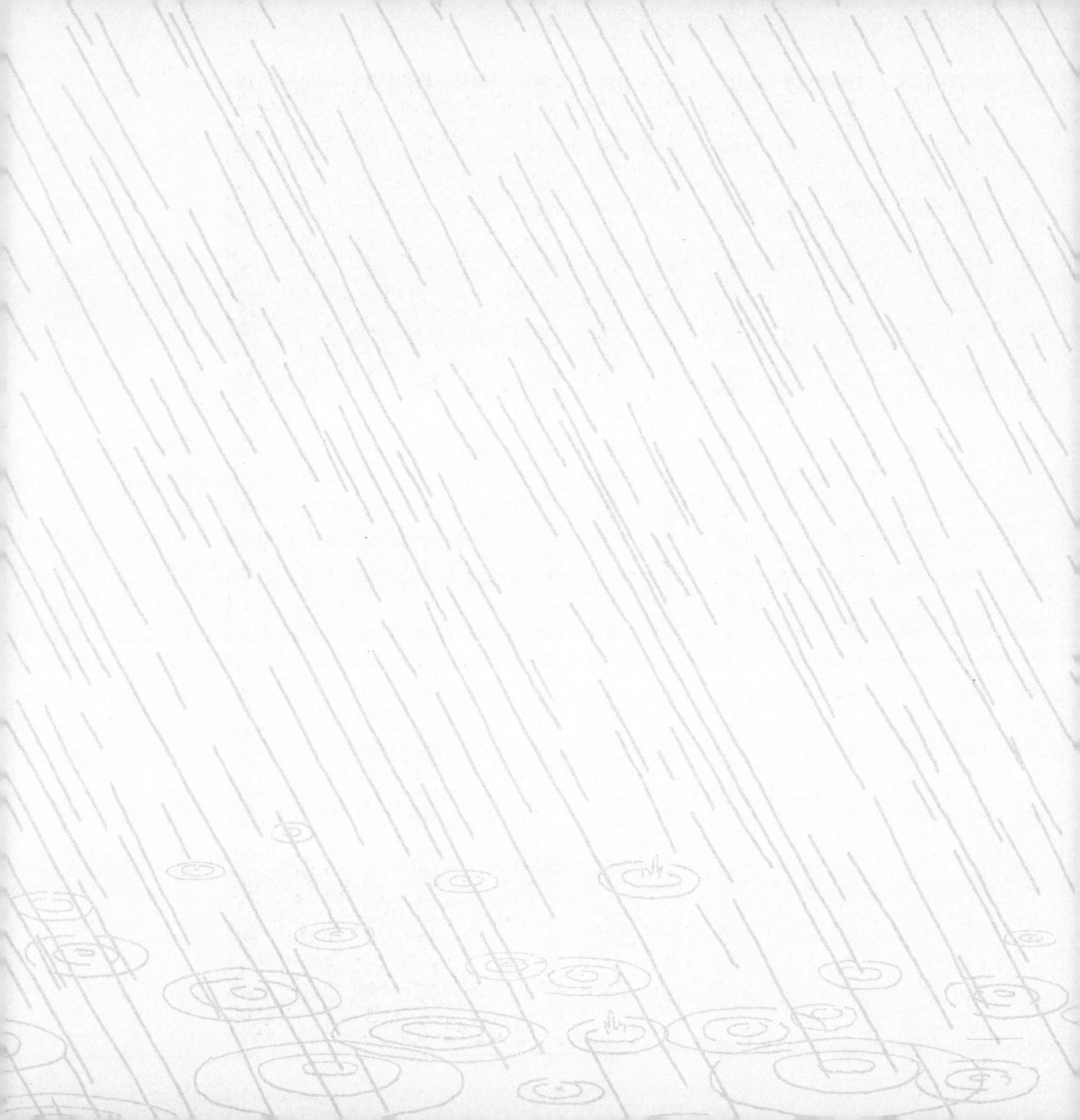

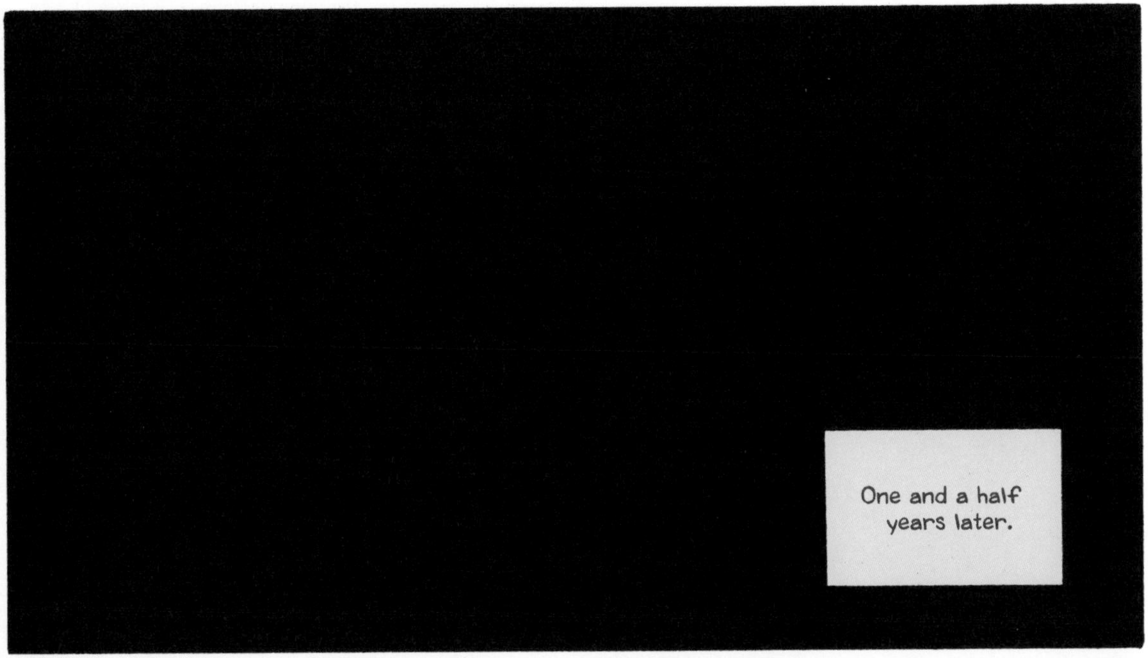
One and a half years later.

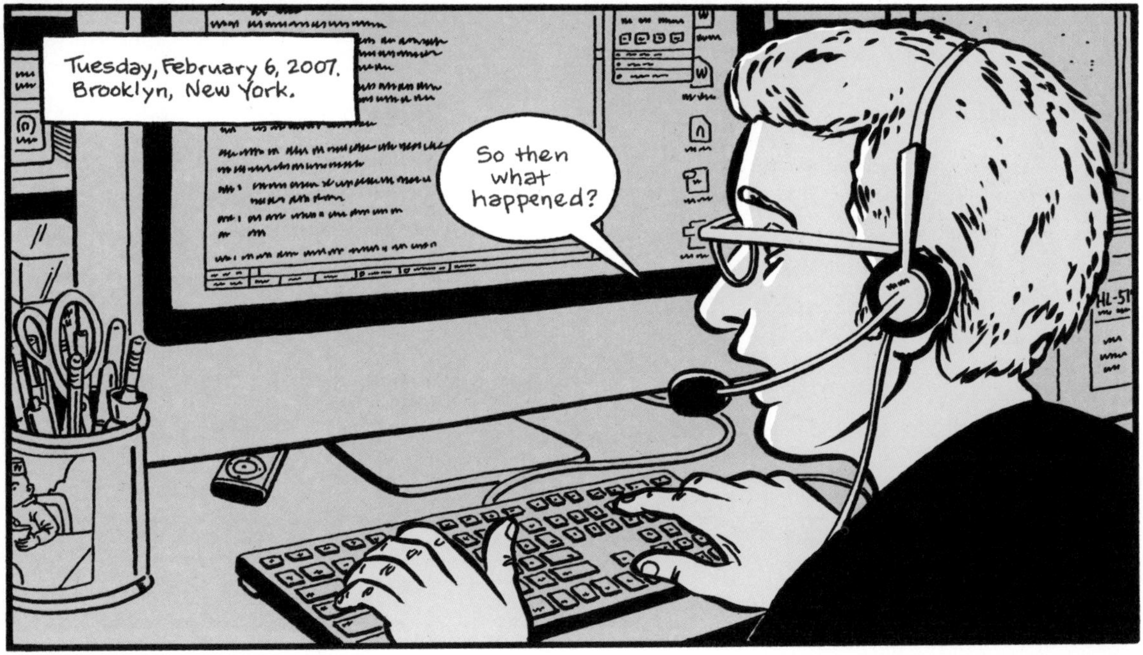
Tuesday, February 6, 2007. Brooklyn, New York.
So then what happened?

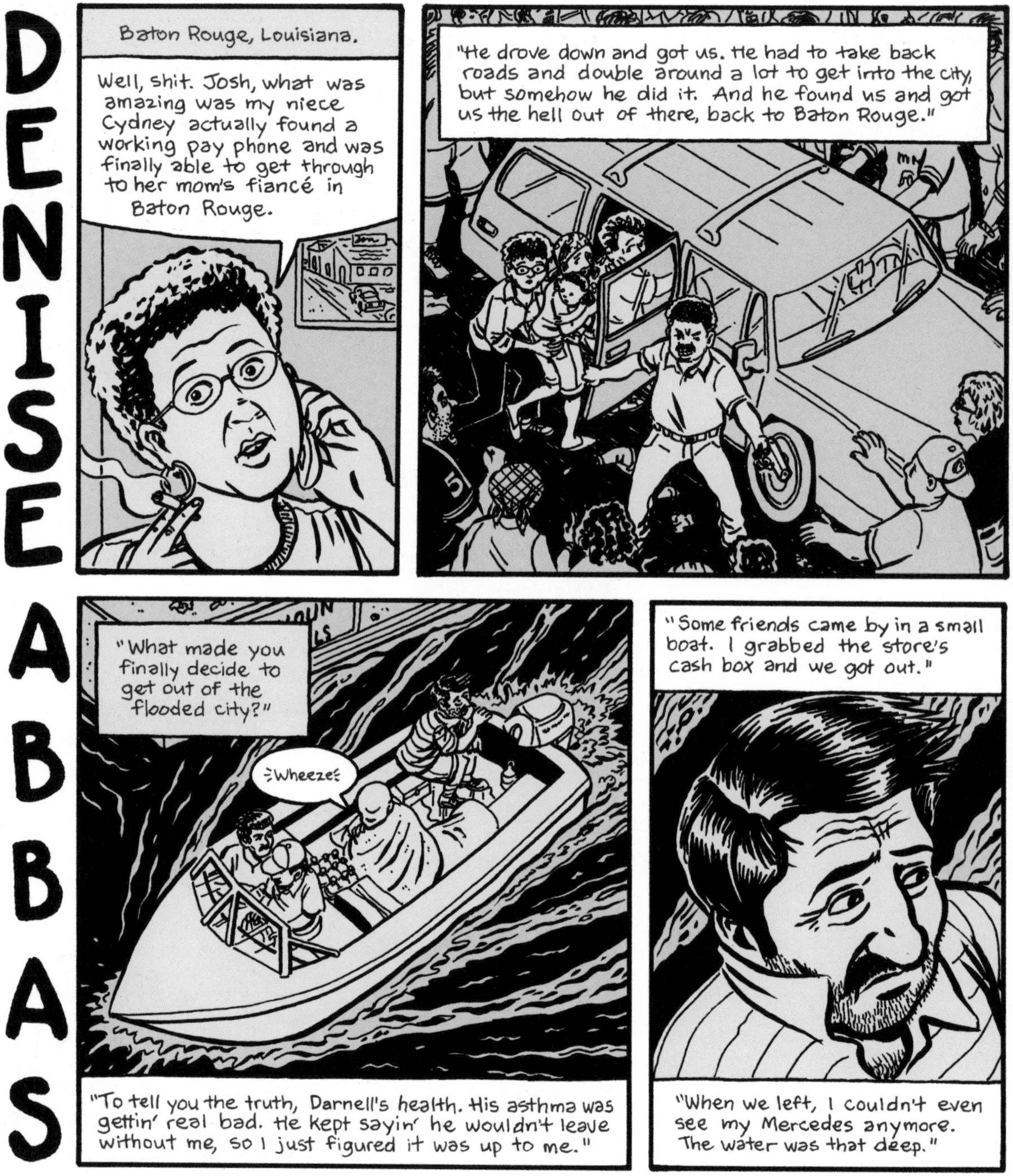
DENISE ABBAS
Baton Rouge, Louisiana.
Well, shit. Josh, what was amazing was my niece Cydney actually found a working pay phone and was finally able to get through to her mom's fiancé in Baton Rouge.
"He drove down and got us. He had to take back roads and double around a lot to get into the city, but somehow he did it. And he found us and got us the hell out of there, back to Baton Rouge."
"What made you finally decide to get out of the flooded city?"
Wheeze
"To tell you the truth, Darnell's health. His asthma was gettin' real bad. He kept sayin' he wouldn't leave without me, so I just figured it was up to me."
"Some friends came by in a small boat. I grabbed the store's cash box and we got out."
"When we left, I couldn't even see my Mercedes anymore. The water was that deep."

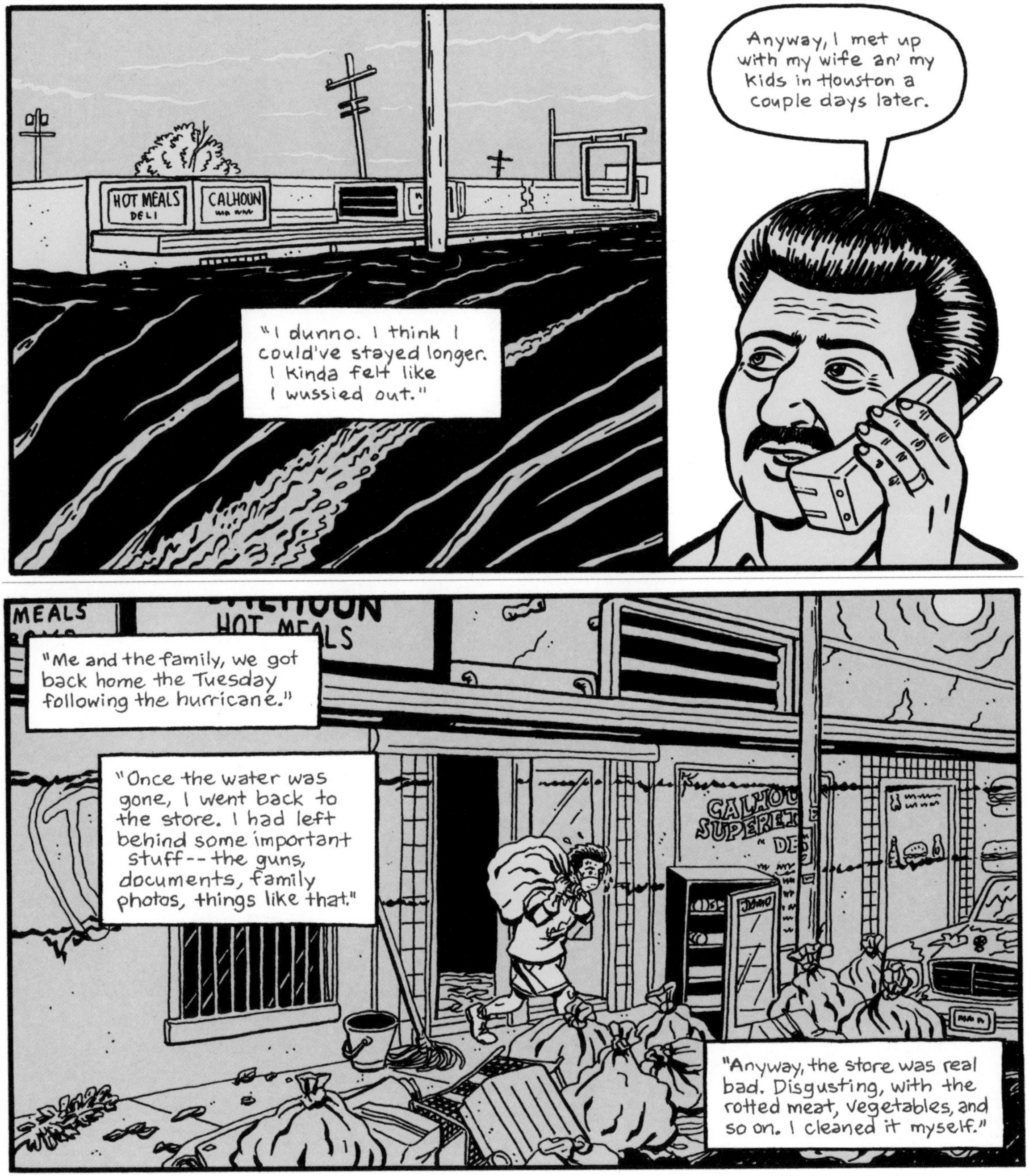
HOT MEALS
DELI
CALHOUN
"I dunno. I think I could've stayed longer. I kinda felt like I wussied out."
Anyway, I met up with my wife an' my kids in Houston a couple days later.
MEALS
HOT MEALS
"Me and the family, we got back home the Tuesday following the hurricane."
"Once the water was gone, I went back to the store. I had left behind some important stuff -- the guns, documents, family photos, things like that."
"Anyway, the store was real bad. Disgusting, with the rotted meat, vegetables, and so on. I cleaned it myself."

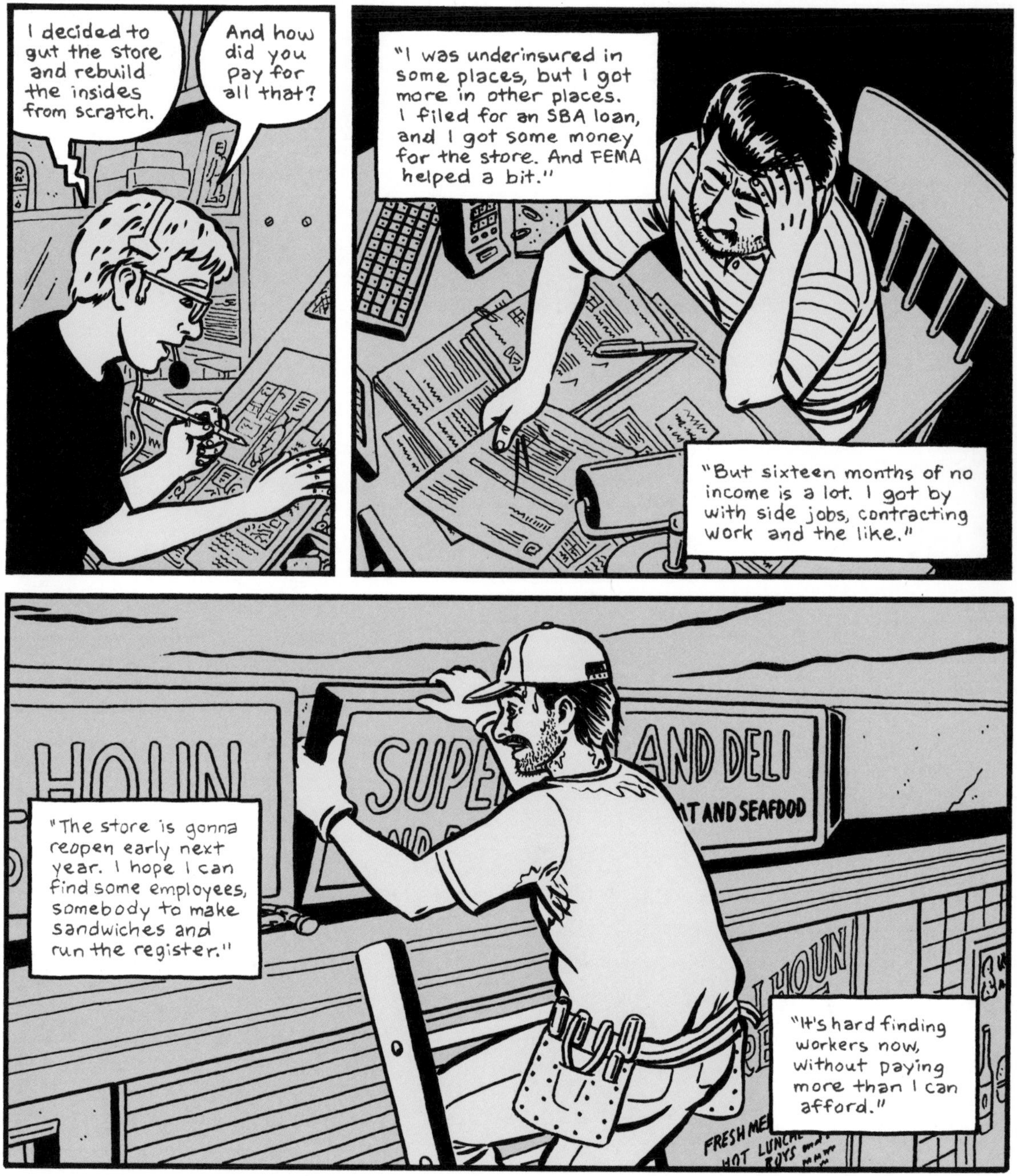
I decided to gut the store and rebuild the insides from scratch.
And how did you pay for all that?
"I was underinsured in some places, but I got more in other places. I filed for an SBA loan, and I got some money for the store. And FEMA helped a bit."
"But sixteen months of no income is a lot. I got by with side jobs, contracting work and the like."
AND DELI
"The store is gonna reopen early next year. I hope I can find some employees, somebody to make sandwiches and run the register."
"It's hard finding workers now, without paying more than I can afford."

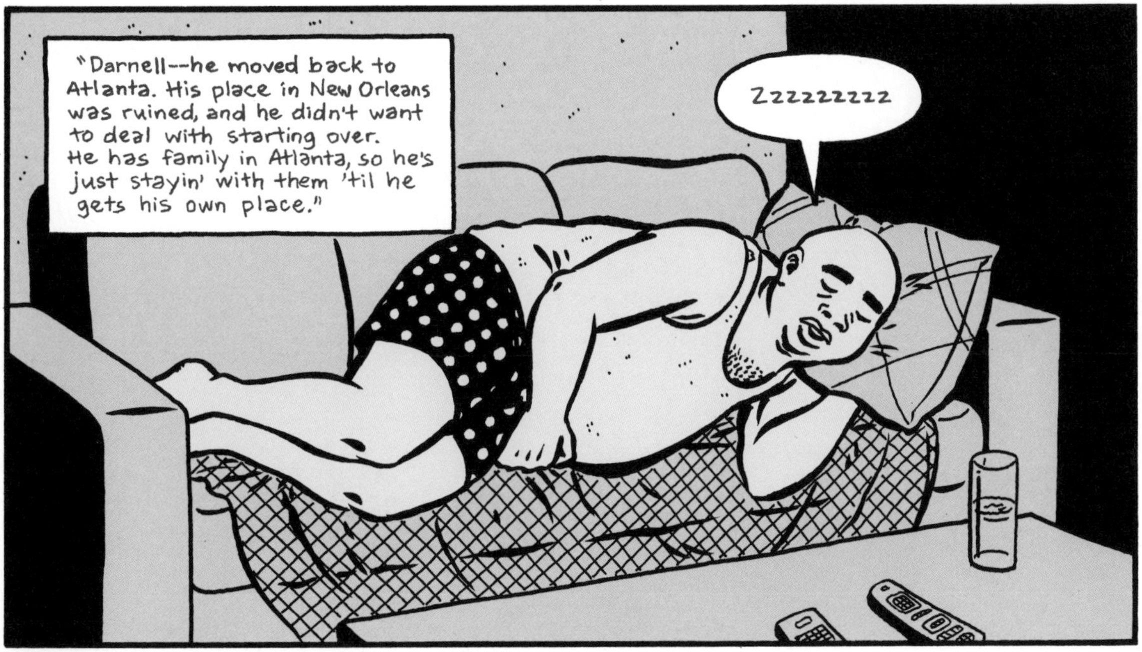
"Darnell--he moved back to Atlanta. His place in New Orleans was ruined, and he didn't want to deal with starting over. He has family in Atlanta, so he's just stayin' with them 'til he gets his own place."
Zzzzzzzzz

THE DOCTOR

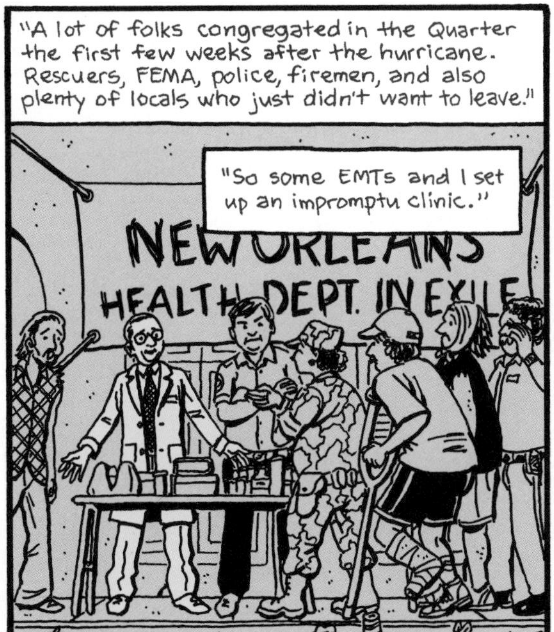
"A lot of folks congregated in the Quarter the first few weeks after the hurricane. Rescuers, FEMA, police, firemen, and also plenty of locals who just didn't want to leave."
"So some EMTs and I set up an impromptu clinic."
NEW ORLEANS
HEALTH DEPT. IN EXILE

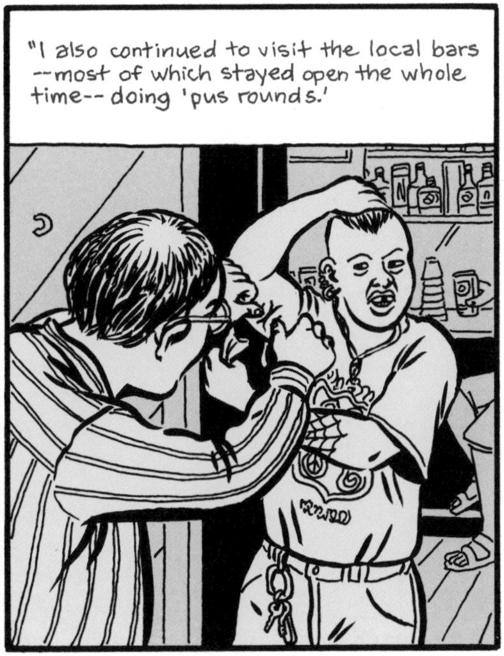
"I also continued to visit the local bars --most of which stayed open the whole time-- doing 'pus rounds.'

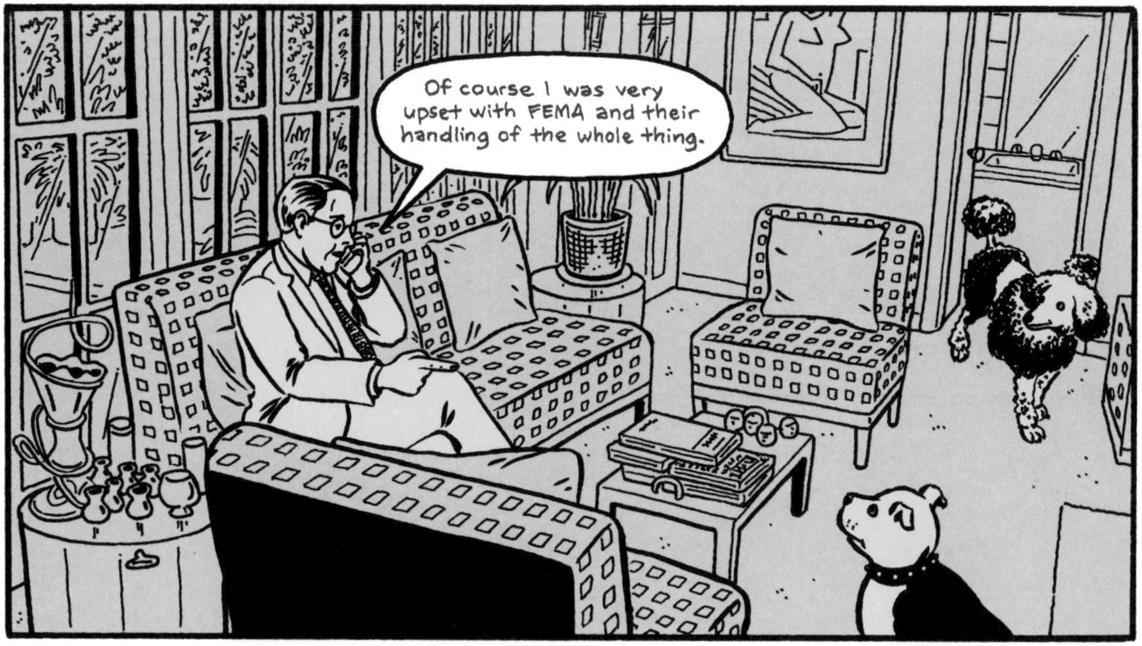
Of course I was very upset with FEMA and their handling of the whole thing.

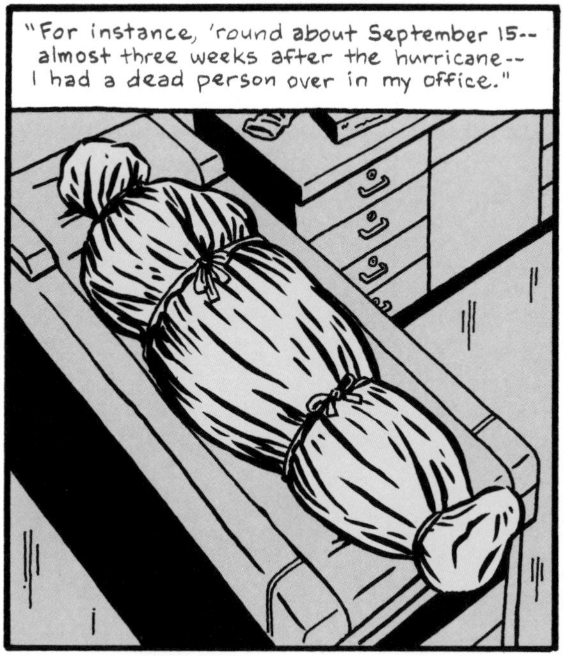
"For instance, 'round about September 15--almost three weeks after the hurricane--I had a dead person over in my office."

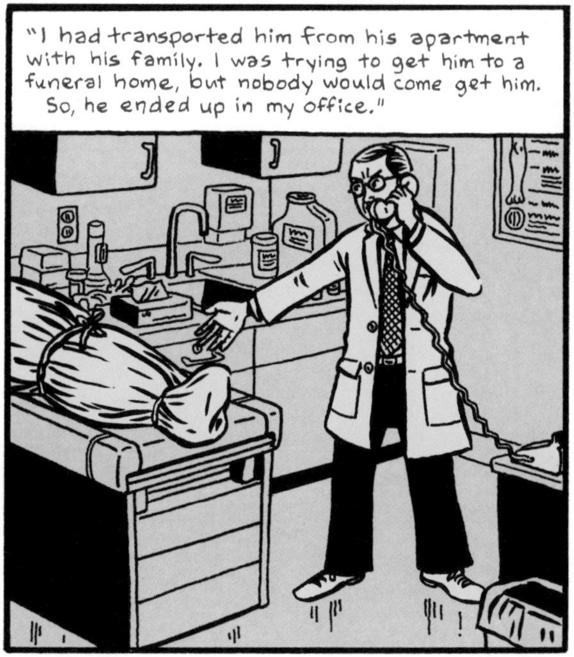
"I had transported him from his apartment with his family. I was trying to get him to a funeral home, but nobody would come get him. So, he ended up in my office."

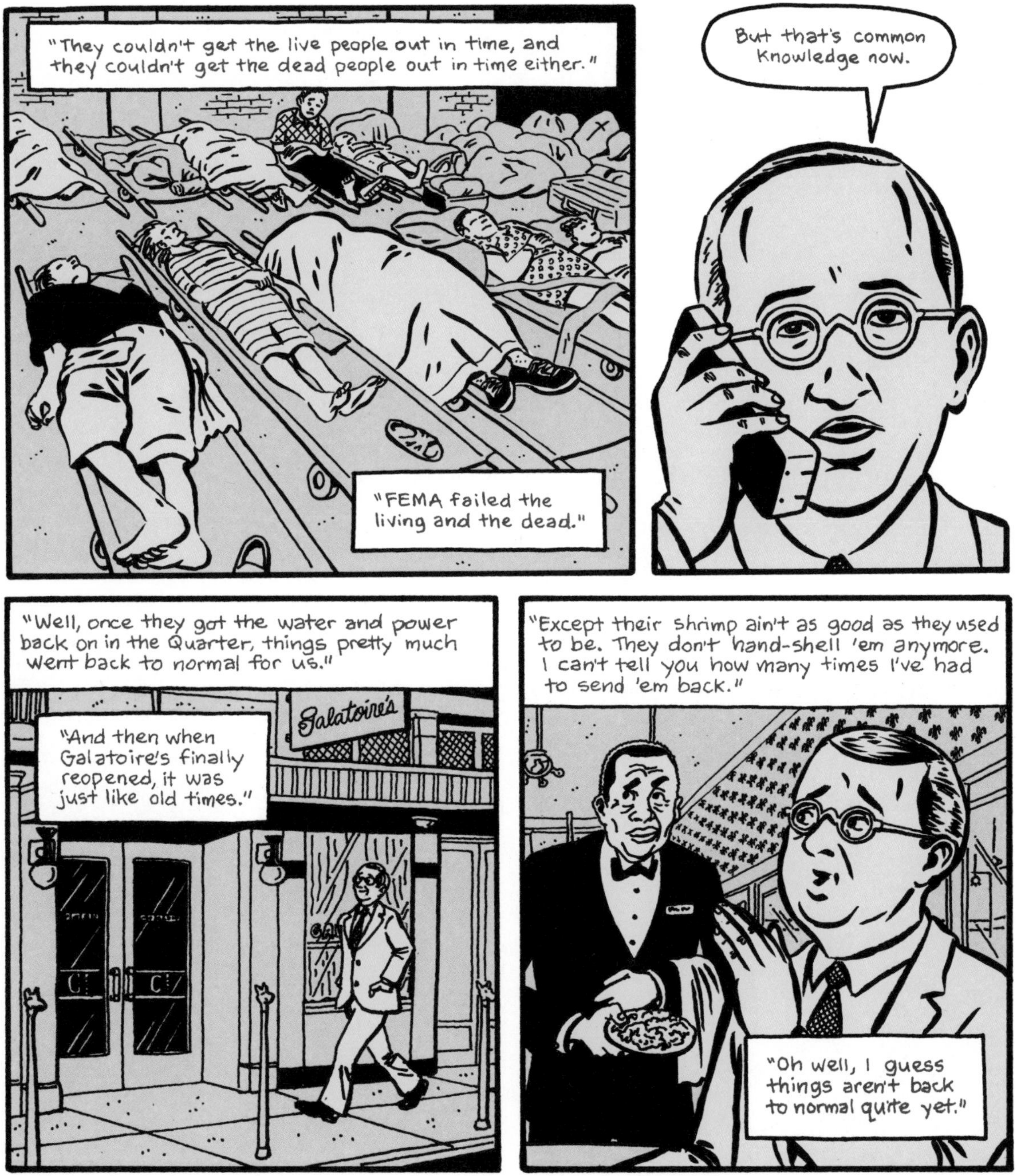
"They couldn't get the live people out in time, and they couldn't get the dead people out in time either."
"FEMA failed the living and the dead."
But that's common knowledge now.
"Well, once they got the water and power back on in the Quarter, things pretty much went back to normal for us."
Galatoire's
"And then when Galatoire's finally reopened, it was just like old times."
"Except their shrimp ain't as good as they used to be. They don't hand-shell 'em anymore. I can't tell you how many times I've had to send 'em back."
"Oh well, I guess things aren't back to normal quite yet."

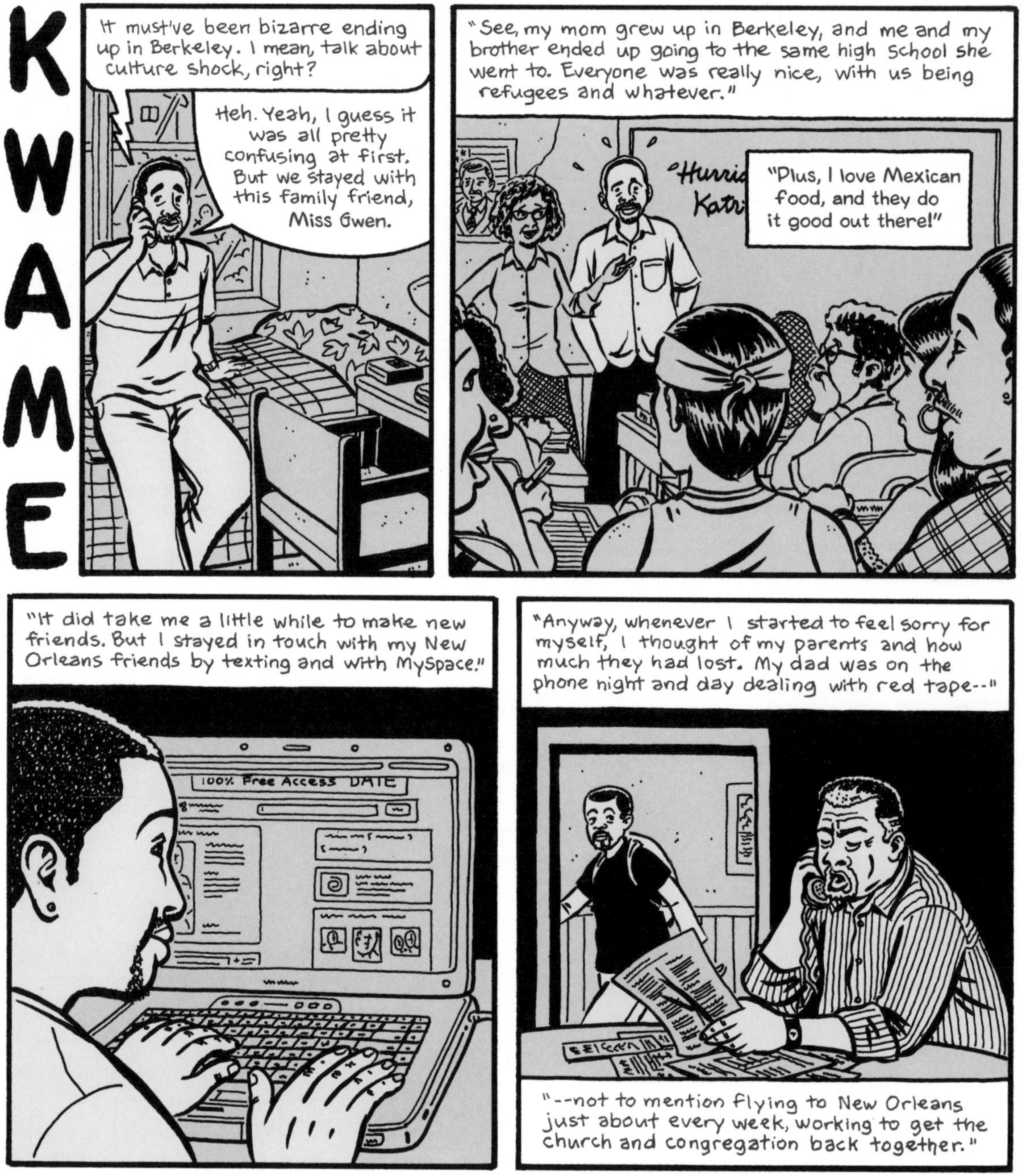
KWAME
It must've been bizarre ending up in Berkeley. I mean, talk about culture shock, right?
Heh. Yeah, I guess it was all pretty confusing at first. But we stayed with this family friend, Miss Gwen.
"See, my mom grew up in Berkeley, and me and my brother ended up going to the same high school she went to. Everyone was really nice, with us being refugees and whatever."
"Plus, I love Mexican food, and they do it good out there!"
"It did take me a little while to make new friends. But I stayed in touch with my New Orleans friends by texting and with MySpace."
100% Free Access DATE
"Anyway, whenever I started to feel sorry for myself, I thought of my parents and how much they had lost. My dad was on the phone night and day dealing with red tape--"
"--not to mention flying to New Orleans just about every week, working to get the church and congregation back together."

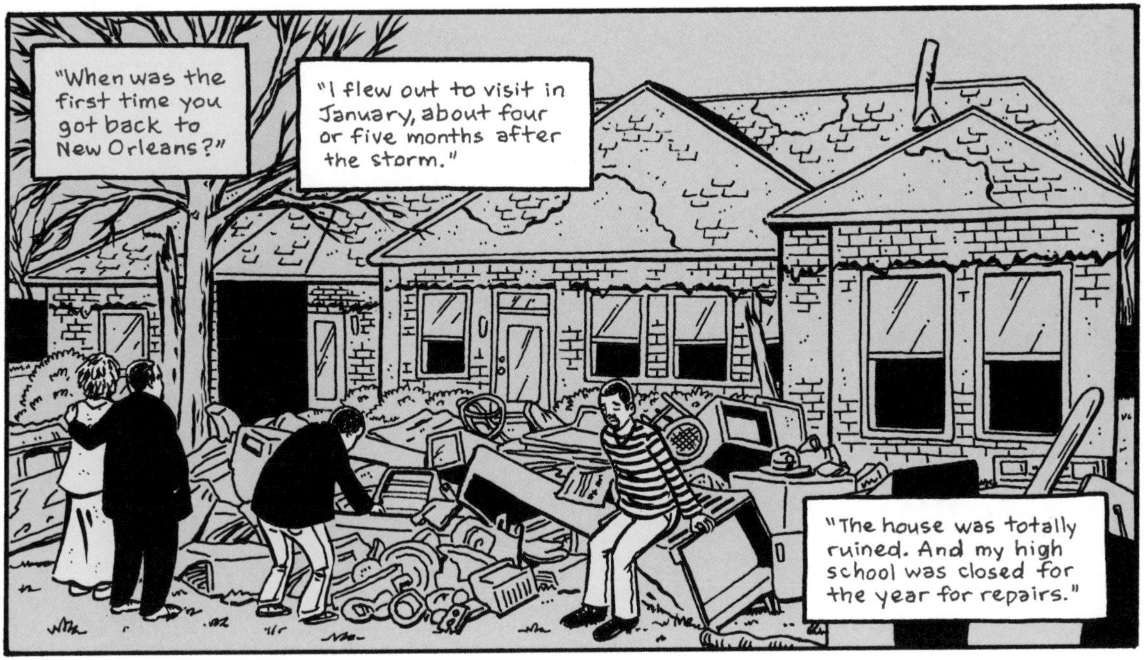
"When was the first time you got back to New Orleans?"
"I flew out to visit in January, about four or five months after the storm."
"The house was totally ruined. And my high school was closed for the year for repairs."

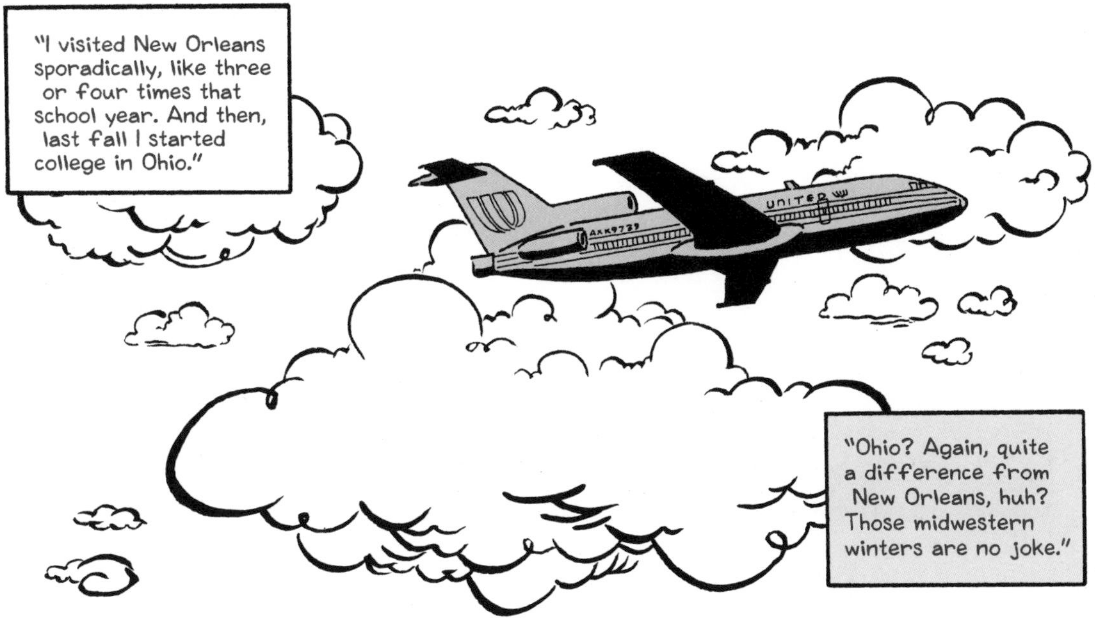
"I visited New Orleans sporadically, like three or four times that school year. And then, last fall I started college in Ohio."
UNITED
"Ohio? Again, quite a difference from New Orleans, huh? Those midwestern winters are no joke."

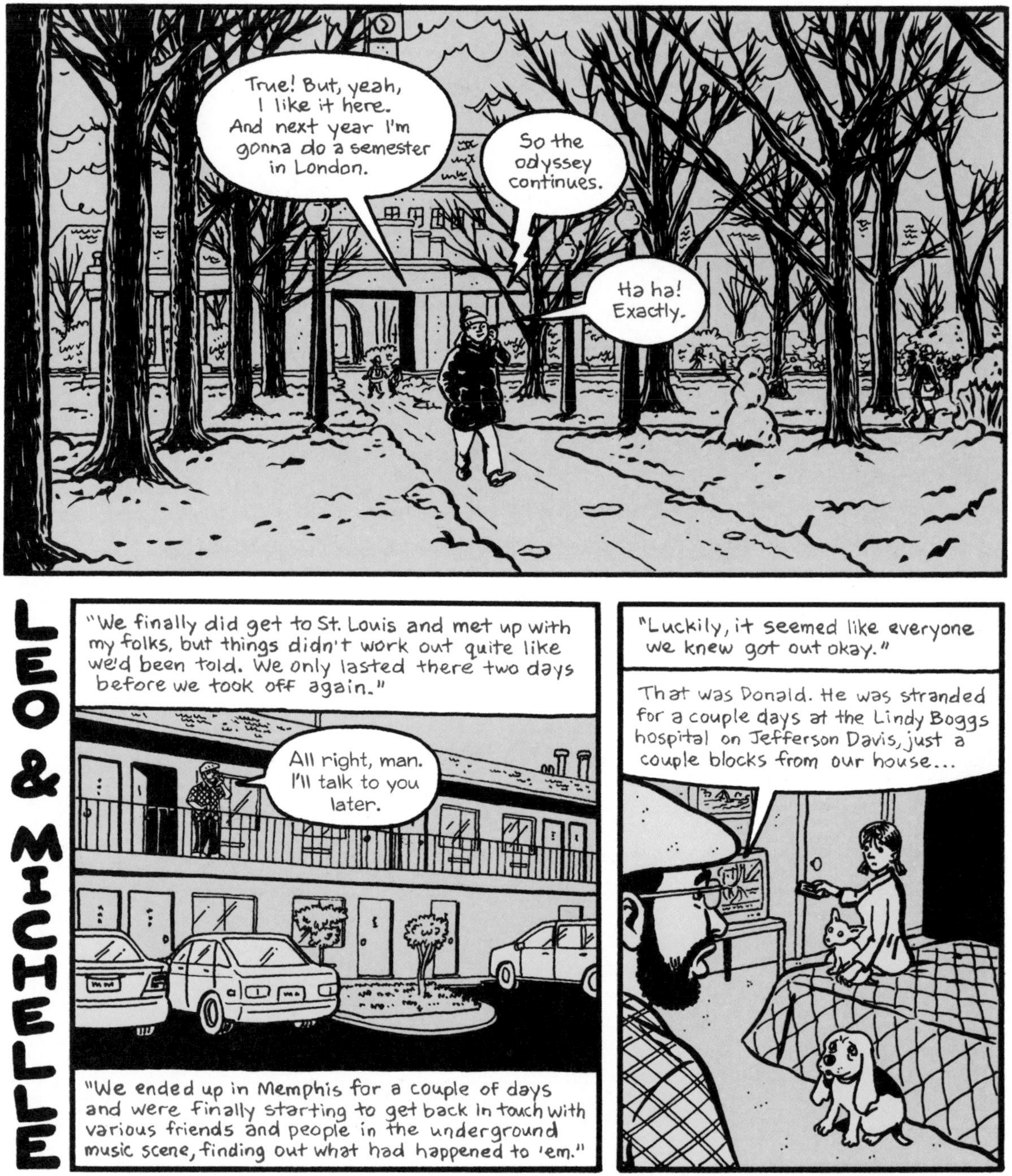
True! But, yeah, I like it here. And next year I'm gonna do a semester in London.
So the odyssey continues.
Ha ha! Exactly.
LEO & MICHELLE
"We finally did get to St. Louis and met up with my folks, but things didn't work out quite like we'd been told. We only lasted there two days before we took off again."
All right, man. I'll talk to you later.
"We ended up in Memphis for a couple of days and were finally starting to get back in touch with various friends and people in the underground music scene, finding out what had happened to 'em."
"Luckily, it seemed like everyone we knew got out okay."
That was Donald. He was stranded for a couple days at the Lindy Boggs hospital on Jefferson Davis, just a couple blocks from our house...

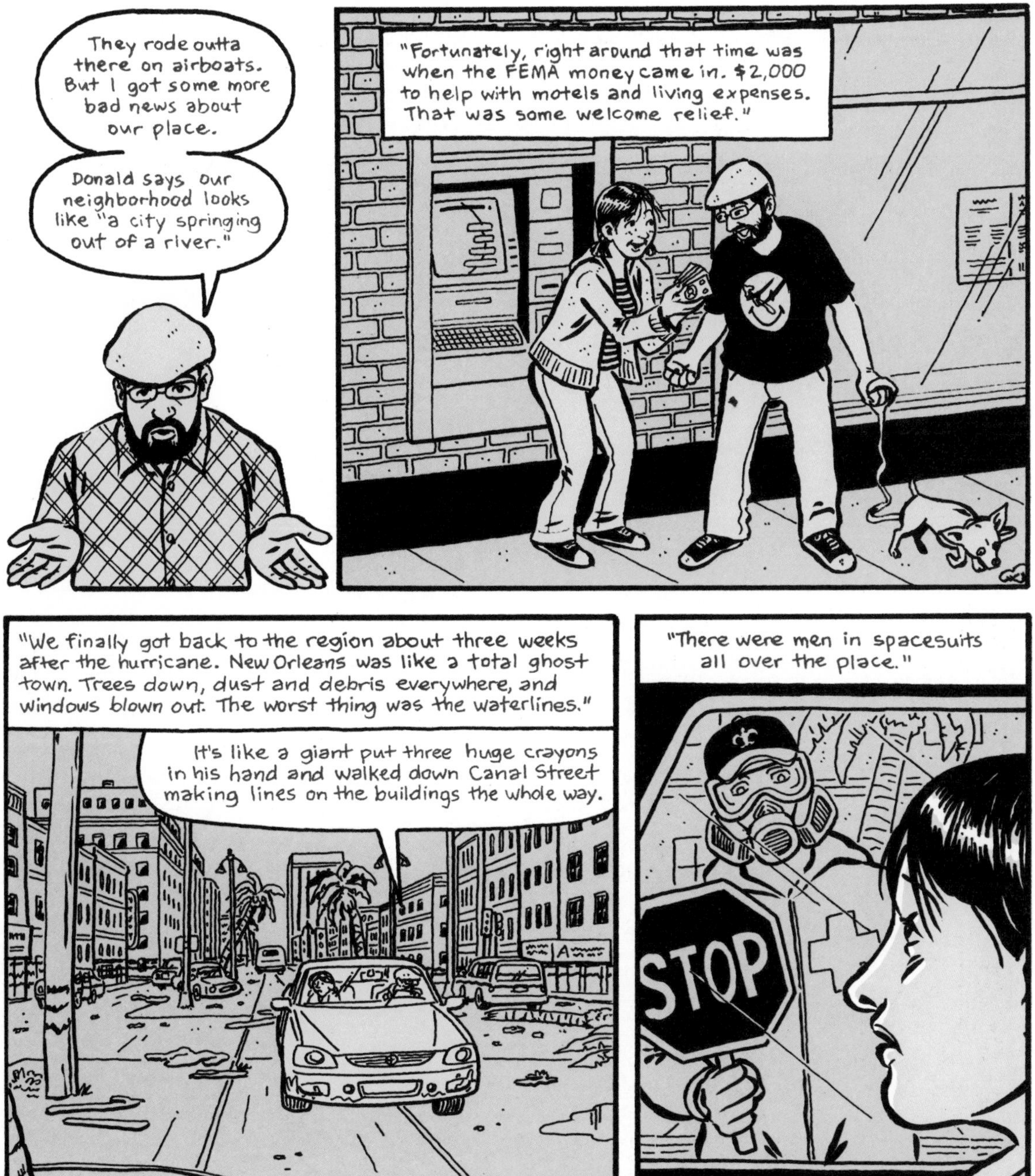
They rode outta there on airboats. But I got some more bad news about our place.
Donald says our neighborhood looks like "a city springing out of a river."
"Fortunately, right around that time was when the FEMA money came in. $2,000 to help with motels and living expenses. That was some welcome relief."
"We finally got back to the region about three weeks after the hurricane. New Orleans was like a total ghost town. Trees down, dust and debris everywhere, and windows blown out. The worst thing was the waterlines."
It's like a giant put three huge crayons in his hand and walked down Canal Street making lines on the buildings the whole way.
"There were men in spacesuits all over the place."
STOP

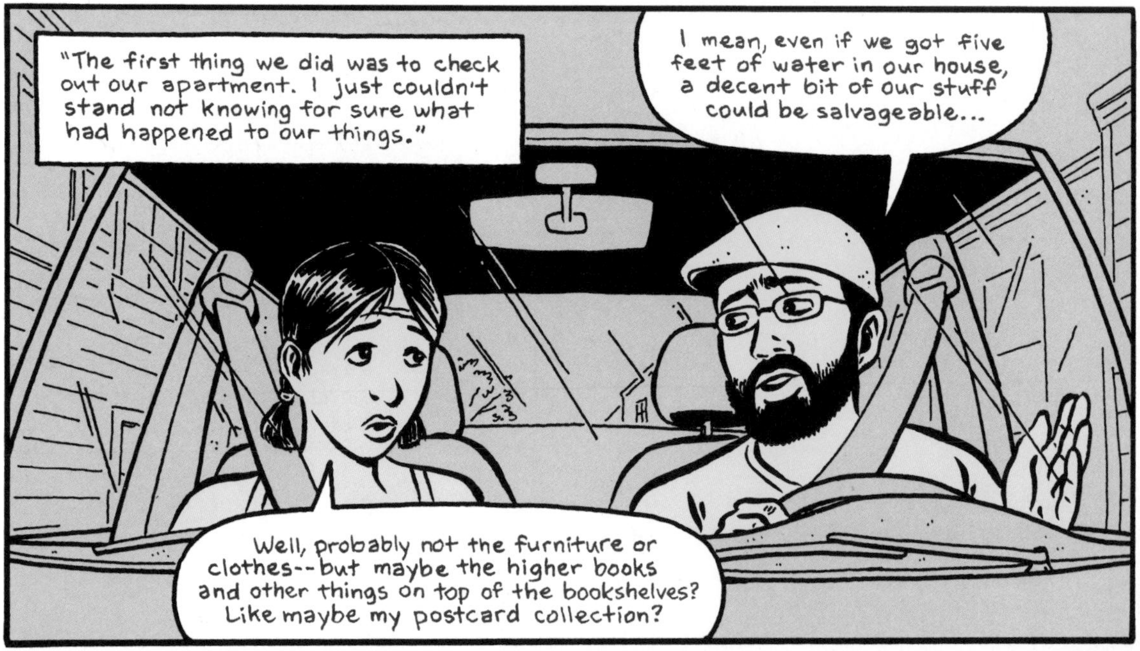
"The first thing we did was to check out our apartment. I just couldn't stand not knowing for sure what had happened to our things."
I mean, even if we got five feet of water in our house, a decent bit of our stuff could be salvageable...
Well, probably not the furniture or clothes--but maybe the higher books and other things on top of the bookshelves? Like maybe my postcard collection?

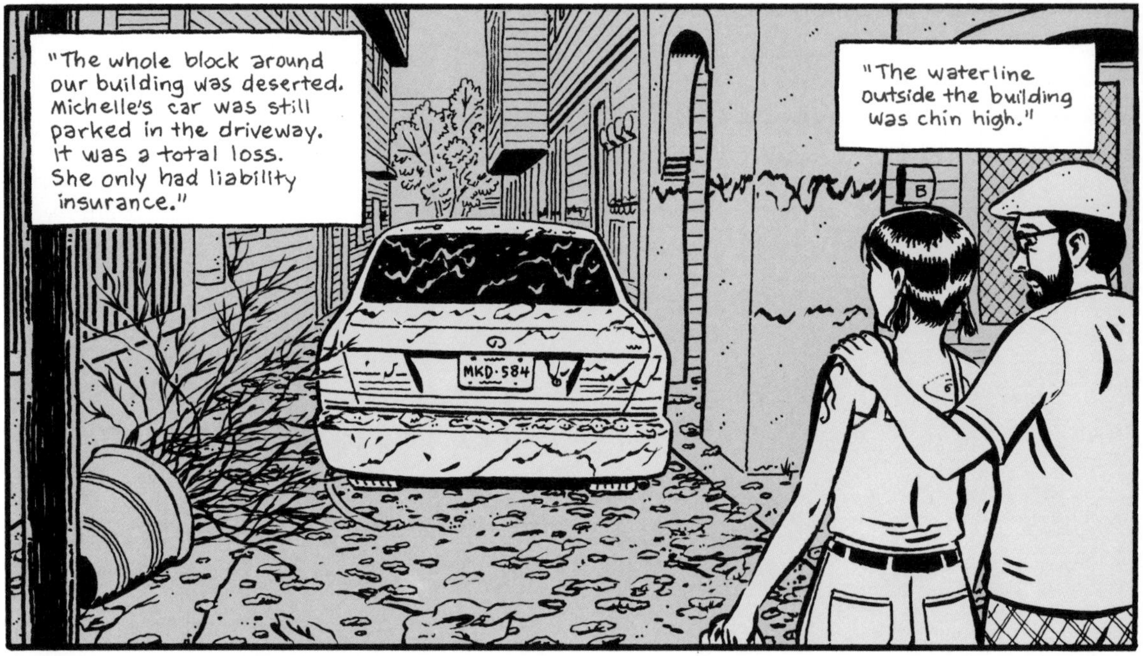
"The whole block around our building was deserted. Michelle's car was still parked in the driveway. It was a total loss. She only had liability insurance."
"The waterline outside the building was chin high."
MKD·584
B

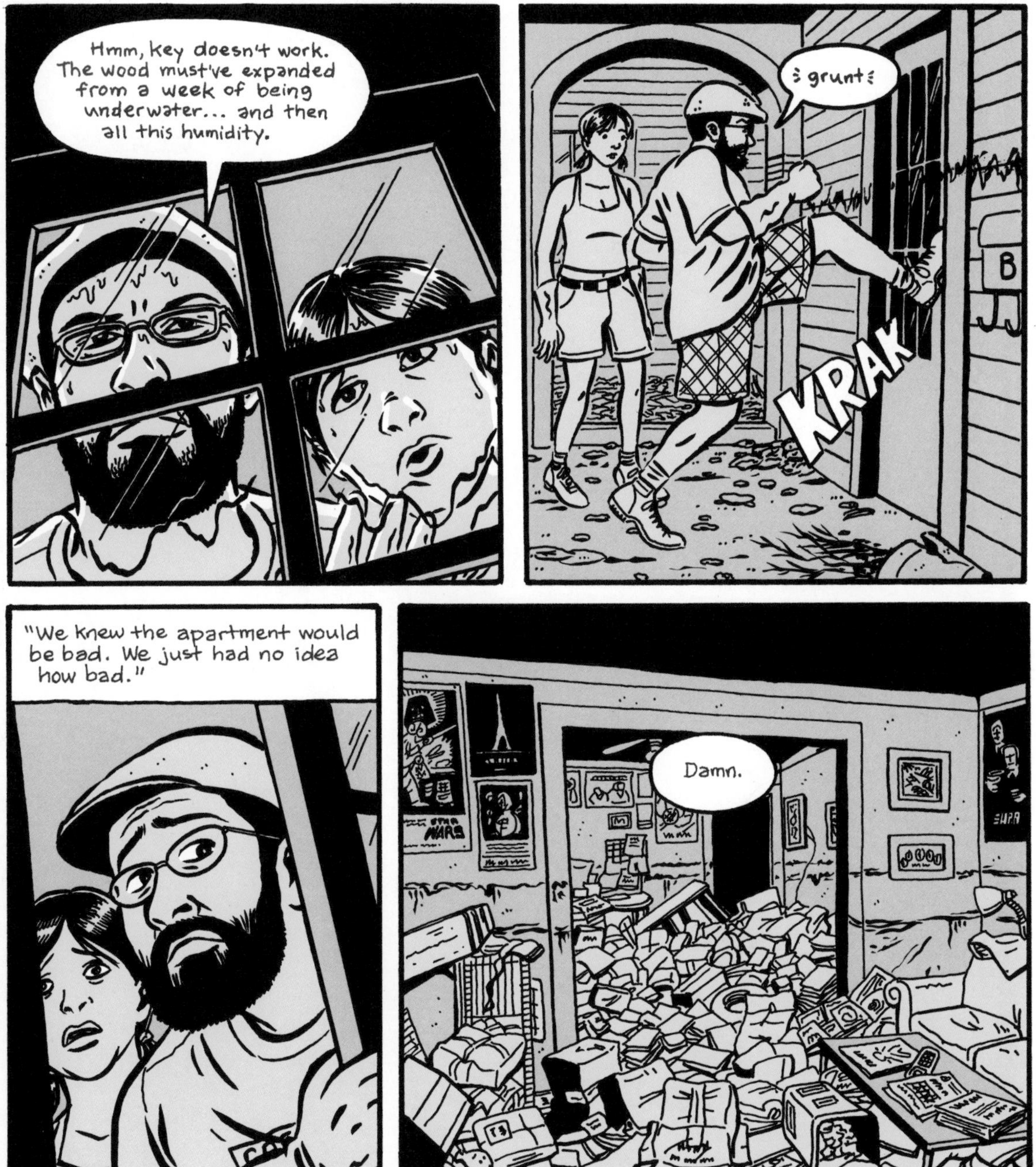
Hmm, key doesn't work. The wood must've expanded from a week of being underwater... and then all this humidity.
grunt
KRAK
"We knew the apartment would be bad. We just had no idea how bad."
Damn.

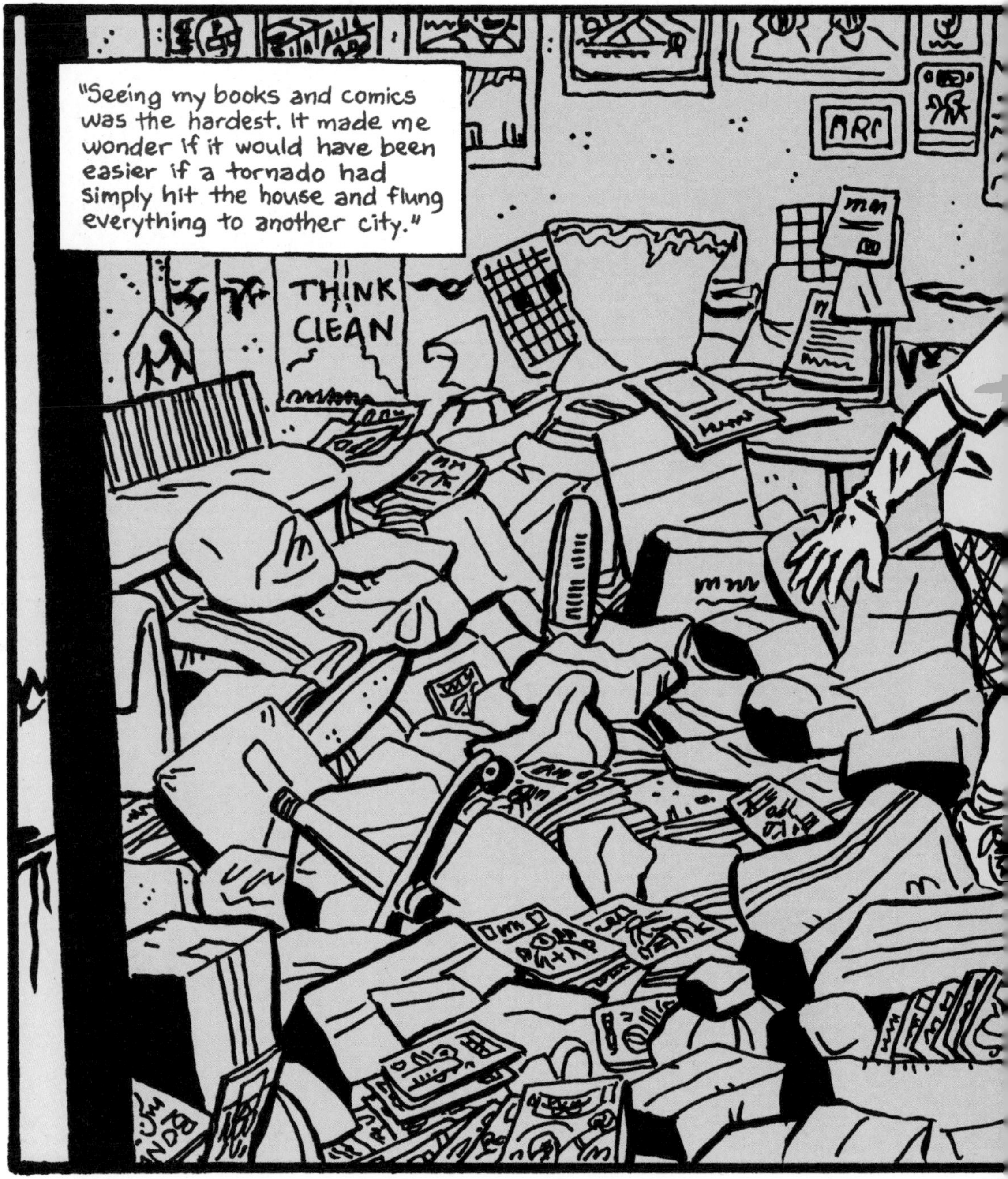
"Seeing my books and comics was the hardest. It made me wonder if it would have been easier if a tornado had simply hit the house and flung everything to another city."
THINK CLEAN

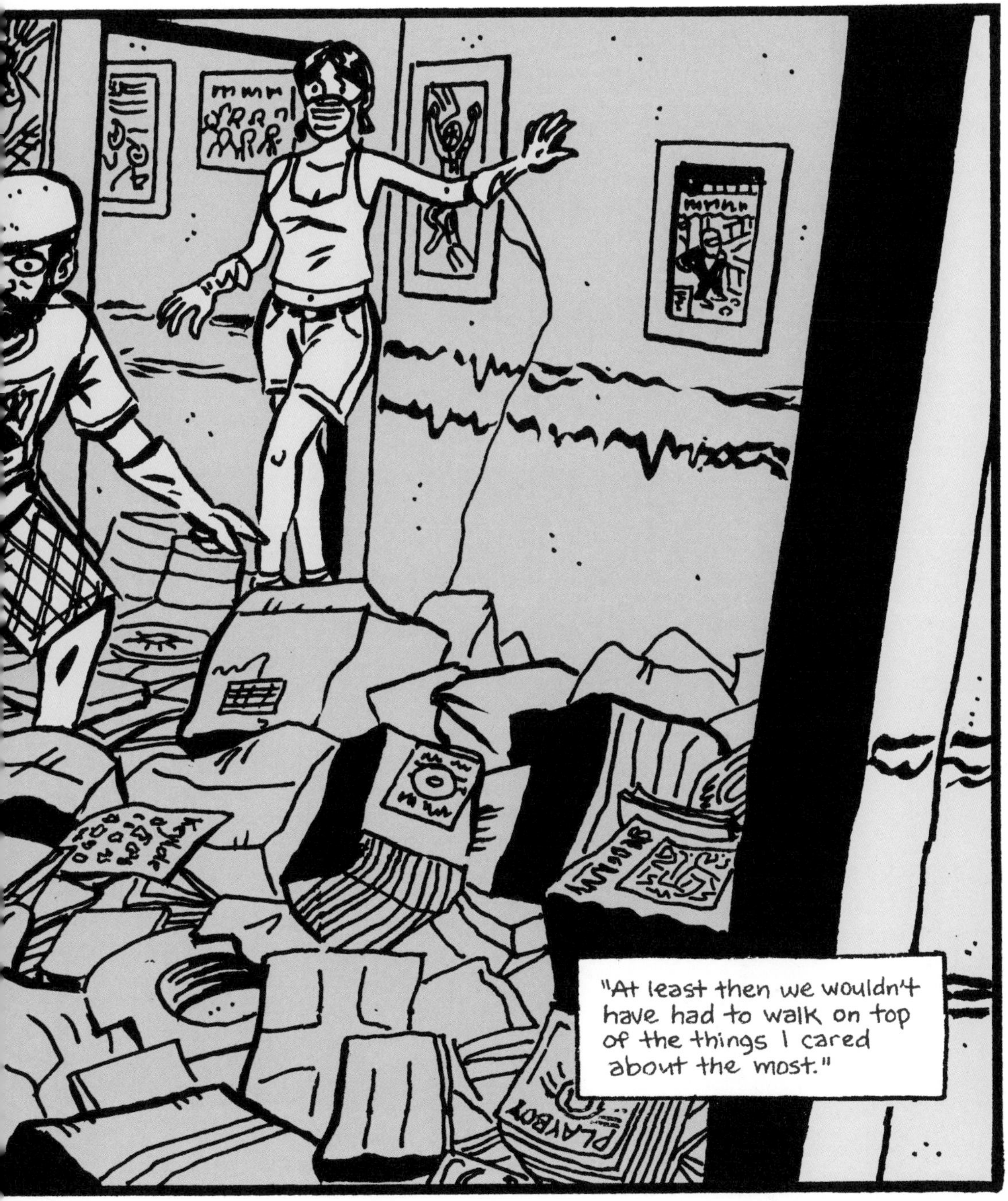
"At least then we wouldn't have had to walk on top of the things I cared about the most."
PLAYBOY

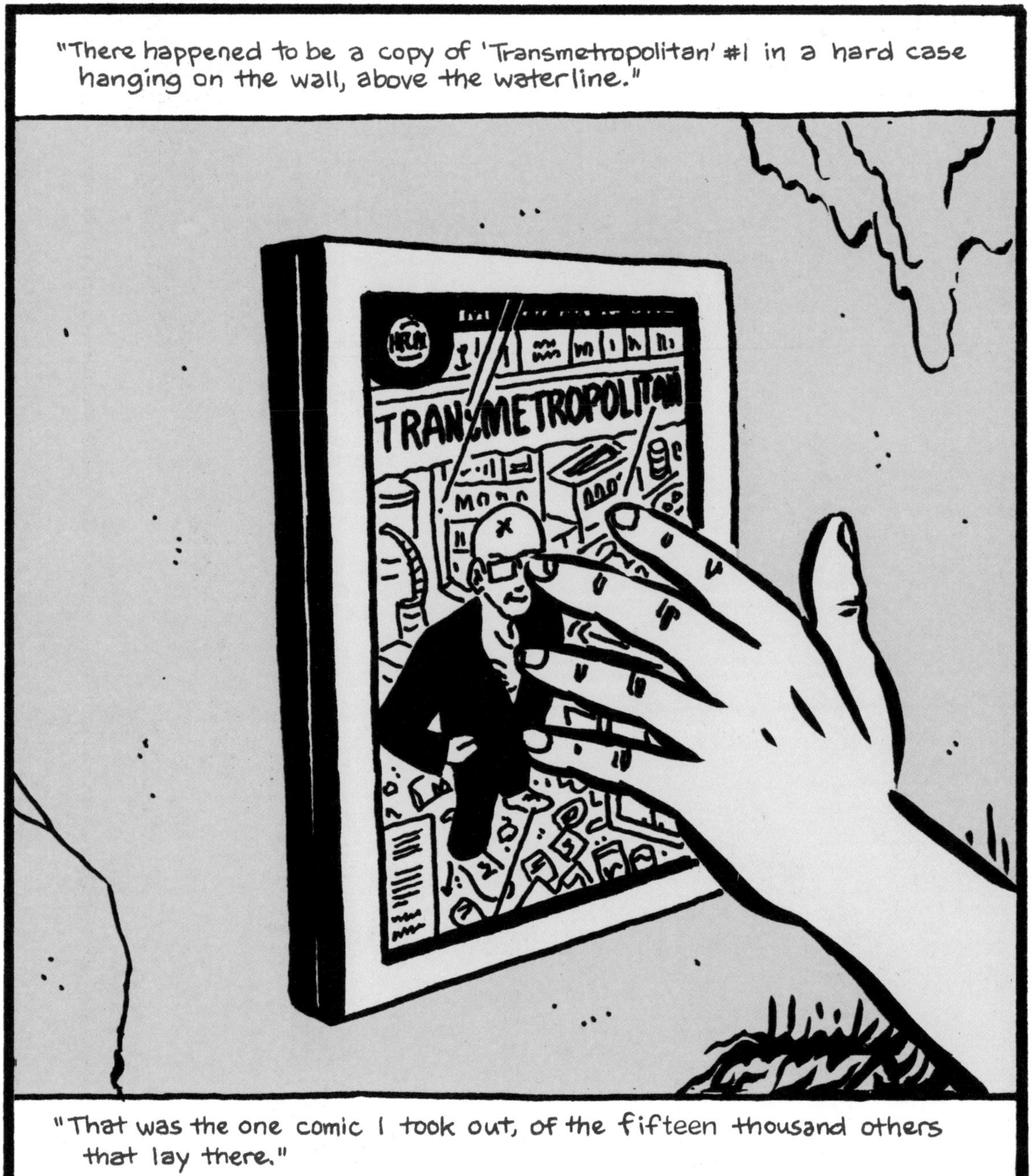
"There happened to be a copy of 'Transmetropolitan' #1 in a hard case hanging on the wall, above the waterline."
"That was the one comic I took out, of the fifteen thousand others that lay there."

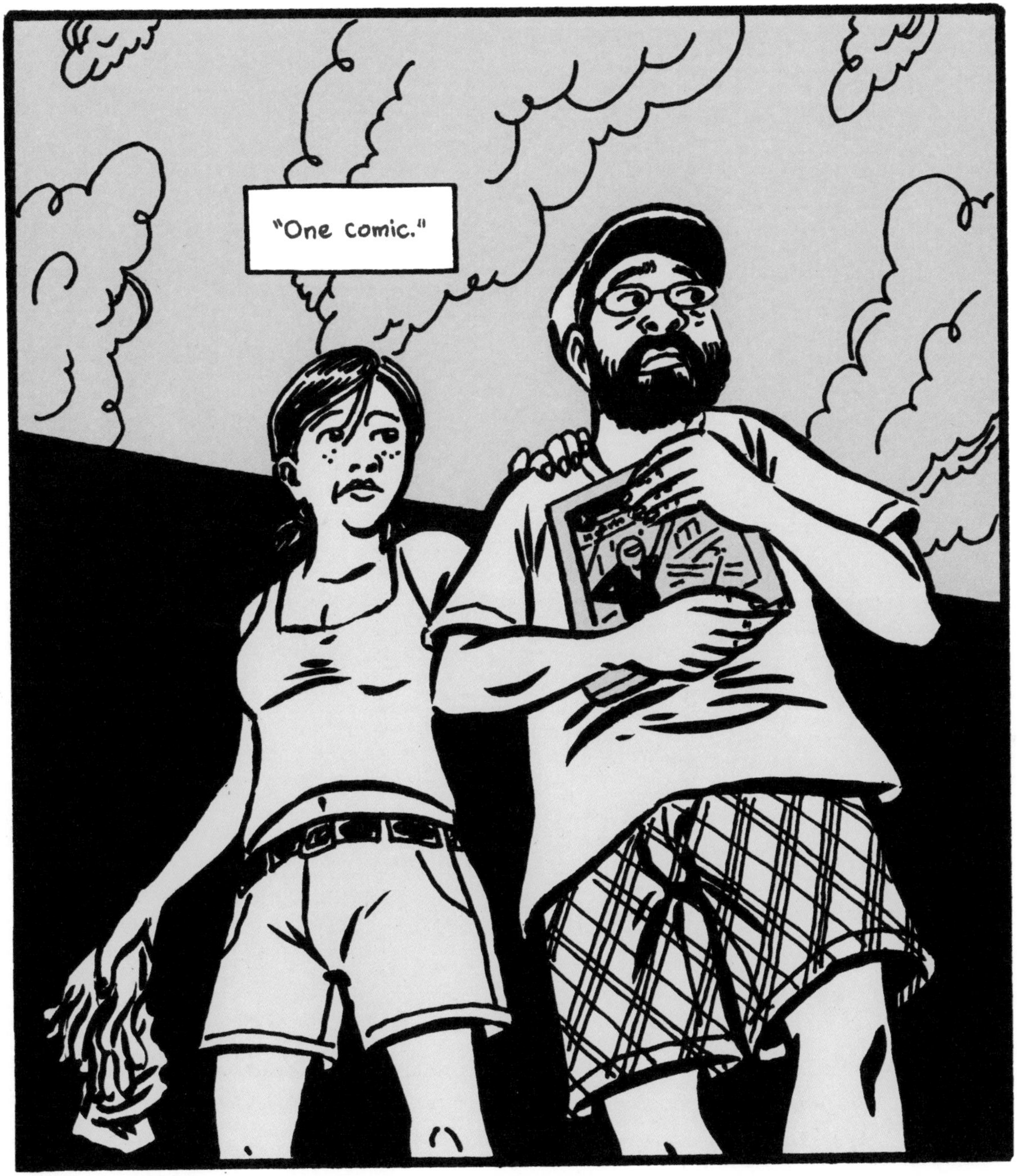
"One comic."

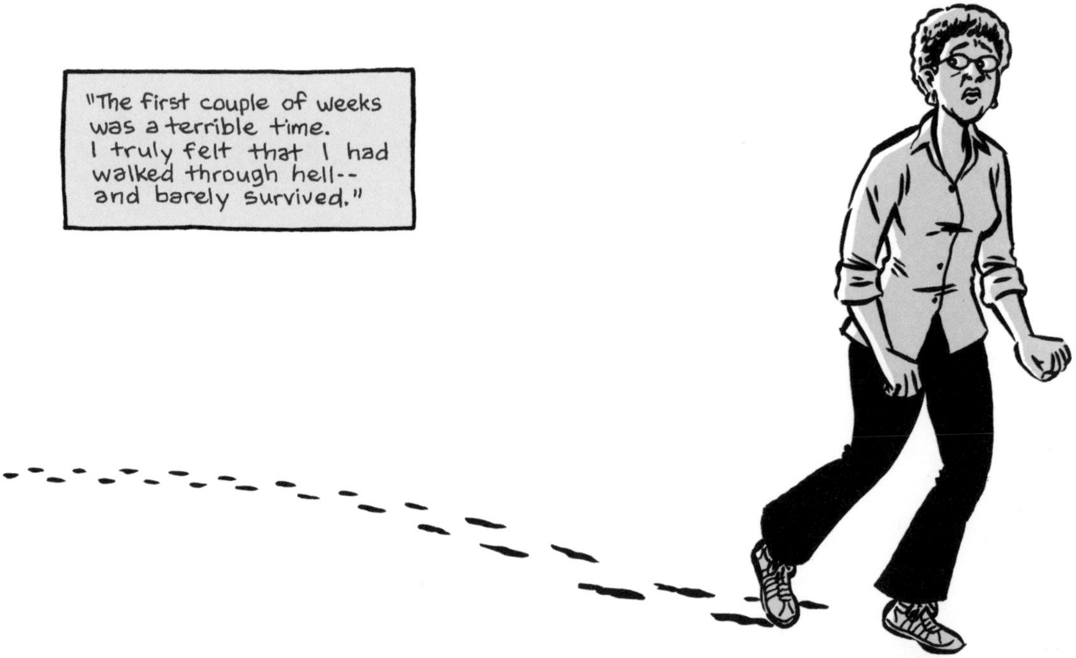
"The first couple of weeks was a terrible time. I truly felt that I had walked through hell-- and barely survived."

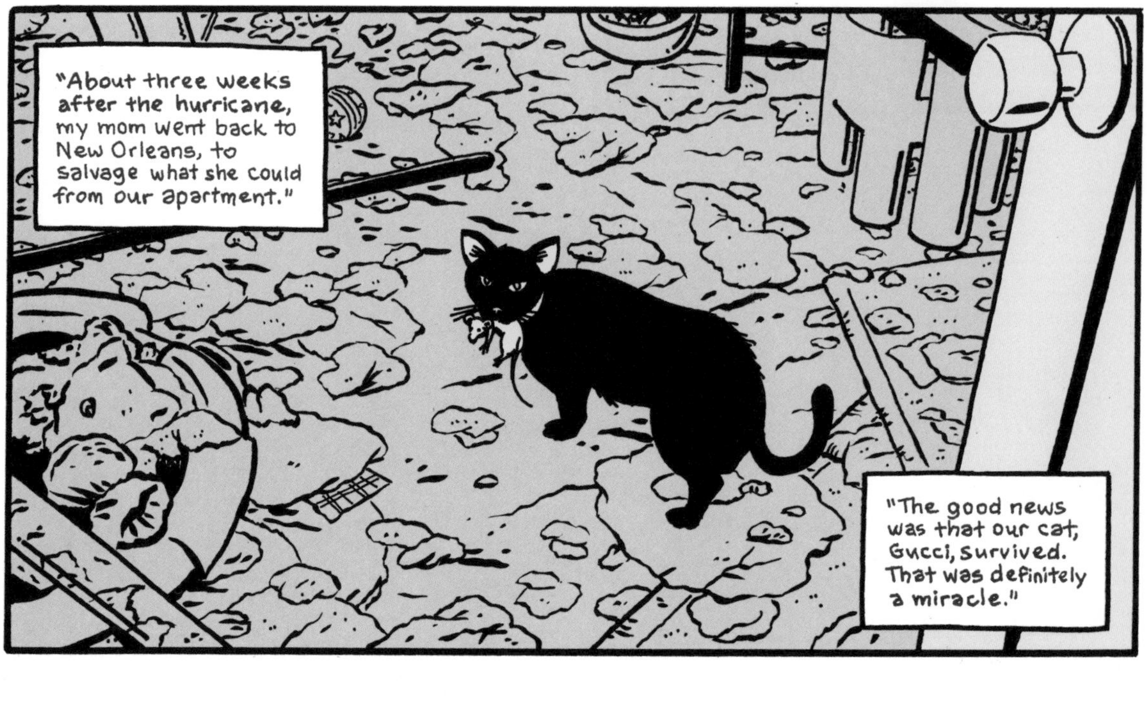
"About three weeks after the hurricane, my mom went back to New Orleans, to salvage what she could from our apartment."
"The good news was that our cat, Gucci, survived. That was definitely a miracle."

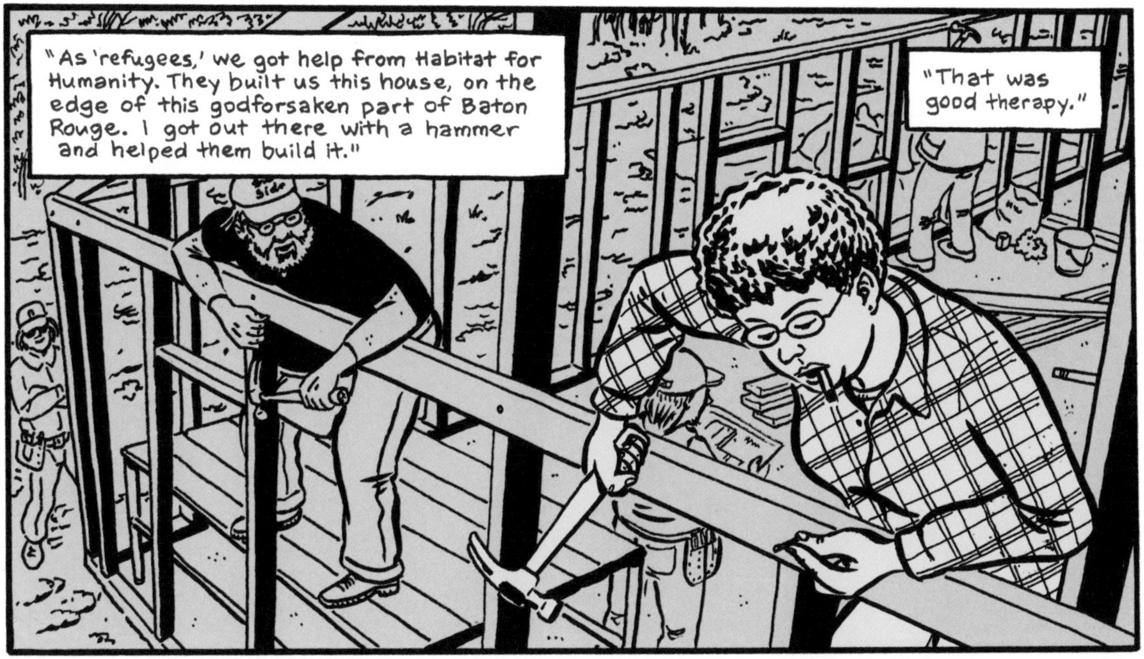
"As 'refugees,' we got help from Habitat for Humanity. They built us this house, on the edge of this godforsaken part of Baton Rouge. I got out there with a hammer and helped them build it."
"That was good therapy."

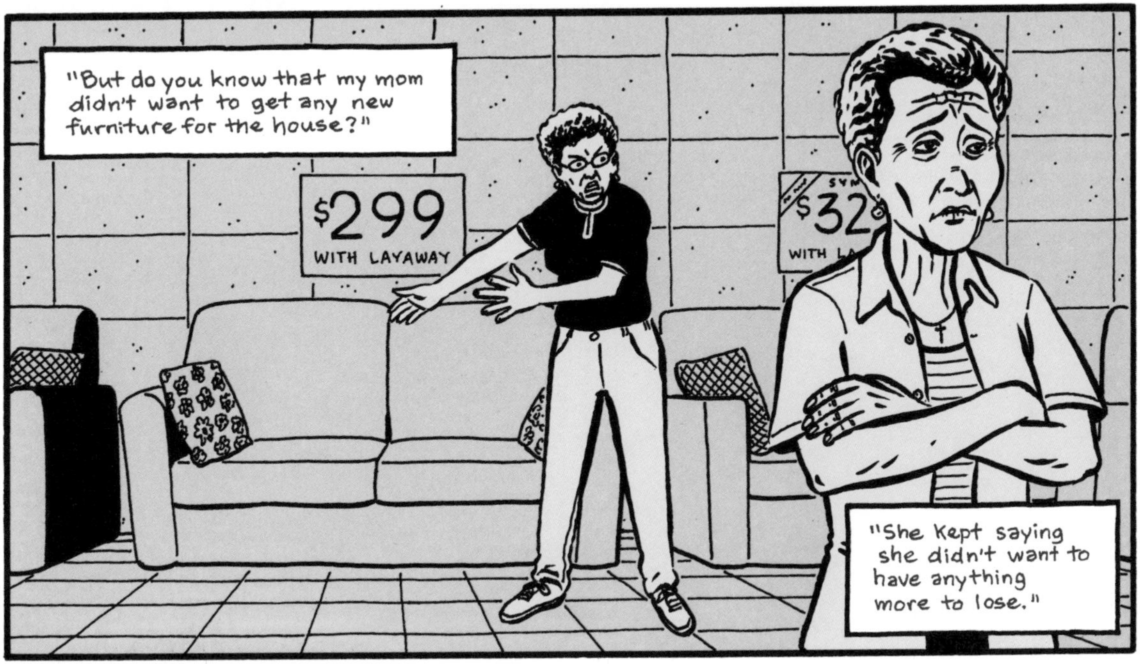
"But do you know that my mom didn't want to get any new furniture for the house?"
$299 WITH LAYAWAY
"She kept saying she didn't want to have anything more to lose."

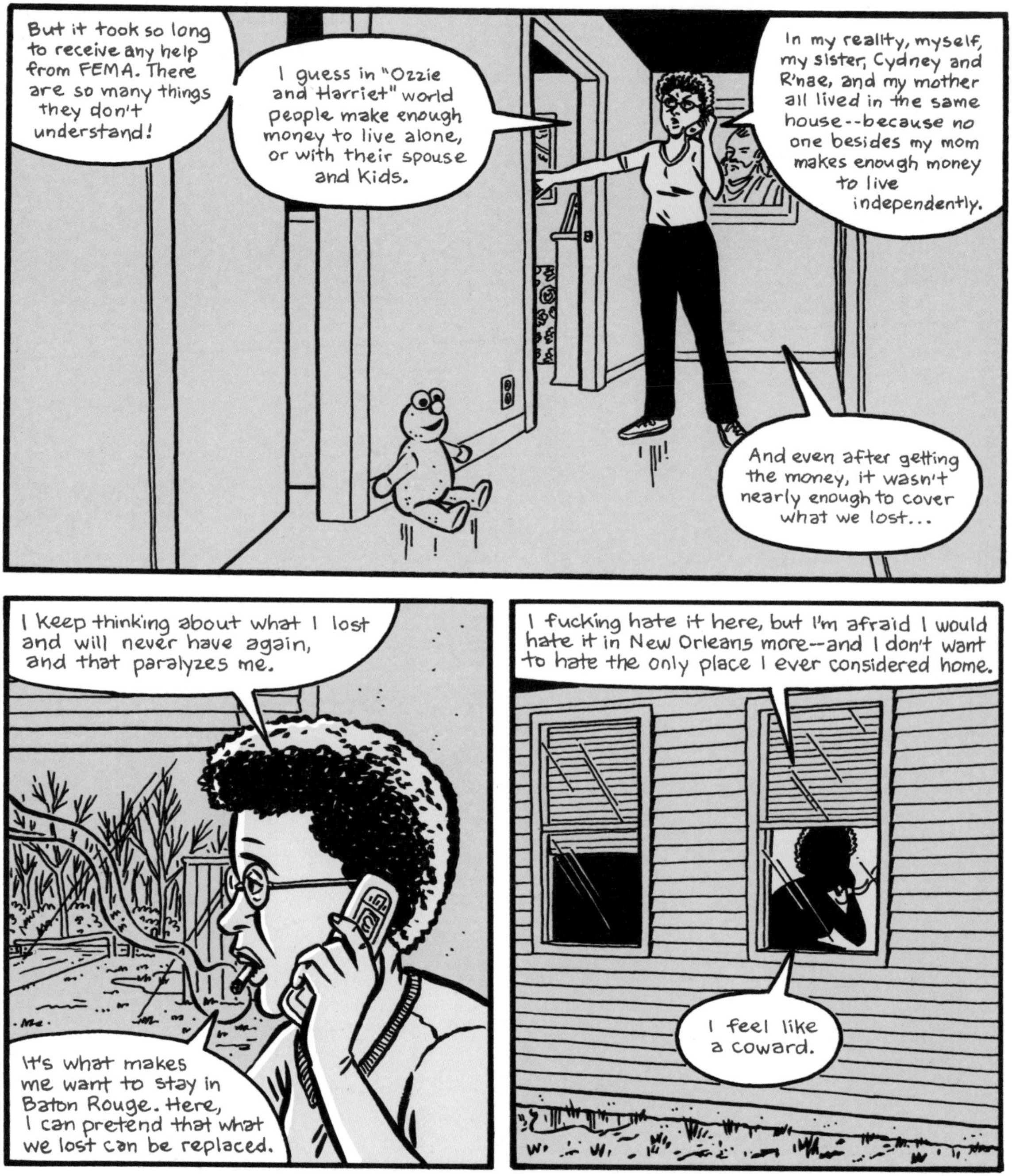
But it took so long to receive any help from FEMA. There are so many things they don't understand!
I guess in "Ozzie and Harriet" world people make enough money to live alone, or with their spouse and kids.
In my reality, myself, my sister, Cydney and R'nae, and my mother all lived in the same house--because no one besides my mom makes enough money to live independently.
And even after getting the money, it wasn't nearly enough to cover what we lost...
I keep thinking about what I lost and will never have again, and that paralyzes me.
It's what makes me want to stay in Baton Rouge. Here, I can pretend that what we lost can be replaced.
I fucking hate it here, but I'm afraid I would hate it in New Orleans more--and I don't want to hate the only place I ever considered home.
I feel like a coward.

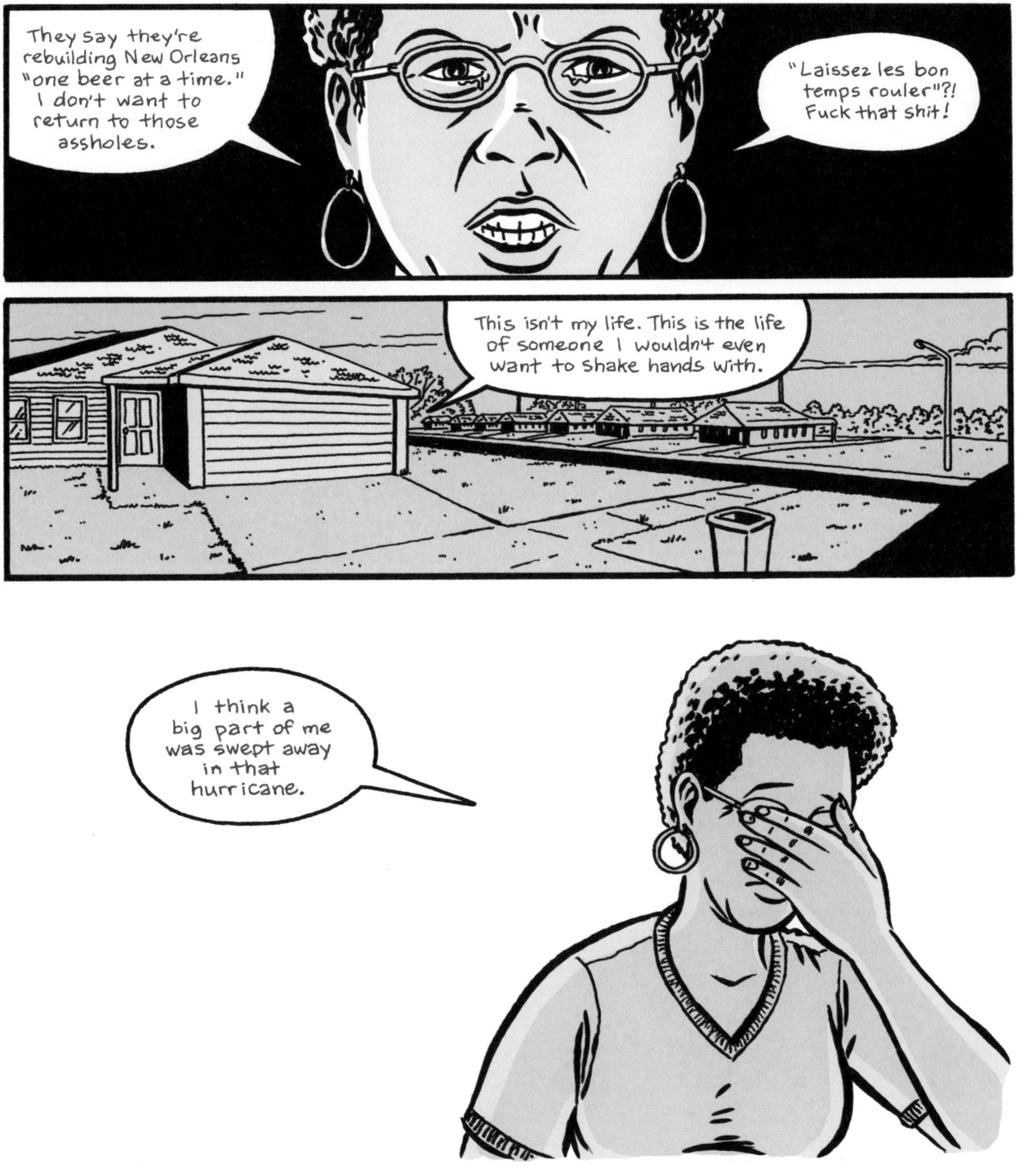
They say they're rebuilding New Orleans "one beer at a time." I don't want to return to those assholes.
"Laissez les bon temps rouler"?! Fuck that shit!
This isn't my life. This is the life of someone I wouldn't even want to shake hands with.
I think a big part of me was swept away in that hurricane.

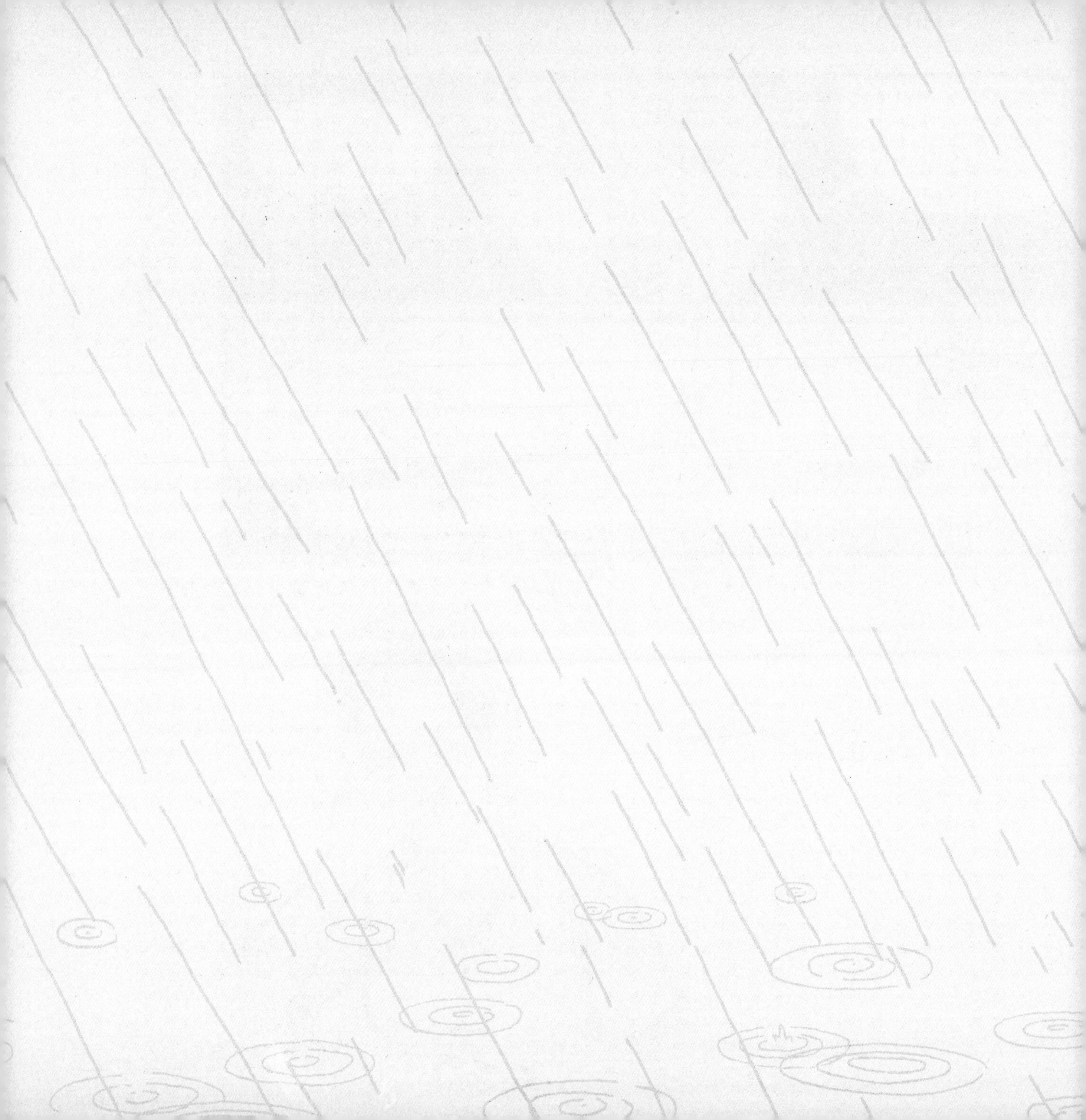

THE RETURN

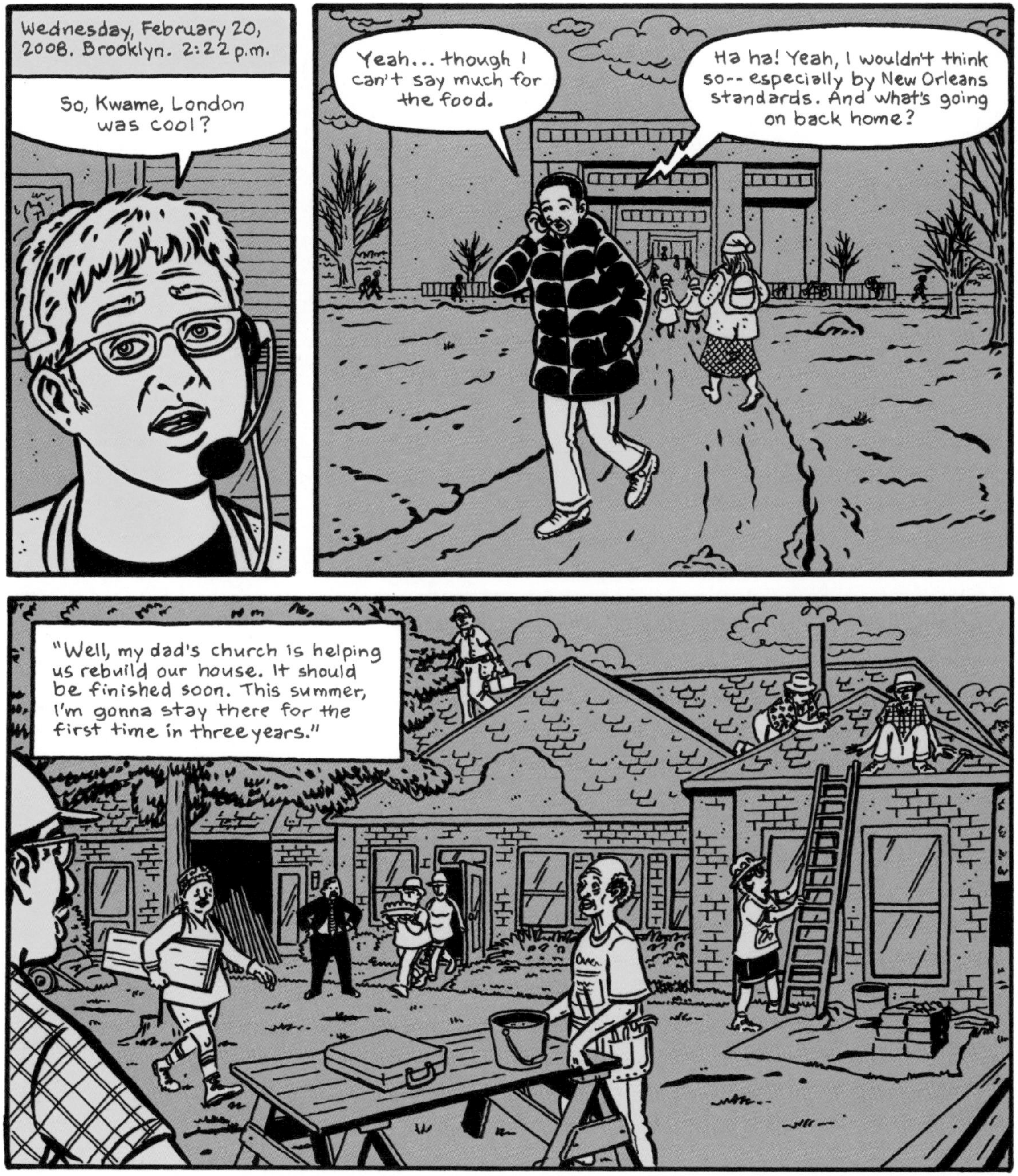
Wednesday, February 20, 2008. Brooklyn. 2:22 p.m.
So, Kwame, London was cool?
Yeah... though I can't say much for the food.
Ha ha! Yeah, I wouldn't think so-- especially by New Orleans standards. And what's going on back home?
"Well, my dad's church is helping us rebuild our house. It should be finished soon. This summer, I'm gonna stay there for the first time in three years."

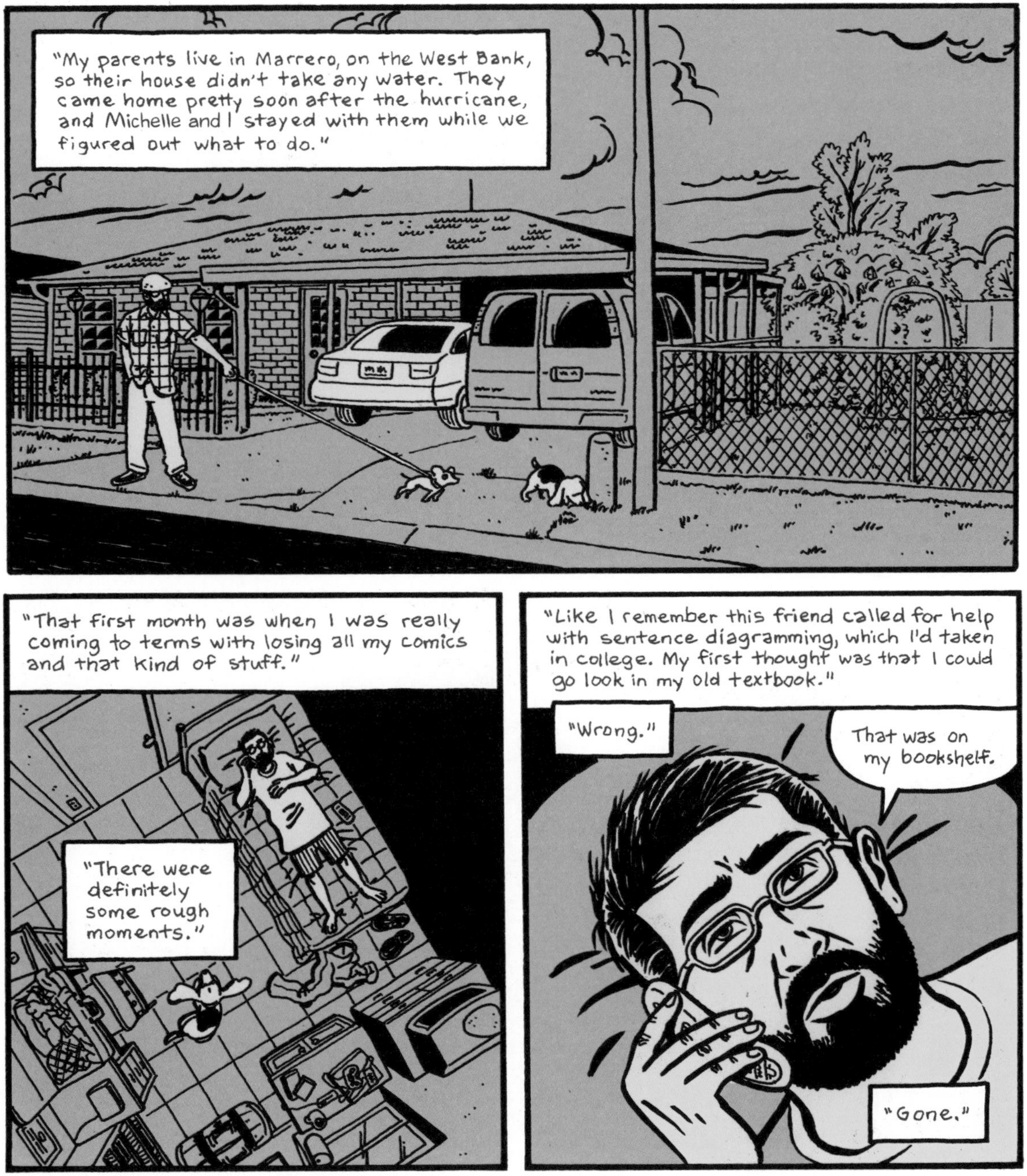

"My parents live in Marrero, on the West Bank, so their house didn't take any water. They came home pretty soon after the hurricane, and Michelle and I stayed with them while we figured out what to do."
"That first month was when I was really coming to terms with losing all my comics and that kind of stuff."
"There were definitely some rough moments."
"Like I remember this friend called for help with sentence diagramming, which I'd taken in college. My first thought was that I could go look in my old textbook."
"Wrong."
That was on my bookshelf.
"Gone."

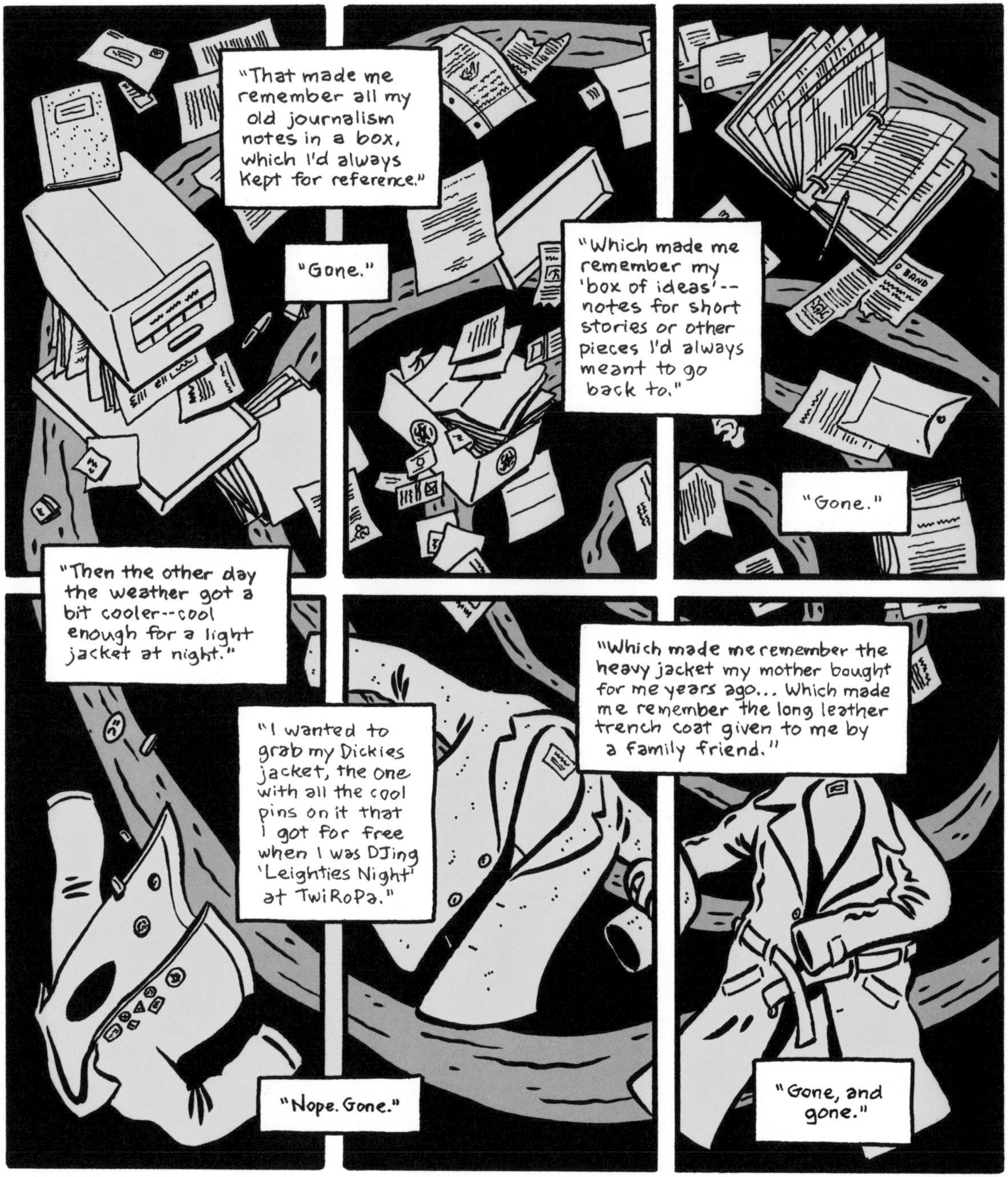
"That made me remember all my old journalism notes in a box, which I'd always kept for reference."
"Gone."
"Which made me remember my 'box of ideas'--notes for short stories or other pieces I'd always meant to go back to."
"Gone."
"Then the other day the weather got a bit cooler--cool enough for a light jacket at night."
"I wanted to grab my Dickies jacket, the one with all the cool pins on it that I got for free when I was DJing 'Leighties Night' at TwiRoPa."
"Nope. Gone."
"Which made me remember the heavy jacket my mother bought for me years ago... Which made me remember the long leather trench coat given to me by a family friend."
"Gone, and gone."

"It was around then that the defections really started to annoy me. I couldn't believe how many people were calling it quits on New Orleans!

"For me, it was never a question that I'd move back somehow.

"For better or worse, I'm married to this place."

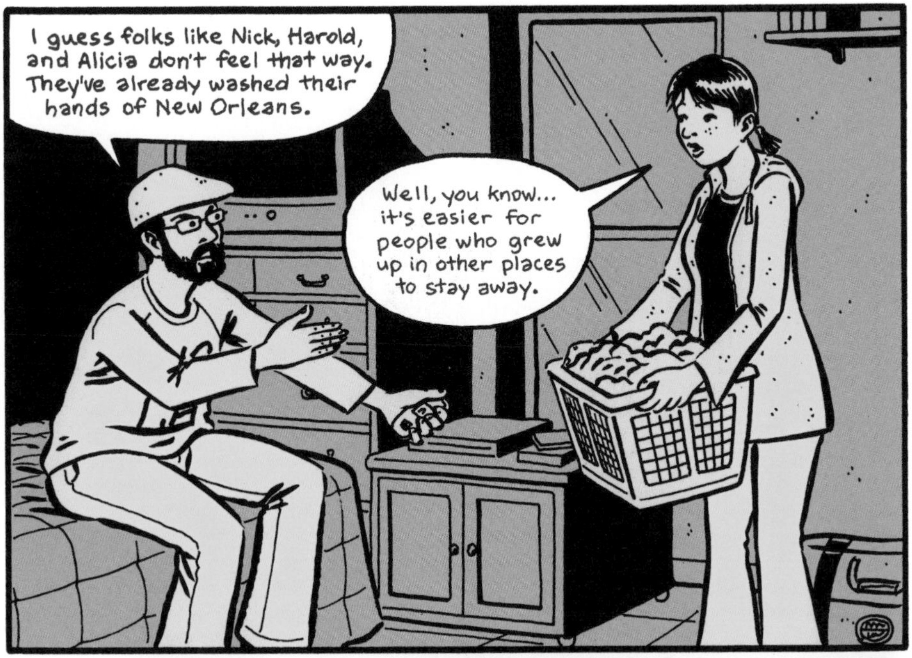
I guess folks like Nick, Harold, and Alicia don't feel that way. They've already washed their hands of New Orleans.
Well, you know... it's easier for people who grew up in other places to stay away.

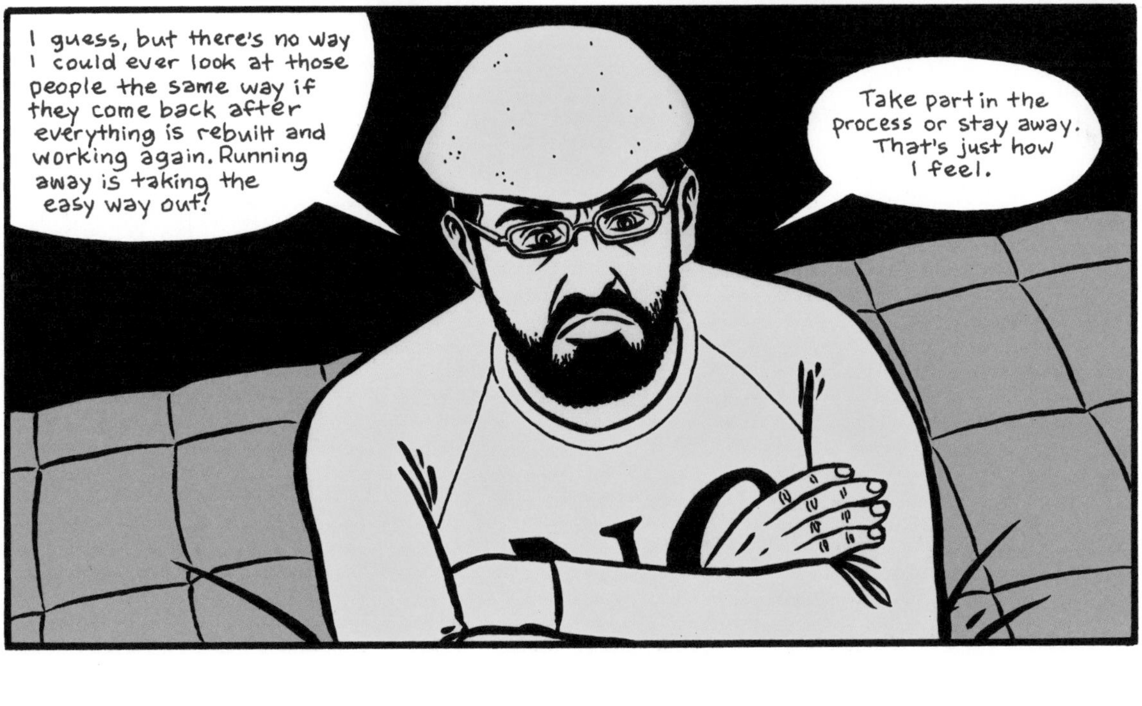
I guess, but there's no way I could ever look at those people the same way if they come back after everything is rebuilt and working again. Running away is taking the easy way out!
Take part in the process or stay away. That's just how I feel.

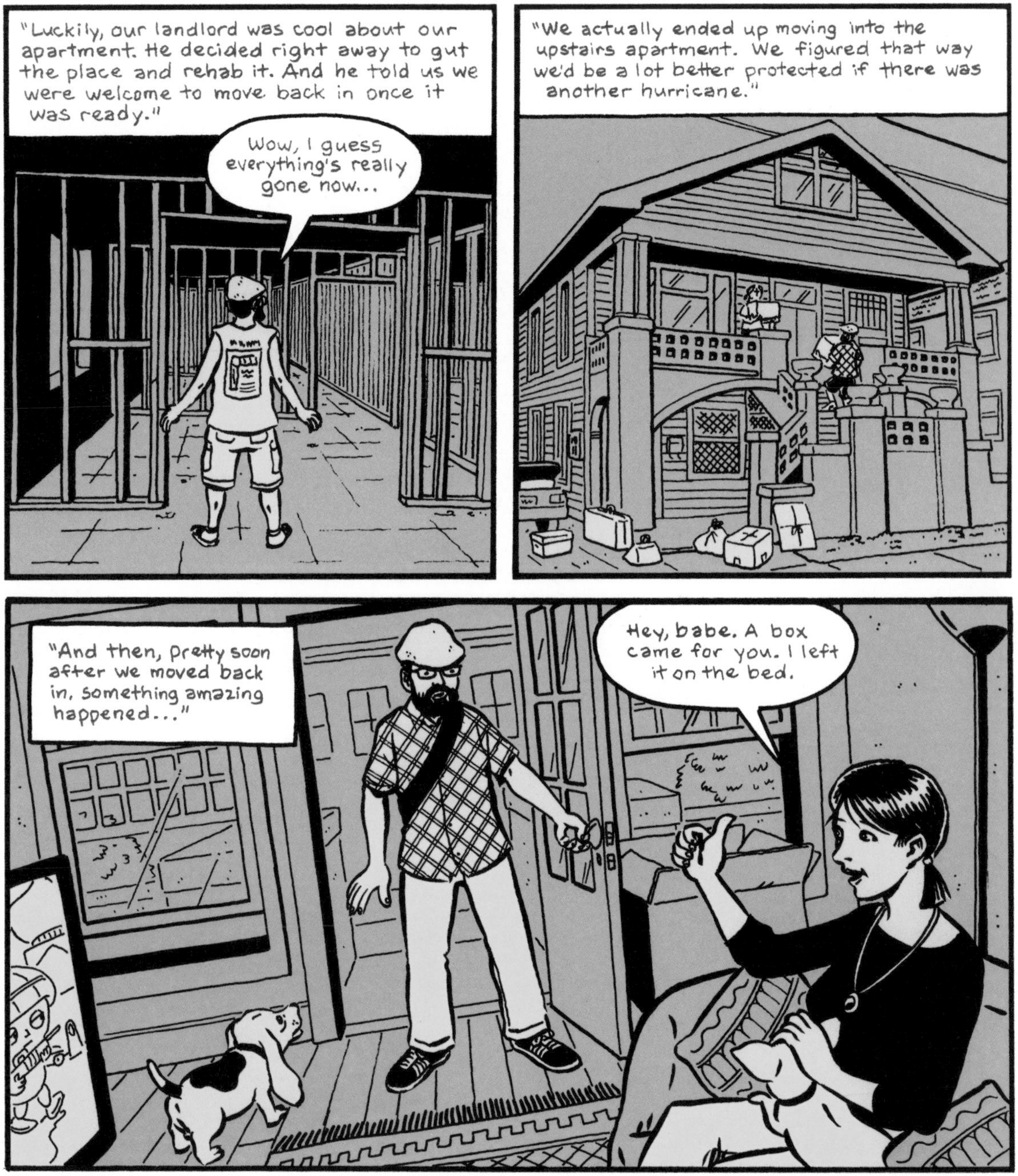
"Luckily, our landlord was cool about our apartment. He decided right away to gut the place and rehab it. And he told us we were welcome to move back in once it was ready."
Wow, I guess everything's really gone now...
"We actually ended up moving into the upstairs apartment. We figured that way we'd be a lot better protected if there was another hurricane."
"And then, pretty soon after we moved back in, something amazing happened..."
Hey, babe. A box came for you. I left it on the bed.

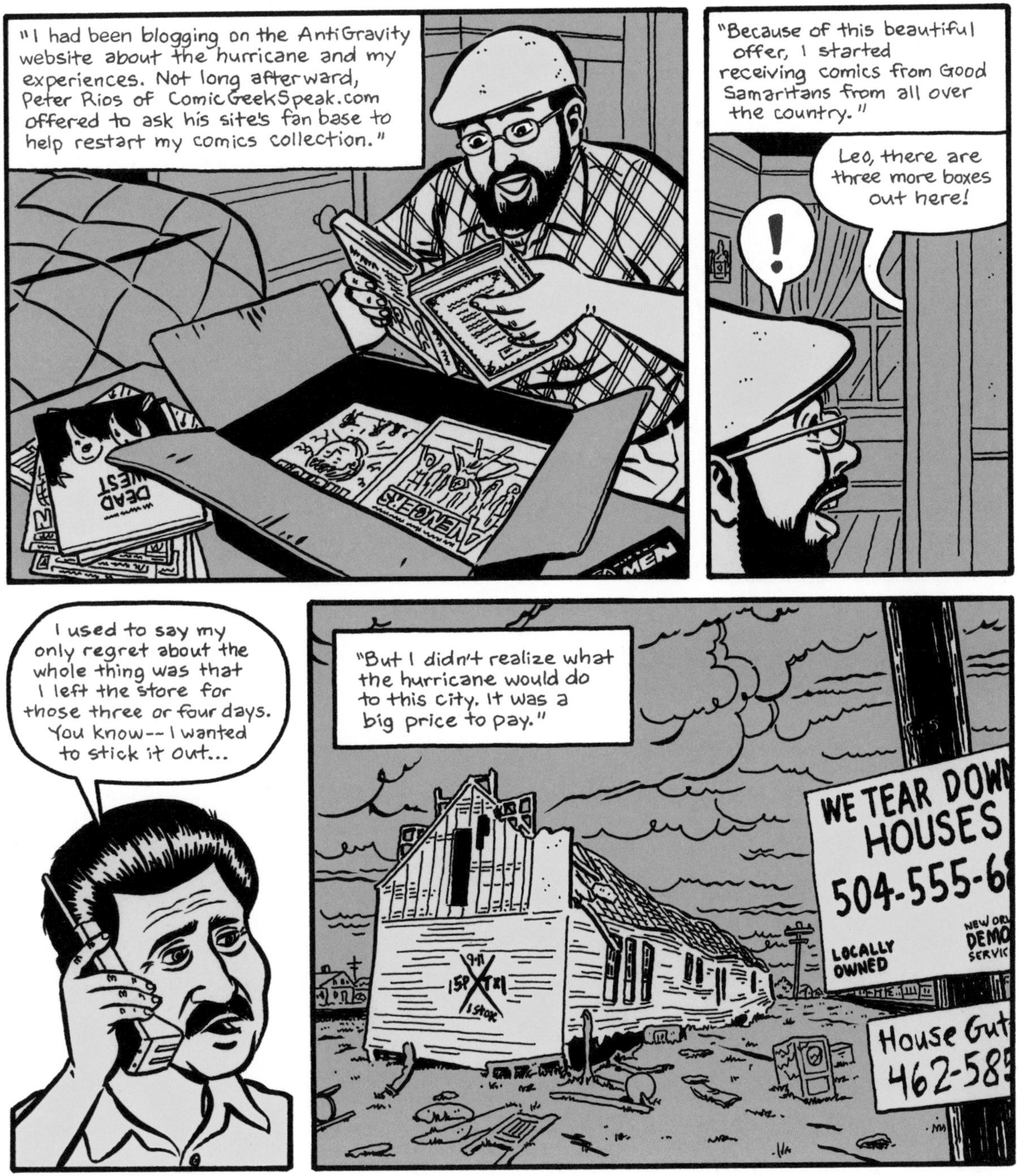
"I had been blogging on the AntiGravity website about the hurricane and my experiences. Not long afterward, Peter Rios of ComicGeekSpeak.com offered to ask his site's fan base to help restart my comics collection."
DEAD WEST
AVENGERS
MEN
"Because of this beautiful offer, I started receiving comics from Good Samaritans from all over the country."
Leo, there are three more boxes out here!
!
I used to say my only regret about the whole thing was that I left the store for those three or four days. You know-- I wanted to stick it out...
"But I didn't realize what the hurricane would do to this city. It was a big price to pay."
WE TEAR DOWN HOUSES
504-555-6
LOCALLY OWNED
House Gut
462-585

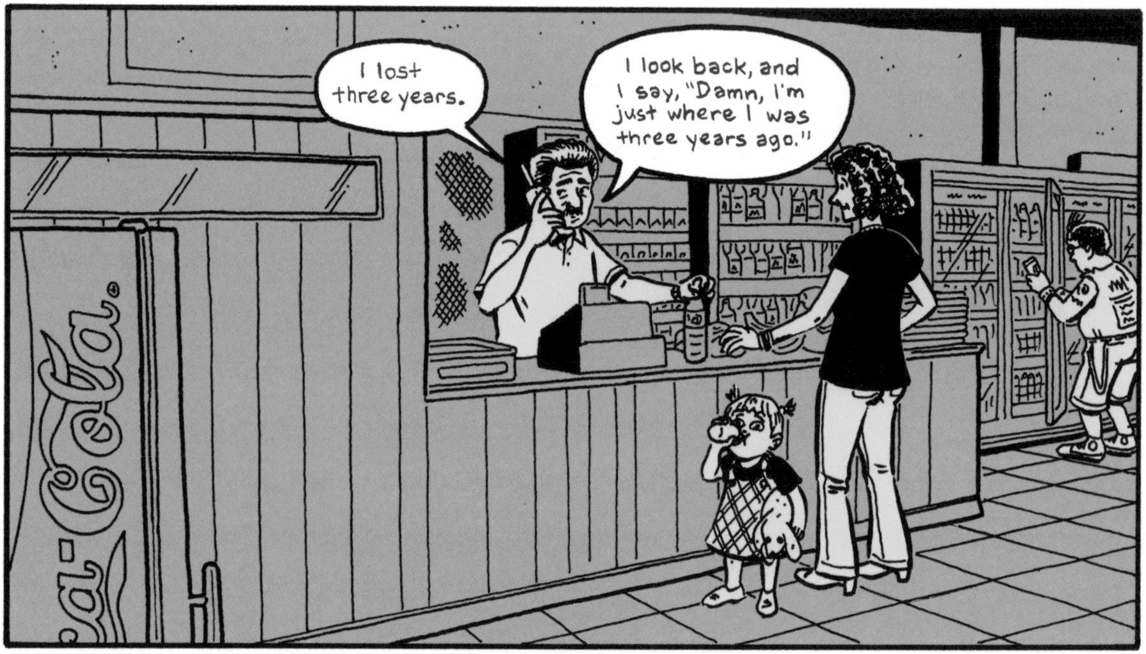
I lost three years.
I look back, and I say, "Damn, I'm just where I was three years ago."

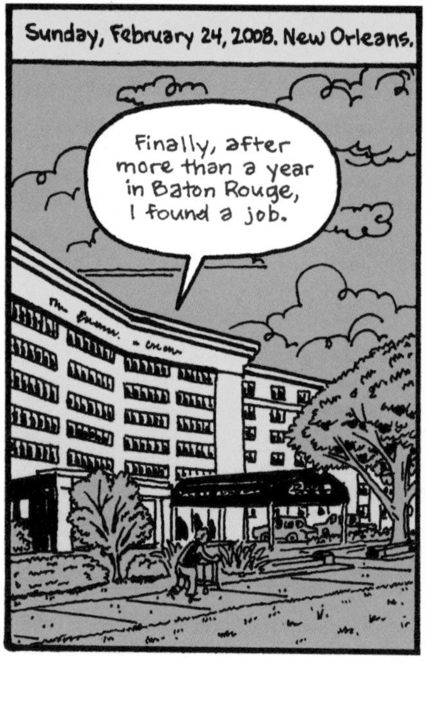
Sunday, February 24, 2008. New Orleans.
Finally, after more than a year in Baton Rouge, I found a job.

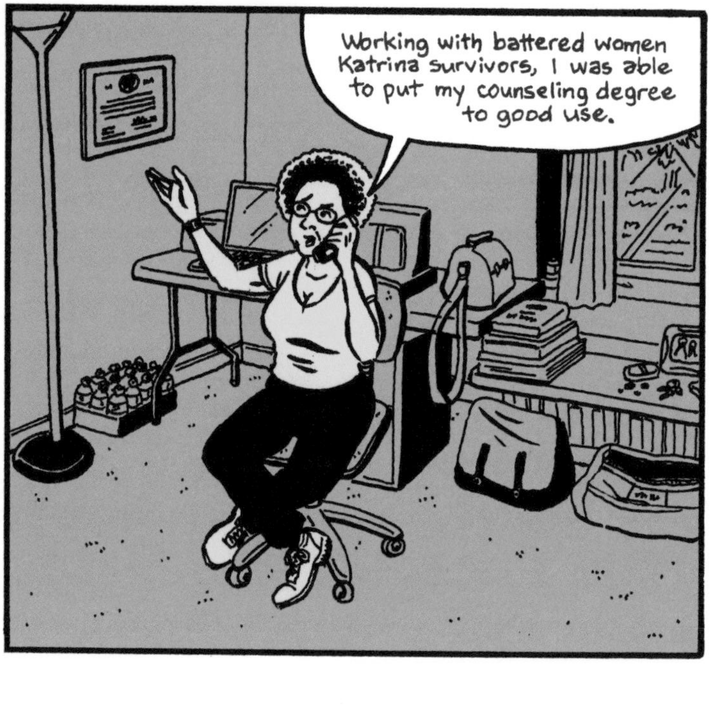
Working with battered women Katrina survivors, I was able to put my counseling degree to good use.

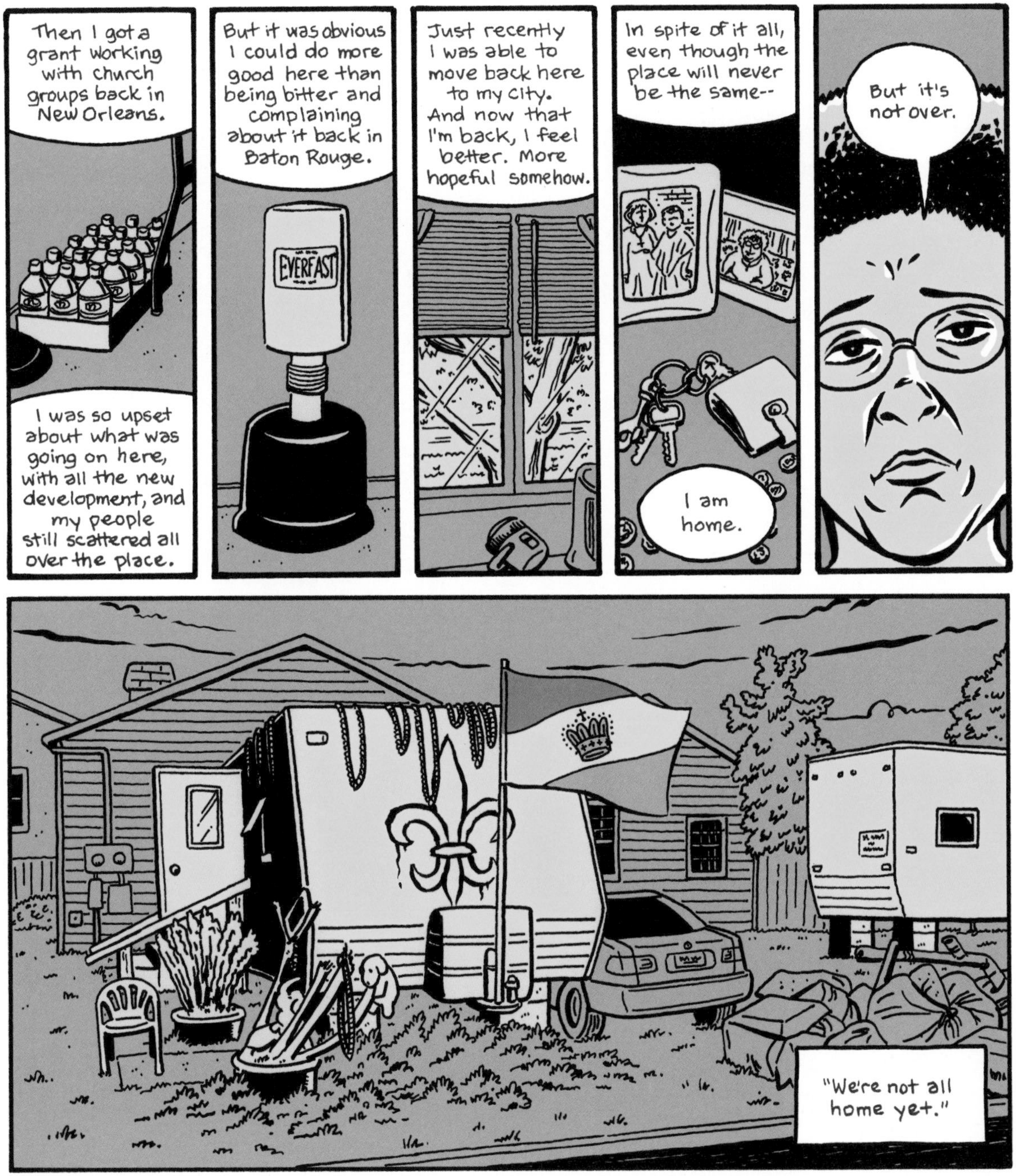
Then I got a grant working with church groups back in New Orleans.
I was so upset about what was going on here, with all the new development, and my people still scattered all over the place.
But it was obvious I could do more good here than being bitter and complaining about it back in Baton Rouge.
EVERFAST
Just recently I was able to move back here to my city. And now that I'm back, I feel better. More hopeful somehow.
In spite of it all, even though the place will never be the same--
I am home.
But it's not over.
"We're not all home yet."

AFTERWORD

DENISE, LEO, MICHELLE, ABBAS, DARNELL, KWAME, and BROBSON (the Doctor) are real people who lived through Hurricane Katrina. The events that occur in "A.D." actually happened to them, and most of the dialogue in this book is taken from our conversations, quotes from interviews, or entries from their blogs. The places and details are real too--down to the DVDs and comics on Leo's shelves and the contents of Abbas's store. (Some names and identifying characteristics, however, have been changed to protect people's privacy.)

"A.D." is my attempt to document the remarkable experiences of the survivors of Hurricane Katrina. The project began in the summer of 2006. Jeff Newelt, the comics editor of the storytelling site SMITH Magazine, had read "Katrina Came Calling," my self-published zine about my time volunteering with the Red Cross in the Gulf Coast after the hurricane. (As a disaster response worker stationed in Biloxi, Mississippi, in October 2005, I delivered hot meals to sections of the city without power, where I met many people who had lost everything in the hurricane, folks who trusted me during that vulnerable time in their lives and who gave me a sense of connection that provided vital background and context for "A.D.") After reading "Katrina Came Calling," SMITH editor Larry Smith asked me to tell the story of Katrina and New Orleans in comics form on his site. I was instantly enthusiastic: I had been deeply affected by my volunteering experience and was looking for a way to bring it to life as a cartoonist. As the project evolved, Larry was instrumental at every stage--from making the first contacts with possible subjects, through all the traveling, interviewing, and decision making, to ensuring that "A.D." was strongly presented on SMITH.

I felt it was important to tell the story from the perspectives of a range of real people who had lived through the storm: well-off and poor, black and white, young and old, gay and straight, male and female. And I knew there were certain key experiences I had to document: evacuating the city, facing the flooding, being trapped at the Superdome or the Convention Center, and losing all your possessions. So my first role as writer/artist of "A.D." was that of a journalist, finding subjects for the story. I talked to friends--and friends of friends--from New Orleans; I spoke with people who ran regional nonprofits and other local organizations; I tracked down accounts of the storm and its aftermath on the radio, in magazines and newspapers, and on the Internet; and I made lots of phone calls and sent lots of e-mails.

Eventually, seven people emerged as the main focus of "A.D." They all had to deal with loss of one kind or another, but each went through Katrina in a different way. I selected Denise after hearing her on a radio program. The mainstream media, in the days following the storm, inaccurately reported roving gangs, shootings, rapes, and murders at the New Orleans Convention Center. Denise witnessed what really happened, how the people there were abandoned by the authorities, and how they did their best to help one another--often with the so-called thugs at the forefront--and I knew Denise's powerful voice had to be front and center in "A.D." I found Leo online. He had been a reader of the blog I kept as a Red Cross volunteer, and when I then read his blog and learned of the loss of his comics collection, I felt an intuitive understanding for him and knew I could bring his and Michelle's story to life. I learned of Abbas and Darnell from a mutual friend, and even though Abbas and I couldn't be more different in our backgrounds and in how we've lived our lives, I totally identified with the series of choices that led to his waterlogged misadventures. (All too similar to some of my own misadventures, like the ones documented in my previous book, "A Few Perfect Hours.") I read about Kwame in my alma mater's alumni magazine. Having led a peripatetic childhood myself, I strongly related to his tale of multiple cross-country displacements. And the Doctor, of course, is a great raconteur--as well as being a key participant in the post-Katrina relief and recovery efforts.

After selecting the subjects, I finally flew down to New Orleans in January 2007 to meet them in person. I took tons of photos, not just of the subjects and their pets, homes, and cars, but also of the still flood-wracked parts of New Orleans. Then it was up to me to weave the characters' stories together in comics form, illustrating the storm and their disparate paths into and through it--while periodically fact-checking with them and keeping up with their changing fortunes.

"A.D." first found a home online when it was serialized on SMITH in 2007-2008. The web version of "A.D.," though significantly shorter than this book, is presented in a way that allows for a multilayered experience. It is seeded with links to podcasts, YouTube videos, archived hurricane tracking reports, and even personal details like the Doctor's favorite mixed drink recipes. "A.D." on SMITH also features video and audio interviews with the characters, a Hurricane Katrina resource list, and an active blog. Check it out at www.smithmag.net/afterthedeluge.

Still, I always planned for "A.D." to be a book. When comics are presented on the web -- often one panel at a time -- something of the gestalt of the comic book is lost: the interplay of the tiers of images on a page, the way a two-page spread can work to frame and augment the drama, and aspects of timing, meter, and rhythm. So when Pantheon offered in the summer of 2008 to publish a book edition of "A.D.," I couldn't wait to get to work on it. The best part about the book, of course, is the opportunity it provides me to expand on the characters' stories -- and to bring them to a whole new audience.

An unexpected reward of the project has been seeing "A.D."'s characters become personally invested in it. For instance, at one point early on, Leo helped out by visiting Abbas's store to take vital reference photos. Denise, Leo, and Kwame have all made media appearances with me, talking about their lives and their participation in "A.D." And last August, Brobson hosted a wonderful release party for "A.D." in his French Quarter home. He, Leo, Michell, Abbas, and Denise have all met each other in person and compared notes about their Katrina experiences.

There are many, many stories about Katrina and its aftermath. Those of the seven people in "A.D." are quite particular and highly personal, but my hope is that they provide a window into a larger world, one that few of us understand and that we'll be trying to make sense of for a long time to come. Denise, Leo, Michelle, Abbas, Darnell, Kwame, and Brobson are still rebuilding their lives -- and the city that they love has a long way to go.

-- Josh Neufeld
Brooklyn, April 2010

ACKNOWLEDGMENTS

Denise, Leo, Michelle, Abbas, Darnell, Kwame, and Brobson, for opening up their lives to my prying brush. Without them, "A.D." wouldn't exist, and any errors or misrepresentations of their experiences are entirely my fault.

My wife Sari Wilson, my partner, creatively and in all other ways. Pantheon editor Lisa Weinert, for her boundless enthusiasm and for helping me see the forest despite the trees. SMITH editor Larry Smith, who sought me out and helped me find the way in. My agent Kate Lee, for her constant encouragement, taking my panicked phone calls, and for always having my back.

The Pantheon krewe: Sara Eagle, Dan Frank, Kathleen Fridella, Keith Goldsmith, Andy Hughes, Josie Kals, Altie Karper, Claire Kelley, Chip Kidd, Lisa Montebello, Jenise Morgan, Jonathan Sainsbury, Peggy Samedi, Anke Steinecke, Hillary Tisman, and Zack Wagman. The SMITH magazine krewe: Tim Barkow, Dave Cirilli, Jeff Cranmer, Cree McCree, Jeff Newelt, and Miles van Meter.

Sara Tchen-Susman, Nicholas Sumida, Leah Feuer, Rachel Rosenfelt, and Ben Moody, for wielding rulers, erasers, pencils, pens, and mice with patience and aplomb.

I am also deeply grateful to Alex Blumberg, Jake Elsas, Randee Falk, Paisley Gregg, Dean Haspiel, Anne Heausler, Kemala Karmen, Seth Kushner, Len Neufeld, Christopher Moscatiello, Charlie Orr, Martha Rosler, Rob Walker, Nancy Wilson, and Robert Wilson.

Google images, Google maps, and Wikipedia were all vital to the project.

Finally, my great thanks to the scores of magazines, newspapers, blogs, and websites that have written about and supported "A.D." in all its forms.

ABOUT THE AUTHOR

JOSH NEUFELD spent three weeks as an American Red Cross volunteer in Biloxi, Mississippi. The blog entries he kept about that experience turned into a self-published book, "Katrina Came Calling," which in turn led to "A.D."

Neufeld works primarily in the realm of nonfiction comics. He is the writer/artist of the Xeric Award-winning graphic travelogue "A Few Perfect Hours (and Other Stories from Southeast Asia & Central Europe)." His work has been featured in "The Vagabonds," "Keyhole," and "Titans of Finance," as well as in numerous comics anthologies, news-papers, magazines, and literary journals. He is a longtime artist for Harvey Pekar's "American Splendor," and his art has been exhibited in gallery and museum shows in the United States and Europe.

Neufeld is currently at work illustrating "The Influencing Machine," written by Brooke Gladstone, co-host of NPR's "On The Media."

Neufeld lives in Brooklyn, New York, with his wife, the writer Sari Wilson, and their daughter.